Rules and Reason
Perspectives on Constitutional Political Economy

Polarization in Western democracies and the collapse of centrally planned economies have led to calls for a redefinition of the state's core functions. This collection explores shifting conceptions of constitutional political economy anchoring the state from the viewpoints of theory, systems, and applications, with a view toward identifying why changes may be desirable and how these might be implemented. Topics in Part I on theory include the writing of constitutions, the dynamic between constitutional order and civil society, the struggle between competitive and protectionist interests, the conflict between protecting expectations and moral evolution, and the role of cultural explanations of constitutional development patterns. Part II on electoral systems and institutions explores the interplay between electoral systems and constitutional engineering, the internal costs of political coalitions, and campaigns in pluralistic elections. Part III investigates the quest for stable, dynamic federal states with particular attention to opportunities and pitfalls in Europe. Nobel Laureate James M. Buchanan offers a foreword to the work and coauthors a chapter on the theory of constitutional rules.

Ram Mudambi is Reader in International Business in the Department of Economics, University of Reading, UK, and Associate Professor at the Fox School of Business and Management, Temple University, Philadelphia, Pennsylvania, USA. His research in constitutional political economy focuses on the effects of electoral rules on political party strategy; his other current research interests include the strategies of multinational corporations and newly public firms, and strategic planning and economic analysis. Professor Mudambi's work has been published in leading journals such as the *Journal of Political Economy*, *Public Choice*, *Strategic Management Journal*, *Journal of International Business Studies*, and the *Journal of Applied Statistics*.

Pietro Navarra is Research Associate in the Institute of Economics and Finance at the University of Messina, Italy. He has served as a Visiting Scholar at the Universities of Pavia, Reading, and California-Irvine and George Mason University. He had also served as a Fulbright scholar at Carnegie-Mellon University. Dr. Navarra's research interests in public choice center on positive models of political budget cycles in Italian elections and the political economy of electoral reforms. He has also studied life-cycle models for the demand for international health services. Dr. Navarra has published in eminent and international journals, including *Public Choice*.

Giuseppe Sobbrio holds the Chair in Public Sector Economics in the Institute of Economics and Finance at the University of Messina. His professional research explores all areas of public economics, focusing especially on public choice and state and local finance. Professor Sobbrio is the author of numerous books, including a widely used Italian textbook on public-sector economics. His scholarly research has appeared in many leading Italian and international journals, including *Public Choice*.

Rules and Reason

Perspectives on Constitutional Political Economy

Edited by

RAM MUDAMBI
University of Reading and Temple University

PIETRO NAVARRA
University of Messina

GIUSEPPE SOBBRIO
University of Messina

CAMBRIDGE
UNIVERSITY PRESS

PUBLISHED BY THE PRESS SYNDICATE OF THE UNIVERSITY OF CAMBRIDGE
The Pitt Building, Trumpington Street, Cambridge, United Kingdom

CAMBRIDGE UNIVERSITY PRESS
The Edinburgh Building, Cambridge CB2 2RU, UK
40 West 20th Street, New York, NY 10011-4211, USA
10 Stamford Road, Oakleigh, Melbourne 3166, Australia
Ruiz de Alarcón 13, 28014 Madrid, Spain
Dock House, The Waterfront, Cape Town 8001, South Africa

http//www.cambridge.org

First published 2001

Printed in the United States of America

Typeface Times Roman 10/12 pt.   *System* QuarkXPress [BTS]

A catalog record for this book is available from the British Library.

Library of Congress Cataloging in Publication Data
Rules and reason: perspectives on constitutional political economy / edited by
Ram Mudambi, Pietro Navarra, Giuseppe Sobbrio.
p.   cm.
Includes index.
ISBN 0-521-65057-7 (hbk.) – ISBN 0-521-65959-0 (pbk.)
1. Economics – Political aspects – Congresses.   2. Constitutional law –
Congresses.   3. Elections – Congresses.   I. Mudambi, Ram.   II. Navarra,
Pietro.   III. Sobbrio, Giuseppe.
HB74.P65   R85   2000
338.9 – dc21   99-053158

ISBN   0 521 65057 7   hardback
ISBN   0 521 65959 0   paperback

R. M.
To Susan

P. N.
To my parents

G. S.
To Paola and Francesco

Contents

Foreword

James M. Buchanan

The conference on Constitutional Political Economy convened in Messina and Taormina in October 1997 was a singular academic-intellectual event. The conference sponsors did an outstanding job in attracting serious research scholars from many countries, all of whom had demonstrated an understanding and appreciation of the importance and relevance of constitutional issues in the world at the end of the century, in both international and national political settings.

In my own introductory remarks at the conference's opening session in Messina, I emphasized the potential significance of the European and Italian venue for such a conference. Europe, at century's end, almost above all else, needs to pay explicit heed to its emerging political structure, which has, to this point, been allowed to evolve through the origin and development of its separate institutional agencies, without constitutional coherence, even as imposed or modeled by those whose task is to bring intellectual-philosophical order into complex organizational reality.

The elementary first step toward constitutional understanding, namely the recognition of the necessary distinction between the choice-operation of the rules or constraints and the choice-operation of ordinary politics within the constraints, has never been characteristic of European attitudes, even those emerging from the academies. The integration of the historic nation-states of Europe requires attention to basic constitutional issues. European research scholars must, by necessity, become constitutionally informed.

I also noted, in my opening remarks, the relevance of the conference venue in Sicily. There has been a general failure on the part of many Europeans to appreciate the implications of genuine European federalism on the internal authority of national governments over citizens. As national governments transfer some elements of sovereignty to the European Union, the potential authority of the regional or provincial governments should increase. And this effect should be especially pronounced for those regions that have historical and geographical claims of autonomy, such as Sicily and Sardinia in Italy and the Basque country and Catalonia in Spain.

Again, at this level of relationship between national and regional governments, the emerging issues are those of constitutional, rather than policy choices. Political economists, political philosophers, political scientists, political sociologists, and constitutional lawyers cannot default on their role in offering assistance in advancing the arguments. In a summary final evaluation, the Taormina conference served to alert scholars everywhere to the recognition that "constitutions matter."

Preface and Acknowledgments

In the short space of less than a decade the political landscape of the world has changed dramatically. The fall of the Berlin Wall has brought into being many states with strong desires but little experience with democracy. In addition, the political climate in many of the world's democracies has been far from still. Italy, New Zealand, and Japan have all undertaken major changes in their electoral systems. Many experts describe the political landscape in the United States as being the most polarized in living memory.

In the former Soviet Empire and in many former authoritarian states, there is the widespread desire to roll back the power of the state and implement the popular will. Simultaneously there is the wish to utilize the second-mover advantages of starting with a clean slate to pick and choose the best system, learning from the experiences of the democratic world. The collapse of the centrally planned economies has also undermined the authority of governments in the democracies of the world. This has led to calls for a re-definition of the core functions of the state. Furthermore, electorates in the democracies are becoming increasingly critical of their political establishments as globalization makes life more and more uncertain. These critiques have fueled demands for changes to limit the powers of political agents and to make them more accountable to their constituents.

In this time of momentous change, we believe that it is valuable to seek the insights of some of the leading thinkers in the area of constitutional political economy into the events taking place on the world stage. With this thought in mind, we organized a conference in Messina and Taormina, Sicily, in September 1997. A great many interesting and original papers were presented and in selecting the works for the current volume we have had to place an emphasis on cohesion. We have attempted to develop three perspectives on constitutional political economy: theory, systems, and applications. We hope that these contributions will provide some insights into why institutional changes may be required and how they might be made, together with some practical illustrations of opportunities and pitfalls in the European context.

This has been a major endeavor and we have incurred substantial debts of gratitude. First and foremost we would like to thank our illustrious contributors, who were generous with both their time and their wisdom. We would like to record our deep appreciation of many conference participants who served as moderators and discussants and many whose ideas are represented in the finished products that are published here. In this connection, we would like mention Fabrizio Balassone, Massimo Bordignon, Giorgio Brosio, Domenico Da Empoli, Valentino Dardanoni, Giuseppe Eusepi, Rafaela Giordano, Arye Hillman, Nino Luciani, Mario Oteri, Fabio Padovano, Giancesare Romagnoli, Norman Schofield, and Michele Trimarchi. Most of all, we would like to single out Charles Rowley, who was always there with advice and guidance.

We would like to thank the Bank of Italy, the National Research Council of Italy, the Banca Nazionale del Lavoro, the Office of the President of the Region of Sicily, the University of Messina and the Messina Opera Universitaria, the Messina Provincial Tourism Authority, and the Municipalities of Messina and Taormina for financial support that made the conference possible. We are also pleased to acknowledge Santa Micali, who served as Vice President of the Organizing Committee. She was ably supported by the administrative employees of the Istituto di Economia e Finanza of the University of Messina, Giuseppe Armaleo, Domenico Cisca, and Teresa Grillo.

Scott Parris and Louise Calabro of Cambridge University Press were unstinting in their support, and we owe them a great deal for shepherding us through the publication process. Finally, no project of this magnitude is completed without a substantial personal cost. Our families have had to endure long absences while this project was under way and we thank them for bearing with us.

Ram Mudambi
Philadelphia, Pennsylvania, USA

Pietro Navarra
Giuseppe Sobbrio
Messina, Sicily, Italy

Contributors

James M. Buchanan
George Mason University, USA

Reiner Eichenberger
University of Zurich, Switzerland

Michael J. Ensley
Duke University, USA

Mikhail Filippov
*California Institute of Technology,
USA*

Francesco Forte
*University of Rome, La Sapienza,
Italy*

Bruno S. Frey
*University of Zurich,
Switzerland*

Bernard N. Grofman
*University of California, Irvine,
USA*

Ram Mudambi
*University of Reading, UK, and
Temple University, USA*

Dennis C. Mueller
University of Vienna, Austria

Michael C. Munger
Duke University, USA

Pietro Navarra
University of Messina, Italy

Peter C. Ordeshook
*California Institute of Technology,
USA*

Chris W. Paul II
*Georgia Southern University,
USA*

Andrew Reynolds
University of Notre Dame, USA

Charles K. Rowley
George Mason University, USA

Pierre Salmon
University of Burgundy, France

Friedrich Schneider
*Johannes Kepler University,
Austria*

Olga V. Shvetsova
*Washington University-St. Louis,
USA*

Guiseppe Sobbrio
University of Messina, Italy

Nicolaus T. Tideman
*Virginia Polytechnic Institute and
State University, USA*

Viktor Vanberg
Albert-Ludwigs University,
  Germany

Alexander F. Wagner
Johannes Kepler University,
  Austria

Allen W. Wilhite
University of Alabama, Huntsville,
  USA

Yong J. Yoon
George Mason University, USA

CHAPTER 1

Constitutional Issues in Modern Democracies

Ram Mudambi, Pietro Navarra, and Giuseppe Sobbrio

Constitutional political economy is an intellectual endeavor in which the notions of efficiency and justice are necessarily balanced. Justice should emerge naturally from a constitutional process, whereas efficiency must be achieved through conscious effort. All the key issues in constitutional political economy relate directly or indirectly to one of these two notions and most to the interplay between the two. Fundamentally, we are concerned with the development of formal "rules" within informal structures in order to regulate all human actions.

Considerations of efficiency are in the realm of positive economics, that is, the analysis of questions of "what is." Notions of justice, however, fall within the purview of normative economics, that is, the examination of questions of "what should be." Constitutional political economy concerns the legal foundations of the market. The legal infrastructure is operationalized through a set of rules and regulations that can be thought of as signals indicating the domains of choice. It follows that these rules influence outcomes – a concern of positive economics. Further, some outcomes are "better" than others, which introduces issues related to comparisons of different sets of rules – a normative consideration.

Public choice is concerned with the development of a rigorous axiomatic general theory of government. In this view, politics is understood as a marketplace for individual exchanges. Within this marketplace, rules and regulations function as constraints on individual and collective action. These rules are implemented according to the institutional framework of the nation-state.

Rules are only as effective as their implementation. Therefore institutions have a critical role to play in determining the actual outcome that emerges from a given legal infrastructure. In this context, Mueller argues that the political institutions of a country determine how well a written constitution can function (Chapter 2).

The human environment is characterized by the inevitability of change. The set of rules and regulations that constrain action must

1

accommodate this fact. However, it is important to recognize that not all rules are equally affected by change. Some fundamental rules are likely to be desirable for long periods of time, while others may only be relevant to particular periods. This generates a hierarchy of rules in terms of the ease with which society will and should allow them to be changed. Rules determined within the confines of ordinary politics can be changed quite easily. However, constitutional political economy is concerned with constitutional rules that rest at the top of this hierarchy and cannot be easily changed.

In a free society, the constitution will be written in such a way that it effectively advances the interests of all citizens. Further, procedures will be adopted to allow the citizens to revise and rewrite these constitutions as their circumstances change and their knowledge grows. As Tideman points out, this growth of knowledge may include changing standards of morality (Chapter 6). When this occurs, as Mueller notes, "written constitutions will not only be shown to matter, but to matter for the good."

The long-term stability and prosperity of a society depends upon its ability to pass valuable information in the form of institutions and ideologies to future generations. Institutions are formal rules constraining human action by making certain behaviors that are inconsistent with the conception of common welfare more expensive. In turn, these effects legitimize the institutions (Buchanan and Tullock, 1962). Ideologies, on the other hand, are informal guides to human action, which provide ready-made templates for right and wrong, good or evil (North, 1981, 1990). By assuming that societies must accumulate knowledge in order to grow and prosper, Munger and Ensley argue that the tension between institutions and ideologies will have a long-term effect on economic growth and prosperity (Chapter 7).

At the heart of constitutional economics is the distinction between the two levels at which choices can be made: the constitutional and the post-constitutional. The first is concerned with choices of rules while the second is concerned with choices subject to rules. In other words, at the constitutional level the rules of the game under which the citizens of a polity wish to live are designed. This perspective implies that the institutions of both the economy and the polity belong to an inclusive constitutional order that may be designated the "political economy." The political economy can be therefore described as the entire set of constraints within which individuals act in pursuing their own objectives.

The trade-off between general and individual objectives leads us to conceptualize the contrast between ordinary politics and constitutional politics. The former is almost necessarily majoritarian, non-consensual, and naturally discriminatory to the extent that the participants promote separable interests. The latter may approach, at least in its ideal form, consensual agreement.

This is consistent with the hierarchical structure of rules we highlighted previously. Thus, ordinary politics deals with the crafting of rules where opposition may be significant, and may change frequently over time, so that the rules themselves must be easily changeable. However, constitutional politics deals with long-lasting rules conceived in the interests of all elements of society so that, ideally, opposition is non-existent. This is guaranteed by making changes possible only through a general consensus.

According to the contractarian conception, the rules for living together are quite literally made up or created in some participatory process of discussion, analysis, persuasion, and mutual agreement. In this conception of social order, the veil of ignorance or uncertainty offers a means of bridging the apparent gap between furtherance of separately defined interests and agreement on the rules that conceptually define the "social contract" (Buchanan and Congleton, 1998). In other words, potential contractors must recognize that the basic rules for social order are explicitly chosen as permanent or quasi-permanent parameters within which social interaction has to take place over a whole sequence of periods. In this framework, contractors may be led to examine rules from behind a "veil of ignorance" (Harsanyi, 1975; Rawls, 1971) or "uncertainty" (Buchanan and Tullock, 1962) with regard to their own interests in future periods. Since future self-interest is either unknown or uncertain, criteria of fairness may replace those of advantage. In this framework, agreement may emerge by a process in which the person who advances an argument in support of one particular rule must invoke criteria that take on elements of general or public interest. The question of legitimization, therefore, requires that the constitutional structure remain categorically distinct from the operation of ordinary politics.

We now proceed to examine the economic component of the overall "political economy" as conceptualized above. It is important to understand and interpret the economy as a constitutional order rather than as an institutional arrangement that has to be evaluated in terms of its relative success or failure in achieving assigned, system-defined objectives. In this context, an "economic constitution" indicates the constitutional order that constrains the actions and transactions of economic agents.

Economic systems exist in a changing environment and they must in one way or another adapt to these changes. Their ability to function and survive depends on their adaptive capacities. The ability of economic systems to adapt and the manner in which such adaptation proceeds critically depends on their underlying economic constitution. As pointed out by Vanberg, the question of how an economic system ought to deal with changes in its environment is at the heart of current political discussions on how to respond to forces of globalization and to internal and external competition (Chapter 3).

It is now widely acknowledged, both in theory and in practice, that the socialist experiment was a costly failure. The false hope that socialism could prove to be a means of achieving fairness in social organization no longer exists. At the other end of the ideological spectrum stands the equally romantic ideal of *laissez-faire*, in which there is no role for the state. In this model freely choosing individuals who have escaped from the Hobbesian jungle create and maintain markets for all goods and services. Any plausibly realistic analysis of social order, whether positive or normative, must be bounded by the limits set by these ideological extremes. The state is neither omniscient nor benevolent but a politico-legal framework that is an essential element in any functioning order of human interaction. The analysis, discussion, and debate then centers on the degree or extent of its political control over, and intervention into, the interaction process (Buchanan, 1989).

In this context, two approaches concerning the nature of civil society have characterized the debate in political philosophy: the Hobbesian trade-off between anarchy and order and the Lockeian contrast between oppression and freedom. For the most part the Hobbesian vision appears to have the ascendancy at the present time. This ascendancy may be seen primarily in the countries emerging from socialism, where the constitutional rule of law has only imperfectly replaced the rigid control of the state. Ironically, in several countries in the West that successfully challenged and defeated the oppression of socialism, the romantic siren call of the Hobbesian state is still tempting to many academics and literati. Rowley argues that on the contrary it is Lockeian ideas of freedom that "offer the most effective basis for the establishment and maintenance of the rule of law and defense of life, liberty, and property. They provide the economic, the political, and the cultural environment most conducive to the flourishing of human talent and the wealth of individuals in society" (Chapter 5).

No existing or proposed political constitution contains sufficient constraints or limits on the authority of the agencies of government over the activities of individuals and groups and, in particular, over their economic activities (Buchanan, 1994). No truly liberal constitution is currently in existence or in prospect. In this sense, all existing constitutions may be tried and found wanting. All constitutions that have been put into place since the eighteenth century, and all that have been reformed, either explicitly or by usage and interpretation since that time, reflect to some degree the romantic image of the benevolent state, whether actual or potential. This is the image introduced by political idealists on the one hand and visionary socialists on the other. Despite this negative assessment, which may seem to be nearly total in its condemnatory sweep, there may be bases for some optimism as one looks far enough forward into the post-socialist epoch and especially into the new century. Economic prosperity and progress can only occur in settings where the activities of government are constitutionally constrained, quite independent of how governmental agents are selected. This realization seems to be finding acceptance virtually in all polities and the pressure of this weight of public opinion will be difficult to resist.

And what of the future? According to Buchanan (1991), the post-socialist century will be marked by a convergence of scientific understanding among economists. This convergence will stand in stark contrast to the controversies that described discourse among political economists in the last century. Questions regarding the sources of earlier controversies in economics, particularly with regard to comparative economic systems will become increasingly important. This is as it should be. Economists must increasingly ask such questions as why economists shared in the "fatal conceit" that socialism represented and why they failed to recognize that incentives remain relevant in all choice settings. This is critical if the mistakes of the past are to be avoided.

The political economy of the future must become more normative. However, the normative focus must be on the constraints within which economic actors, individually and corporately, make choices among alternatives. The accompanying, and indeed prior, positive analysis must involve comparisons among alternative sets of constraints or rules. In this setting, it is to be expected that constitutional economics will command increasing scientific attention.

References

Buchanan, J. M. 1989. "The Economy as a Constitutional Order." In Werner Sichel, ed., *The State of Economic Science: Views of Six Nobel Laureates.* Kalamazoo: Upjohn Institute, pp. 79–96.

1991. "Economics in the Post-Socialist Century." *Economic Journal,* 101(404): 15–21.

1994. "Notes on the Liberal Constitution." *Cato Journal,* 14(1): 1–9.

Buchanan, J. M., and Congleton, R. D. 1998. *Politics by Principle Not Interest.* New York: Cambridge University Press.

Buchanan, J. M., and Tullock, G. 1962. *The Calculus of Consent: Logical Foundations of Constitutional Democracy.* Ann Arbor: University of Michigan Press.

Harsanyi, J. C. 1975. "Can the Maximin Principle Serve as a Basis for Morality? A Critique of John Rawls' Theory." *American Political Science Review,* 69: 594–606.

North, D. 1981. *Structure and Change in Economic History.* New York: W. W. Norton.

1990. *Institutions, Institutional Change, and Economic Performance.* Cambridge: Cambridge University Press.

Rawls, J. 1971. *A Theory of Justice.* Cambridge, Mass.: Harvard University Press.

PART I

CONSTITUTIONAL THEORY

Part I is made up of contributions that examine the theoretical under-pinnings of constitutional political economy. Do constitutions matter? Mueller's answer to this fundamental question is that they can matter, although they do not necessarily do so. The many Brazilian constitutions have had limited impact. In the former USSR, the constitution had some admirable sounding sections but did not produce an admirable political system. In contrast, ancient Athens, the Weimar Republic, and Costa Rica are three cases where constitutions have had important effects. The main message of this chapter is that written constitutions can matter in how well the political institutions of a country function.

Vanberg focuses on economic systems and the framework of rules and institutions that constrain the actions and transactions of economic agents. He argues that this framework, which may be called an "economic constitution," determines the ability of the system to adapt to a changing environment. This insight is used to analyze the current debates on globalization and the conflict between protectionist and competitive interests. The analysis of Buchanan and Yoon can be understood as a more abstract approach to the issue of a changing environment. In particular, dropping the "natural" distinction between rules (constraints) and outcomes within such rules, the argument is made for choosing constitutional variables (constraints) based on efficiency considerations.

The bipolar world during the Cold War pitted the free democracies of the West against socialist dictatorships. During this period, the social-ist states offered the Hobbesian goal of order, while the democracies adopted the Lockeian perspective. Ironically, Rowley points out that the failure of the socialist system has been accompanied by a drift from Lockeian to Hobbesian principles among leading political philosophers. He assesses the implications for sound constitutional political economy of the Lockeian approach that attaches supreme importance to the preservation of life, liberty, and property. Tideman continues on this theme, noting that the definition of property itself is subject to current codes of morality and that these can change, as in the case of slavery. The constitutional protection of property must therefore allow for moral evolution.

Finally, which features of a society really matter and which can we ignore as merely reflecting idiosyncratic differences in custom or taste? If a society manages to identify some rules or practices that matter, how can it ensure that this knowledge is preserved? Munger and Ensley attempt to answer these questions, offering a means of analyzing how societies differ and how they maintain differences in rules and preferences over time. They conclude that the long-term stability and prosperity of a society depends upon its ability to pass valuable information in the form of institutions and ideologies to future generations. Institutions are knowledge in the form of constraints, whereas ideologies are guides to choice. The interaction between institutions and ideologies is an important variable for understanding stability and economic progress.

CHAPTER 2

On Writing a Constitution

Dennis C. Mueller

> Someone once said that there are two sorts of people: Those who view
> the world as consisting of two sorts of people, and those who do not.
> Edmund S. Phelps

There are two sorts of students of politics: those who believe that constitutions have important consequences for a country's political history,
and those who think they do not. I am one of those who believe that constitutions *can* matter, although they do not necessarily do so. After convincing you of this, I shall draw out some of the implications for
constitutional design, and for the design of the process by which the constitution gets written.

It is uncontroversial that constitutions *need not* matter. Brazil has had
more than eighty constitutions and most Brazilians probably would not
be able to identify any one of them that had a significant effect on the
country. The constitution of the former USSR had some admirable
sounding sections but did not produce an admirable political system. If
a constitution is ignored, it cannot have an impact.

But not all constitutions have been ignored. I begin by describing
three cases where constitutions did matter. Two had good consequences,
one not so good.

I   Three Cases Where Constitutions Mattered

A   Ancient Athens

Democracy was invented during the sixth century b.c. in Attica through
a series of reforms begun by Solon and largely completed by Cleisthenes.[1] Prior to and during much of this century Attica was ruled by
individuals (tyrants) and groups (oligarchies) drawn from the aristocracy.

This chapter draws heavily on my book *Constitutional Democracy* (1996).
[1] The discussion of this event is based mainly on Meier (1990) and Farrar (1988).

9

These aristocrats were the heads of various clans (*phylae*). The *phylae* were defined by a combination of kinship and geography that made them natural coalitions for redistributional, rent-seeking activities. Rent seeking in Attica pitted tribe against tribe, city against countryside, economic interest (e.g., agriculture) against economic interest; patterns familiar from other times and places. Cleisthenes proposed a set of reforms, a constitution, that destroyed these patterns. He divided Attica into small geographic political units called *demes*. Each *deme* contained about sixty citizens. New *phylae* were defined by combining *demes* from different parts of Attica, *demes* from different clans and with different economic interests.

Cleisthenes obviously understood the costs that factional strife places upon a community. Like Madison over two millennia later, he sought institutional reforms to neutralize the harmful effects of faction.[2] His solution was to redefine the *phylae* to transform them from coalitions representing narrow tribal, geographic, and economic interests into coalitions that included a broad cross-section of the interests of the citizens of Attica, what Olson (1982) would call encompassing organizations. The interests that members of a newly defined *phyle* had in common were those that all citizens of Attica had in common. Cleisthenes' constitution "by its admirable mixture of all the elements [of Attican society], guaranteed the concord and welfare of the community."[3]

Attachment to the larger community was further strengthened by the rules in Cleisthenes' constitution for selecting representatives to the Council, a kind of executive committee of the Assembly of all citizens. Members of the Council served for one year and were chosen by lot from each *deme*. Every citizen had a chance of serving on the Council, and over time many did. The Council included citizens from all parts of Attica and from all economic groups, and it evolved into the most important decision-making body in Attica. Its broad-based membership engendered in the citizenry an interest in the community and a sense of responsibility for its welfare. Since the Council met in Athens, the interests of the whole of Attica and of Athens became intertwined.

During the sixth century B.C. the political concept, *isonomy*, developed. This word came to connote both the democratic constitution of Athens and the equality of rights of its citizens, the notion that all citizens were equal before the law (Meier, 1990, pp. 152–62). The invention of democracy in Athens gave all citizens a stake in the welfare of the polis that they defended by actively participating in politics and by serving in the military when required. It was on the strength of this

---

[2] James Madison, like many of the other Founding Fathers, was a student of politics from the classical period. Thus, it is likely that his ideas about faction and how to curb its detrimental effects were influenced by Cleisthenes' reforms.

[3] Attributed to Pericles by Plutarch as quoted by Meier (1990, p. 61).

citizen participation that Athens would rise to dominance over the next two hundred years.

Cleisthenes' reforms transformed Attica from a country of squabbling clans and geographic and economic interests with a political system that was preoccupied with zero-sum redistribution, into the world's first democracy. Athens became a powerful empire whose politics was redirected toward positive-sum activities, a political community in which citizens actively participated and which rewarded them for their participation.

What led the Athenians to gamble on a set of proposals of such novelty as those put forward by Cleisthenes? Kitto (1957, pp. 106–7) argues that the Greeks had such confidence in the creative powers of the human mind and enthusiasm for that which was new, that one should not be surprised by their willingness to adopt radically new political institutions, especially since they were invented by one of their admired citizens. For our purposes, it is not important *why* they adopted Cleisthenes' constitution, but *that* they did and consciously so. In so doing, they created the world's first constitutional democracy, a polity that at its zenith would become the standard for all future democracies. Those who regard constitutions as inconsequential must bear the burden of proof that Athens' glory in the fifth and fourth centuries would have been just as great had Cleisthenes never proposed his constitutional reforms, or the Atticans had not adopted them.

B   The Weimar Republic

Bad constitutional structures have also had important consequences. The Weimar Constitution is often cited as an example, and it is, but not necessarily for the reasons usually given.

The weakness of the Weimar Constitution most frequently mentioned was the electoral system that produced a multiparty Parliament and allowed parties on both the far right and the far left to take seats. The number and diversity of the parties made it difficult for the Parliament to function effectively over the last five years of the Republic's life (Hermens, 1951, 1963).

The causal links between electoral rules, number of parties, and political stability are not direct, however.[4] *More* parties were represented in the German Parliament of 1912 under a plurality system of the kind associated with two-party government than during the Weimar Republic (Lakeman, 1974, pp. 208–13). Nor is it clear that such a system would have prevented the Nazis' rise to power. Indeed, a British-style first-past-

---

[4] See, my discussion in *Constitutional Democracy*, chs. 9–11. All future references to this book will be as *CD* followed by chapter numbers.

the-post system invariably over-allocates seats to the biggest parties. Such a system would certainly have transformed the Nazis' 37 percent of the popular vote in 1932 to an even larger fraction of seats in the Parliament, and therefore might even have accelerated Hitler's seizure of power.

In addition to the number and diversity of parties in the German Parliament during the Weimar Republic, at least four other factors contributed to its demise: (1) the unusually divisive issues the Parliament faced, (2) policy errors, (3) the method of cabinet formation, and (4) the power of the president in relation to the Parliament. The third and fourth factors are a direct result of provisions in the Weimar Constitution.

The defeat in World War I and the humiliating terms of the Versailles Treaty afforded nationalistic and authoritarian parties a basis upon which to build support. The treaty saddled Germany with occupational forces, large reparation obligations, and constraints on future military programs. The nationalistic parties and those committed to maintaining democracy and good relations with other countries were continually divided over reparation and rearmament issues (Eyck, 1963, chs. 5, 6).

In 1927 the Parliament passed an extremely generous system of unemployment insurance under the optimistic premise that the economy would soon improve and unemployment would fall (Eyck, 1963, pp. 135ff.). At the same time it voted large salary increases for all civil servants. Such fiscal optimism and generosity to political supporters is frequently observed in democratic countries and is a common cause of budget deficits. These actions resulted in a severe financial crisis following the economy's collapse in the early 1930s, and became a further source of parliamentary strife.[5] Add to these subsidies for farmers and interregional transfers, and one finds that much of the attention of the German Parliament in the late 1920s and 1930s was devoted to inherently divisive distributional questions (Eyck, 1963). Although no constitution could have allowed the German Parliament to sail through this troubled period without some strife, a different structure could have deterred the Parliament from focusing so heavily upon zero-sum redistribution policies (*CD*, 6, 7, and 16), and prevented it from myopic and fiscally irresponsible actions (*CD*, 17).

Under the Weimar Constitution the President selected the Chancellor, who then selected the other members of his cabinet (Eyck, 1962, ch. 3). The cabinet did not need to be approved by a majority of the Parliament. On several key occasions proposals of the cabinet were voted down by the cabinet members' own parties (Eyck, 1963; Lepsius, 1978). The division of legislative and executive authority *within the Parliament* allowed under the Weimar Constitution, and the paralysis it caused,

---

[5] The decline in output in Germany between 1929 and 1931 was comparable to that in the United States, and much greater than elsewhere in Europe (Childs, 1980, p. 44).

helped to destroy popular support for parliamentary democracy in the Weimar Republic.

The feature of the Weimar Constitution that contributed the most to the impotence of the government and the demise of the Republic, however, was the division of authority between the president and the Parliament. In building a strong presidency into their Constitution, the Weimar Convention had sought to achieve the kind of stability the United States had experienced with its strong presidential system (Eyck, 1962, p. 72). Max Weber was one of the intellectuals at that time who favored a strong president to counter the political paralysis that might arise when power is shared in a multiparty parliament (Peukert, 1991, p. 39). In the Weimar Constitution, the president's power stemmed from his authority to disband the Parliament and call new elections, and to rule by decree in the interim and in other emergency situations. The octogenarian President von Hindenburg made repeated use of this authority in the waning years of the Republic undermining both the effectiveness of the Parliament and the legitimacy of the government. The most serious failure of the Weimar Constitution was the ambiguous and contradictory division of authority among the president, the chancellor, and the Parliament (Lepsius, 1978, pp. 47–50; Carstairs, 1980, pp. 165–6). The president could appoint the chancellor and dissolve the Parliament but could not legitimately implement a program (although he could and did govern by decree on several occasions). The chancellor could form a cabinet and propose a program but could not necessarily get it through the Parliament. The rank and file of the Parliament could block legislation but, with the leadership of several parties in the cabinet, was unable to initiate and pass legislation.

Many Latin American constitutions have also been modeled after that of the United States, but as with the Weimar Constitution have included electoral rules that produce multiparty parliaments, the consequence being that neither the parties in the parliament nor the president can deliver the programs they promise during election campaigns. Constitutional divisions of authority between president and parliament have often resulted in political paralysis, and have undoubtedly contributed to political instability in Latin America and the recurring appearance of dictators there, as they did in Germany sixty years ago.[6]

C   Costa Rica

Not all Latin American countries have been plagued by political and economic instability and recurring lapses into dictatorship, however. Costa Rica has the highest income, health, and education levels of any country

---

[6] See Linz and Stepan (1978).

in Central America. It also has the longest and deepest democratic traditions (Seligson, 1990, pp. 455–6). It was a dictatorship from 1870 to 1882 but returned to democracy at that end of that interval (Ameringer, 1982, p. 17). When the president refused to step down following a close election in 1948, a brief civil war ensued and democracy was reestablished. With this brief exception the Costa Ricans have experienced democratic government for more than a century. There are several possible explanations for Costa Rica's relative economic and political success. One important reason is certainly the rather small indigenous population that it has (Ameringer, 1982, pp. 3–4). This accident of history has spared it the kind of ethnic distributional struggles between those of European and American descent that have contributed to political and social instability in Mexico, Peru, Brazil, and elsewhere in Latin America. Another explanation, however, is its constitutional history.

Following the civil war of 1948 a specially elected constitutional assembly drafted a new constitution for Costa Rica (Ameringer, 1982, p. 37) repeating the procedure followed when the first constitution was drafted in 1812 (Seligson, 1990, p. 460). We shall argue in Section IV in favor of having a separately chosen assembly for writing a nation's constitution. Costa Rica, like other Latin American countries, has its problems of crime, deficits, and inflation (Ameringer, 1982, ch. 6). But in this country, these problems are unlikely to give rise to a military dictatorship. Costa Rica's constitution of 1949 removed the danger of military dictatorship by abolishing the military. The absence of dictatorship in at least one Latin American country almost certainly has its roots in that country's constitution and is another illustration of the point that constitutions can matter.

D   Lessons

This brief look at three cases in which constitutions have significantly impacted the course of political history in a country provide the following two lessons. First, the stability of a political system may be jeopardized if its representative institutions are mostly concerned with divisive distributional issues, rather than the potentially consensual, positive-sum issues that are a democratic government's raison d'être. I do not imply here that some redistribution activity is not part of the legitimate work of government, but rather that support for a democratic system will be eroded if its day-to-day activities are dominated by distributional issues.

The second lesson is that the rules by which representatives are selected, the relationship between the executive and the legislative branches, and other aspects of the parliamentary process (like, for example, the voting rule used by the parliament) may determine the effectiveness of the government, which in turn can impact its stability.[7]

II   The Constitutional Convention

If constitutions matter, and if they can have good and bad consequences, then the question is, how can we get a constitution that can and does have desirable consequences?

One solution is to find a Cleisthenes, who is capable of designing the kind of political system a country needs, and to adopt the system he designs. I do not know enough about Greek history to determine what motivated Cleisthenes or what gave him his ideas. But we all know that individuals such as Cleisthenes and James Madison are extremely rare, and most societies are probably too timid to follow their radical proposals when they do happen along. Waiting for or finding a person who will propose the ideal constitution is not a promising option.

The Greeks had to invent a constitution, because they had to invent democracy. Every democratic government since the Greeks has had the luxury of copying at least in part the constitutions of its predecessors. The first truly democratic governments to form following the Greeks were arguably the city-states of Renaissance Italy. They copied the Greeks in their use of lotteries to select representatives to their governing councils.[8]

The fundamental idea that a community should be formed by compact among its members was developed by the religious sects that sprang up in Europe during the Reformation.[9] Some of those that fled to America to avoid religious persecution brought the idea with them, and it evolved here into the notion that political communities should be founded by contract. The United States' constitutional experience embodied this

---

[7] Here I am obviously in disagreement with the thrust of the arguments of Robert Dahl (1998). The preconditions for democracy do not strike me as radically different in pre–World War II Germany from other European countries, but Germany's combination of presidential and parliamentary democracy made its government particularly impotent in dealing with the different questions it faced.

Costa Rica was spared some of the distributional frictions that its neighbors had, because of its relatively small native population, but in other respects it had the same preconditions for democracy as they did. Its success as a stable democracy must be attributed to the form of its democratic institutions and the way in which they were created. Moreover, some features of its constitutions, e.g., the early inclusion of universal education, helped to create in Costa Rica some of the "preconditions" for democracy Dahl and others stress.

[8] For an interesting and approving account of democratic institutions in Florence, see Schwartz (1988, ch. 7).

[9] The first written *political* constitution that was ever proposed was probably that put forward by the Levellers in 1647 (Wooton, 1990).

idea (Arendt, 1963, pp. 164–78). The American colonists also brought with them the idea, which developed in Tudor England, that it was not people but places (corporations) that were to be represented (Eckstein, 1963, p. 248; Huntington, 1968). The separation of powers built into the U.S. Constitution was clearly an adaptation of the division of authority between king and parliament that had been evolving in Great Britain. The truly innovative stroke in the U.S. Constitution was the introduction of federalism (Riker, 1964, 1987).

The next great invention in constitutional design was proportional representation in the middle of the nineteenth century. It caught on quickly and by the beginning of the twentieth century was incorporated into the constitutions of almost all European democracies. The Weimar Constitution, as already noted, was an unhappy marriage of European proportional representation and the United States' separation of powers through a presidential system.

Thus most constitutions have been a packaging and repackaging of ideas and institutions found elsewhere, with the occasional innovation appearing as conceptions of representation and democracy evolved. Sometimes the package seems to work, sometimes as in the Weimar Constitution it explodes. The U.S. Constitution is regarded by many, although certainly not all, as one of the more successful packagings. Let us therefore briefly examine its creation to try to find a clue as to the cause of its success – and failures.

III   The Philadelphia Convention

There is a wide range of views regarding the motives and abilities of the men who assembled in Philadelphia during the summer of 1787 and as to the quality of the product they produced. At one pole, we have an observer no less astute than Alexis de Tocqueville asserting that

> The assembly which accepted the task of composing the second Constitution was small, but George Washington was its President, and it contained the finest minds and the noblest characters that had ever appeared in the New World.

At the other pole, we have Charles Beard (1913) and his many followers, who regard the convention as a cabal of wealthy land and slave owners out to protect their property.

Public choice is built on the premise that all individuals pursue their self-interest. The public-choice approach, when applied to the participants of the Philadelphia convention, would inquire first as to the narrow, personal interests of the participants, and thus would seem to favor the interpretation of Charles Beard. Men like Cleisthenes and Madison, who appear to be concerned with advancing the welfare of society or perhaps, more cynically, their place in history, do come along from time to time, however. Such was the case in Philadelphia, and consequently all actions taken at the convention cannot be explained by narrow self-interest.

It is clear, however, that many delegates did weigh more heavily the interests of the state that sent them than those of the country at large. This "constituent bias" helps account for both Houses of Congress having geographic representation, and for one of them being gerrymandered. The Constitution's treatment of slavery also reflects a concern by the delegates from states where slaveholding was important to protect this "peculiar institution." In these and perhaps still other ways,[10] the institutions embedded in the original Constitution reflect narrower interests of a regional or economic nature. Both aspects of the Constitution have had negative consequences for future generations.

The most obvious example of this is the Constitution's treatment of, or more accurately failure to treat, the slavery issue in a way that was viable in the long run. The Civil War is a direct consequence of this failure.

The effects of geographic representation have been more subtle and slower to materialize. It is now apparent, however, that geographic representation transforms each member of the House and Senate into a lobbyist for his district or state and an ombudsman for its residents (Mayhew, 1974; Fiorina, 1977). The resulting porkbarrel politics contributes to the waste and inefficiency of government. It also plays a role in the increasingly prevalent deadlocks between Congress and the president that prevent the government from undertaking policies, like deficit reduction, that have broad popular support. The president represents a national constituency; each member of Congress represents a local constituency. On some issues, like spending reductions and tax increases, it appears that the two (and sometimes three when the House and Senate cannot agree) often cannot come together.

Buchanan and Tullock (1962) discuss constitutional choices under the premise that the individuals writing the constitution are uncertain about their future positions. The setting is analogous to Rawls's (1971) original position, and the constitution Buchanan and Tullock describe as being written in this setting has certain fairness properties in common with Rawls's social contract. It is obvious, however, from the Constitution's treatment of slavery and modes of representation that the delegates in Philadelphia were not behind a Rawlsian veil of ignorance when they dealt with these questions. Calvin Jillson (1988, p. 16), claims that the delegates at the Philadelphia convention did "base their decisions on impressions regarding the more diffuse and general interests of the community" when they could not "see clearly what differences [their] choices

---

[10] See tests and discussion in McGuire and Ohlsfelt (1986) and McGuire (1988).

... would make to them as individuals, or to their states and regions."
The Bill of Rights, although not agreed to in Philadelphia, would seem
to be an example of this, and so it and some other parts of the Constitution arguably do have the elements of fairness and justice of the kind
about which Buchanan, Tullock, and Rawls have written.[11] In those areas
where the delegates were unsure of the best course to take for their own
or their constituents' interests, they tried to advance the interests of
everyone.

If then we would like the constitution to advance the interests of *all*
future citizens, to be a kind of contract among *all* citizens for their mutual
advantage, the lessons of Philadelphia would appear to be clear. We must
choose delegates who represent all of those who will live under the
constitution and who *think of themselves as representatives of all future
citizens*.

IV   Choosing a Constitutional Convention

A   *The Separate Election of Delegates*

The most straightforward way to ensure that all future citizens are represented at the constitutional convention is to choose delegates in an
election with the entire nation designated a single electoral district.
Defining the entire nation as a single district is desirable under the
assumption that people with particular interests or particular views
about the constitution might be found anywhere in the country. If this is
not a good assumption, if people with particular interests are clustered
together in separate geographic areas, then representation by geographic
district is obviously more appropriate. In this case the polity being
formed is more of a confederation, however.

Given the special nature of the constitutional convention, desirable
candidates might include individuals who have not been and/or may not
become candidates for public office (e.g., noted scholars with expertise
in law or political science, former jurists and elected officials, members
of the press, from television, etc.). They may, therefore, not be members
of a political party, or at least not closely associated with one. A method
of electing delegates in which the voters vote for individuals rather than

---

[11] Landes and Posner (1975) would disagree. They see the Constitution as designed to facilitate Congress's selling legislation to interest groups. They interpret the First Amendment "as a form of protective legislation extracted by an interest group consisting of
publishers, journalists, pamphleteers, and others who derive pecuniary and non-
pecuniary income from publication and advocacy of various sorts" (p. 893). By extension, the Sixth Amendment guaranteeing those arrested a speedy trial becomes the first
successful effort by lawyers to drum up business.

for parties is thus most appropriate as, for example, the single-transferable-vote procedure. Indeed, the outcome of the convention is likely to be better if its delegates are *not* viewed as members of a particular party whose life before *and after* the convention is tied to the fortunes of that party. If the constitution is to advance the interests of *all* future citizens, then it must be written by people who are willing to encompass the interests of others along with their own. Representatives of particular interests who anticipate having to win the votes of these "constituents" in the future will be less inclined to compromise these interests and thus may jeopardize the success of the convention.

B   *The Constitutional Convention as a Jury*

The most democratic method for choosing members of a constitutional convention would be by some random selection method for which all citizens were eligible. Such a selection procedure would have two major advantages. First, as is the intent with a jury, it is the procedure most likely to produce impartial delegates, delegates who do not have to run for reelection, have not been selected to represent a particular set of interests, and whose interests are probably unknown to most of the electorate. These delegates are the most likely to take into account the long-run interests of all future citizens and agree to a compromise. Although they are not selected because they represent particular interests, they would by the nature of the selection process be representative of all citizens. The random selection of representatives in fifteenth-century Florence appears to have made all citizens feel that they were a part of the government, and that their interests were represented. It also appears to have led representatives to identify with the common interests of Florence (Schwartz, 1988, ch. 7). Random selection of delegates to a constitutional convention could have the same effects and thereby enhance the likelihood that citizens accept the constitution as theirs.

A convention composed of average citizens would lack expertise, of course. This deficiency could be remedied, as with an elected set of delegates, by appointing experts as consultants or additional members.

It is difficult to imagine a constitutional convention being formed by random selection following a revolution or the collapse of a dictatorial regime. Time is of the essence in such situations, and a convention that is more clearly representative and in possession of the necessary competence would be favored. If, on the other hand, the adopted constitution required periodic new constitutional conventions empowered to amend or replace the existing constitution, the delegates to these subsequent conventions could be randomly selected. The pressure of time would not be severe in this case, nor would the cost of failure. A convention might meet for a full year,[12] with the existing constitution as a status quo. If a convention agreed to amendments or an entirely new constitution, they or it would be adopted; otherwise the existing constitution would continue in effect.

## C	The Parliament as a Constitutional Convention

When an elected parliament exists it, or a subset of it, becomes an obvious body to serve as a constitutional convention. Historically, most constitutional conventions have been constituted from an existing parliament. In some cases, as in East Europe after the collapse of Communism, parliaments are chosen[13] and charged with both running the country and writing its constitution at the same time. In others, an existing parliament may be asked (say, by the chief executive) or feel compelled to write a new constitution by the circumstances of the moment.

Having an existing parliament also serve as a constitutional convention has the great advantage of saving time. When a country is in an anarchy of sorts, or faces the real threat of anarchy, both the short-run tax and expenditure decisions a polity makes, and the long-run choice of its rules have to be made. If a body with a legitimate claim to represent all of the people exists, why not use it to handle both sets of questions? The parliament is also quite likely to contain some of the expertise needed to write the constitution.

There are severe dangers in a parliament's also serving as a constitutional convention, however. First, having two important tasks to fulfill, it may do one or both badly. To the extent that the nation faces a crisis following a revolution or regime collapse, short-run problems are likely to be severe and draw the bulk of the energies of the parliament, with constitutional questions getting short shrift. Such is the case in East Europe today.

Second, as elected representatives, and ones who hope to be elected again, members of parliament may be less willing to compromise by sacrificing the interests of their constituents. The delegates from Delaware to the Philadelphia convention that drafted the U.S. Constitution had been instructed not to compromise on the issue of the proportional representation (PR) of cities (by area) in the legislature. This proved to be

---

[12] Thus, a person randomly chosen as a delegate would be asked to take a full year out of his life to participate in the constitutional convention. The hardship of this could be compensated for financially. In a country in which democracy and citizenship were prized, most would presumably relish the opportunity to participate in a national event that occurs only once, twice, or at most three times in their lifetime – the chartering of their country's political future.

[13] The original selection of parliaments in East Europe after 1989 did not always result in all parliamentary seats being filled by popular vote.

an effective stratagem to bring about the "Great Compromise" of each state having the same number of representatives (two) in the upper house. But had a greater consensus been required for approval of the Constitution, the Delaware delegation's intransigence could have stood in the way of obtaining the final objective (Berns, 1988, pp. 136–7). More generally, the voting patterns at the Philadelphia convention reveal that delegates voted a combination of their own personal interests and those of their constituents (McGuire, 1988). Some delegates to the *Assemblée Constituante* to draft a new constitution for France in 1789 were also given specific instructions on how to vote on certain issues by the estates they represented. In the interests of compromise some French delegates reinterpreted their mission as that of representing the whole nation (Elster, 1991, p. 27). If delegates adhere rigidly to the interests of their constituents, the exercise is doomed to failure if these interests cannot be made to coincide. In Philadelphia, Delegate Gorham of Massachusetts, arguing for ratification of the Constitution by separately elected state conventions, clearly recognizes the relative advantage of separately elected constitutional conventions. "Men chosen by the people for the particular purpose, will discuss the subject more candidly than members of the Legislature who are to lose power which is to be given up to the Genl. Govt." (quoted by Riker, 1987, p. 18). This advantage is illustrated by the experience of Costa Rica, whose 1949 Constitution was drafted by a specially elected Constituent Assembly. Despite the country's being ruled by a military junta at the time, the Assembly appears to have been able to undertake its assignment free of external pressure. "The document owes its existence to debate and compromise, and not to the domination of a single group."[14]

The third danger is that a member of parliament chooses to advance neither the interests of the whole nation nor of his constituents but only those of himself. In particular, parties and their members may opt for constitutional rules that favor their chances for reelection once the constitution is implemented. The largest party favors a two-party system, smaller parties a multiparty system. Large and medium sized parties favor high minimum cut-offs on the fraction of the vote a party must win before it can claim seats; tiny parties want low cut-offs. Well-known and popular politicians favor procedures that allow voters to vote for specific individuals, like the single-transferable-vote procedure. Uncolorful or disliked leaders of major parties favor party-list procedures in which voters only choose among the parties. This motivation is the simplest to understand and appears closest to the truth based on the historical evidence.[15]

---

[14] Ameringer (1982, p. 38). See also Bird (1984, ch. 10).
[15] See Elster's (1993) discussion.

The 1974 constitution of Sweden, although drafted by a commission, was a compromise between the until then dominant Social Democratic Party and the leading opposition parties. Olof Ruin (1988, pp. 320–1) argues that "the agreement . . . hammered out [did not] rest on any version of the right constitutional framework for an advanced welfare society of the Swedish type. Rather, the agreement was characterized by calculations from different quarters of what maximally favored and disfavored their own political party. The Swedish version of constitutional politics appeared as the interest politics of political parties *par excellence.*"

Members of the different parties in Italy that existed prior to Mussolini's takeover met after World War II and drafted a constitution designed to protect incumbent parties (e.g., by allowing them to reward their supporters with patronage of various sorts). It has served the parties' interests well, particularly those of the Christian Democrats, who have been in every government since. How well it has served the Italian citizens is another matter (Spotts and Weiser, 1986, esp. pp. 4–8). Out of frustration with the performance of the Italian political system several attempts at constitutional reform have been made. In one of these, the Bozzi Commission, appointed in November of 1983, proposed reforms that were defeated by a constellation of party interests that feared the parties would be weakened by the changes (Hine, 1988, pp. 218–23).[16]

Although the West German, post–World War II constitution has probably served its citizens better than Italy's citizens have been served by theirs, the same kind of jockeying for post-constitutional advantage was visible at the convention in Bonn (Merkl, 1963, pp. 90–103).

The Spanish Constitution of 1978 was drafted by a committee composed of representatives from both houses of parliament with all parties represented except the Basque National Party. Although consensus was a primary objective from the start, and one that was largely obtained (Leorente, 1988), the different parties did have an eye on their likely positions in the post-constitutional government. The two largest parties (the Union of the Democratic Center and the Spanish Socialist Workers Party) favored and succeeded in getting a constructive motion of censure into the constitution over the vigorous opposition of the smaller parties

---

[16] In spring of 1992, Italians voted for outsider parties on both the left and the right (e.g., the Lombard League, the Greens) in an obvious rebuke of the Christian Democrats and other mainstream parties that had formed the chain of governments since World War II. The election was widely interpreted as a new demand for constitutional reform. Substantial electoral reforms were enacted in 1993, the effects of which are still being felt (Mudambi, Navarra, and Sobbrio, 1999). However, the discussion of constitutional reform in Italy continues to be led by those in politics, and so the chances of meaningful reform remain dim.

(Bonime-Blanc, 1987, p. 77). This rule stipulates that the prime minister cannot be voted out of office unless a replacement is agreed upon. In favoring the rule, the two largest parties in Spain were increasing the likelihood that the governments, of which they expected to be a part, would not easily fall.

All of the constitutions that established democracy in the major Latin American countries have been written by standing parliaments or conventions dominated by the major parties or political interests of the participants (Geddes, 1990). All reflect these interests. For example, proportional representation has generally been adopted at times of significant political transition, when both larger parties that feared significant future declines in strength and small ones expected to benefit from such a shift.

Even more conspicuous illustrations of crass political self-interest occur when the parliament can choose the electoral rules. In France, parliament has the authority to select the electoral rules. The French routinely shift from single- to multi-member district representation according to the expectations of the parties controlling a particular seating of Parliament as to which formula will best serve their interest in the next election (Carstairs, 1980, pp. 176, 185; Knapp, 1987).

The absence of a constitution gives the British Parliament the authority to choose electoral rules by default. The proposal to switch to PR has surfaced on several occasions during the last century in the United Kingdom. These proposals have inevitably met with a cool reception by the party that was the largest or expected to be the largest in the next election (and thus the beneficiary of a disproportionate allocation of seats under the single-member-per-district representation formula). With opposition from the largest one or two parties in the British Parliament almost a certainty, proposals for PR are doomed to fail. As Dicey observed long ago, in Great Britain constitutional issues and party politics are intertwined.[17]

D   Conclusions

For politicians, as for Vince Lombardi's football teams, "winning is the only thing." A politician's striving after victory can lead to desirable outcomes. In a two-party system, each party tries to put forward a platform that is preferred by a majority of voters to the opposing party's platform. In a multiparty system a party must take positions that a given block of voters finds superior to those of all other parties. The necessity to run for reelection constrains individual candidates and their parties to take positions that appeal to at least some groups of voters.

---

[17] Bogdanor (1988, pp. 70–1). See also Carstairs (1980, pp. 195–6).

But the incentives of a person elected to parliament who finds himself in a constitutional convention are quite different. The constitutional convention is a one-time occurrence. The views of those who elected a representative to parliament regarding provisions in the constitution may not be homogeneous, and in any event are probably unknown to the member of parliament. Indeed, they may be unknown to the citizens themselves, since constitutional conventions are such rare events. Thus, an elected member of parliament, whose long-run political career is, he hopes, in parliament, may ignore the interests of both those who elected him and the citizenry at large when making his constitutional choices, at least as these choices pertain to parliamentary elections and the chief executive. A career politician attending a constitutional convention for one time may choose simply to advance his future political prospects.

This likelihood is enhanced when one considers the decision calculus of the voter. He has voted for someone (or some party) now in the parliament. The person(s) he voted for is (are) now part of a constitutional convention that votes to establish a system of representation that the citizen believes is not in his best long-run interests. The next parliamentary elections are held under the new set of rules. Does the voter vote against the persons (party) he formerly supported because of their actions in the constitutional convention, or does he treat those actions as sunk costs and vote for the person or party that will best represent his interests in the next parliament? The latter is clearly the rational thing to do, and if he does it and if his representative knows he will do it, he has complete discretion to write the constitutional rules to maximize his long-run prospects in the parliament. And that is what the record indicates has been done.

These considerations suggest that it is better to elect a separate group of people to the constitutional convention than to have the constitutional convention formed by those elected to serve in the parliament.[18] The rational voter realizes that a different set of issues is to be decided at a constitutional convention, and thus that a different type of person should be chosen to participate. Given the one-shot nature of the convention, the voter knows that, once elected, her representative will be free to vote as he pleases at the convention. The citizen wants, therefore, to elect persons noted for their integrity as well as their honesty and judgment – qualities not always found in those who choose politics for a career. Once the delegates are selected, the citizen can only trust and hope that the magnitude of the task the constitutional convention faces causes the delegates to discharge their duties responsibly.

---

[18] Moreover, it would be wise to prohibit a delegate from holding public office for a fixed interval after the convention.

V   Amending the Constitution

In addition to writing the first constitution, the convention must decide how the constitution is to be rewritten over time or perhaps even replaced in toto. There are several options here. (1) Provision is made for the periodic convening of a constitutional assembly with the authority to amend or replace the existing constitution. This assembly could be governed by the same rules as the first convention, or one could establish new rules. (2)Provision is made for calling a new convention upon some fraction of the citizens or parliament or states demanding it. Once convened it has the same powers to amend or replace the existing constitution. (3) The constitution can be amended by referendum. (4)The constitution can never be changed, and all ambiguities and boundary disputes are settled by the judiciary. (5) Some combination of the above four is an option.

The same issues regarding selection of delegates arise under (1) and (2) as for the original convention. The case against a parliament's serving as a constitutional convention is even stronger when the convention is called under an existing working constitution. Time and the threat of anarchy should not be as pressing concerns, and the polity can afford the luxury of convening an assembly that functions independently of the parliament.

If the constitution is a form of contract among the citizens, the likelihood that it advances the interests of *all* of them is greater if a substantial majority of the citizens or delegates to the constitutional convention must approve it for it to take effect.[19] If the consensual nature of the constitution rests on the size of the majority that ratifies it, and this consensus is to be preserved, then the same supramajority should be required to amend it as was originally required to ratify it.[20] This requirement, coupled with the inability to amend a referendum proposal once made, makes amendment by referendum an unlikely occurrence.

Another potential disadvantage of amendment by referendum arises from the likelihood that the original set of provisions in the constitution obtained their supramajority as a package, that is, as a result of vote trades. If B traded her vote on free speech for A's vote on abortion, and the article on abortion is subsequently amended to B's disapproval, B will have given A her vote rather than traded it. If B anticipates such a successful referendum effort, she will be unwilling to trade her vote in the constitutional convention, and the likelihood of obtaining the required majority on a package of rights falls. This consideration favors

[19] Buchanan and Tullock (1962) require unanimous consent for this reason, as does Rawls (1971) for his social contract.
[20] Charlotte Twight (1992) demonstrates that constitutional revisions in practice are seldom consensual.

the reconvening of a full convention to amend the constitution rather than piecemeal amendments by referendum,[21] so that whole packages of changes involving new trades replace previous packages.[22] However, if reconvening constitutional assemblies is made difficult if not impossible, allowing constitutional change through referenda may be a superior way of updating the citizens' constitutional contract than entrusting all changes to their agents in the judiciary.

The latter is nevertheless the simplest and potentially quickest procedure for keeping the constitution up to date. It suffers from two main defects. First, the court with final authority to settle constitutional disputes must consist of but a handful of individuals, and is thus a very small sample of the population. Its judgment may diverge from that of the larger population, just as any small sample mean can diverge from the population mean.

Second, even if a decision made by the court is exactly the decision that a newly convened convention or the citizens by referendum would have made, there may be an advantage in reaching this decision by one of the more circuitous routes. If the constitutional convention is properly constituted, the citizen *knows* that he has been fairly represented. He can observe and consider the arguments on all sides of the issue as it is debated; debates among members of a court are never observed. The citizen knows, and presumably accepts, that the original constitution was ratified by a substantial majority and that any changes in it require the same majority. Changes cannot be made by simple majorities as is generally true of courts. In a referendum the citizen participates directly, and is exposed to arguments on all sides of the issue. The more time-consuming amendment procedures should generate a better understanding of the decisions made and thereby conviction that the correct decision has been made. In so doing, they are more likely to maintain citizen consensus on the provisions of the constitution and compliance with its provisions.[23]

---

[21] The Swiss hold the record for constitutional amendments (119 through September of 1993, Schweizerische Bundeskanzlei, 1987; Moser, 1993) and as a consequence their constitution gets "longer, more chaotic, in places more ridiculous each year" according to Christopher Hughes (1988, p. 279). The Swiss amendment procedure requires a majority of voters *and* a majority of cantons to approve an amendment before it passes. Although this rule is stronger than a straight simple majority requirement, it is considerably weaker than the 75 percent or so required majority envisaged here, and thus leads to more successful amendment efforts.

[22] An interesting example of how compromise can and does occur in the writing of a constitution is presented by Przeworski's (1988) account of Sweden's first constitution.

[23] Bruce Ackerman (1991) argues that the Supreme Court amended the U.S. Constitution fundamentally in the 1860s and the 1930s by changing its interpretation of the Constitution's language. The "amendments" have been precipitated by significant shifts in the thinking of large majorities of Americans at these two junctures of American history as to what the Constitution should be:

VI   Conclusions

The main message of public choice is that institutions matter. The main message of this chapter is that written constitutions can matter in how well the political institutions of a country function. If this proposition is valid, then it most certainly is valid for the United States, the oldest continuously functioning democracy with a written constitution in the world. For this its constitution and the institutions it defined deserve credit.

To substantiate this point one might cite (1) the Commerce Clause, which under the expansive interpretation of the Supreme Court turned the United States into a giant customs union and thereby facilitated its becoming the richest country in the world; (2) its federalist structure, which allowed it to expand territorially and to grow in population without being strangled by a centralized and bureaucratic national government; (3) the Bill of Rights, which along with the liberal interpretations of the Supreme Court have made the United States the world's model of a free society; and (4) the separation of powers, which provided the judiciary with the independence and authority both to interpret the Constitution on the citizens' behalf and to reinterpret it to prevent its otherwise inevitable obsolescence.

But one can also cite some failures. The Constitution's treatment of slavery and an illiberal interpretation of it by the Supreme Court in the Dred Scott decision led to one of world history's bloodiest wars. The geographic mode of representation defined by the Constitution, coupled with expansive interpretations by the Supreme Court of the federal government's authority relative to the states, has over time undermined the nation's federalist structure resulting in a bloated federal government that does far too many things that should be left to states or cities or simply left undone: a separation of powers between the executive and legislative branches that too often causes stalemates that prevent the federal government from doing that which it should.

One might object that geographic representation and checks and balances have been in place since the Republic's founding, and yet problems of porkbarrel politics and governmental deadlocks seem of recent origin. There are several points to observe in this regard.

First, some problems *have* been around for a long time, but at lower levels of government. Governmental waste and corruption were widespread in the nineteenth century, but at state and local levels. The federal

As a positive analysis of U.S. history, Ackerman's interpretation is most convincing. But it raises serious normative questions. How large a majority of the popular vote in presidential elections suffices for the Court to amend the Constitution? What should be done if the Court fails to heed the majority? To what extent does a minority remain party to the constitutional contract if the contract can be amended whenever a substantial majority so chooses?

government accounted for only 3 percent of GDP in 1929. Even if half of the federal government's budget was wasted in 1929, this would have amounted to only $1^1/_2$ percent of GDP. The same degree of governmental waste today amounts to 12 percent of GDP.[24] The failures of the federal government are more prominent today than they were during the first 150 years of the republic, because the federal government is much more prominent.

The growth of the federal government in the last half century was facilitated by the Supreme Court's reinterpretation of Section 8 of Article I of the Constitution in *U.S. v. Butler* (1936). Section 8 limits the Congress of the United States to eighteen rather narrowly defined powers. But, in *Butler* the court ruled that "the power of Congress to authorize appropriations of public money for public purposes is not limited by the direct grants of legislative power found in the Constitution."[25] The door was thereby opened to the growth in federal government expenditures that was to follow.

Although the constitutionally defined relationship between the president and Congress is not much different now than it was two hundred years ago,[26] the deadlock that it can produce is considerably worse today as a result of the growing parochialism of the Congress. When voters held the *parties* responsible for the performance of government, a presidential landslide would sweep many from the president's party into the House and Senate. Not only would these newcomers be beholden to the president for their past success, but they would realize that if the president did not perform well, the next landslide could sweep them out. But porkbarrel politics and ombudsmen activities have severed the link between a congressional candidate's success and that of his party or the president. To a considerable degree "*Congress* [has become] *composed of professional officeholders oblivious to the changing political sentiments of the country*," and oblivious to those sentiments to which the president responds.[27] Each marches to its own mandate.

Thus, the failures of the U.S. representational system have become significant only in the aftermath of the Supreme Court's 1936 reinterpretation of the Constitution, which allowed the federal government to

---

[24] The 50 percent figure seems to correspond to what the average American estimates the waste in government to be. For example, 75 percent of the 1,512 individuals questioned in a *Washington Post*–ABC poll in October of 1991 believed "that people in government waste a lot of money we pay in taxes." When asked how much is wasted, the average reply was 49 cents out of every dollar (Balz and Morin, 1991).

[25] As quoted by Niskanen (1992, p. 14) upon whom this discussion draws.

[26] The important exception being of course that the Senate was not directly elected two hundred years ago, and thus could exercise the greater detachment and statesmanship envisaged for this *upper* House by the Constitution Framers.

[27] Quote is from Fiorina (1977, p. 14), italics in the original.

expand its activities greatly. This expansion coupled with geographic representation led to the present overcentralization of government, and this centralization coupled with geographic representation strengthened the link between congressional representatives and their constituents at the expense of ties to party and president, further advancing the deadlock aspect of the checks and balances system.

The problems the United States' political institutions create do lead from time to time to efforts to change the Constitution. A balanced-budget amendment, a line item veto for the president, and similar proposals surface and resurface as the country struggles with consequences of the structure designed for it over two hundred years ago. While such changes might certainly help, none proposed so far goes to the heart of the matter. To tackle the problems created by the United States' political institutions head on, a new constitutional convention would need to be called, and a new constitution written.

The very success the Constitution has had in making the United States what it is today unfortunately stands in the way of changing the Constitution to make the country still better. Although many Americans have been frustrated in recent years by particular interpretations of the Constitution by the Supreme Court, most today still undoubtedly view the Constitution with a degree of reverence and awe. Many fear that were a new constitutional convention called, it would in most likelihood not be capable of improving on the constitution that already exists. Indeed, it might not even come close to doing as well. This fear is, I suspect, shared by many political scientists. It is a sad commentary on our ability to learn from our mistakes and on the contributions political science and related disciplines have made over the last two hundred years to our understanding of the consequences of different political institutions.

But the United States is not the end of the world. The events in Eastern Europe and the former Soviet Union since 1989 have awakened an interest in having democratic institutions in every part of the world that does not have them. In other places where democratic institutions exist but have not been performing well, like Italy and Japan, fundamental constitutional changes are also being tried or discussed. In most cases direct citizen involvement has been minimal, and one fears that the new constitutions like the old will do better advancing the interests of those who actually do write them, than of the citizens they hypothetically serve. But with so many experiments going on, one must hope that in a few cases more direct citizen involvement occurs. Constitutions will be written which effectively advance the interests of all citizens, and procedures will be adopted to allow the citizens to revise and rewrite these constitutions as their circumstances change and their knowledge grows. If and where this occurs, written constitutions will not only be shown to matter but to matter for the good.

References

Ackerman, Bruce A. 1991. *We the People*. Cambridge, Mass.: Belknap Press.

Ameringer, Charles D. 1982. *Democracy in Costa Rica*. New York: Praeger.

Arendt, Hannah. 1963. *On Revolution*. New York: Viking Press.

Balz, Dan, and Morin, Richard. 1991. "A Tide of Pessimism and Political Powerlessness Rises." *The Washington Post*, Nov. 3, p. A1 ff.

Beard, Charles A. 1968. *An Economic Interpretation of the Constitution of the United States*. New York: Macmillan (orig. pub. 1913).

Berns, Walter. 1988. "The Writing of the Constitution of the United States." In Robert A. Goldwin and Art Kaufman, eds. *Constitution Makers on Constitution Making: The Experience of Eight Nations*. Washington, D.C.: American Enterprise Institute for Public Policy Research, pp. 119–53.

Bird, Leonard. 1984. *Costa Rica*. London: Sheppard Press.

Bogdanor, Vernon. 1988. "Britain: The Political Constitution." In Vernon Bogdanor, ed. *Constitutions in Democratic Politics*. Aldershot, England: Gower, pp. 53–72.

Bonime-Blanc, Andrea. 1987. *Spain's Transition to Democracy*. Boulder, Colo.: Westview Press.

Buchanan, J. M., and Tullock, G. 1962. *The Calculus of Consent*. Ann Arbor: University of Michigan Press.

Carstairs, Andrew McLaren. 1980. *A Short History of Electoral Systems in Western Europe*. London: Allen & Unwin.

Childs, David. 1980. *Germany since 1918*. New York: St. Martin's Press.

Dahl, Robert. 1998. *On Democracy*. New Haven, Conn.: Yale University Press.

Eckstein, Harry. 1963. "Introduction: The Impact of Electoral Systems on Representative Government." In Harry Eckstein and David E. Apter, eds. *Comparative Politics*. New York: Free Press, pp. 247–54.

Elster, Jon. 1991. *Arguing and Bargaining in Two Constituent Assemblies*. Stores Lectures, Yale Law School, New Haven, Conn., mimeo.

_____ 1993. "Constitution-Making in Eastern Europe: Building the Boat in the Open Sea." *Public Administration*, 71 (Spring/Summer): pp. 169–217.

Eyck, Erich. 1962. *A History of the Weimar Republic*, vol. 1. Cambridge, Mass.: Harvard University Press.

_____ 1963. *A History of the Weimar Republic*, vol. 2. Cambridge, Mass.: Harvard University Press.

Farrar, Cynthia. 1988. *The Origins of Democratic Thinking*. Cambridge: Cambridge University Press.

Fiorina, M. P. 1977. *Congress: Keystone of the Washington Establishment*. New Haven, Conn.: Yale University Press.

Geddes, Barbara. 1990. "Democratic Institutions as Bargains among Self-Interested Politicians." Mimeo, University of California at Los Angeles.

Hermens, Ferdinand A. 1963. "The Dynamics of Proportional Representation." In Harry Eckstein and David E. Apter, eds., *Comparative Politics*. New York: Free Press, pp. 254–80; reprinted from *Democracy or Anarchy?* South Bend, Ind.: University of Notre Dame, 1938, pp. 15–74.

_____ 1951. *Europe between Democracy and Anarchy*. Notre Dame, Ind.: University of Notre Dame.

Hine, David. 1988. "Italy (1948): Condemned by Its Constitution?" In Vernon Bogdanor, ed. *Constitutions in Democratic Politics*. Aldershot, England: Gower, pp. 206–28.

Hughes, Christopher. 1988. "Switzerland (1875): Constitutionalism and Democracy." In Vernon Bogdanor, ed. *Constitutions in Democratic Politics*. Aldershot, England: Gower, pp. 277–89.

Huntington, Samuel P. 1968. *Political Order in Changing Societies*. New Haven, Conn.: Yale University Press.

Jillson, Calvin C. 1988. *Constitution Making: Conflict and Consensus in the Federal Constitution of 1787*. New York: Agathon Press.

Kitto, H. D. F. 1957. *The Greeks*. Baltimore: Penguin Books.

Knapp, Andrew. 1987. "Proportional but Bipolar: France's Electoral System in 1986." *West European Politics*, 10 (Jan.): pp. 89–114.

Lakeman, Enid. 1974. *How Democracies Vote*, 4th ed. London: Faber and Faber.

Landes, William M., and Posner, Richard A. 1975. "The Independent Judiciary in an Interest-Group Perspective." *Journal of Law and Economics*, 18 (Dec.): pp. 875–901.

Leorente, Francisco Rubio. 1988. "The Writing of the Constitution of Spain." In Robert A. Goldwin and Art Kaufman, eds. *Constitution Makers and Constitution Making*. Washington, D.C.: American Enterprise Institute, pp. 239–65.

Lepsius, M. Rainer. 1978. "From Fragmented Party Democracy to Government by Emergency Decree and National Socialist Takeover: Germany." In J. L. Linz and A. Stepan, eds. *The Breakdown of Democratic Regimes*. Baltimore: Johns Hopkins Press, Part II, pp. 34–79.

Linz, J. L., and Stepan, A., eds. 1978. *The Breakdown of Democratic Regimes*. Baltimore: Johns Hopkins University Press, pp. 34–79.

Mayhew, D. R. 1974. *Congress: The Electoral Connection*. New Haven, Conn.: Yale University Press.

McGuire, Robert A. 1988. "Constitution Making: A Rational Choice Model of the Federal Convention of 1787." *American Journal of Political Science*, 32 (May): pp. 483–522.

McGuire, Robert A., and Ohsfeldt, Robert L. 1986. "An Economic Model of Voting Behavior over Specific Issues at the Constitutional Convention of 1787." *Journal of Economic History*, 46 (March): pp. 79–111.

Meier, Christian. 1990. *The Greek Discovery of Democracy*. Cambridge, Mass.: Harvard University Press.

Merkl, Peter H. 1963. *The Origin of the West German Republic*. New York: Oxford University Press.

Moser, Peter. 1993. "Why Is the Political System of Switzerland So Stable?" Mimeo, University of St. Gallen, Switzerland (Nov.).

Mudambi, Ram, Navarra, Pietro, and Sobbrio, Giuseppe. 1999. "Changing the Rules: Political Competition under Plurality and Proportionality." *European Journal of Political Economy*, 15(3): 547–67.

Mueller, Dennis C. 1996. *Constitutional Democracy*. Oxford: Oxford University Press.

Niskanen, William A. 1992. "The Case for a New Fiscal Constitution." *Journal of Economic Perspectives*, 6 (Spring): pp. 13–24.

Olson, Mancur, Jr. 1982. *The Rise and Decline of Nations: Economic Growth, Stagflation, and Social Rigidities*. New Haven, Conn.: Yale University Press.

Peukert, Detlev J. K. 1991. *The Weimar Republic*. London: Penguin Press.

Przeworski, Adam. 1988. "Democracy as a Contingent Outcome of Conflicts." In Jon Elster and Rune Slagstad, eds. *Constitutionalism and Democracy*. Cambridge: Cambridge University Press, pp. 59–80.

Rawls, J. A. 1971. *A Theory of Justice*. Cambridge, Mass.: The Belknap Press of Harvard University Press.

Riker, William H. 1964. *Federalism: Origins, Operation, Significance*. Boston: Little, Brown, and Co.

——. 1987. "The Lessons of 1787." *Public Choice*, 55 (Sept.): pp. 5–34.

Ruin, Olaf. 1988. "Sweden: The New Constitution (1974) and the Tradition of Consensual Politics." In Vernon Bogdanor, ed., *Constitutions in Democratic Politics*. Aldershot, England: Gower, pp. 309–27.

Schwartz, Nancy L. 1988. *The Blue Guitar*. Chicago: University of Chicago Press.

Schweizerische Bundeskanzlei. 1987. *Referendumsvorlagen, Dringliche Bundesbeschlüsse, Volksinitiativen, Volksabstimmungen, 1848–1974* (with Nachtrag, May 1, 1974–Oct. 15, 1980), Bern.

Seligson, Mitchell A. 1990. "Costa Rica." In Howard J. Wiarda and Harvey F. Kline, eds. *Latin American Politics and Development*, 3rd ed. Boulder, Colo.: Westview Press, pp. 455–66.

Spotts, Friedrich, and Weiser, Theodore. 1986. *Italy: A Difficult Democracy*. Cambridge: Cambridge University Press.

Twight, Charlotte. 1992. "Constitutional Renegotiation: Impediments to Consensual Revision," *Constitutional Political Economy*, 3 (Winter): pp. 89–112.

Wootton, David. 1990. "Leveller Democracy and the Puritan Revolution." In J. H. Burns, ed. *The Cambridge History of Political Thought, 1450–1700*. Cambridge: Cambridge University Press, pp. 412–42.

CHAPTER 3

Constitutional Order and Economic Evolution: Competitive and Protectionist Interests in Democratic Society

Viktor Vanberg

1   Introduction

Economic systems exist in an environment, and they must, in one way or another, adapt to the conditions and changes in their environment. Their ability to function and survive depends on their adaptive capacity. This problem has existed throughout the ages for all economic systems. It has, however, without a doubt become especially topical in recent times through the accelerated economic integration worldwide and the increasing globalization of markets.[1] Discussions, under headings such as "institutional sclerosis," of the present difficulties that European welfare states encounter in a world of increasing global competition illustrate this fact.[2]

The ability of economic systems to adapt to changes in their environment, and the manner in which such adaptation proceeds, critically depend on their *economic constitution*, that is, on the framework of rules and institutions that constrain actions and transactions of economic agents within a jurisdiction as well as their transactions with actors outside. External influences always affect an economic system through their impact on the behavior of persons within the respective jurisdiction. And what we describe as a system's adaptation to its environment is, in the final instance, always a matter of reactions of individual persons to changes in the environment – whether these reactions occur through separate individual responses or through organized collective choices, and whether they occur as adaptive responses on the sub-constitutional

---

[1] Killick (1995b: 2): "There is thus an ever-present need to respond to – and take advantage of – such changes in the economic environment. The imperative to do so has been intensified in recent decades as economic interdependence among nations has increased, with the rise of trade and international capital movements relative to domestic economic activities."

[2] Killick (1995c: 379f); Heuss (1990: 97f).

level or as changes in the economic constitution itself. Decisive for the adaptive capacity of an economic system are the ways in which its economic constitution channels the efforts of individual actors in their private as well as in their public political capacities.[3]

The purpose of this chapter is to discuss, from a constitutional economics viewpoint and in general terms, the fundamental problem of adaptation that economic systems face vis-à-vis the constantly changing economic conditions in their environment. Central to constitutional economics is the distinction between two levels at which choices can be made, the *constitutional level* of rule choice and the *sub-constitutional level* of strategy choice within rules. Applied to the notion of economic systems as "social niches" we can distinguish, accordingly, between the collective, political choice of the economic constitution for a jurisdiction, and the choices economic agents make within the constraints defined by the economic constitution. In a system of several levels of jurisdictions this distinction is to be understood, of course, as a relative distinction. What is a matter of constitutional choice at one level of jurisdiction can be viewed as sub-constitutional choice in relation to a more inclusive level of jurisdiction.

The question of how an economic system ought to deal with changes in its environment is at the heart of current political discussions on how to respond to the forces of globalization and to the competition among jurisdictions that they induce. From a constitutional economics perspective, this question can be examined as a problem of how to design a desirable economic constitution for a jurisdiction, or, in other words, as a problem of choosing the "rules of the game" under which the citizens of a polity may wish to live.

2   Jurisdictions as Constitutional Niches

While economic systems have to adapt to the conditions of their respective environment, they are at the same time themselves an expression of the human effort to adapt the environment to *human needs*. People tend not to simply accept their environment as given, but strive to alter it according to their own preferences. This is true for both the social and the natural environment. To the extent that the shaping of an economic constitution (or, more generally, the design of the framework of rules of a jurisdiction) is a matter of deliberate political choice, it can be viewed as the attempt to create something like a *social* or *con-*

---

[3] Speaking of "adaptively efficient institutions," Pelikan (1995: 177, 188) notes: "Extensive social learning, restructuring and adapting may keep going on in a society with stable institutional rules – provided that they are . . . 'adaptively efficient' . . . that is, to effectively provide for sufficient flexibility and adaptability of the structure over the range of the states that the world may happen to assume."

stitutional niche that affords its inhabitants in some respects a more desirable or more hospitable social environment than would otherwise be the case.

The term *economic system* is used here to connote a *jurisdiction* or *polity*, which has a relevant degree of authority to choose the *economic constitution* within its boundaries. Though one may primarily think of nation-states as jurisdictions, the arguments to be developed here can be generalized to other kinds of jurisdictions, be they sub- or supra-national, such as local communities; states in a federal system; or international arrangements. As already indicated, the term *economic constitution* is used here to denote the entire framework of rules which are binding for all the members, constituents or *citizens* of a jurisdiction, and which are of relevance with regard to their economic activities and transactions. It is the difference between the internally enforced economic constitution or framework of rules, and the rules in force (or not in force, respectively) outside the jurisdiction, which – from a constitutional economics perspective – sets a jurisdiction apart from its surrounding environment.[4] An economic constitution limits the permissible economic activities within a jurisdiction in a way comparable to the way that the rules of a game limit the permissible strategies and actions of its players.

When economists talk about the *efficiency* of transactions or cooperative arrangements, the normative standard that they typically have in mind, explicitly or implicitly, is the extent to which the persons concerned are able to satisfy their wants. Applied to economic constitutions the same criterion implies that constitutions should be judged in terms of their capacity to further the well being of the persons living under them. This notion corresponds to the principle of "internal" legitimization that we associate with democratic polities as self-governed associations that are supposed to promote the shared interests of their members or citizens. Since the citizens are the final judges on what promotes their interest, their voluntary agreement to the respective economic constitution is the ultimate source of legitimization and the ultimate criterion for whether the constitution does, in actual fact, serve their common interests.[5]

A jurisdiction's choice regarding its framework of rules can be seen as an expression of the constituents' efforts to actively adapt their environment to their preferences (i.e., to create a more hospitable niche). The members of a jurisdiction are, of course, not limited to the option of taking the environment outside of their jurisdictional "niche" as given, but they can seek, in cooperation with the constituencies of other

---

[4] Depending on the degree of difference between the internal order of rules and externally valid rules (or, respectively, non-existent rules), this separation can be more or less pronounced.

[5] I am, of course, referring here to the contractarian paradigm of constitutional economics that has been advanced most systematically by James M. Buchanan (1991).

jurisdictions, to create, on a more inclusive jurisdictional level, a more hospitable constitutional environment surrounding their own jurisdiction, an environment that serves their preferences better than what would otherwise exist. In this sense one can think of the designing of constitutional environments as a contractual process occurring on several levels through which, at the borders of existing jurisdictions, possibilities exist to improve the hospitability of the given environment through binding rules on a more comprehensive level.[6] Regardless of on which level the efforts of constitutional design occur, they must, of course, account for the constraints imposed upon them by the respective environment, and they can only address such aspects of the environment which can actually be changed by way of collective, political choice. In accordance with the "internal" criterion for legitimization of constitutional regimes, it is always the preferences of the members or citizens at the respective jurisdictional level that provide the measuring rod against which the efficiency of economic constitutions is to be judged.[7]

I shall speak of *constitutional interests* or *constitutional preferences* when I refer to citizens' interests with regard to the framework of rules under which they want to live. To be sure, persons as citizens are not interested in rules per se but in the consequences that follow from observing particular rules. Their constitutional preferences are informed by their "outcome interests," that is, by their preferences regarding the outcome patterns that they expect to result from alternative rules. This means that persons' constitutional preferences will be informed by their *fallible* theories about the working properties of rules. In other words, persons' constitutional preferences may be *ill informed* in the sense that they may be based on mistaken expectations about the kind of outcome patterns that certain rules will tend to produce. Accordingly, persons' constitutional choices may well be inconsistent with their outcome preferences, a fact that is of relevance for issues to be discussed later in this chapter.

The problem to be examined here pertains to the demarcation of an economic system as a "social niche" from its economic environment. As noted, this issue lies at the heart of the current political discussion on the

---

[6] For a more detailed discussion of this notion with regard to the design of competition orders, see Vanberg (1995).

[7] To regard the preferences of the members of a jurisdiction as the normative standard for judging the legitimacy of a jurisdiction's constitutional order is not the same as saying that the interests of non-menbers who may be negatively affected by internally legitimized rules are completely irrelevant under normative aspects. It only means that such "externality" problems have to be addressed at the appropriate jurisdictional level, on which the "external interests" are included in the relevant constituency. Agreement can, of course, have legitimizing force only for the group of persons who are in fact in agreement. How, with regard to a particular issue, the relevant constituency is to be defined is a separate matter.

"globalization of markets" and "competition among jurisdictions." Nation-states, in their efforts at shaping the economic constitutions within their jurisdiction, have always been subject to constraints that international trade and mobility of productive resources impose on their discretion in matters of constitutional choice. Yet, such constraints have recently grown stronger, due to the forces of globalization, that is, due to political and institutional changes as well as advancements in communication and transportation technologies that have contributed to making economic opportunities outside of domestic jurisdictions more easily accessible, creating increasingly global markets for goods, services, and productive resources. These developments do not only mean that firms are facing stronger worldwide competition, they also mean that national economic constitutions are coming under more intense competition, in the sense that their comparative qualities, relative to each other, more speedily translate into economic effects within the respective jurisdictions (Vanberg and Kerber, 1994).

Quite obviously, as globalization leads to intensified competition among national economic constitutions it imposes constraints on the power of governments to sustain existing constitutional provisions, or to legislate constitutional reforms, in response to domestic demands, and not all constitutional preferences that citizens at various jurisdictional levels may harbor, need to be viable in the sense that the respective economic constitutions can be sustained in the environment in which they exist. This raises the question of how national governments *can* respond, and how national constituencies *may want* their governments to respond, to the challenges of globalization. In what follows I shall examine some of the arguments that are relevant to this issue.

3   The Classical Free-Trade Argument as Constitutional Advice

Since Adam Smith most economists have stressed the advantages that persons can realize in an open and competitive economy. Their arguments in support of this claim can be viewed as advice in matters of constitutional choice.[8] They inform citizens on why it is in their best interest to prefer a competitive and open economic order as opposed to protectionist regimes. The focus of these arguments is on the wealth effects made possible by the increase in the division of labor that goes along with expanding markets. Smith and his followers emphasized the relevance of an appropriate legal order for the functioning of markets and, in this sense, they certainly recognized the role of jurisdictions as "constitutional niches." Yet, it was in the complete openness of jurisdictions

---

[8] This is certainly what Smith (1981: 468) had in mind when he spoke of political economy as "the science of a legislator."

to economic transactions that they saw the constitutional regime most beneficial to the interests of the jurisdictions' members.

In a completely open economic system, intrajurisdictional economic activities are by necessity always fully adapted to the alternative options available outside the jurisdiction. Given completely open access to potentially more advantageous outside options, the cooperative arrangements and exchange relations within a jurisdiction have to constantly adapt to the ever changing external conditions, and the internal structure of economic activities will always develop toward a pattern that reflects the relative advantage of internal and external options. In other words, a completely open economic system would always tend to be fully adapted to its economic environment.

The economists' unshakable confidence in the advantages of free trade notwithstanding, there have always been critics who have held reservations about certain consequences of competitive openness. The primary source of such reservations is, quite obviously, the constant pressure to adapt to changing circumstances that people in an open economic system have to endure. In an open economic system, internal economic activities are forced constantly to adapt to the externally available alternative options, and resources are always induced to search for their most profitable employment opportunities. Whereas the classical economic argument sees this as the particular advantage of an open economic system, human beings experience this as a burden imposed upon them. Indeed, there are probably few people who enjoy knowing that their own income prospects and the value of their material and human capital are constantly being threatened by economic changes outside (as well as inside) of their jurisdictions, changes that may force them to find alternative, and possibly less remunerative, employment possibilities for their resources. It is not difficult to understand the wish to avoid exposure to such competitive pressures, and this wish is the reason for the universal demand for protection.

It does not come as a surprise then that, in academic as well as in public discourse, one often encounters arguments that, in one way or another, put forward the diagnosis that a completely competitive and open economic constitution can by no means be claimed to be desirable for people, but that it is, in fact, rather hostile toward human needs.[9] In

---

[9] Jones (1995: 95ff.) refers to this issue when he raises the question, "(w)hether a world of completely open markets would be hospitable" (ibid.: 96), and when he remarks: "Whereas a stagnant society will miss some advantages, a society in a perpetual state of rapid factor mobility runs a risk of trading-off stability for the sake of febrile adaptability. The 'optimality band' within which it may be desirable to operate has scarcely been located, but the political disinclination to open all borders to all goods, services and factors of production seems more than the result of compounding sectional interests. It is the understandable reaction of people who are being urged to hurry towards a goal the posts of which are always moving." Which alternatives the people have in this regard,

this context, the need for social integration, stability, and security are mentioned, all of which are allegedly in conflict with the flexibility, the risks, and the restlessness of open competitive systems. The concept of the *social market economy* and the creation of the welfare state were obviously motivated by the intention to set up a constitutional framework that would offer a more hospitable "niche" to the entirety of human needs than a system of open competition.[10] In recent socio-philosophical discourse it is in particular the advocates of *communitarianism* who stress that the modern liberal market order disregards the aspects of human needs mentioned above, and that this order is therefore defective and in want of repair.

The issues raised here are about matters of constitutional choice, and the relevant measure in questions of constitutional choice are the *constitutional interests* of the citizens of the respective jurisdictions. The political economist can provide information that may help citizens to make better informed constitutional choices and to realize more successfully their constitutional interests. Yet he cannot tell citizens which constitutional interests they should pursue, except in the sense of pointing out to them that the pursuit of their constitutional preferences may lead to consequences that they dislike. Since citizens may evaluate alternative economic constitutions not only in terms of economic efficiency but in terms of other criteria as well, the economist's arguments about the preferability of competitive orders can be no more than conjectures about the kind of order that people find preferable, if they have a clear understanding of the relevant alternatives, that is if their constitutional preferences are informed by an adequate understanding of the outcome patterns that alternative rules will tend to produce. However, the ultimate judgment, of which economic constitution is desirable to them must always be reserved to their own constitutional choices.[11]

4 Consumer Interests, Producer Interests, and Citizenship Interests

An important aspect of the kinds of interests, which are potentially in conflict with competitive openness, seems to concern advantages that

and how these alternatives are to be assessed in light of their constitutional interests, is the problem to be dealt with here.

[10] Neuber (1995: 120) points to the national differences with regard to how much concern is given to "security-needs": "(O)ne could argue that the US economy is more flexible ... than, say, that of Germany. The state presence in the economy is lower, regulation is less pervasive, and contracts are more flexible, particularly in the labor market. The inherent flexibility is bought at the cost of more uncertainty (less welfare state, more open competition, fewer institutional safeguards)."

[11] Here, of course, the question emerges on which "acts of choice" can be seen as the most reliable indicators for the constitutional preferences of the citizens. This question will be addressed in a later section.

persons can realize only through mutually binding agreements or commitments, that is, through some *renunciation of flexibility*. Openness to the environment means access to alternatives, and to enhance competition means to provide for easier access to alternatives. There are occasions, however, in which persons may wish to commit to mutual constraints, that is, to bind themselves if others do likewise. By entering contractual agreements people always limit to a certain extent their leeway in decision making and thus their access to alternatives, and they do so because they hope for advantages that can be achieved through the mutual renunciation of their full range of flexibility.[12]

In markets we can find innumerable cases in which actors are willing to enter mutually binding agreements or commitments (such as long-term sales contracts, employment contracts, partnership agreements, etc.) that limit, for example, the parties' freedom to change their counterparts in trade relations or cooperative ventures as new opportunities arise. Such instances of mutual self-binding in markets prove that persons may voluntarily choose to sacrifice to some extent their freedom of choice in exchange for gains from commitment. Under the market paradigm, voluntary contracts are the main instrument of social coordination, and economic relations are constantly subject to revision in response to the emergence of better alternative options. Yet, at the same time the market is an arena of action where actors have the option to bind themselves mutually in a voluntary manner. The market principle of voluntary coordination includes the possibility that actors enter voluntarily *constitutional* agreements the very purpose of which is the renunciation of sub-constitutional freedoms of decision. The processes on the sub-constitutional level (e.g., the giving of orders and their being obeyed as a means of coordination within a firm) are indirectly legitimized through the voluntary consent to the contractual arrangement by everybody involved.[13] When entering contractual arrangements of mutual self-binding, those involved have to weigh the disadvantages resulting from the limitation of their own freedom of choice against the advantages to be gained from the other participants' commitments. The different kinds of contracts to be found in markets reflect these considerations.[14]

[12] It is the central notion of constitutional political economy that mutual (as well as unilateral) commitments may bring advantages that could not be realized otherwise.

[13] Though this cannot be discussed here in any detail, it should at least be mentioned that a number of questions can be raised here: How can one measure the degree to which the consent to a contractual arrangement is voluntary? What is relevant, the voluntary consent at the time of the original contract-making only, or, instead, the ongoing voluntary consent to the continuation of the arrangement? If the latter is the case, what are then reliable indicators for voluntariness?

[14] It is in itself a question of constitutional choice, which kinds of contracts should be considered legitimate, or should be enforced by the apparatus of the state. The question of whether the directly concerned parties agree voluntarily to a contract on the sub-

The role that voluntary consent among participating actors plays as a legitimizing principle can be easily misunderstood if the distinction between the constitutional and the sub-constitutional decision levels is not adequately observed. Market and free-trade regimes are not self-legitimizing in the sense that the voluntary nature of the transactions performed within their framework could be considered to legitimize not only these transactions themselves but also the regimes as such. With their voluntary consent to *transactions within* a market framework persons express their agreement to these transactions not their agreement to the constitutional framework within which the transactions take place. Whether or not they would like to live under a competitive market or free-trade regime, as opposed to some alternative constitutional arrangement, is a question of their *constitutional* preferences, preferences they do not express through the decisions they make under the auspices of such a regime. It would be by no means inconsistent for someone to advocate a protectionist regime, but at the same time, under free-trade conditions, to prefer to purchase foreign goods over domestic products. The latter is a question of sub-constitutional interests, and the first a question of constitutional interests.

If actors in markets, through their voluntary consent to mutual constraints, reveal that they do not in all regards prefer the advantages of complete flexibility and freedom of choice to advantages that are attainable through binding commitments, then one should allow for similar considerations to apply to matters of constitutional choice on the level of political communities or jurisdictions. In this sense one cannot rule out a priori as a possible explanation for protectionist provisions that the members of a jurisdiction find it to be in their best interest to enter mutually binding agreements which, on the one hand, limit their own flexibility to respond to economic opportunities emerging outside of their jurisdiction, but which, on the other hand, as a result of the same obligations on part of their fellow citizens, shelter them from extra-jurisdictional competition. Economists may well suspect that such preferences for a protectionist "insurance arrangement" can only be based

constitutional level must therefore be distinguished from the question of whether the citizens of a jurisdiction may want to decide, on a constitutional level, that certain contracts are invalid, irrespective of whether the parties to these contracts agree to them voluntarily. Thus, while it is well conceivable that contracts of enslavement could come into existence in a completely voluntary fashion, there may nevertheless be good reasons for citizens to come to the conclusion, on the constitutional level, that contracts of such a nature should be invalid. The decisive question on the constitutional level is how the nature of the demarcation between admissable and inadmissable contracts impacts on the functional characteristics of the respective economic order. Which limitations of the freedom of contract are desirable to the members of a jurisdiction is in the final consideration a question of their *constitutional interests*, i.e., of their interests regarding the kind of constitutional regime in which they desire to live.

on misperceptions of the true costs of such arrangements. Yet they cannot rule out, in principle, the possibility that the citizens of a jurisdiction may still consider a regime of this sort to be in their constitutional interest, even after they have diligently weighed all relevant costs and benefits.

In economics the issue of protectionism is generally discussed in terms of the conflict between our constitutional interests as consumers and our interests as producers. The argument that Adam Smith and many economists after him have made consists essentially of the following two claims. First, it is producers who are interested in protection, while consumer interests are best served by a competitive, free-trade regime. Second, consumer interests should take precedence over producer interests, since it is only in order to consume that we produce.[15] From a constitutional economics perspective this argument can be refined by putting the issue as a matter of constitutional choice, asking what kind of economic constitution, a protectionist or a free-trade regime, citizens could agree on who take into account that they are typically on both sides of the issue, as producers – in their roles as investors, employees etc. – as well as consumers. In constitutional economics terms the classical free-trade argument can be restated as the conjecture that only as consumers citizens share a *common constitutional interest*, namely an interest in a competitive, free-trade regime, while in their protectionist producer interests they are typically divided, as these interests aim at *protectionist privileges* rather than at general constitutional provisions equally applicable to all producers.

If one looks at the issue of protectionism in the preceding sense only as a matter of consumer interests versus producer interests, it seems as if protectionist interests can only be interests in protectionist *privileges*. Accordingly one might be inclined to conclude that there are no protectionist provisions that could be claimed to be in citizens' *common* constitutional interest, and, hence, that there are simply no protectionist interests that citizens could be expected to share. This conclusion would, however, unduly rule out the possibility that people may harbor protectionist interests that are motivated by interests other than the interests of producers in protectionist privileges. Yet we cannot rule out a priori the possibility that citizens *in their capacity as citizens* rather than as producers, may share an interest in maintaining certain characteristics of their jurisdiction that they wish to be guarded by protectionist provisions. In order to contrast them to producer interests in protectionist privileges,

---

[15] The well-known passage in Smith (1981: 600) reads: "Consumption is the sole end and purpose of all production; and the interest of the producer ought to be attended to only so far as it may be necessary for promoting that of the consumer. The maxim is so perfectly self-evident, that it would be absurd to attempt to prove it."

one can think of such potentially common protectionist interests as *citizenship interests*.[16]

5   Protectionist Privileges and Rent Seeking

Obviously, we need to draw a distinction between two varieties in which protectionist interests may appear, namely, on one side, as *partial* interests in protectionist *privileges* and, on the other side, as *common* interests in *non-discriminatory, general* protectionist provisions. In their first variety, protectionist interests are directed at protectionist privileges that are granted, in a discriminatory fashion, to particular persons or particular groups in the jurisdiction, but not to others. Though one can expect their beneficiaries to have an interest in such protectionist privileges, it is difficult to think of reasons why the non-privileged should consent to such discriminatory regimes, if they have a clear understanding of the nature of such provisions.[17] In their second variety, protectionist interests are directed at protectionist provisions that apply equally to all citizens and in which all share a common interest. Whether such common protectionist interests do in fact exist, and how one can, in practice, tell them apart from interests in protectionist privileges, is the issue to be discussed in the remainder of this chapter.

When confronted with the need to adapt to changes in external economic conditions that negatively affect the returns from their current use of resources, the members of a jurisdiction face basically two alternative options. One alternative consists in leaving it to the individual actors themselves separately to adapt to such changes by accepting a loss in income, or by reestablishing their competitiveness through reducing costs and/or improving quality, or by finding alternative employment for their respective resources. The second alternative consists in attempts to spare those who are directly affected the necessity to adapt by taking collective provisions, be it by shielding them through protectionist measures from external competition, or be it by subsidizing them in order to compensate for the consequences of competition. Whichever alternative is chosen, the necessity to adapt to the change in environmental conditions cannot be evaded. Choosing the second alternative means only that the burdens of adaptation are being diffused and made anonymous, by

---

[16] I have adopted this term from Kincaid's (1992) discussion of what he describes as a conflict between "consumership and citizenship." On this issue see also Vanberg (1997).

[17] It is, to be sure, conceivable for protectionist privileges that are granted exclusively to particular groups to be, nevertheless, in the common constitutional interest of all citizens of the respective jurisdiction. Yet, it is not easy to think of an example that can be plausibly assumed to fall in that category, though such things as farm subsidies are sometimes claimed to enjoy broad support in the population at large. In any case, this possibility will not be considered here.

imposing them on the large, anonymous groups of consumers and taxpayers. This alternative certainly looks enticing to those directly affected
in any concrete case. Granted as a privilege, such protection is clearly
advantageous to the privileged in the sense that any particular group will
prefer enjoying the protection over not receiving it. This does not mean,
however, that protection is an attractive regime when applied as a
general rule. In considering this issue, the members of a jurisdiction have
to take into account the overall working properties of a protectionist
regime, including the problems of rent seeking that occur whenever governments or legislative bodies of a jurisdiction hold the power to bestow
protection or subsidies on certain groups.

Calls for protection voiced in the political process typically seem
to reflect producer interests, aimed at protectionist privileges. Special-
interest groups seek to attain protection for themselves. They do not
lobby for protectionist measures to be extended without distinction to
all members of the jurisdiction. It should be obvious that neither Adam
Smith nor other economists advocating free trade have overlooked the
fact that protectionist regulations that are restricted to particular persons
or groups can be advantageous to them and that the prospective beneficiaries can therefore be expected to launch efforts to secure protection
for themselves. It is not controversial that privileges can be in the constitutional interests of the privileged. The issue is why the non-privileged
should give their consent to such regimes. Why should they agree to an
"insurance arrangement" that provides protection against external competition for others but not for themselves? An order of protectionist
privileges cannot be considered, in the sense noted, to be equivalent
to mutually binding commitments in markets, commitments to which
all parties voluntarily agree. Protectionist provisions could be said to be
equivalent to such voluntary mutual commitments only in cases in which
they are indeed in the common constitutional interest of all citizens.
Behind the classical free-trade argument stands, in its final conclusion,
the thesis that one can hardly find examples for protectionist regulations
that can plausibly be claimed to lie within the common constitutional
interest of all the members of a jurisdiction.

Protectionist privileges always involve the usage of the coercive apparatus of the state for the transfer of income from others to those favored
by the regulation. In contrast to income derived from production or free
exchange in the market, protection income relies on forcible transfers.
Subsidies involve forcible transfers from taxpayers to the recipients;
tariffs or other trade restrictions involve forcibly hindering or completely
denying actors access to extra-jurisdictional economic opportunities to
the benefit of the "protected." Juxtaposed to the protectionist privileges
of one group, therefore, always stands the "exploitation" of others who,
through state-coercion, are denied otherwise accessible advantages. The

better the chances are of attaining protection privileges through the political process, the stronger the incentives will be for actors in the jurisdiction to shift their efforts away from the realization of income through market performance and into the attainment of such privileges (or into warding off measures that provide privileges for others). The fatal consequences this process has for the potential of wealth creation within the respective jurisdiction have been, under the rubric of "privilege seeking," a principal concern of the Freiburg School of Law and Economics (Vanberg, 1998), and they are the central theme of the theory of "rent seeking" (Buchanan et al., 1980).

The theory of rent seeking complements and reinforces the classical free-trade arguments by focusing on the dynamics of the political process in jurisdictions in which protectionist privileges can be attained. The theory points to the fact that even if conceivably protectionist provisions might be found that lie in the common constitutional interest of all the members of a jurisdiction, citizens may still be ill advised to allow for protectionist provisions to be attained through the political process, as long as that process cannot be trusted to be sufficiently reliable in sorting out protectionist provisions that are indeed in their common, citizenship interest from those that bring advantages only for some and disadvantages for others, or possibly even disadvantages for everybody involved. The critical issue is therefore, how – by what procedure – it is to be decided which demands for protectionist measures are actually in the common interest, and how – by what procedure – citizens can protect themselves against the implementation of measures that discriminate against them to the benefit of others, or that are detrimental to all of them. If there is no practical procedure available that sufficiently guards against these risks, the interests of all members may well be better served by not allowing for any kind of protectionism than by allowing for possibly desirable protection, while running the risk of ending up with a bundle of measures undesirable in the sum of its impact.

The desire of single groups to gain protection from competition for themselves but at the same time to enjoy the advantages of an open economic system is, as noted before, not hard to understand. Yet, by separately seeking protectionist privileges for themselves, they jointly produce an outcome that is desirable for none of them. As the theory of rent seeking shows, the members of a jurisdiction in which the political process permits protectionist privileges to be granted are caught in a multi-person prisoner's dilemma (Schelling, 1978, ch. 7). For each single group the striving for such privileges is the dominant strategy, but by choosing this strategy they bring about an outcome that serves nobody's interests. If citizens had to decide between the resulting system of widespread protection and a regime generally open to competition, they would have good reasons to choose the latter. But in the real political process they are not faced with a choice of this kind. Here they are confronted with the choice of whether to seek to secure protectionist privileges for themselves or to abstain from such rent seeking. Whether they choose the one option or the other will typically not be decisive in determining which kind of overall regime they will end up living in. By their own separate abstention from rent seeking they cannot prevent the dynamics of the political process from drifting toward a state of pervasive protectionism, which is not even desirable to the "beneficiaries" of the protectionist regulations when compared to the conditions that would prevail in an open competitive system.

6   The Co-Evolution of Constitutional Niches and Their Environment

Economic systems co-evolve with their environment. From an evolutionary perspective one can interpret the economic constitution of a jurisdiction as part of the selection environment that conditions the behavior of economic agents within the jurisdiction. If, following Karl Popper (1994), we look at all acts of living beings, including human actions, as problem-solving activities, then the issue under analysis here can be described like this: economic behavior deals, in the most general sense, with problems of scarcity. The economic constitution of a jurisdiction defines important aspects of the problem environment that persons within the jurisdiction confront. Constitutional constraints channel their attempts at problem solving in a certain manner by defining which strategies persons can legitimately use in their competition for scarce rewards and also by posing problems that they have to overcome. For example, queuing in lines for sought-after scarce goods was one of the characteristic consequences of the framework of rules in place in the former socialist systems, and it was one of the major everyday problems that persons in these systems had to deal with.

At the heart of evolutionary thought is the concept of *population dynamics*, that is, the notion that a species, as a population of individuals, changes its composition (the distribution of individual characteristics) over time as an outcome of the interaction of continuous variation and selective retention, a process that results in the population becoming better adapted to the problem environment or, in other words, in its increased problem-solving capacity. In this sense evolutionary competition can also be viewed as a process in which knowledge or problem-solving know-how is created.[18] The decisive mechanism here is that individual traits that allow for better problem solutions – or that, in other words, are better adapted to the problem environment – provide to their

---

[18] For more detail compare Kerber (1996, 1997).

bearers better chances for reproduction, that is, better chances of having their traits represented in future generations, while the opposite is true for less effectively adapted characteristics.

The evolutionary population model can be usefully applied to the notion of economic systems or jurisdictions as "constitutional niches" and to their evolution over time. In terms of the population model one can think of the different strategies that economic agents within a jurisdiction employ, in dealing with the various kinds of problems they face, as populations of problem-solving trials that may be more or less well adapted to the kinds of problems that they are meant to solve. In this setting the economic constitution of a jurisdiction represents an important part of the relevant problem environment to which the agents' problem-solving efforts are, in varying degrees, adapted. The better adapted they are, the higher chances are that they will be retained by the actors using them and that they will be imitated by others, and the better will be their survival prospects.

The notion that a jurisdiction's economic constitution is an important part of the problem environment that economic agents within the jurisdiction face, and the idea that the nature of the economic constitution will affect the ways in which intra-jurisdictional populations of problem solutions will evolve over time, can, of course, be applied to the various adjacent levels in a world of multiple jurisdictional levels. Thus, one can view the various patterns of private economic activity within the constitutional framework of a nation-state as a population of tentative problem solutions in their respective constitutional niches. Similarly, one can view the various legal provisions of the member states of a federal union as populations of tentative problem solutions within the federal jurisdiction with its constitutional framework. In a system with several levels, the constitutional rules at one level define relevant aspects of the problem environment within which the populations of problem-solving strategies at the lower jurisdictional levels evolve.

People always strive, within the constraints that they face, to improve their condition, according to what they consider desirable and in accordance with their knowledge about possibly auspicious strategies. In the present context this means that people will always strive to solve the problems they confront in ways that appear most promising to them – whatever kind of economic system or "constitutional niche" they find themselves in.[19] In this process they not only seek to adapt their problem-solving strategies to the conditions defined by the economic constitution (as well as to the conditions set up by other characteristics of the jurisdiction), they also seek to adapt these conditions, as far as is possible, to

---

[19] Alchian (1977: 16) speaks of "(a)daptive, imitative, and trial-and-error behavior in the pursuit of 'positive profits.'"

their own preferences. *The efficiency and viability of an economic constitution will depend on its ability to channel the problem-solving efforts of the respective jurisdiction's citizens in socially productive directions.*

7   Protectionism and Perverse Selection

In a paper dealing with the "transformation" of formerly socialist economies Pavel Pelikan (1992) has used an evolutionary approach, similar to the perspective adopted here, to explain the failure of socialist systems. Analogous to the distinctions between the *order of rules* and the *order of actions*, or between the constitutional and the sub-constitutional levels of choice, Pelikan distinguishes between the framework of rules (R) which limits the actors' range of permissible strategies within an economic system and the patterns or structures of behavior (S) which evolve within a given framework of rules. In the sense noted above, Pelikan also views the distinction between R and S as a relative distinction that can be applied to any two neighboring levels in a world with multiple levels of jurisdictions, and he also stresses that the processes of change occurring on the various levels can be viewed as evolutionary processes, that is, as the evolution of frameworks of rules (R-evolution) and as the evolution of patterns of behavior within the rule frameworks (S-evolution).[20]

As Pelikan (1992: 51) argues, critical for the relative performance of alternative economic systems is the channeling effect that their respective R has on the evolution of their S or, in other words, in which direction their R steers the S-evolution.[21] In his view the enhancement of the efficiency or problem-solving potential of an economic system is dependent upon the availability of a framework of rules in which evolutionary experimentation and learning by trial-and-error selection are allowed to take place. As the paramount reason for the failure of socialist systems he diagnoses, accordingly, the "catastrophic influence" the framework of rules R had on the S-evolution in these systems.[22] In the terminology used here, this negative impact would have been felt in the deficient evolution of the population of problem-solving strategies, and of patterns of economic behavior and organizations within the framework of socialist economic constitutions. As Pelikan (1992: 53) puts it: "All socialist Rs

[20] Pelikan (1992: 43): "S-evolution consists of changes in the population of agents, or changes in the network of their relationships, or both.... R-evolution consists of changes of law and custom."

[21] The idea that "different Rs must be judged above all for their influence on S-evolution" is stressed by Pelikan (1992: 44) as the core claim of his essay. In this context, see also Mndambi et al. (2001) for a similar analysis applied to the case of Italy.

[22] Pelikan (1992: 44): "It was the poor performance of their Rs that caused the socialist economies to fail and ... it was the disastrous influence of these Rs on S-evolution that was the main cause of this poor performance."

then turn out to have the double disadvantage ... that ... they raise greater obstacles to potentially successful trials, and at the same time are less strict at eliminating committed organizational errors. As the effects of this double disadvantage cumulate over time, the S evolved under a socialist R will increasingly be scourged by backward industries and mediocre or outright wasteful firms."[23]

In the framework of socialist economic constitutions, just as in all other social environments, people seek to improve their lot. They use their creativity to find new and possibly better solutions to the problems confronting them. And they learn, through their own experience and, indirectly, through the experiences of others, which problem-solving strategies deliver the most desirable results. In the socialist regimes too the population of problem-solving strategies evolved over time toward better adaptation to the problem environment imposed by the socialist rules of the game. The principal deficiency of the collapsed socialist systems was that the creativity and adaptive abilities of the people were forced under a system of rules that steered their problem-solving efforts into socially unproductive or even destructive directions.[24] The populations of problem-solving strategies (behavioral dispositions, forms of organization, etc.) that have grown under these conditions, but that are maladapted to their new economic environment, pose the transformation problem that the former socialist economies have to solve.

Stated differently, one can see the fundamental flaw of the socialist systems in that they created a "perverse" problem environment or selection environment, perverse in the sense that they tended to encourage strategies of economic behavior that were rational for the individual actors, given the problem environment that they faced, but which eroded the economic viability of the systems themselves. It is this problem of perverse selection that is of interest in the present context. The failure of the socialist economies exemplifies, in a particularly drastic manner, a general problem that ought to be considered when the potential benefits and costs of protectionist provisions are under examination. It is a problem that reinforces the warning against protectionism that the classical free-trade and the rent-seeking arguments imply.

Far from being confined to the socialist economies, the problem of "perverse selection" can also be found in Western economies. It is probably one of the principal causes of the ubiquitously diagnosed crisis of

---

[23] Neuber (1995: 115) identifies the "innovative deficit of the socialist economies" as the "crucial distinguishing factor between market economies and planned economies: innovation is a decentralized process, requiring an adequate 'selection environment.'"

[24] Similarly Neuber (1995: 112) states: "(T)he stereotypical understanding of planned economies fails to recognize that much of the behavioral, and consequently structural, rigidity that could be observed was in itself the result of rational adaptation by economic agents to the prevailing structure."

the social welfare state. Perverse selection is at work when the rejection of economic "mistakes" is hindered by preserving unprofitable structures through protection and subsidies, at the direct or indirect expense of profitable industries and enterprises, thereby eroding the economic base of the latter. As Jones (1995: 95) puts it: "The cost of protectionism is evident. It is the classic instance of reinforcement of unadaptability."

Perverse selection environments are like "social traps" (for example, the prisoner's dilemma) in that a conflict exists between what is advantageous or rational for persons to do when they choose individually and separately, and what is in their common interest. If one of the principal positive functions of government is to help citizens avoid or correct social dilemmas, then the problem with "perverse" constitutional frameworks is that they do exactly the opposite; that is, they *create* social dilemmas. In jurisdictions or "social niches" that place their members in perverse selection environments, persons' rational, adaptive strategy choices are steered into a direction that increasingly erodes the viability of the "constitutional niche." The problem of perverse selection results typically from efforts to make a jurisdiction a hospitable social niche for economic activities that would not be able to survive outside of the protective environment, under competitive conditions. To be sure, as noted before, every economic constitution is an expression of the attempt to create, inside a jurisdiction, an environment that is hospitable to the activities that citizens want to encourage. Furthermore, as noted, attempts at creating more hospitable social environmental conditions by constitutional means can be undertaken at various, more or less inclusive, jurisdictional levels. Yet all such efforts are subject to the constraint that the respective constitutional frameworks have to be viable within their environment. And their viability (this is the essence of the preceding argument) is always dependent on the directing effects that they have on the evolution of their internal populations of problem-solving strategies.

8   Protectionism, Citizenship Interests, and Globalization

In a world in which actors are free to choose the jurisdictions or constitutional regimes in which to allocate their productive resources, one should expect the matural process to select against protectionist privileges and in favor of regimes that are more in line with the constitutional interests of those making the choices. Even if economic agents were initially inclined to opt for economic constitutions that discriminate in their favor, in such a world they would eventually come to opt for non-discriminating constitutions because they would learn from experience that jurisdictions that grant them privileges will not be attractive to the non-privileged parties who would have to fund their privileges. And in the absence of these parties an economic constitution that grants privileges is not even attractive to the would-be privileged.[25]

Since the increase of possibilities of choice for productive resources between alternative jurisdictions is a principal feature of the process of "globalization," the latter can be said to bring the real economic world closer to the above conceptual model of free choice among jurisdictions. This again means that the kinds of constraints that the model world imposes on protectionist policies should also show their effects in a world of increasingly global markets. The easier it is for resources to move between jurisdictions, the lower the willingness of their owners will be to accept less advantageous conditions in one jurisdiction compared to those in the jurisdiction next door.[26] This again induces, as noted earlier, competition among economic constitutions as mobile resources will seek out jurisdictions that offer them the most hospitable constitutional environments. The critical issue in the present context is whether such competition can be expected to select against protectionist privileges only, in which case it could be said to help citizens realize their common constitutional interests, or whether it will also tend to select against constitutional provisions that all citizens would benefit from, a claim that is often made, for instance, in the current debate on the future of the "Sozialstaat" in Germany.

As globalization facilitates mobility of resources across jurisdictions, one should expect it to select against protectionist privileges.[27] It is,

---

[25] Not only would, in such a world of voluntary choice among constitutional orders, the discriminating orders suffer from a loss of members. The non-discriminating but inefficient orders would also lose members to the same degree in which information about the relative efficiency of alternative regimes becomes available.

[26] Jones (1995: 100f.) emphasizes the importance that historically competition among jurisdiction has had for Europe, and he stresses its parallelism to today's globalization of competition: "Europe's mosaic of little polities, its emergent system of nation-states, was immensely interconnected and competitive. . . . The polities of Europe were separately ruled but leaky: capital, entrepreneurship, technology and labour circulated among them. These productive factors did not, however, need to shift *en masse*. Shifts at the margin were all that were required to nudge most rulers away from damaging acts of expropriation. . . . There was in effect a single market for information. . . . When a policy was deemed ineffective or worse, it could be avoided. When it was thought good, it would be copied. The ebb and flow of factors around the European-cum-Atlantic world had some of the consequences loved or loathed in the globalized market of today: international rivalry to retain or attract them, tamed governments, curbed their taxing power, and infringed their sovereignty, although they scarcely knew it and had to pretend otherwise." Jones (ibid.: 101) adds the interesting remark: "How Europe's governments reasserted a considerable part of their sovereignty during the nineteenth century is another story. They went on straining to create nationhood out of the ethnic and linguistic fragments."

[27] Streit (1995: 374) points out the limitations that the competition of jurisdictions for mobile resources imposes on national policies and remarks that the forces of globalization make it increasingly difficult for national governments to favor particular group interests through regulation.

however, not obvious at all why it should pose a threat to protectionist provisions that reflect common citizenship interests, that is, provisions that are desirable for all members of the jurisdiction because they make it a more attractive constitutional niche for all of them. If there exist generally advantageous protectionist provisions, provisions that are indeed in the common interest of the constituency as a whole, they should be able to evolve and to be maintained in a regime of free choice among jurisdictions. The relevant test of whether protectionist measures are not just serving the privileges of some while being disadvantageous to others, but, instead, do actually contribute to making a jurisdiction a more desirable social niche for all citizens, lies, ultimately, not in whether such provisions are sought after and can be attained in the political process, but rather in the attractiveness of the respective jurisdiction as a "constitutional niche." To the extent, for instance, that the regulations of the German Sozialstaat do in fact constitute, as some claim, generally desirable jurisdictional characteristics, they should be an asset rather than a liability in inter-jurisdictional competition. If the claim is true, it is not clear why such constitutional provisions should be threatened by globalization. It is, therefore, somewhat paradoxical, if those who make the claim at the same time call for protectionist measures in order to defend the German Sozialstaat against the threats of global competition.

Likewise, it would seem that communitarian claims about constitutional interests that remain uncovered by competitive market regimes ought to be proven, in the final instance, under the conditions of competition between jurisdictions, that is, by actual choices that persons make in the "market" for alternative constitutional orders. It is certainly true that feelings of uneasiness with "modernity" in general, and with market competition in particular, are often expressed, but such complaints are, in and by themselves, not convincing proof that the persons who express them are prepared to pay the price which life in a "communitarian order" (whatever that may be) would call for. The relevant test would be, indeed, the willingness to give preference to "communitarian jurisdictions" over alternative orders. In the final instance, the only reliable indicator for the constitutional interests that people truly do have in common would seem to be their voluntary participation in particular regimes, in the presence of available alternative options.

9   Conclusion

Economic systems co-evolve with, and within, their environment, and they cannot exclude themselves from the necessity to adapt to ever-changing environmental conditions. That they cannot evade the necessity to adapt does not mean, however, that constituents could not seek to create for themselves, at various jurisdictional levels, constitutional niches that reflect their preferences for the kind of socio-political-economic world that they would like to live in. In creating their jurisdictional niches constituents will have to find, though, a sustainable balance between their own constitutional preferences and the viability constraints that their environment imposes on them, constraints that, to be sure, may themselves be subject to constitutional agreements on more inclusive jurisdictional levels, but that cannot be all changed at will. Pelikan speaks in regard to this issue of, as he calls it, the "wisdom condition" in institutional choice.[28]

Globalization seems to pose, in this regard, a particularly difficult problem to democratic political processes that, using Hirschman's (1970) "exit and voice" terminology, can be described as follows: The more mobile resources are, the less incentive their owners will have to incur the costs of relying on the political voice mechanism to protect their interests, and the more they will tend to use, for that purpose, their less costly exit options. Conversely, the less mobile resources are, the less can their owners rely on the exit mechanism to protect their interests, and the more incentives they have to make use of the political voice mechanism. This would tend to give the interests of owners of less mobile resources a greater weight in the political process compared to the interests of owners of more mobile resources. To the extent, however, that the long-term income-earning prospects of the less mobile resources are dependent on the presence of complementary mobile resources and, accordingly, on their jurisdictions' ability to attract such resources, the more reason they should have to see to it that their jurisdictions provide hospitable environments for mobile resources. In other words, their long-term interests would require the owners of less mobile resources to use their political voice to promote the interests of the owners of mobile resources, who themselves have lesser incentives to make their voices heard in the political process.

Whether one can expect the democratic process in modern welfare states to be capable of such "fiduciary representation" of the interests of mobile resources, to benefit the long-run common interests of the less mobile and immobile resources, is somewhat doubtful. It would require that politicians who advocate reforms that make a jurisdiction more attractive to mobile resources have a better chance of winning elections than politicians who cater to the short-term interests of the immobile or

---

[28] Pelikan's (1995: 189) "wisdom condition" says that viable institutions "must also be able to induce the members of the society to choose objectives that do not destroy the basis on which continuing existence of the institutions depends." As Pelikan (ibid.: 200) notes: "For example, much as medicine has found that the preference for longevity is incompatible with the preference for smoking, the social sciences should be able to find that the preference for civilization and welfare (in the broadest meaning of the term) is incompatible with the preference for certain types of institutions."

less mobile resources. If that were the case, the forces of *inter-jurisdictional* competition for mobile resources and the forces of *intra-jurisdictional* competition for political office would work in concert. What may be happening in fact, however, is that these forces pull in opposite directions, that is, that proposals for reforms that respond to the demands of inter-jurisdictional competition do not make for a platform that helps politicians to win elections.

References

Alchian, Armen A. 1977. "Uncertainty, Evolution and Economic Theory." *Economic Forces at Work*. Indianapolis, Ind.: Liberty Press, pp. 15–35.
Buchanan, James M. 1991. *The Economics and Ethics of Constitutional Order*. Ann Arbor: University of Michigan Press.
Buchanan, James M., et al., eds. 1980. *Toward a Theory of the Rent-Seeking Society*. College Station: Texas A&M University Press.
Heuss, Ernst. 1990. "Evolution and Stagnation of Economic Systems." In K. Dopfer and K.-F. Raible, eds., *The Evolution of Economic Systems: Essays in Honour of Ota Sik*. New York: St. Martin's Press, pp. 91–9.
Hirschmann, Albert O. 1970. *Exit, Voice and Loyalty*. Cambridge, Mass.: Harvard University Press.
Jones, E. L. 1995. "Economic Adaptability in the Long Term." In T. Killick, ed., *The Flexible Economy – Causes and Consequences of the Adaptability of National Economics*. London and New York: Routledge, pp. 70–110.
Kerber, Wolfgang. 1996. "Recht als Selektionsumgebung für evolutorische Wettbewerbsprozesse." In B. Priddat and G. Wegner, eds., *Zwischen Evolution und Institution – Neue Ansätze in der ökonomischen Theorie*. Marburg: Metropolis-Verlag, pp. 301–30.
1997. "Wettbewerb als Hypothesentest: Eine evolutorische Konzeption wissenschaffenden Wettbewerbs." In K. V. Delhaes and U. Fehl, eds., *Dimensionen des Wettbewerbs*. Stuttgart: Lucius, pp. 29–78.
Killick, Tony, ed. 1995a. *The Flexible Economy – Causes and Consequences of the Adaptability of National Economies*. London and New York: Routledge.
1995b. "Relevance, Meaning and Determinants of Flexibility." In T. Killick, ed., *The Flexible Economy – Causes and Consequences of the Adaptability of National Economics*. London and New York: Routledge, pp. 1–33.
1995c. "Conclusions: Economic Flexibility, Progress and Policies." In T. Killick, ed., *The Flexible Economy – Causes and Consequences of the Adaptability of National Economics*. London and New York: Routledge, pp. 365–94.
Kincaid, John. 1992. "Consumership versus Citizenship: Is There Wiggle Room for Local Regulation in the Global Economy?" In B. Hocking, ed., *Foreign Relations and Federal States*. London and New York: Leicester University Press, Mudanbi, Ram, Navarra, Pietro, and Sobbrio, Giuseppe. 2001. *Rules, Choice, and Strategy*. Aldershot, England: Edward Elgar. pp. 27–47.
Mudambi, Ram, Navarra, Pietro, and Sobbrio, Giuseppe. 2001. *Rules, Choice, and Strategy*. Aldersshot, England: Edward Elgar.
Neuber, Alexander. 1995. "Adapting the Economies of Eastern Europe: Behavioral and Institutional Aspects of Flexibility." In T. Killick, ed., *The Flexible Economy – Causes and Consequences of the Adaptability of National Economics*. London and New York: Routledge, pp. 111–53.

Pelikan, Pavel. 1992. "The Dynamics of Economic Systems, or How to Transform a Failed Socialist Economy." *Journal of Evolutionary Economics*, 2: 39–63.

——— 1995. "Competition of Socio-Economic Institutions: In Search of the Winners." In L. Gerken, ed., *Competition among Institutions*. New York: St. Martin's Press, pp. 177–205.

Popper, Karl R. 1994. *Alles Leben ist Problemlösen*. Munich: Piper.

Schelling, T. C. 1978. *Micromotives and Macrobehvaior*. New York: W. W. Norton.

Smith, Adam. 1981 [1776]. *An Inquiry into the Nature and Causes of the Wealth of Nations*. Indianapolis: Liberty Classics.

Streit, Manfred E. 1995. *Freiburger Beiträge zur Ordnungsökonomik*. Tübingen: J. C. B. Mohr (Paul Siebeck).

Vanberg, Viktor. 1995. "Ordnungspolitik und die Unvermeidbarkeit des Wettbewerbs." In H. H. Francke, ed., *Ökonomischer Individualismus und freiheitliche Verfassung*. Freiburg: Rombach, pp. 187–211.

——— 1997. "Subsidiarity, Responsive Government and Individual Liberty." In K. W. Nörr and Th. Oppermann, eds., *Subsidiarität: Idee und Wirklichkeit – Zur Reichweite eines Prinzips in Deutschland und Europa*. Tübingen: J. C. B. Mohr (Paul Siebeck), pp. 253–69.

——— 1998. "Freiburg School of Law and Economics." In P. Newman, ed., *The New Palgrave Dictionary of Economics and the Law*. London: Macmillan.

Vanberg, Viktor, and Kerber, Wolfgang. 1994. "Institutional Competition among Jurisdictions," *Constitutional Political Economy*, 5: 193–219.

CHAPTER 4

The Efficacy of Arbitrary Rules

James M. Buchanan and Yong J. Yoon

I Introduction

The analytical core of constitutional political economy is located in the categorical distinction between two sets: (1) alternative constraints or rules and (2) alternative positions or outcomes attainable within separately defined constraints. Almost all discussion has proceeded on the presumption that there exists some "natural," or empirically derived, basis for this distinction. The familiar explanatory reference is to ordinary games (poker, tennis, basketball), where there is surely universal recognition of the distinction between "the rules," which indeed define the game itself and which must be explicitly chosen through some process, and the outcomes or solutions that emerge from the interdependent choices among strategies made by the players whose behavior is constrained by the rules that are chosen.

The extension to politics is not so simple as it may appear to be, even to those who share the American sense of constitutional order, with its categorical difference between constitutional law and ordinary legislation. Here the distinction between the choice among constraints and choices made within constraints becomes evident, but the analogy from ordinary games breaks down because outcomes within rules are explicitly chosen; political outcomes do not emerge from the interdependent choices made by separate participants as is the case in ordinary games. Nonetheless, the distinction remains central to the analytical exercise. And, in an even broader perspective, political philosophers who seek to ground political legitimacy in consent or agreement must necessarily place the formation of the basic social contract at a level or stage of choice that is categorically separate from the give and take of ordinary politics.

We do not challenge the usefulness of analyzing the implications of the rules-within-rules distinction in these several "natural" settings. (There is no suggestion that we throw out much earlier work.) The simple

We are indebted to Mancur Olson and Robert Tollison for helpful suggestions.

point promised here is only that of suggesting that the distinction may also be efficacious in non-natural settings. That is to say, rules may be efficiency enhancing even in situations where there is no clear demarcation between levels or stages of choice. Even in those situations where the rules-within-rules distinction cannot readily be discerned and applied, there may exist prospective gains to all participants from action that separates, arbitrarily, one set of potential variables from another, thereby effectively "constitutionalizing" a subset. The analysis has practicable relevance for ongoing discussions about such issues as the balanced-budget amendment or, indeed, many proposals to include more constraints in the political constitution.

The discussion here is related, indirectly at least, to two separate research programs in decision theory. Herbert Simon (1957) has long been associated with the behavioral hypothesis that individuals "satisfice" rather than "maximize". A possible rational derivation for such behavior is suggested by the adoption of dimension-reducing rules. Ron Heiner (1983) has located the origins of predictable human behavior in the inability of individuals to choose as if they are error free in complex (many-dimensional) settings. The prospects for costly errors are decreased by the adoption of rules.

In Section II, we summarize the reasons for rules and contrast the efficiency reason implied by the analysis here with other familiar constructions. In Section III, we present the basic analysis through emphasis on the complexity of the dimensionality of the collective-choice set. This is illustrated using a stylized three-person, three-public good model. Section IV compares the two- and three-dimensional models for collective choice in more detail. The constitutional calculus is addressed in Section V, and the chapter is concluded with Section VI.

II   Reasons for Rules

The focus of attention on the potential efficacy of arbitrarily selected rules allows us to identify a reason for rules that is conceptually quite different from those that are emphasized in the theory of self-control, on the one hand, and the theory of protective constitutionalism, on the other. In the first of these settings, the individual, even in social and behavioral isolation, may prefer to impose constraints on his or her own behavior in order to forestall expedient reaction to the creation of temptation that is deemed to be potentially damaging from some enlightened perspective. (The story of Ulysses and the Sirens offers the example from classical mythology; Elster, 1979.) In the second setting, that which more or less defines the domain of constitutional political economy, the individual agrees to constraints on his or her own behavior in social or collective interaction in order to secure the anticipated benefits of constraints on the behavior of others. (See Brennan and Buchanan, 1985; Buchanan, 1975.)

In some respects, an even more basic reason for rules stems from the recognition that rules are efficiency enhancing, either individually or collectively, where neither of the familiar arguments above is fully applicable. As members of the human species, we make and follow rules in order to reduce, perhaps dramatically, the complexity of the choices that we might otherwise confront. As members of a collective unit, we may adopt rules (we may agree to constitutionalize some collective-choice parameters) in order to reduce the resource wastage that the complexity of a less-constrained politics would necessarily involve.

III   Rules and the Dimensionality of Collective Choice

A rule operates to reduce the dimensionality of the choice set. If this is acknowledged, the economist is immediately prompted to ask: How could any decrease in the number of available choice alternatives possibly be efficiency enhancing, per se, apart from the two familiar arguments noted above? The answer is located in the possible effects on the costs of choice itself.

This result may be illustrated in a simple example with discrete values. First, we remain at the level of personal choice, or personal ordering prior to expression of choice itself. Suppose that there are three potential-choice variables (three dimensions) and that each variable may take on each of three possible values. There are twenty-seven alternatives in the unconstrained choice set. In ordering these alternatives, the individual must carry out some cursory comparative examination of each alternative. Even if each step in the process requires only a nanosecond, the costs of making the ordering clearly could be reduced by a dimensional shrinkage of the set. If one of the three variables should be fixed in value, the choice set is decreased from twenty-seven to nine members; the costs of ordering are clearly lowered.[1]

Our primary emphasis is not on the costs of individual orderings of alternatives. It is instead on the possible efficacy of arbitrary rules (of constitutionalization) in settings of interaction where collective choices must be made. The proposition advanced here is that a reduction in the number of dimensions that defines the size of the choice set decreases the costs of making choices, both for individuals as separately considered and for the collectivity in the aggregate. Hence, even if there is no "natural" distinction to be drawn between rules (constraints) and other members of the set among which choices are to be made, the arbitrary introduction of such a distinction may be utility increasing.

---

[1] The search algorithm in computer science is illustrative. An ordering of 27 numbers requires 351 operations; an ordering of 9 numbers requires only 36 operations.

We can again introduce the example with three variables, each of which can take on any one of three discrete values. But these variables are now public goods that must be shared among three persons; each person must adjust to the same value for each of the goods. For a simple illustration, think of three students who must share a dormitory room with thermostat setting, lights-out time, and visitor access as three separate variables. Again there are twenty-seven possible outcomes.

Consider, now, the costs of reaching a collective decision. Assume that each of the three persons (*A*, *B*, and *C*) has a most preferred position or outcome, defined as one solution in the three-dimensional choice space, and that these most preferred positions differ as among the three. If we do not allow for the introduction of a partitionable good, with which side payments might be made, there will be no agreement on a unique solution. Some decision rule will be necessary.

Suppose that the effective constitution dictates that decisions for the group are to be made by simple majority voting, and, indeed, in public attitudes this rule becomes "natural" in settings where collective choices must be made. In the model as described, there are twenty-seven positions that might be set, one against the other, in a sequence of pairwise majoritarian comparisons. Initially, we may neglect the endogeneity of the process through which alternatives are presented for voting choices. In the non-constrained case, there would be 351 separate voting comparisons to be made.[2] Each of these "elections" would, necessarily, use up resources.

Suppose, now, that one of the three variables is "constitutionalized" by fixing a value that is to remain invariant over the collective choice as among the remaining options. This step reduces the number of positions or outcomes from 27 to 9 and reduces the number of possible pairwise majoritarian voting choices from 351 to 36.

If we recognize that the alternatives presented for collective choice emerge endogenously from proposals made by the participants themselves, many of the possible pairwise voting comparisons will never arise. No majority coalition will advance for consideration any alternative in which all of its members (in the three-person collectivity, both members of the potential majority) receive lower payoffs than in other feasible alternatives. (For further discussion and analysis, see Buchanan, 1995a, 1996.) The majority non-dominated set of positions will be a subset of all positions. The complexity involved in reaching collective choices is less than might be suggested in models that neglect the endogeneity of choice alternatives.

We want to suggest, however, that the cost-reducing effect of decreasing the dimensionality of the space remains. Consider now basically the

---

[2] In general, there are $m(m - 1)/2$ voting comparisons where m is the number of alternatives. (See Black, 1958.)

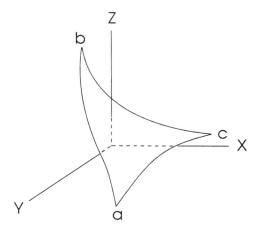

Figure 1. Bliss points: three-person three-public goods.

same example as before, only let us drop the assumption of discrete values and allow for continuous variation along each of the dimensions. Commence, as before, with a three-person, three public goods example. The space has three dimensions, and the bliss point of each participant is defined in this space. We may think of connecting these three positions in the three-dimensional space by tracing the contract loci and thereby creating a three-sided roughly triangular simplex or manifold in three-space. (See Figure 1.) This construction allows us to depict the set of majority non-dominated positions. The subset of positions that remains majority non-dominated are those positions that lie along the boundaries of the triangular simplex located in the three-dimensional space. Any position that does not lie along such boundaries will be dominated, *for any majority*, by a position or positions on the boundaries. Hence, no such position will ever be presented for a vote by any prospective coalition. (See Buchanan and Yoon, 1997.)

IV   From Three to Two Dimensions

For multi-dimensional collective choice there will be no majority equilibrium, and the collective outcome will cycle as among all the positions defined by the boundaries of the simplex. We seek now to answer the question: How will a reduction in the number of dimensions reduce the costs of collective choices?

As before, assume that one of the three variables is now "constitutionalized" by imposing a fixed value on one of the three variables. As depicted in Figure 2, the collective-choice setting in two dimensions lends

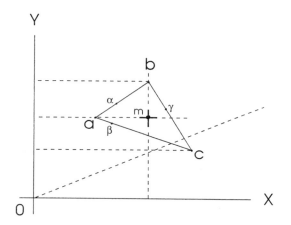

Figure 2. Constrained bliss points.

itself to geometrical illustration. The plane surface becomes a cut through the initial three-dimensional space at the selected value for the parameterized variable.

In the more familiar plane geometry here, the positions labeled a, b, and c are *constrained* bliss points for the three persons A, B, and C. Or, stated differently, these positions may be thought of, roughly, as projections of the non-constrained bliss points in three-dimensional space onto the two-dimensional plane. (Strictly speaking, the bliss points are projections from three-space only on the assumption that iso-utility surfaces are spherical.)

Again, the familiar majoritarian cycle in two-space will occur as among all positions along the boundaries of the triangular figure defined by the three loci. And, similarly as in the three-dimensional setting, these boundary positions make up the majority non-dominated set in the constrained space. (When an additional dimension is parameterized, leaving the domain for collective choice uni-dimensional, majority rule produces a unique equilibrium. Duncan Black's median voter theorem applies, even in the presence of coalitions, as Yoon, 1997, has shown.)

The proposition we advance is that the costs of collective decision, even in the absence of a majority equilibrium in the reduced-choice set, are lower than in the higher dimensional setting. There are, as already noted, two separate components in this cost reduction: the first for each participant separately and the second for all persons in the aggregate. The change in dimensionality reduces the private costs for each person in the ordering of feasible alternatives. Indeed, the very necessity of locating some higher dimensional bliss point is obviated by the shrinkage of the feasible set. It seems plausible to suggest that persons may be able to evaluate alternatives in the reduced set *without* explicit derivation of the total higher dimensional ordering. For illustration, if the three variables are designated as x, y, and z, the fixing of a value for z, say, at z^*, requires that the individual order only those (x, y) alternatives that are in the constrained subset. The more inclusive ordering over the whole set that includes other values for z than z^* is unnecessary, and, if at all costly, will not be carried out.[3]

The second component of cost reduction as the dimensionality of the choice set is decreased is more significant. As noted, and as depicted in Figure 2, there is no majoritarian equilibrium even in the setting where one of the initial three variables is "constitutionalized" at a specific value. Over the sequence of votes, outcomes will cycle continuously among all positions shown on the boundaries of the triangular figure defined by the three contract loci. If we assume that, quite apart from the cost of the individual orderings discussed, there is some cost involved in the cycling-voting process itself, we can begin to sense the impact of the dimensional shift.

Why does the cycle occur? And what generates a change from one position or outcome to another? Consider the coalition AB and assume that a position, say, α, in Figure 2, has been reached. This position is dominated for members of the differing coalition, AC, by, say, β. To get to this new position, individual C will be motivated to propose β as an alternative to α, and any such action undertaken by C must involve some cost. A specific proposal, like β must be formulated and presented, and importantly, C must make efforts to persuade A to defect from the coalition with B that has sustained the α position. Rent-seeking costs, defined in some inclusive sense, will be incurred in each and every link in the cyclical rotation.

To elaborate our point here, consider, now, how these rent-seeking costs might be changed as the dimensionality of the choice set is increased from two to three. Majority voting will generate continuous cycling in either case. But rent-seeking investment in the aggregate will vary directly with the dimensionality of the choice set. This relationship stems from that between effort and anticipated reward. In the three-dimensional space of our illustration, each person will expect to attain a position closer to his or her bliss point, when successful in attaining membership in the majority coalition than would be the case in the con-

---

[3] The ordering among the alternatives in the constrained subset, where only x and y are variables, may vary with the parameterized value for z. But such absence of independence creates no problem here, since the alternatives outside the constrained subset are genuinely irrelevant, by contrast with the Arrow setting that requires ordering over the whole set (Arrow, 1951).

strained two-dimensional model. Majoritarian rent seeking (Buchanan, 1995b) will clearly be higher in the three- than in the two-dimensional setting. And, of course, in the aggregate, most, if not all, such investment measures social wastage of productive resources.

If we acknowledge, as we must, that costs must increase as the dimensionality of the collective choice set is expanded, and for both of the reasons noted, we are prompted to examine prospects for possibly off-setting increases in benefits. And at this point it seems clear that public-choice theorists, most of whom are economists, have generalized too readily from the evident advantages of increasing dimensionality in the presence of fully partitionable and marketable private goods to infer comparable advantages in public- or collective-choice settings where, by definition, partitionability and exchangeability are absent.

Consider the problem as faced by a member of a collectively organized group, one that has its collective choice set limited to some arbitrarily determined small number of dimensions. What might be expected to be gained by "deconstitutionalizing" one or more parameters, thereby allowing majority voting to determine values for one or more of the variables that were previously fixed, at least quasi-permanently, by constitutionally enforced mandate? An individual might anticipate that, if successful in attaining membership in a dominant majority coalition, a position somewhat closer to his or her higher dimensional bliss point will be reached than that which was possible in the constrained subset, even as a member of a successful coalition. Against such an anticipated benefit, however, the individual must reckon on the prospect that a position even further away from the idealized point might be selected when minority rather than majority status is his or her lot. There seems to be no clear argument in logic here to suggest that the participant in collective action secures a net increase in utility from an increase in the dimensionality of the choice set.

V   Constitutional Calculus

Consider a person who is a participant in a continuing constitutional convention, out of which collective outcomes emerge that dictate the partitioning of the set of collective-choice variables into those that are constitutionalized and those that are not constitutionalized and hence left to the workings of ordinary in-period majoritarian politics. Values for the first set are to be chosen constitutionally and these values are to remain invariant over a whole sequence of periods. These variables become parameters within which ordinary politics takes place. Values for the second set of variables are to be left open for determination, period by period, through standard political processes, which we assumed to be majoritarian.

The focus of our analysis in this chapter is on arbitrary rules, by which we mean that, initially, there is no clearly defined "natural" division between the two sets of collective-choice variables, no classificatory scheme that commands immediate and universal assent. We assume that the inclusive set, N, of collective-choice variables is sufficiently large to ensure that period-by-period majoritarian choice will be predictably complex and will involve both cycling among alternatives (absence of equilibrium) and investment in rent seeking aimed at forging successful majority coalitions.

The individual as participant in this constitutional setting must confront choices that require consideration of three interdependent questions. First, should some subset of the N collective-choice variables be constitutionalized? Second, if some variables are to be converted into rules, what particular variables should be included? Third, for each variable to be included, what should be set as the constitutionalized value that is to be held in place at least quasi-permanently?

It is clear that these choices are not independent, one from the other. If a single variable is to be constitutionalized but only at some extreme value, the participant might never agree to include it in the subset. But, over some range of value, constitutionalization of this variable might be acceptable. Other variables might preferably be constitutionalized, at least over some ranges for their own values. And, even if a particular variable might qualify for constitutionalization, standing alone, it might fail the test if a sufficient number of other variables are included in the subset of constraining rules.

It seems analytically straightforward to model the individual's maximizing problem as she confronts setting values for the three interdependent choice options. If a person is a constitutional dictator, she would choose that subset of variables for constitutionalization that would most effectively meet her preferences, and these would be parameterized at her most preferred specific values. Each person's "constitutional bliss position" may be conceptually defined. But, of course, these positions would differ as among participants. The setting is the familiar one in which "trades" must be made if potential agreement is to be reached. In general, no person is likely to secure her separately defined constitutional optimum. But under many configurations of preferences along with predicted costs, there may be sufficient intersections of interest to ensure that some subset of collective-choice variables will command general agreement for constitutionalization.

Consider the basic three-person, two public goods diagram. Assume that the iso-utility contours are concentric around the three bliss points. Under simple majoritarian voting, there will be a continuous cycle among all the positions defined by the three loci. All positions either inside or outside the triangular area, *abc*, will be dominated for any majority.

Consider, now, a proposal that one of the two variables, Y or X, be parameterized, or constitutionalized, and that majority voting be used to determine the remaining variable, thereby eliminating the cycle and generating the unique median result.

What is the opportunity set that will face the three participants, such that they may consider this proposal? This opportunity set will consist of positions that lie along the two intersecting middle lines of optima. Any position that does not lie on these lines cannot be attained under the institution being proposed.

If there is any cost of the cycling process, including outlay on majoritarian rent seeking, there may be positions in this opportunity set that will be Pareto-Wicksell preferred to cycling among positions on the three loci. To the extent that these costs are in some sense roughly symmetrical among all three participants, the subset of positions in the opportunity set that Pareto-Wicksell dominate the cycling results would tend to lie close to the intersection, as indicated by the heavily shaded segments of the middle lines of optima in Figure 2.

Both initial locations of the bliss points and possible asymmetries in relative costs may, of course, affect the results. Participants who find the cycling process relatively less costly will not find the constitutionalization of a variable to be desirable unless such a rule change will differentially advantage them, thereby making any agreed upon outcome more toward their own bliss points.

Constitutionalization of a collective-choice variable need not imply that a value for that variable is uniquely set. Constitutionalization implies only that the variable in question is fixed separately and independently from ordinary in-period determination through majority voting procedures. For example, and especially if there are interdependencies among the variables, constitutionalization may consist in tying the value of one variable to another. Again, referring to the illustration in Figure 2, the value for Y could be set at one-half the value for X, hence requiring that all solutions lie along the dotted line, with the median preference along this imposed dimension made finally controlling.

VI   Conclusion

The analysis calls attention to the question of possible determination of an efficient constitutional structure in those settings beyond those where there exists the "natural" distinction between constraints and end-states, that is, between properly constitutional and post-constitutional variables. How many variables should be placed beyond the ordinary politics that operate within a set of quasi-permanent constraints or parameters? And if some variables are to be constitutionalized, which variables should these be? And, for those that are placed in the subset, what values should be left?

We have done little more than suggest outlines of the research program that might be devoted to exploration of these questions. As the preceding discussion suggests, however, the burden of proof seems to rest on the argument that would support increases in the number of variables that are opened for ordinary political determination, period by period, through the operation of majoritarian decision-making institutions.

Defenders or proponents of relatively unlimited majoritarian democracy may suggest that the analysis presented in this chapter fails to reckon on the possible positive value assigned to political participation, as such. Even if persons recognize the costs of collective choice as related directly to the dimensionality of the space and also recognize the relatively limited, if any, direct benefits from expanding this space, they may still prefer to allow ordinary politics to operate in an un-constrained n-space than in any constrained space that is less than n-dimensional. They may do so because they place some positive value on conscious collective determination, period by period, of all collective-choice values, as opposed to existence under the quasi-permanent constraints of what they consider to be arbitrary rules.

Note that the analysis and discussion here are not about the extent to which the economy is politicized, that is, the extent to which the economy is subject to political-collective choices for the values of variables to be imposed coercively on all members of the politically organized group. Instead, the analysis is limited to the constitutional/post-constitutional breakdown within the politicized sector itself, and especially when consideration extends beyond the "natural" parameters that impose orthodox limits on political processes.

In both public and academic discourse and debate over the proposed balanced-budget amendment to the United States Constitution, particularly that which took place in the 1980s and 1990s, arguments were advanced to the effect that "too much should not be placed in the constitution." The analysis of this chapter implies the contrary thrust; it implies that possibly more, not less, might be constitutionalized and on straightforward efficiency grounds.

The argument supplies an underlying logical basis for Hayek's (1979) proposal to separate the collective choice of the distribution of tax shares from those of budgetary composition and aggregate size. His specific suggestion involved delegation of tax-share distribution to a designated "upper" legislative body, members of which meet more stringent qualifications and serve longer terms, while budgetary choices remain within the domain of ordinary parliamentary assemblies. If translated and transplanted to an American setting, Hayek's proposal might be interpreted as calling for an effective constitutionalization of tax-sharing arrangements. (See also Brennan and Buchanan, 1981.)

Our primary emphasis here has not, however, been on the particular politics or political structure for any collectivity at any time. The analysis does imply that, to the extent that the division between variables to be constitutionalized and those left in the domain for ordinary majoritarian politics is arbitrary, perhaps as emerging from the particularized history of a polity, the overall efficacy of differing political orders may not critically depend on what is and what is not constitutionalized. Our central point, as noted, has been limited to the elaboration of a reason for rules that may not have been given sufficient attention. Even arbitrary rules may be, within limits, efficiency enhancing because they may serve to reduce the "churning" (de Jasay, 1985) that becomes all too characteristic of modern majoritarian politics.

References

Arrow, Kenneth J. 1951. *Social Choice and Individual Values*. New York: Wiley.

Black, Duncan. 1958. *Theory of Committees and Elections*. Cambridge: Cambridge University Press.

Brennan, Geoffrey, and Buchanan, James M. 1985. *The Reason of Rules: Constitutional Political Economy*. Cambridge: Cambridge University Press.

——— 1981. "The Tax System as Social Overhead Capital: A Constitutional Perspective on Fiscal Norms." In Dieter Biehl, Karl W. Roskamp, and Wolfgang F. Stolper, eds., *Public Finance and Economic Growth*. Detroit: Wayne State University Press, pp. 46–56.

Buchanan, James M. 1975. *The Limits of Liberty: Between Anarchy and Leviathan*. Chicago: University of Chicago Press.

——— 1995a. "Foundational Concerns: A Criticism of Public Choice Theory." In José Casas Pardo and Friedrich Schneider, eds., *Current Issues in Public Choice*. Cheltenham, England: Edward Elgar, pp. 3–20.

——— 1995b. Majoritarian Rent Seeking. Working paper, Center for Study of Public Choice, George Mason University, Fairfax, Va.

——— 1996. Rule Feasibility and Rule Dominance. Working paper, Center for Study of Public Choice, George Mason University, Fairfax, Va.

Buchanan, James M., and Yoon, Yong J. 1997. Constitutional Geometry. Working paper, Center for Study of Public Choice, George Mason University, Fairfax, Va.

de Jasay, Anthony. 1985. *The State*. Oxford: Basil Blackwell.

Elster, Jon. 1979. *Ulysses and the Sirens: Studies in Rationality and Irrationality*. Cambridge: Cambridge University Press.

Hayek, Friedrich A. 1979. *Law, Legislation and Liberty*, vol. 3, *The Political Order of a Free People*. Chicago: University of Chicago Press.

Heiner, Ron. 1983. "The Origin of Predictable Behavior," *American Economic Review* 73 (No. 4, September): 560–95.

Simon, Herbert A. 1957. *Models of Man: Social and Rational.* New York: John Wiley & Sons.

Yoon, Yong J. 1997. Coalitions and the Median Voter Theorem. Working paper, Center for Study of Public Choice, George Mason University, Fairfax, Va.

CHAPTER 5

Constitutional Political Economy and Civil Society

Charles K. Rowley

1   The Constitutional Premise

A constitution is here defined as a set of rules that determine the political institutions of a society (Mueller, 1996: 43). Since a society is defined in terms of the existence of such a set of rules, every society, whether democratic, oligarchic or autocratic, has a constitution.

All societies emerge from some pre-society form that is here called a state of nature, which itself influences the nature and behavior of individuals. In this sense, all constitutions evolve over time and are not to be conceived as rational constructs, even though most scholars of constitutional political economy (Buchanan and Tullock, 1962; Rawls, 1971; Buchanan, 1975; Mueller, 1996) analyze constitutions from a constructivist rationalist perspective, ignoring the evolutionary process.

The importance of evolution is most clearly evident in the example of the United Kingdom, whose unwritten constitution has evolved over more than two millennia. This constitution has been and is being forged by successful and unsuccessful invasions from outside, by bloody civil wars and by the building and then the dismantlement of a great Empire, as well as by a slow, essentially non-violent, post-1688 shift from autocratic monarchy to constitutional monarchy.

The importance of constructivist rationalism is most clearly evident in the case of the United States, whose written constitution, which embraced much of the antecedent English common law, was chosen consciously by a property-owning white male minority elite, was written by design and with purpose and was then imposed upon a largely unen-

I should like to thank Maria Pia Paganelli for research assistance. The essay benefitted from helpful comments received at the Conference on Constitutional Political Economy held in Taormina, Sicily in September 1997. The helpful commentary of Nicolaus Tideman is especially valued. Financial support is acknowledged from The John M. Olin Center for Employment Practice and Policy, from The Sunmark Foundation and from the Earhart Foundation.

franchised population. This constitution has survived, in terms of periodically amended parchment if not in terms of political reality, only because the more populous northern states denied secession rights clearly implicit in that parchment and imposed a military dictatorship upon the South following successful invasion.

In imposing that outcome, President Lincoln repeatedly violated the parchment of the Constitution, relying on arguments of military necessity for example, to eliminate the right to habeas corpus, to imprison state legislators inclined to secession and to take out, though ultimately not to serve, an indictment of Chief Justice Roger Taney of the United States Supreme Court. The Great Emancipator freed the slaves only at the high price of partially enslaving free men (Hummel, 1996).

The important lesson to be learned from the history of the two most attractive and longest-standing constitutions of the modern world – both incidentally primarily Anglo-Saxon in origin – is that neither of them emerged even in some remote sense as the outcome of unanimous consent. Rather they were forged by elites, imposed upon the majority without consultation and amended by the bloody forces of internal and external conflict. In a sense, nevertheless, the fact that both constitutions have long survived suggests that they contain within themselves features that prove to be attractive to populations much more extensive than those that forged them.

This essay explores the process of constitutional evolution, therefore, from radically opposed social-contract perspectives and reviews the consequences of such constitutional processes for the establishment and the maintenance of civil society. It also recognizes that conflict as well as consent is an ever-present partner of constitutional evolution.

2   Two Spectra in the Political Philosophy of Civil Society

The collapse of the Soviet Empire, beginning in 1989, and the subsequent efforts made by many central and eastern European countries to construct or to reconstruct civil societies out of the shambles left behind by communism, has inspired many Western intellectuals to revisit the concept of civil society and to ask themselves whether this concept may speak also to the condition of the West in the post-communist world order. In so doing, it has become apparent that the concept of civil society has many meanings – indeed, that it offers a very broad tent capable of sheltering a multitude of diverse systems.

In this essay I review the concept of civil society from a constitutional perspective focussing on the central ideas of two great English political-philosophers of the seventeenth and early eighteenth centuries, Thomas Hobbes and John Locke. These two scholars, although utilizing essentially the same vocabulary of the civil-society notion, in fact outline two categorically opposed visions of society.

Two great spectra have dominated political philosophy certainly since the midsixteenth century (Bobbio, 1993: 29). The spectrum favoured by Thomas Hobbes was that between anarchy and order. For Hobbes order was the predominant objective that justified civil society. The spectrum favoured by John Locke was that between oppression and freedom. For Locke, freedom was the predominant objective that justified civil society.

For the most part, the Hobbesian vision appears to have the ascendancy at the present time not only in the countries emerging from socialism, but also in the countries of the West that successfully challenged and defeated the socialist vision. I shall argue, to the contrary, that the ideas of John Locke offer the most effective basis for the establishment and maintenance of civil society. A strictly limited government, of separated powers with authority that extends only to the maintenance of the rule of law, and the defense of life, liberty and property provides the economic, the political and the cultural environment most conducive to human flourishing and the wealth of the individual in society.

3   The State of Nature

The starting point for a discussion of the concept of the state of nature is the conceptual model of natural law theory employed by all the major political philosophers from Thomas Hobbes to G. W. F. Hegel. This conceptual model is built on the supposed dichotomy between the state of nature and civil society. Its characteristic features are as follows, paraphrased from Bobbio (1993: 1–2):

1. The state of nature is a non-political condition of mankind and represents the starting point for any analysis of the origins of the state.
2. The constitutive elements of the state of nature are individuals, who do not live in society, but who are characterized by varying degrees of sociability. Families may also exist in this state.
3. Individuals (families) are free and equal (at least in principle) in the state of nature.
4. The state of nature and civil society are opposed to one another. Civil society arises to correct or to eliminate shortcomings in the state of nature.
5. Any shift from the state of nature to civil society does not occur by necessity, because of the nature of things. It takes place through voluntary and deliberate acts on the part of individuals who are concerned to leave the state of nature. In this sense, civil society is not natural but an artifact.
6. The principle through which civil society becomes legitimate is consent.

Despite some protestations to the contrary, there has never been a historical transformation from the state of nature to civil society through the process idealized in this conceptual model. "The image of a state that arises through the reciprocal consent of individuals who are originally free and equal is a pure construct of the intellect" (Bobbio, 1993: 3).

The conceptual model outlined above differs sharply from the alternative conceptual model which acted as a basis of reference for political philosophers who preceded the natural law theorists and who derived their thinking from Aristotle's *Politics*:

> When several villages are united in a single complete community, large enough to be nearly or quite self-sufficing, the state comes into existence, originating in the bare needs of life, and continuing in existence for the sake of the good life. And therefore, if the earlier forms of society are natural, so is the state, for it is the end of them, and the nature of a thing is its end. . . . Hence it is evident that the state is a creation of nature, and that man is by nature a political animal. (Aristotle, *Politics* Bk. I: ch. 2: 1252)

This view of the state was carried forward by political philosophers over many centuries, through the Dark and the Middle Ages and into the post-Renaissance era, until the beginning of the seventeenth century and the seminal writings of Thomas Hobbes. As Bobbio (1993) demonstrates, the Aristotelian approach is evident in the writings of Marsilius of Padua in the Middle Ages, and in the writings of Bodin in 1606.

Writing in the early seventeenth century, also, Johannes Althusius still defines the city as a public association that differs from the various private associations in that it is an aggregation of lesser associations. The universal association, he refers to as the state: "Human society becomes differentiated into states by progressing from private to public societies according to fixed steps" (Althusius [1608]/1932: v). In all these interpretations, the principle of legitimization of political society is not consent, but rather it is necessity. It was against this formidable tradition that Thomas Hobbes was to launch a powerful attack.

The Hobbesian Perspective

Thomas Hobbes was born in 1588 in Malmesbury, Wiltshire, and died in 1679, some nine years before the Glorious Revolution. He is widely regarded as the most formidable of English political philosophers, not least because "his doctrine is at once so clear, so sweeping, and so disliked" (Macpherson, 1962: 9). This reputation was established by three major publications that spanned the length of the English Civil War. The first of these was *Elements of Law*, completed and circulated in manuscript in 1640, and published in two pirated parts in 1650. Hobbes fled to

Paris in November 1640, fearful of being implicated in the Long Parliament's attack on the Earl of Strafford. He published his second major work, *De Cive*, in Paris in April 1642 and his seminal book, *Leviathan*, also in Paris in April 1651 some two years after the execution of King Charles I. Within six months of this latter publication, Hobbes was excluded from the French court of the dead king's son, Charles Stuart.

In February 1652, Hobbes returned to London and to the dictatorship of The Lord Protector, Oliver Cromwell. He remained in England following the Restoration of the Stuart dynasty in May 1660 until his death in December 1679. It is not at all surprising, in such circumstances, that Hobbes focussed attention in his political philosophy upon the dichotomy between the state of nature and civil society and that his perspective on the state of nature was less than benign.

The three major political works cited above offer identical descriptions of the state of nature. In each book, Hobbes focusses on the objective conditions in which man finds himself in the state of nature, conditions which are independent of his will, and on the human passions that at least partially are fuelled by those objective conditions. Hobbes presents his arguments in chapter XIV, Part I of *Elements*, in chapter I of *De Cive*, and in chapter XIII of *Leviathan*.

The principal objective condition is that individuals are equal de facto by nature. Being equal, they are capable of perpetrating the greatest of evils upon each other, namely death. The second objective condition is the scarcity of commodities, which together with equality, generates a permanent state of reciprocal lack of trust. This lack of trust causes each individual to prepare for war and to make war, if necessary, rather than to sue for peace. The third objective condition is the *ius in omnia*, the right to all things which nature gives to anyone living outside civil society. Since there is no criterion to distinguish between mine and thine, every individual has the right to appropriate all that falls into his power, or at least all that is useful to his own preservation. The combination of these three conditions inevitably generates "a situation of merciless competition, which always threatens to turn into a violent struggle" (Bobbio, 1993: 39).

This natural danger is intensified by the fact that individuals are dominated by passions, the gift of evil nature, which incline them to unsociability. Hobbes does not have a favourable view of his fellow men. For example, in *Leviathan*, he divides men into those devoted to covetousness and those devoted to sloth, remarking that these "two sorts of men take up the greatest part of mankind" (*Leviathan* XXX: 224).

In *Elements*, Hobbes stresses the characteristic of "Glory, or internal gloriation or triumph of the mind" (*Elements* I, 9; 1: 28), because this is the passion "which proceedeth from the imagination or conception of our *own power*, above the power of him that contendeth with us" (*Elements* I, 9; 1: 28). Since some men possess this passion and demand superiority over their fellow men, conflict is inevitable in the state of nature.

In *Leviathan*, Hobbes identifies three causes of conflict: competition, which makes men fight for gain; diffidence, which makes them fight for security; and glory, which makes them fight for reputation (*Leviathan* XIII: 81). Ultimately, what drives one man against another is the unending quest for power.

In *Leviathan*, Hobbes clarifies the fundamental problem of political science as the problem of power: "So that in the first place, I put for a general inclination of all mankind, a perpetual and restless desire of power after power, that ceaseth only in death" (*Leviathan* XI: 64). He identifies two kinds of power, namely natural power, which depends on capacities of body or mind, and instrumental power, which depends on other means such as wealth, reputation, or friends.

The state of nature as defined by Hobbes is terrifying because the desire for power creates a situation that is a state of war. Indeed, the state of nature is the state of war of all against all: "Hereby, it is manifest, that during the time men live without a common power to keep them all in awe, they are in that condition which is called war; and such a war, as is of every man, against every man" (*Leviathan* XIII: 82).

This "war of all against all" is confined by Hobbes to three specific circumstances that comprise the state of nature, conditions that are historically verifiable (Bobbio, 1993: 41–2). First, there is the circumstance of primitive societies, epitomized by the barbarian populations of antiquity and the savage populations of some areas of the Americas in his own time. Primitive societies live in a condition which precedes the passage from the state of nature to civil society and which we may label pre-political. Second, close to the heart of Hobbes is the case of civil war, which occurs when a state already exists, which dissolves for a variety of reasons. In this case, the passage is from civil society to anarchy, a situation that we may label *anti*-political. Third is the situation of international society where relations between the states are not regulated by a common power. This is a situation which occurs *among* political powers.

Of these three situations, only one really concerned Hobbes, namely civil war. He never believed that the universal state of nature was the primitive condition. Indeed, in his discourse with Bishop Bramhall, Hobbes argues that: "it is very likely to be true, that since the creation there never was a time in which mankind was totally without society. If a part of it were without laws and governors, some other parts might be commonwealths" (*EW* Vol. 5: 183–4).

Although he refers to the Americas both in *De Cive* and in *Leviathan*, he ends the latter reference with an important statement: "Howsoever, it may be perceived what manner of life there would be, where there were no common power to fear, by the manner of life, which men that have formerly lived under a peaceful government, use to degenerate into, in a civil war" (*Leviathan* XIII: 83). It was left to Hegel, another realist, to focus upon international society as a Hobbesian state of nature (Bobbio, 1993: 43).

Hobbes means by state of war not only a condition of violent conflict between men but also a state of precarious peace, in which the peace is preserved only by reciprocal fear: "For as the nature of foule weather, lieth not in a showre or two of rain; but in an inclination thereto of many days together: so the nature of war, consisteth not in actual fighting; but in the known disposition thereto, during all the time there is no assurance to the contrary (*Leviathan* XIII: 82). The "war of all against all" therefore should be construed to identify that condition in which large numbers of men live in fear of violent death because of the absence of a common power over them:

> Whatsoever therefore is consequent to a time of warre, where every man is enemy to every man; the same is consequent to the time wherin men live without other security, than what their own strength and their own invention shall furnish them withal. In such condition, there is no place for industry; because the fruit thereof is uncertain: and consequently no culture of the earth, no navigation, nor use of the commodities that may be imported by sea; no commodious building; no instruments of moving or removing such things as require much force; no knowledge of the face of the earth; no account of time; no arts; no letters; no society; and which is worst of all, continuall feare, and danger of violent death; And the life of man, solitary, poore, nasty, brutish and short. (*Leviathan* XIII: 83)

The Lockeian Perspective

John Locke was born in 1632 and died in 1704, his life spanning one of the most turbulent periods in English history, from the seventh year of the reign of Charles I to the third year of the reign of Queen Anne. Like Hobbes, Locke spent part of his life on the continent, first in France from 1675 to 1679, where he fought against tuberculosis, and second in exile in Holland from 1683 to 1689 when the Glorious Revolution had already swept James Stuart from the throne.

Unlike Hobbes, however, the turbulence of Locke's times failed to impress upon him a black judgement of mankind in the absence of some common authority. In part, this difference in judgement was the product of a different experience. For Locke was only ten years old when the

Civil War began and was still a schoolboy at Westminster School when Charles I was executed. In contrast, Hobbes, who was born in 1588, was a middle-aged man at the time of this traumatic event.

Locke's most important discourse on natural law is to be found in his earliest unpublished text, *Questions Concerning the Law of Nature* (1664) written when he was a young scholar at Oxford University. However, his most important insights into the state of nature are to be found in his more mature work in political philosophy, *Two Treatises of Government*, probably drafted in 1679–81 but published much later, in 1690.

The concept of the state of nature is the fulcrum of Locke's *Second Treatise*, from which Locke launches his account of political obligation, his justification of civil society, his case for limited political power, and his arguments concerning justified insurrection against unlawful government. In this sense "[t]he state of nature defines for Locke the boundaries of the political" (Simmons, 1993: 13). An understanding of Locke's concept of the state of nature is essential to any understanding of his perspective on the political relationship.

For Locke, the state of nature is the state into which every man is born. It is "a *state of perfect freedom* to order their actions, and dispose of their possessions, and persons as they think fit, within the bounds of the law of nature, without asking leave, or depending upon the will of any other man" (Locke, II, para. 4). This does not imply an absence of effective government. Man may live under highly effective government and yet remain in the state of nature, if such government is illegitimate.

Although Locke clearly states that "*Want of a common judge with authority, puts all men in a state of nature*" (para. 19), and "Men living together according to reason, without a common superior on earth, with authority to judge between them, is *properly the state of nature*" (ibid.), the existence of a common judge evidently is a necessary but not a sufficient condition for civil society. For the state of nature is compatible with the existence of contractual integrity: "For 'tis not every compact that puts an end to the state of nature between men, but only this one of agreeing together mutually to enter into one community, and make one body politick" (para. 14).

It is also compatible with the existence of a common judge, where that common judge is illegitimate, based perhaps upon foreign conquest, or upon domestic tyranny: "But *conquest* is as far from setting up any government, as demolishing an house is from building a new one in the place" (para. 175) and "whosoever in authority exceeds the power given him by the law, . . . ceases in that to be a magistrate, and acting without authority, may be opposed, as any other man, who by force invades the right of another" (para. 202). Even individuals living under legitimate government remain in the state of nature if they are minors, visiting aliens or persons of defective reasoning.

Unlike Hobbes, Locke defines a state of nature based upon relationships between men, relationships characterized by a strong moral content. Specifically, the law of nature defines this moral implication: "Thus the law of nature stands as an eternal rule to all men" (para. 135) and "the *fundamental law of nature* being *the preservation of mankind*, no humane sanction can be good, or valid against it" (*ibid.*).

Although Locke does not discuss in detail the law of nature in the *Second Treatise*, the general form of the duties implied by this law is clear, namely, the duty to preserve oneself and others: "The *state of nature* has a law of nature to govern it, which obliges every one: And reason, which is that law, teaches all mankind, who will but consult it, that being all equal and independent, no one ought to harm another in his life, health, liberty, or possessions" (para. 6).

The law of nature implies that the state of nature is not a state of license, but rather is characterized by duties and obligations to which all men are subject: "But though this be a *state of liberty*, yet it is *not a state of licence*" (para. 6). Man has the right, in the state of nature, to punish appropriately those who transgress his natural rights: "the *execution* of the law of nature is in that state, put into every mans hands, whereby every one has a right to punish the transgressors of that law to such a degree, as may hinder its violation" (para. 7).

The Lockeian state of nature is by no means as bleak as that posited by Hobbes. "It is a state of limited safety and considerable uncertainty, a state of significant but not desperate "inconveniences," a state to which only certain limited forms of political society will be preferable" (Simmons, 1993: 26).

In Locke's view, the state of nature may take many forms, depending in part upon the level of development of the society. In the case of the primitive society, with no ownership of land and few movable possessions, Locke concedes that monarchy may prove to be an acceptable form of government (para. 107). For the more advanced society, with property in land, money, commerce, and the like, the safeguards required against governmental abuse of power preclude simple monarchy but may justify some form of more limited government (para. 111).

In this regard, the natural right to property that exists for individuals in the state of nature plays a crucial role. Locke's theory of property rests on the notion that "every man has a *property* in his own *person*" (para. 27). From this he concludes that whatever man removes out of the state of nature, by mixing his labor with it, becomes his property "at least where there is enough, and as good left in common for others" (para. 27). Leaving aside the debate over this proviso, the natural right to property thus established in the state of nature places severe limits on the kind of government to which any property-holding individual will consent when civil society is formed.

4   Civil Society as Social Contract

The century which commenced with Hobbes's *Leviathan* in 1651 and which ended with Rousseau's *Du Contrat Social* in 1762 was the great age of the doctrine of the social contract, the age in which the theory of natural law was developed and illuminated as the basis from which the social contract is implemented. It was the age during which two separate concepts of social contract were disentangled, with powerful implications for the notion of civil society.

The earlier idea of the social contract, emphasized by the medieval schoolmen, and by most of the Catholic and Calvinist theorists of the late sixteenth and early seventeenth centuries, focussed on the notion of the *pacte de gouvernement* or the contract of government. In this theory, government is based on a contract between the ruler and his subjects. Many thinkers stopped at this point without reflecting on the prior relationship that must exist between the members of society who presumably have agreed among themselves to the subjection implied by such a compact.

The later idea of the social contract emphasized by Hobbes, Locke and Rousseau, focussed attention upon the *pacte d'association* or the contract of society, the pact which creates society itself, which may preclude any contract of government and which, at least, must be prior to such a contract. Hobbes, Locke, and Rousseau did not concern themselves at all with the contract of government but centered attention exclusively on the contract of society.

The community formed by a contract of society may indeed be self-governing, without any distinction between ruler and subject. This in essence is the theory of Rousseau. Alternatively, the community, once formed, may appoint a fiduciary government, with which it makes no contract, but which it may dismiss for breach of trust as it interprets such trust. This, in essence, is the theory of Locke. Yet again, the community, once formed, may hand over all its rights and powers to a sovereign *Leviathan*, which makes no contract with it whatsoever, and which, therefore, is not subject to a contract of government. This, in essence, is the theory of Hobbes.

The Hobbesian Perspective

Hobbes believed in natural law. The dilemma of man in the state of nature, therefore, is constituted, not by the absence of morality, but by the total frustration of that morality as a consequence of insecurity (Warrender, 1957: 103). This intolerable state of affairs cannot be ended by men joining together in small or even in large numbers, since their distrust of each other would not be eliminated by such action. Reason comes to the rescue of men who wish to leave this precarious state. As used by Hobbes, reason is the capacity to calculate so that, given certain premises, man necessarily derives certain conclusions.

Right reason suggests to man a set of rules, the laws of nature, which aim at securing a peaceful cohabitation. These rules are subordinate, however, to a first, fundamental rule that prescribes the seeking of peace, since the laws of nature cannot be upheld in the absence of this condition. It follows, therefore, that there is only one way to make the laws of nature effective and to force individuals to act according to their reason and not according to their passions. This way is to establish a power so irresistible that it makes any contrary action disadvantageous (Bobbio, 1993: 46).

This irresistible power is the state. To achieve peace, man must leave the state of nature and enter into civil society. The state is a product not of nature but of the human will. To be effective, the compact that creates the state must be among many and not among few individuals. It must be permanent and not temporary. The only way to constitute a shared power is for all to consent to sacrifice their own power and to transfer it to one person. Henceforth, this person will have full authority to prevent each man from harming others by exercising his own power.

As a consequence of this covenant of union, individuals acquire fundamental obligations typical of the *pactum subiectionis*, namely the obligation to obey all commands of the holder of power: "*I authorize and give up my right of governing myself, to this man, or to this assembly of men, on this condition, that thou give up thy right to him, and authorize all his actions in like manner*" (*Leviathan* XVII: 112).

In Hobbes's interpretation of this *pactum subiectionis*, the parties are the individuals who agree with each other to subject themselves to a third party, who does not participate in the contract. In a sense, Hobbes merged the two contracts which are the foundations of the state (Bobbio, 1993: 48). From the viewpoint of the agents, it is a *pactum societas*. From the viewpoint of its content it is a *pactum subiectionis*.

The power handed over to the supreme authority comprises the supreme economic power (*dominium*) and the supreme coercive power (*imperium*). "There is no power on earth" says the verse in the Book of Job, which describes the sea monster Leviathan, "which is equal to it" (Job 41: 24). In Hobbes's view, this sovereign power must be irrevocable, absolute, and indivisible if it is to fulfill its purpose of ensuring peace throughout civil society.

In *Leviathan*, Hobbes clearly focusses attention on the spectrum from anarchy to order and comes down decisively in favour of order. This judgement is essentially hostile to any philosophy of liberty. It is true that Hobbes's Leviathan emerges through individual consent, but that does not make his philosophy individualistic in any modern sense. Hobbes relies entirely upon right reason to direct the energies of Leviathan through the use of science and language to ensure the peace. Hobbes even advocates state utilization of public instruction to control the beliefs of its citizens in pursuing this ultimate goal.

The Lockeian Perspective

Locke was a more political animal than Hobbes, more directly involved in the politics of his day. In particular, the period 1679–81, when the *Two Treatises* most probably was written, was the time during which he was actively involved with the Earl of Shaftesbury in an attempt to have the brother of King Charles II, a Catholic, excluded from the line of succession to the Throne. To achieve this end, it was essential for Locke to appeal to the landed gentry, to convince them that action against the Crown was not a mortal sin, and that it was justified by the unlawful actions of the Monarch.

Hence, Locke argues for a natural right to property, not a right created by the recognition and guarantee of a community. He also recognizes, in the state of nature, three imperfections – namely, partial judgements, inadequate force for the execution of judgements and variety of judgements passed by different men in similar circumstances. Three things are necessary to remedy these imperfections – namely, a judicature to administer law impartially, an executive to enforce the decisions of the judicature, and a legislature to lay down a uniform rule of judgement (Barker, 1947: xxi).

In order to secure these remedies, man must enter into civil society, and thereby must "give up every one his single power of punishing to be exercised by such alone as shall be appointed to it amongst them; and by such rules as the community, or those authorised by them to that purpose, shall agree on" (Locke, II, para. 127). Note that, unlike Hobbes, Locke does not argue that man must give up *all* his rights, and certainly not his right to property.

Artifacts in the form of civil society cannot possess rights naturally. Only by consent can individuals divest themselves of their natural rights and subject themselves to the authority of the state: "For no government can have a right to obedience from a people who have not freely consented to it" (para. 192). By consent, Locke means the actual personal consent of the mature individual (Simmons, 1993: 60). Even then, the state only has the powers that have been delegated to it. The influence of the Levellers on Locke's thinking is strongly evident, in this respect:

> The *supream power cannot take* from any man any part of his *property* without his own consent. For the preservation of property being the end of government, and that for which men enter into society, it necessarily supposes and requires, that the people should have *property*, without which they must be suppos'd to lose that by entring into society, which was the end for which they entered into it, too gross an absurdity for any man to own. (para. 138)

In several places in the *Second Treatise*, Locke professes in unambiguous language that the legislative power is the supreme power in government. "This *legislative* is not only the *supream power* of the commonwealth, but sacred and unalterable in the hands where the community have once placed it; nor can any edict of any body else, in what form soever conceived, or by what power soever backed, have the force and obligation of a *law*, which has not its *sanction from* that *legislative*, which the publick has chosen and appointed" (para. 134).

Although the legislature is supreme, however, its powers are strictly limited. It may be removed or altered by the people: "yet the legislative being only a fiduciary power to act for certain ends, there remains still *in the people a supream power* to remove or *alter the legislative*, when they find the *legislative* act contrary to the trust reposed in them" (para. 149). In particular, the legislature may be removed by the people "whenever they shall be so foolish, or so wicked, as to lay and carry on designs against the liberties and properties of the subject" (ibid.).

Locke was careful throughout the *Second Treatise* to emphasize that removal or change of government does not in itself imply the destruction of the civil society. Such destruction occurs, according to Locke only when a country is invaded and its inhabitants retreat into the state of nature (para. 211). Locke does not envisage that the community itself, which in his view would be dominated by those with property, could ever abuse its power.

In the *Two Treatises*, Locke clearly focusses attention on the spectrum from freedom to oppression and comes down decisively in favour of freedom. The state is so severely constrained by Locke's civil society that it cannot invade the liberty of the individual without placing itself in a state of war with the people. Majoritarian democracy, in the modern sense of that term, is trumped by the rights of the individual, and is forever proscribed from the drift towards Leviathan that characterizes all late twentieth-century Western democracies.

5   Late Twentieth-Century Hobbesian Constitutional Political Economy

Few modern Hobbesians would share openly with Thomas Hobbes the view that individuals should willingly hand over all their rights and authority to Leviathan. Some would simply argue in favor of a democracy in which the legislature is the dominant branch of a government elected by some form of majority vote principle. None would be completely comfortable with a limited government in which individual rights always trumped democracy.

The Perspective of Robert Nozick

In 1974, Robert Nozick became the favourite son of the libertarian movement as a consequence of the publication of *Anarchy, State, and Utopia*. Nozick grounded his case for the minimal state in a strong assumption of value pluralism, concluding that there was indeed a Utopia, one best society for *everyone* to share, even though there would not be one kind of community and one kind of life led in this Utopia. Utopia is a framework for utopias: "So is this all it comes to: Utopia is a free society? Utopia is not just a society in which this framework is realized. . . . It is what grows spontaneously from the individual choices of many people over a long period of time that will be worth talking eloquently about" (Nozick, 1974: 332).

According to Nozick (1974: 333) this minimal or night-watchman state is "the only morally legitimate state, the only morally tolerable one." It is the state ideally designed to accommodate the aspirations of untold dreamers and visionaries:

> The minimal state treats us as inviolate individuals, who may not be used in certain ways by others as means or tools or instruments or resources; it treats us as persons having individual rights with the dignity this constitutes. . . . How *dare* any state or group of individuals do more. Or less. (*ibid.*)

In 1989, Nozick recanted his earlier writing and condemned his 1974 book as "a book of political philosophy that marked out a distinctive view, one that now seems seriously inadequate to me" (Nozick, 1989: 17). In *The Examined Life*, Nozick effectively changes direction, vaulting from the freedom versus oppression to the anarchy versus order spectrum. Nozick clearly prefers order to anarchy and accepts the Hobbesian implications of this choice.

Nozick now suggests that the very question "How can I be free?" is rooted in excessive egotism. Authority has legitimacy to the extent that those commanded feel obligated therefore to obey. A leader is required to resolve competition among goals. Indeed, only under very special circumstances can society avoid the need for such leadership.

The Examined Life (1989) displays a yearning for unity and order that is typically Hobbesian in nature. It is this yearning which leads Nozick into a full-scale retreat from the minimal state, with all its potential disorder. Democratic institutions are viewed as vehicles through which individuals express the values that bind them together, which forge their solidarity as a group (ibid.: 287). In Nozick's judgement, the zig-zag of politics is the new ideal, preferable to complete dictatorship on the one hand and to anarchy on the other.

The Perspective of John Gray

Throughout his early career, John Gray forged a reputation as a leading English classical liberal. His writings on the scholarship of John Stuart Mill (Gray, 1976), Isaiah Berlin (Gray, 1980), and Friedrich von Hayek (Gray, 1981) placed him forthrightly in the classical liberal camp. Unlike Nozick, Gray never embraced the concept of the minimal or nightwatchman state. Yet, consistently, he embraced a notion that individual liberty represented an important and worthwhile ethical goal (Rowley, 1996: 3–4).

In 1989 Gray wrote off that intellectual capital and pronounced that his long-term project to define classical liberalism and to provide it with a sound foundation in ideology had been an unqualified failure: "The enterprise ended in failure. The upshot of the arguments developed in these essays is that the political morality that is constitutive of liberalism cannot be given any statement that is determinate or coherent and it has no claim to reason" (Gray, 1989: vii).

Gray (1989: 239–61) systematically explores the various arguments that purport to ground classical liberalism in a set of universal principles – utilitarian, rights-based, contractarian, the nature of knowledge and human flourishing – and finds each of them unconvincing. This outcome, he argues, is not to be lamented "since liberal political philosophy expresses a conception of the task and limits of theorizing that is hubristic and defective" (Gray, 1989: vii).

Gray's hostility to classical liberalism rests on a judgement that liberalism, which in its applications to personal conduct aims for toleration, even for pluralism, in its political demands becomes an expression of intolerance, since it denies the fact that many different kinds of government may contribute to human well-being. In societies characterized by pluralism of values, Gray suggests that liberalism is either dictatorial or incoherent.

In such circumstances, according to Gray (1989: 262): "We are left with the historic inheritance of liberal civil society." This inheritance is a complex structure of practices and institutions, embracing a system of private or several property, the rule of law, constitutional or traditional limitations on the authority of government, and a legal or moral tradition of individualism.

In *Post-Liberalism* (1933), John Gray returns to his thesis that classical liberalism as a doctrine with aspirations to universal prescriptive authority is dead. All that remains is "the historic inheritance of civil society that has now spread to most parts of the world" (Gray, 1993: 314). Even this inheritance is by no means the exclusive contribution of classical liberalism.

By civil society, Gray means a number of things. First, it is a society that is tolerant of diversity of views and in which the state does not seek to impose any comprehensive doctrine. In this sense, Calvin's Geneva was not a civil society, nor were any of the totalitarian societies of the twentieth century, notably Germany's Third Reich and the USSR.

Second, it is a society in which both government and its *subjects* (Gray's term) are restrained in their behavior by the rule of law. A state in which the will of the ruler is the law cannot be a civil society. From this perspective, one would not expect Gray to endorse the Hobbesian vision. However, any such expectation would be wrong.

Third, civil society is characterized by the institution of private and several property. Societies in which property is vested in tribes or is owned collectively cannot be civil societies, since they foreclose on the diversity of individual endeavors. In this respect, Gray appears to endorse capitalism. Yet even this inference is wrong. Gray proceeds to advocate municipal, village, and co-operative forms of ownership of capital as greatly superior to capitalism for Japan and for post-communist Russia.

The criteria set out by Gray are capable of both a narrow and a catholic definition of civil society. Gray (1993) makes it clear that he prefers the broad-tent definition. The societies of North America and Western Europe clearly qualify (though his dislike of the United States is evident). One senses that something is wrong, however, when Gray adds a range of societies, past and present, that in no sense satisfy his own criteria: Tsarist Russia, Meiji-period Japan, Bismarckian Prussia, Duvalier's Haiti, Singapore, South Korea, and Taiwan.

Evidently, something other than Lockeian principles is driving this judgement. Close inspection suggests that Gray has shifted from a classical liberal to a Hobbesian framework of analysis. John Gray has become obsessed with the need for order and is willing to tolerate a degree of oppression to achieve that state of affairs.

For example, in his essay on Hobbes, Gray comments that "there is an arresting contemporaneity about many of Hobbes's insights that we can well profit from" and "[f]ar from being an anachronistic irrelevance, Hobbes' thought is supremely relevant to us, who live at the end of the modern era whose ills he sought to diagnose" (Gray, 1993: 3). In Gray's judgement (ibid.), "the modern state has failed in its task of delivering us from a condition of universal predation or war of all against all into the peace of civil society."

In its weakness, Gray argues, the modern state has re-created in a political form that very state of nature from which it is the task of the state to deliver us: "In this political state of nature, modern democratic states are driven by *a legal and political war of all against all* (Gray's italics) and the institutions of civil society are progressively enfeebled (ibid.). The paradox of the Hobbesian state he suggests is that, whereas its authority is unlimited, its duty is minimal, namely the maintenance of civil peace.

Gray finds much to praise in the writings of Michael Oakeshott. He notes with approval, for example, that Oakeshott rejects, as a prime example of rationalism in politics, the attempts by Locke, Kant, and John Stuart Mill to fix the proper scope and limits of government determinantly once and for all.

He endorses Oakeshott's judgement that the proper limits of government cannot be determined by reasoning from first principles. The image of human life that Oakeshott conveys to him is not that of a problem to be solved or a situation to be mastered. It is an image of individuals lost in a world in which their vocation is to play earnestly and to be earnest playfully, living without thought of any final distinction.

Gray does not end his philosophical journey with Hobbes's *Leviathan* or with Oakeshott's critique of purposefulness. Instead, he seeks out an anchor in a concept of civil society derived from the scholarship of Buchanan. Gray is especially attracted to Buchanan's proceduralist, contractarian approach and by the fact that Buchanan does not privilege liberty from the outset. Gray delights in the fact that contractarian choice will not plausibly yield a Lockeian, Nozickean, or Spencerian minimal state and, furthermore, will not endorse unencumbered Lockeian rights.

Although Gray acknowledges that Buchanan's contractarian approach will usually enhance individual liberty, he concludes that it cannot give universal protection to the personal or civil liberties that are central to the Western tradition. This limitation is welcomed by Gray: "It is far from self-evident, and sometimes plainly false, that the institutions and civil liberties of even limited democratic government are always and everywhere appropriate and defensible" (Gray, 1993: 61). Here again, Gray's longing for order trumps any residual concern for liberty as he continues his slide towards Hobbesian authoritarianism.

The Perspective of James M. Buchanan

Foremost among Hobbesian constitutional political economists is James M. Buchanan, whose 1977 book *The Limits of Liberty* foreshadows all work in this genre. The book was an intellectual response to the grave political situation in the United States during the early 1970s, an attempt to re-establish the contractarian vision of constitutional democracy within an environment disrupted by serious political upheaval. To this end Buchanan reached out to Thomas Hobbes's *Leviathan* (1651), replacing Hobbes's reliance upon an almighty sovereign with his own vision of a limited constitutional democracy to search out the phoenix of social contract from the ashes of political conflict.

Following the logic of Hobbes, Buchanan grounds his analysis in a state of nature characterized by an absence of property rights and of law. Within this adverse environment, a natural distribution is seen to emerge, dependent upon the relative skill, cunning, strength, and good or bad fortune of the various individuals therein located.

Because individuals expend resources on predation and defense, under such circumstances, each may recognize the prospect for increasing his utility, at least in absolute terms, through the mechanism of a social contract designed to establish civil society. Mutual gains are possible through such an agreement, even though the particular assignment of property rights will be dependent on bargaining skills and other factors, including, of course, the initial natural distribution.

In the Hobbesian model utilized by Buchanan there are considerable differences among individuals in the precontractual setting. Therefore, post-contract inequality in property and in human rights must be predicted. This post-contract outcome will not normally be stable. Once reached, one or more parties to the agreement may find it advantageous to renege on or to violate the terms of the contract.

In essence, each individual may confront a prisoner's dilemma in which he expects to benefit by breaching the terms of the agreement. If this prisoner's dilemma is to be avoided, it must be anticipated in the social contract itself, and incentive-compatible contracts must be established at that stage.

The prisoner's dilemma may extend even to the enforcement aspects of the social contract. If the individuals themselves are responsible for enforcement, the incentive to renege continues. If an external agent is empowered to enforce, then who monitors that external agent? In a sense this exposes the bankruptcy of the Hobbesian approach from the viewpoint of classical liberalism (although Buchanan, 1977, does not explicitly recognize this implication).

Because Buchanan does not envisage a social contract that limits the state to the role of referee, but rather anticipates a regulatory and productive state that exists also to correct market failure, he must confront in his analysis the prospect that individuals may fail to constrain the size and power of such a state once established. Since he also recognizes the impracticability of governing by universal consent in a world character- ized by positive transaction costs, he also must acknowledge that the majority vote rule may result in budgetary excess. He must confront the very real prospect that even a constitutionally constrained democracy may burst out of those constraints and transform itself into a Hobbesian sovereign.

Buchanan's solution to the social dilemma created by the alleged col- lapse of constitutional constraints in the United States is process ori- ented. He looks to a contractarian revival, mistakenly, in my view, finding encouragement in John Rawls's book, *A Theory of Justice* (1971). However, in *The Limits of Liberty*, Buchanan rightly rejects the artificial setting required by Rawls and focuses on the prospects for genuine con- tractual renegotiation among real individuals who are not equals at the stage of deliberation.

In this renegotiation, Buchanan envisages that those with property, who fear that their rights will be abrogated by those without property operating through the majority vote, may agree to a once-and-for-all transfer of wealth in return for a genuinely new constitution that overtly limits fiscal transfers. He does not confront, in this analysis, the prospect that the payment of *Danegelt* does not ease but rather tends to exacer- bate the demand for transfers in any real-world society.

Buchanan ultimately concludes that some mid-point between anarchy and Leviathan is indeed attainable, and that the allegedly discredited principles of laissez-faire and socialism can indeed be replaced "when successfully negotiated social contract puts 'mine and thine' in a newly defined structural arrangement and when the Leviathan that threatens is placed within new limits" (Buchanan, 1977: 180). Whether or not such a solution can be derived logically from a Hobbesian vision of mankind is highly debatable. Certainly, Hobbes (1651) did not think that it was possible.

The Perspective of Robert Bork

In his 1996 book, *Slouching towards Gomorrah*, Robert Bork adopts a Hobbesian perspective on recent developments in the United States, which is much more pessimistic than that of Buchanan. In the United States, Bork sees a Western civilization that has been in a process of degeneration for the better part of forty years. Degeneration is evident, he claims, in religion, the arts, law, scholarship, education, entertainment and morality. Only with respect to its economy can the United States be called healthy at the end of the twentieth century.

The enemy, he claims, comes from within in the form of modern liberalism, "a corrosive agent carrying a very different mood and agenda than that of classical or traditional liberalism" (Bork, 1996: 4). Yet, this modern liberalism is the offspring of classical liberalism, the consequence of the collapse of the tempering forces of authority and tradition that once held degeneration in check.

The twin defining characteristics of modern liberalism, according to Bork, are radical egalitarianism (equality of outcomes) and radical individualism (no limits to personal gratification). These characteristics are incompatible since equality of outcomes requires coercion whereas gratification of desires requires liberty. If they are to operate simultaneously, they must be kept apart when they compete. American culture has evolved to accommodate this separation.

Radical egalitarianism rules in fields where superior achievement is possible and would be rewarded except for coercion. Quotas, affirmative action, and feminism, Bork claims, are obvious examples. Radical individualism rules when there is no prospect that achievement will produce inequality. Sexual activities and popular culture, he claims, are obvious examples. Both impulses are antagonistic to the traditional morality of civil society. Radical egalitarianism stimulates the growth of government, whereas radical individualism erodes the constraints on responsibility, without which liberty becomes license.

In responding to this perceived collapse of civil society in the United States, Bork resorts to proposed constitutional reforms, albeit much more pragmatic and less philosophical than those of Buchanan. In so doing, he focusses almost exclusively on the anarchy versus order spectrum. Specifically, Bork recommends a major contraction in the separation of powers, a mechanism that the Founding Fathers relied upon to limit the powers of the federal government.

In Bork's view, "It is arguable that the American judiciary – the Supreme Court, abetted by the lower federal courts and many state courts – is the single most powerful force shaping our future. In its cultural-political role, the Court almost invariably advances the agenda of modern liberalism" (Bork, 1996: 96). To return the judiciary to constitutional legitimacy, Bork argues in favor of a constitutional amendment "making any federal or state court decision subject to being over-ruled by a majority vote of each House of Congress" (117). There in one stroke would go the rule of law and with it any residual protection for minorities from the majority vote.

More specifically, Bork advocates the abrogation of First Amendment Rights, in order to maintain social order: "Any serious attempt to root out the worst in our popular culture may be doomed unless the judiciary comes to understand that the First Amendment was adopted for good reasons, and those good reasons did not include the furtherance of radical personal autonomy" (153). The power that such an abrogation would offer to any federal government bent on becoming Leviathan is entirely ignored in Bork's unequivocal commitment to order and his rejection of liberty for citizens of the United States of America.

The Hobbesians' Dilemma

If man is as amoral and if the state of nature is as devoid of civilization as Hobbes and his followers argue, then there is little or no prospect of establishing limited government by social contract. Hobbes recognized this in noting that individuals would contract with each other to hand over all their rights to Leviathan, which itself would not be bound by the contract, but which would be expected to maintain peace. In a sense, the social contract becomes an act of constructivism, since there is no foundation upon which a society might be expected to evolve in the absence of some rationalist intervention. Individuals retain no rights in such a settlement, other than those allowed by the state as an act of noblesse oblige.

No doubt there are many regions of the world in the late twentieth century where this Hobbesian solution might be universally endorsed. In Europe, the shambles that was once Yugoslavia comes to mind. In Asia, the more backward regions of the former USSR, and Cambodia, are likely candidates. In the Middle East, Syria, Iraq, Iran, and Lebanon are outstanding candidates. Much of sub-Saharan Africa also qualifies. By and large, however, it is not to these regions of the world that the late twentieth-century Hobbesians address their arguments.

The advanced countries of the West are all endowed with a lengthy history of civil society, characterized by the recognition of property rights, individual rights, and the rule of law. In such circumstances, the dire prophecies of the Hobbesians about the collapse of civil society and the need to restore it through powerful government are misplaced. In such advantageous environments, civil society can best be protected not by extending but by retrenching the power and authority of the state.

6   Late Twentieth-Century Lockeian Constitutional Political Economy

In the late twentieth century there are few economists and few political philosophers who subscribe unequivocally to Locke's arguments in favor of a minimal state empowered only to maintain the life, liberty, and property of those who consent to leave the state of nature and to enter into civil society. Nevertheless, that small group of scholars, in my opinion, offers the best prospect for the maintenance of liberty in societies that currently appear to value order more highly than individual freedom and that increasingly are willing to invade the rights to life, liberty, and property through the process of democracy.

The Perspective of Anthony de Jasay

In his 1996 monograph *Before Resorting to Politics* Jasay suggests that the question whether freedom is valuable ought not to enter into a properly thought-out political doctrine. Instead, we should start with a presumption against coercion: "The basic rule is that a person is presumed free to do what is feasible for him to do. This presumption is subject to two compatibility conditions. One relates a person's proposed actions to his own obligations, the other to harm to others" (Jasay, 1996: 23). Where these conditions are satisfied, the defendant is relieved of the burden of proof that his action is admissible.

If utilities cannot be compared across individuals, as the Pareto principle indicates, utilitarian consequentialism, which has encouraged the growth of government on grounds of market failure, is simply out of place. No balance can be struck between the good and the bad consequences of intervention. This leads Jasay to deploy his first warning to those who would engage in consequential politics: "first, avoid doing harm" (ibid.: 10).

In this view, given the presumption against coercion, Jasay argues that a political authority is not entitled to employ its coercive powers to impose value choices upon society. The guiding principle in such circumstances can only be: "*When in doubt, abstain*" (ibid.: 11). This principle holds even where a democratic majority shares a value judgement that would endorse coercion, given that rival value judgements are held among the minority. To implement this presumption, given the malleability of practical politics, requires "at least some non-procedural, strictly substantive limitation of social choice" (12).

If this principle is accepted, Jasay argues, coercion is legitimate only "when it is positively invited by the prospective coercee" (16). Notably, such endorsements will be forthcoming when individuals attempt to resolve prisoners' dilemmas through the medium of the state. Political associations may be deemed desirable in such circumstances to "lay down a 'property rights scheme,' including rules of property, liability and tort" (17).

Each individual is endowed by fate with a set of potential actions that are feasible. Some of these alternatives are inadmissible because they would harm others in a way that would constitute a tort. Other alternatives are inadmissible because individuals have contracted with others not to implement them. Every other feasible act is admissible (29–30).

From this perspective, the late-twentieth-century view that the state is called upon to play a redistributive role is erroneous. Given that the balancing act is inadmissible, redistribution cannot serve as a warrant for coercion. This has powerful implications for Jasay's (1996) theory of property rights. Although Jasay is certainly not a Lockeian scholar, his theory of property rights exhibits distinctly Lockeian characteristics.

According to Jasay, property is partitioned among individuals before resorting to politics. It is not some kind of a common pool resource that remains permanently under the control of the political process. Once property is owned, its voluntary transfer takes place either in exchange or as a unilateral gift. Original ownership arises on the basis of first possession, not for natural law reasons posited by Locke, but as a matter of expediency in conformity with Jasay's general rule outlined above: "taking first possession of a thing is a feasible act of his that is *admissible* if it is *not a tort* (in this case not trespass) and violates no right" (37).

According to Jasay, two alternative acts vest ownership in the performer, namely finding and keeping and enclosure. In either case, there is no moral requirement that the lucky or the diligent should recompense others less lucky or less diligent as long as no tort has been committed. In this sense, property originates in a liberty, it remains a liberty, and its growth and distribution are the result of agreement. The Lockeian nature of this argument is clear.

The Perspective of Rasmussen and Den Uyl

Unlike Jasay (1996), who avoids moral arguments in his case for avoiding resort to politics, Douglas Rasmussen and Douglas Den Uyl (1991) resort to Aristotelian ethics in defense of the Lockeian right to life, liberty, and property. Following Aristotle, they emphasize the importance of human flourishing as the ultimate moral objective. For human beings to flourish, they must be autonomous or self-directed. If the individual is to achieve well-being, or as Aristotle called it *eudaimonia*, he can do so only by living rationally or intelligently. *Eudaimonia* is defined as the satisfaction of right desire, those desires that lead to successful human living (Rasmussen and Den Uyl, 1991: 36).

From this perspective, Rasmussen and Den Uyl argue that Lockeian rights "are the only meta-normative principles that can provide for a compossible set of moral territories that the highly individualized and self-directed character of human flourishing demands" (ibid.: 129). These rights, therefore, are derived from the recognition that human beings are individuals who cannot be ends-in-themselves except through their own self-directed behavior. This is a powerful argument for those who are unwilling to accept the quasi-religious defense of private property mounted by Locke in *The Two Treatises of Government*.

Rasmussen and Den Uyl recognize that Aristotelean political philosophy cannot be classified as classically liberal. Liberty is not one of the core values of antiquity. In order to draw from Aristotle an essence that is favorable to liberty, they reject his view that moral perfection is the true standard of cooperation and replace it with the notion that the natural right to liberty is a social and political condition necessary for the possibility of moral perfection. They claim that Aristotelian tradition "is perhaps the only remaining unexplored source for providing liberalism with the kind of secure moral footing it desperately needs" (ibid.: 225).

The Perspective of Friedrich von Hayek

In his 1973 book, *Law, Legislation and Liberty*, Hayek argues that social theory begins with – and has a purpose only because of – the discovery that there exist orderly structures which are the product of the action of many individuals but are not the result of human design. Rather, these structures are the result of individuals adapting to circumstances that affect directly only some of them and which, in their totality, need not be known to any individual.

Crucial to Hayek's notion of constitutional political economy is the role played by the common law as just such a complex order that has evolved spontaneously over time without any overt human design. Hayek has argued that the common law possesses the central characteristics of *Nomos*, the law of liberty in that it reflects the necessary conditions of the rule of law.

In his judgement, all authority, indeed society itself, derives from the law. The power to legislate, for example, presupposes recognition by individuals of common rules which determine that power and which also limit it. In this sense, customs and traditions precede formal constitutions, and if a constitution does not properly reflect those customs and traditions it is invalid.

Hayek recognizes that judge-made law will be perfected by the deliberate efforts of judges, or by others learned in the law, by the laying down of new rules: "Indeed, law as we know it could never have fully developed without the occasional intervention. . . . to extricate it from the dead ends into which the gradual evolution may lead it, or to deal with altogether new problems" (Hayek, 1973: 100). Yet, it remains true that the system of rules as a whole does not owe its structure to the design of either judges or legislators. It is the outcome of a process of evolution. In this sense, Hayek sides with Kant's emphasis on the purposeless character of the rules of just conduct and rejects the utilitarian emphasis on purpose as the central feature of the law.

A Modern Lockeian Synthesis

It is my judgement that an appropriate combination of the ideas of John Locke and of the contemporary "Lockeians" whose work has been outlined in this section offers the best hope of restoring civil society in the advanced nations of the West. Although Richard Epstein does not claim to be a Lockeian, his 1995 book, *Simple Rules for a Complex World*, encapsulates much of the necessary synthesis.

Epstein endorses the wisdom of Locke with respect to property rights claiming that "In all affairs, decentralization of ownership necessarily follows from the principle of self-ownership. Its functional roots are so powerful that it should be treated as a moral imperative" (Epstein, 1995: 60). This principle is the first pre-requisite for civil society.

The second pre-requisite is a sound rule governing the acquisition of property. Here again, a variant of Locke, Jasay, and Rasmussen and Den Uyl suffices: man takes what he can get. This is the common law of first possession for land or the rule of capture for wild animals and for material things. Where the chain of title is broken beyond recognition, rules of adverse possession or prescriptive right effectively restore the chain.

These rules of individual autonomy and first possession together constitute the original position against which all subsequent exchanges must be evaluated. Societies that distance themselves from these rules are not civil societies. However, as Epstein correctly recognizes, these rules alone will not suffice. Additional rules are necessary to govern the process of voluntary exchange. Laws that confirm freedom of contract encourage individuals to seek out mutual gains from trade. In this respect, the classical common law of contract, which required offer, acceptance, and consideration, provided a sound rule. In such a system, contracts can be set aside only on grounds of infancy, insanity, duress, fraud, or mutual mistake.

The fourth rule required by civil society is one that protects individuals from third-party effects. This rule forms the basis of the law of tort. As Epstein puts it: "In its crudest and simplest form, the irreducible core of this body of law can be succinctly expressed: 'keep off'" (ibid.: 91).

In its early common law form, this rule was designed to prevent trespass, larceny, murder, rape, and other invasions of private property. In the case of intentional torts, strict liability is clearly appropriate. Whether, in the case of accidents, the rule should take the form of negligence with contributory negligence or strict liability (Epstein favors the latter) is a matter of debate. The crucial requirement is that of proximate cause. If such a rule functions well there is no need for criminal law, which places a much more active role on the state.

Epstein adds rules to this list that provide an active role for the state. In my view this is wrong. The four rules spelled out above provide a viable basis for a civil society characterized by a minimal state. They offer a stable legal order that is adaptable to variations in behavior, custom, and other practices across different societies. They secure individual autonomy, they require responsible behavior, they foster mutual gains from trade, and they protect individuals against third-party transgressions. Indeed, they provide the best possible foundation for a free yet ordered society in which the state is strictly confined to a night-watchman role.

7   Conclusion

If individuals are to flourish in civil society, the nature of the constitution on which that civil society is grounded is institutionally extremely important. This essay has argued that individuals flourish best in a society characterized by government constitutionally constrained to a night-watchman role. Such constraints will hold only where individuals must personally consent to join a given civil society, as they attain majority, and where individuals and groups remain free to secede from any civil society that fails to limit itself to a minimalist role. In such circumstances, the constitution will be self-enforcing.

Inevitably, governments dissatisfied with the lack of power that such a constitution imposes periodically will ignore the constraints of the parchment and will place themselves in a state of war with the people. Rules alone cannot prevent such an act nor can they guarantee the restoration of the minimal state following attempts to overthrow it. That is the ongoing tragedy of the human condition.

Nevertheless, I strongly believe that if a minimal state were to remain in being sufficiently long for human flourishing to take place, the large majority of the people would take up arms against any government that attempted to destroy the liberties to which they had become accustomed. If such an uprising were to be put down by overwhelming force, well at least they would have tried.

References

Althusius, J. [1608]/1932. *Politica methodice digesta*. Cambridge: Cambridge University Press.
Aristotle. 368–348 B.C./1941. *The Basic Works of Aristotle*. Ed. R. McKeon. New York: Random House.
Barker, E. 1960. *Social Contract: Locke, Hume, Rousseau*. Oxford: Oxford University Press.
Bobbio, N. 1993. *Thomas Hobbes and the Natural Law Tradition*. Chicago: University of Chicago Press.

Bodin, J. [1606]/1962. *De la Republique.* Cambridge, Mass.: Harvard University Press.

Bork, R. 1996. *Slouching towards Gomorrah.* New York: Regan Books.

Buchanan, J. M. 1977. *The Limits of Liberty.* Chicago: University of Chicago Press.

Buchanan, J. M., and Tullock, G. 1962. *The Calculus of Consent.* Ann Arbor: University of Michigan Press.

Dunn, J. 1980. *Political Obligation in Its Historical Context.* Cambridge: Cambridge University Press.

Epstein, R. A. 1995. *Simple Rules for a Complex World.* Cambridge, Mass.: Harvard University Press.

Ferguson, A. [1767]/1980. *An Essay on the History of Civil Society.* Ed. L. Schneider. New Brunswick, N.J.: Transaction Publishers.

Fukuyama, F. C. 1992. *The End of History and the Last Man.* New York: The Free Press.

Gray, J. 1976. "John Stuart Mill and the Future of Liberalism." *The Contemporary Review* 220 September.

——— 1980. "On Negative and Positive Liberty." *Political Studies* 28.

——— 1981. "Hayek on Liberty, Rights and Justice." *Ethics* 92 (1), October.

——— 1989. *Liberalisms: Essays in Political Philosophy.* New York: Routledge.

——— 1993. *Post-Liberalism: Studies in Political Thought.* Princeton, N.J.: Princeton University Press.

Hayek, F. von. 1973. *Law, Legislation and Liberty,* Vol. 1. London: Routledge and Kegan Paul.

Hobbes, T. [1642]/1839–45. *De Cive.* Ed. W. Molesworth. *The English Works of Thomas Hobbes.* Vol. 2. London.

——— [1650]/1839–45. *Elements of Law.* Ed. W. Molesworth. *The English Works of Thomas Hobbes.* Vol. 4. London.

——— [1651]/1839–45. *Leviathan.* Ed. W. Molesworth. *The English Works of Thomas Hobbes.* Vol. 3. London.

——— [1655]/1839–45. Ed. W. Molesworth. *The English Works of Thomas Hobbes.* Vol. 5. London.

Hume, D. [1741–2]/1987. *Essays, Moral and Political.* Ed. E. F. Miller. Indianapolis: Liberty Press.

Hummel, J. R. 1996. *Emancipating Slaves, Enslaving Free Men.* Chicago and La Salle: Open Court.

Jasay, A. de. *Before Resorting to Politics.* The Shaftesbury Papers 5. Aldershot, England: Edward Elgar Publishing.

Kant, I. [1781]/1963. *Critique of Pure Reason.* Trans. Norman Kemp Smith. New York: St. Martin's Press.

Klaus, V. 1996. *Transforming toward a Free Society.* Presentation at a meeting of the Mont Pelerin Society, Vienna, Austria.

Kumar, K. 1993. "Civil society: An inquiry into the usefulness of an historical term." *British Journal of Sociology* 44 (3).

Locke J. [1664]/1990. *Questions Concerning the Law of Nature.* Ed. Robert Horwitz, Jenny Strauss Clay and Diskin Clay. Ithaca, N.Y.: Cornell University Press.

——— [1690]/1960. *Two Treatises of Government.* Ed. P. Laslett. Cambridge: Cambridge University Press.

Machan, T. 1975. *Human Rights and Human Liberties.* Chicago: Nelson-Hall.

Macpherson, C. B. 1962. *The Political Theory of Possessive Individualism.* Oxford: The Clarendon Press.

Marsilius of Padua. 1967. *Defensor Pacis*. Toronto: University of Toronto Press.

Mill, J. S. [1859]/1989. *On Liberty*. Ed. S. Collini. Cambridge: Cambridge University Press.

Mueller, D. C. 1996. *Constitutional Democracy*. New York: Oxford University Press.

Nozick, R. 1974. *Anarchy, State and Utopia*. New York: Basic Books.

——— 1989. *The Examined Life: Philosophical Meditations*. New York: Simon and Schuster.

Rasmussen, D., and Den Uyl, D. 1991. *Liberty and Nature: An Aristotelian Defense of Liberal Order*. La Salle: Open Court.

Rawls, J. 1971. *A Theory of Justice*. Cambridge, Mass.: Belknap Press.

Rousseau, J. J. 1762/[1966]. *The Social Contract*. Ed. G. D. H. Cole. London: Dent.

Rowley, C. K. 1989. "The Common Law in Public Choice Perspective." *Hamline Law Review* 12(2): 355–83.

——— 1990. "The Reason of Rules". *Annual Review of Conflict Knowledge and Conflict Resolution* Vol. 2: 195–228.

——— 1996. "What Is Dead and What is Living in Classical Liberalism." In C. K. Rowley, ed., *The Political Economy of the Minimal State*. Aldershot, England: Edward Elgar Publishing.

——— 1998. State of Nature and Civil Society. In *The New Palgrave Dictionary of Economics and the Law*, ed. Peter Newman. New York: Macmillan, 514–23.

Simmons, A. J. 1993. *On the Edge of Anarchy*. Princeton, N.J.: Princeton University Press.

Smith, A. 1776/[1991]. *An Inquiry into the Nature and Causes of the Wealth of Nations*. Collector's Edition. Norwalk: The Easton Press.

Tocqueville, A. de. [1835–40]/1966. *Democracy in America*. Ed. J. P. Mayer and M. Lerner. New York: Harper Collins.

Warrender, H. 1957. *The Political Philosophy of Hobbes: His Theory of Obligation*. Oxford: The Clarendon Press.

CHAPTER 6

The Constitutional Conflict between Protecting Expectations and Moral Evoluation

Nicolaus Tideman

1   The Possibility of New Moral Insights That Necessitate Redistribution

The main point of this chapter is simple: Unless the process that generates a constitution is perfect, there should be provision for the possibility of changing the constitution. It is true that the stability provided by constitutions is valuable. By limiting the opportunities for transient majorities to redistribute, constitutions protect property rights. The resulting stability promotes efficiency by reducing rent seeking. But as valuable as stability is, it is not lexically more valuable than the chance to incorporate new moral understandings into a constitution. And when a society perceives the need to incorporate a new moral understanding into its constitution, a disappointment of pre-existing expectations is likely to be necessary.

Perhaps the point seems so simple that it does not even need to be stated. How could anyone doubt that it will sometimes be appropriate to change a constitution and that some will lose in the process? However, associated issues are complex enough that some elaboration is warranted.

The first point to be made is that disagreement about what constitutes an improved understanding of a moral imperative is nearly inevitable at the time when the new understanding is emerging. History reveals that such improvements in our understanding do occur and that they are controversial when they occur.

Three hundred years ago virtually no one questioned the propriety of slavery. Even John Locke, that most articulate advocate of human freedom, invested in slaves. But over the course of the eighteenth and nineteenth centuries, amid extreme controversy in some times and places, slavery was nearly eliminated from the world. With a bit of a lag, a consensus gradually evolved among humanity that slavery was

97

wrong, indeed that no distinctions in civil rights based on race could be justified.

Two hundred years ago almost no one thought that women should be allowed to vote. Amid extreme controversy in some times and places, they were granted voting rights. Now virtually no one argues that women should be denied any rights that men have. We have not yet arrived at a consensus about what equality of the sexes means, but we are near a consensus that we should strive for it.

The next point to be made is that it would not be reasonable to expect constitutional changes that reflect new moral understandings to be made as approximate Pareto improvements. It would have been possible to end slavery in a way that made almost no one noticeably worse off as compared to his or her expected utility under slavery. It would merely have been necessary to declare the slaves free, provided that they made reasonable progress on paying debts to their former masters equal to their market value as slaves, and that they used their first earnings to buy insurance policies that would compensate their former masters in the event that they died or became incapacitated before they finished paying the debts. But such an end to slavery would never have satisfied the impulse that inspired its abolition.

Ending slavery was not an issue of economic efficiency or voter preferences. Slavery needed to be ended because so many people could not in good conscience participate in a legal system that enforced slavery. If slavery was wrong, there was no basis for requiring persons subjected to slavery to purchase their freedom. They had to be recognized as unconditionally free. Others would need to bear the loss from the fact that those formerly recognized as the owners of slaves would no longer be allowed to appropriate the product of slave labor. Who should bear the loss?

2   Assigning the Costs of Moral Accidents

In addressing this question, it is helpful to employ ideas from the theory of accidents. We now see that the perpetuation of slavery was a moral accident. To reduce the likelihood of future moral accidents, it is sensible to assign the costs of accidents to some or all of the persons who could have prevented them. Costs might also reasonably be assigned to anyone who benefited from the accidents. Among the prominent candidates for bearing the cost would be those who captured people and sold them into slavery, those who bought, sold, and transported slaves, those who held slaves, those who passed and enforced laws perpetuating slavery, those who bought products produced with slave labor, those who sold goods to persons involved in the selling or holding of slaves, and so on. Anyone who received an inheritance derived from slavery could be called upon to relinquish it as well. Emphatically not on the list are the slaves themselves and any person who came of age without an inheritance after slavery ended. They did not cause slavery. Thus it was wrong of Britain, in ending slavery in the 1830s, to compensate those who were historically regarded as the owners of slaves, with funds from general revenues and with a rule permitting them to work the slaves for a few more years, during which time many slaves were worked to death.

There are particular advantages to assigning the cost of the end of slavery to those who thought of themselves as slave owners. It is administratively more efficient than other possibilities, because it means leaving the costs where they fall. More importantly, the idea that slavery might be seen to be wrong, and that then the costs of ending slavery might be left where they fall, provides a continuing incentive for those involved in slavery to cease.

Contrary arguments can be made. From a utilitarian perspective, concentrating the losses leads to greater felt cost than if the same losses are dispersed. Uncertainty in rights makes it more difficult to effect the transactions that lead to efficient resource allocation. And the persons historically regarded as the owners of slaves will generally be a politically powerful group, who may exercise their power to perpetuate slavery far longer if they must bear the full cost of freeing slaves than if the cost is shared.

Furthermore, when social arrangements look exploitative, defenders of historical institutions will often argue that there is another perspective from which those arrangements promote efficiency. For example, slavery has been defended as a Pareto improvement from an environment in which those defeated in war are killed. Another example comes from the theory of the origin of government advanced by Mancur Olson. He theorizes that autocratic governments originated in an environment of roving bandits, when some potential bandits decided that there was a greater gain in becoming stationary bandits and protecting the victims from roving bandits (Olson, 1993).

The Russian Mafia today can be understood, in many cases, as promoting efficient resource allocation by preventing the dissipation of rent through competition. For example, Old Arbat Street in Moscow was for many years a place where artists would sell their wares to tourists. But to operate there, artists were required to pay the Mafia gang that controlled the street. The fees collected by the Mafia served to ration the space to an efficient number of artists. Without that rationing device, there would have been an excess of artists crowding the street and interfering with each other inefficiently. And people would have been getting up at 2:00 in the morning to get space before anyone else claimed it. In these circumstances, the Mafia action served to prevent the dissipation of the rent and did not reduce the net incomes of artists. If there were no public-good aspects of the provision of art, it could be argued that complete efficiency was achieved by this "spontaneous" private appropriation of rent.

The person who wishes to abolish such exploitative institutions as slavery, autocratic governments, and Mafia protection schemes, without compensation for those who derive income from them, can be asked to explain why it is right to terminate these incomes without compensation, when the development of the institutions served to improve allocative efficiency.

The answer comes in two parts. Part of the answer is that slavery, autocratic government, Mafia protection, and other exploitative institutions are second bests. Slavery may be better than the killing of those who are defeated in war, but magnanimity by victors or an end to war is better. And once slavery starts, it generates enslavement of the weak who would otherwise be safe. Autocratic government may be better than suffering the predation of roving bandits, but government that reflects a sense of community among the governed is certainly better. Mafia protection of Old Arbat Street artists may be better than chaotic appropriation of selling space, but public collection of rent for the use of selling space is better. The fact that these institutions may be improvements on what would otherwise have existed does not imply that they should continue to exist when yet better institutions become feasible.

The second part of the answer is that if one is tempted to suppose that the income from the indefinite duration of an exploitative institution is needed to induce people to invest efficiently in creating the institution, that temptation should be resisted. If the developer of an exploitive institution were able to capture exactly the full increase in aggregate income from its development, and if the profit in developing such an institution depended on receiving the increase in income for all eternity and not just until a better institution became feasible, and if the time when the better institution became feasible was independent of whether the first institution was developed, then it would not be worthwhile to develop the institution in the first place. In these circumstances a right in perpetuity is like a perpetual patent on something that would have been discovered by someone else if not by its first inventor. In the same way that a perpetual patent can motivate excessive expenditures on inventive activity, a perpetual right to benefit from an exploitative institution induces excessive investments in exploitation.

If you believe that a little extra incentive for the creation of property rights does no harm, there are reasons for disagreeing. Those who develop exploitive institutions are not limited to collecting the increase in aggregate income from the development of those institutions. If they sometimes promote efficiency, they more generally steal unboundedly. There is no need to worry about insufficiency of the incentive to exploit. When we are able to replace an exploitive institution with a better one, we should not be concerned about the efficiency consequences, or the justice, of disappointing the financial expectations of those who counted on the continuation of exploitation.

Returning to earlier points, there is the utilitarian argument that a concentrated loss produces a greater felt cost than the same loss when spread. While this is true, general attention to this argument would lead to complete leveling. We refrain from spreading costs for the sake of creating incentives.

Next is the argument that uncertainty in rights adds to transactions costs and therefore impedes the efficient allocation of resources. This too is true but need not stop us. During the course of the U.S. Civil War, the market price of slaves rose and fell with the fortunes of the Confederacy. But improving the efficiency with which those who thought of themselves as slave owners allocated slave labor would not have been a sufficient reason to guarantee them against loss from the end of slavery.

More serious is the argument that, since those who benefit from exploitation will use their considerable power to perpetuate it, a greater good is achieved by buying them off. Insurance companies often pay to retrieve stolen property from persons they believe to be thieves, to avoid the greater cost of compensating the victims of thieves. As a financial proposition, compromise with principle can pay.

But there are enduring costs. Truth is often a casualty as well. If one were dealing with a straightforward iniquitous person (a professional blackmailer or kidnapper, perhaps), who would acknowledge that his position was without moral justification and represented nothing more that a selfish effort to extract what he could from his position of power, then one could readily weigh the costs and benefits, and bow to power if that was less costly. But if one is dealing with persons who style themselves the owners of slaves and want acknowledgment that they are justly entitled to compensation for the taking of "their property," then concession may cloud the perception of right and wrong for a long time. Concession in this case comes at a great price. This is what makes it worthwhile to fight for the establishment of principle instead of cutting a deal with those who perpetuate iniquity.

3   The Possibility of a Right of Secession

But slavery is long gone. Of what relevance, you may ask, are such arguments today? I suggest that, some time in the next century or two, a number of moral issues as momentous and contentious as slavery will rise to public consciousness and pose the same issues of moral advance versus the protection of financial interests that might be thought of as property rights.

Consider the issue of secession. While there is often a correspondence between the borders of a nation and the set of persons who want to identify with a particular nationality, there are many instances when the preponderance of persons in a region would strongly prefer not to be part of the nation that exercises sovereignty over them – Chechens in Russia, Basques in Spain, Kurds in Turkey, Iran, and Iraq, Kashmiris in India, Catholics in Northern Ireland, Hungarians in Serbia, Romania, and Slovenia, Corsicans in France, Palestinians in Israel, Christians in Sudan, and so on around the globe. The particular locations of national borders are primarily the result of wars. In many cases, the only justification that can be given for borders apart from "If you try to take what I claim, I'll kill you" is that any acknowledgment that borders were subject to question would lead to interminable conflict, so we are better off abiding by what we have than allowing the question to be opened.

But this puts the advocates of maintaining existing borders in the potentially uncomfortable position of needing to support every "reasonable" government that seeks to suppress its secessionists. This then necessitates an evaluation of the reasonableness of the complaints of every minority with regard to language, religion, education, the provision of public services, marriage rules, child-rearing practices, tolerated intoxicants, and every other area of social life about which people can disagree. The person who wants to support the efforts of a government to suppress its secessionist minorities must be able to say that in every area where the government imposes a rule on the minority, no right that the minority ought to have is violated. It is becoming increasingly difficult to sustain a claim that it is possible to know what rights minorities deserve. I predict that within a century, humanity will come to a consensus that the right of a defined unit to secede from a larger governmental entity is a basic human right, that no nation or administrative sub-unit is entitled to cling to control of a compact sub-unit whose citizens are united in their desire not to be controlled by the larger entity.

Already we may be seeing the first signs of this. Czechoslovakia was peacefully partitioned into the Czech Republic and Slovakia, although the fact that this seems to have been mutually desired makes it less evidential for the thesis. The Kremlin acquiesced with only a little grumbling to the dismantling of the USSR. Here one might propose that with democracy looming, it was valuable for Russians to ensure that they would not become a minority in their own nation. After some fighting, the international community pressured the remnants of Yugoslavia to accept the departure of Slovenia, Croatia, and Bosnia. Canada seems to acknowledge implicitly that if the people of Quebec really want to no longer be part of Canada, they may have their way. When Quebecoi insist that Native American tribes that want to remove their tribal lands from the jurisdiction of Quebec must never be allowed to do so, they sound inconsistent. This is not enough evidence to make a convincing case, but it may be straws in the wind. Still, in so many other cases, there is little if any general international support for the efforts of secessionists.

4   The Complementary Right of Equal Access to Natural Opportunities

One of the factors that make the case for secession difficult is the problem of regional inequality in natural resources. When the people who called themselves Biafrans sought to secede from Nigeria in the 1960s, the morality of their claim was undermined by the fact that, if they had succeeded, they would have taken disproportionate oil resources from the rest of Nigerians. The limited support for the efforts of the Chechens to separate from Russia is explained in part by the understanding that, even though the Chechens have been abused by Russians for centuries and have never fully acceded to their incorporation into Russia, if Chechnya were allowed to separate from Russia, that would create a precedent that would make it difficult to oppose an effort by the people of the sparsely populated Yakutsia region of Eastern Siberia, rich in oil and diamonds, to insist that they too have a right to be a separate nation.

Perhaps, a general recognition of a right of secession will need to wait for another component of moral evolution: recognition that all persons have equal claims on the value of natural opportunities. If this were recognized, then any nation or region with disproportionately great natural resources would be seen to have an obligation to share the value from using those resources with those parts of the world that have less than average resources per capita. This would eliminate the desire to appropriate natural resources as a reason for secession and as a reason for opposing secession.

Signs of recognition of the equal claims of all persons on the use of natural opportunities are slim. One can point to John Locke:

> Whether we consider natural Reason, which tells us, the Men, being once born, have a right to their Preservation, and consequently to Meat and Drink, and such other things, as Nature affords for their Subsistence: Or Revelation, which gives us an account of those Grants God made of the World to Adam, and to Noah, and his Sons, 'tis very clear, that God, as King David says, Psal. CXV. xvi, has given the Earth to the Children of Men, given it to Mankind in common.

Locke goes on to say that every person has a right to himself, and therefore to the things of value that are created by combining his efforts with natural opportunities, "at least where there is as much and as good left in common for others." He then argues that with so much unclaimed land in America, no one can justly complain if all of Europe is privately appropriated. Locke does not address the question of how rights to land should be handled if there is no unclaimed land.

Thomas Jefferson (1813), writing on the subject of patents, said,

> But while it is a moot question whether the origin of any kind of property is derived from nature at all, it would be singular to admit a natural and even an hereditary right to inventors. It is agreed by those who have seriously considered the subject, that no individual has, of natural right, a separate property in an acre of land, for instance.

Henry George said,

> The equal right of all men to the use of land is as clear as their equal right to breathe the air – it is a right proclaimed by the fact of their existence. For we cannot suppose that some men have the right to be in this world and others no right.
>
> If we are all here by the equal permission of the creator, we are all here with an equal title to the enjoyment of his bounty – with an equal right to the use of all that nature so impartially offers. This is a right which is natural and inalienable; it is a right which vests in every human being as he enters the world, and which during his continuance in the world can be limited only by the equal rights of others.

General recognition of the equal rights of all to the use of land and other natural opportunities is hard to find. When the powerful nations of the world got together to eject Iraq from Kuwait, very little was heard of the bizarreness of supposing that the Emir of Kuwait and his relatives had a right to all the oil that lay under Kuwait. Some recognition of equal rights to the use of natural opportunities can be found in the proposed Law of the Sea Treaty, which would have had all nations benefiting from the granting of franchises to extract minerals from the sea. From an economic perspective, the treaty was flawed by the fact that it would have created an artificial scarcity of seabed mining activities in order to raise revenue. The United States opposed it, and it was not implemented. But it did suggest general recognition of global equal rights to at least those natural opportunities that no one has yet begun to use.

One impediment to the recognition of equal rights to the use of natural opportunities is that some system of assessment would be needed to identify the transfers that would compensate for unequal access to natural opportunities. Another impediment is that a system of rewards for those who discover new opportunities would be needed. But if there were a will to address them, these technical difficulties could be solved adequately, as they are in jurisdictions such as Alberta, Canada, that claim all mineral rights for the government.

5   Power, Population, and Process

There are two other difficulties that are more serious. First, the existing distribution of recognized exclusive rights to natural opportunities (land, mineral resources, fishing rights, water rights, etc.) is the outcome of a game of power, and those who have won at this game have great power and are loathe to part with their winnings. Second, Malthusian analysis has led people to expect that if the value of exclusive use of natural opportunities were distributed equally, population would expand until everyone was at a subsistence level.

There is a solution to the second problem, contained in the idea that all persons have equal rights to the use of natural opportunities. If the crowding effects of additional persons outweigh the beneficial effects of greater economies of scale, then any region that has an above-average population growth rate is appropriating more than its share of the scarce natural opportunity to be a parent. The costs that this region thereby imposes on other regions can justly be subtracted from what would otherwise be its claim on the value of using natural opportunities. Each region could then decide for itself whether to pass those costs on to individual couples who decide to conceive children.

Similarly, when a region imposes costs on others through interregional pollution, the costs so imposed should be subtracted from the region's claim to the value of exclusive use of natural opportunities.

The great challenge is to overcome the entrenched power that benefits from continued blindness to moral necessity. The mechanism must not be force of arms, for that entails too great a risk of installing a new power elite who would be as unprincipled as the first. Nor should the mechanism be the power of majorities, through legislation and referenda, for these processes can also be used for the selfish aggrandizement of those who control them. It is good that constitutions prohibit the taking of property without just compensation. It is to be hoped that courts will interpret such restrictions as prohibiting taxes that take all of the value of things currently regarded as property.

When respect for a newly understood moral truth requires the disappointment of previously protected expectations, those who would push their fellow citizens to incorporate that truth into the governmental process should be obliged to have their ideas reviewed in a constitutional amendment process that will ensure that they will be adopted only if a broad consensus on them is achieved. When people are ready to see a new moral truth, that truth can overcome such a hurdle.

References

George, Henry. *Progress and Poverty*, Book VII, ch. 1 (pp. 338–9 in many editions).

Jefferson, Thomas. 1813. Letter to Isaac McPherson, August 13.

Locke, John. 1690 (1960). P. Lasle (ed.) *Two Treatises of Government, Second Treatise*, para. 25. Cambridge: Cambridge University Press.

Olson, Mancur. 1993. "Dictatorship, Democracy and Development." *American Political Science Review* 87 (Fall): 567–76.

CHAPTER 7

Ideological Competition and Institutions: Why "Cultural" Explanations of Development Patterns Are Not Nonsense

Michael J. Ensley and Michael C. Munger

I   Introduction

Why do some societies prosper and grow? Why do other societies stag-nate, though they have equal or superior endowments of natural and human resources? It is not surprising that social scientists do not fully agree on precisely which economic variables are most important. What is interesting is the growing consensus that, even if we *could* identify all the economic variables, they would still be insufficient to explain growth and development. If this is true, what are the omitted factors?

An analytical theory of "culture" is a crucial part of the answer. "Analysis" of culture may seem like an oxymoron, of course. Cultural explanations have been marginalized in the theoretical literature, and for good reason. Those who study economic development, or comparative politics, are skeptical of giving a residual a name and then calling it a variable. Persson and Tabellini had it right: Explanations for growth cannot be random effects, admitting of no further analysis.

> Economic policy is not a random variable that varies freely across coun-tries. Rather, policy is the result of deliberate and purposeful choices by individuals and groups, who have specific incentives and constraints. If we maintain that it is policy differences that explain growth differ-ences, what we ultimately have to explain is why these deliberate and purposeful choices differ systematically across countries. To us, the most promising avenue toward such an explanation is to be found in the study of political incentives and political institutions. (Persson and Tabellini, 1992: 5)

The authors thank participants in the Political Science Graduate Studies Colloquium at Duke University, Scott Basinger, Robert Bates, Roger Congleton, Scott de Marchi, Ron Heiner, William Keech, Robert Keohane, Robert Tollison, and Gordon Tullock for com-ments and suggestions that improved the early versions of this chapter. We offer special thanks to Peter Lange, who made very significant comments and suggestions. In any case, for all the above, the usual caveat applies.

Culture should not automatically be dismissed as just an idiosyncratic *residual* variation in growth (or some other measure of economic activity) after all systematic economic components of that activity have been controlled for. Such systematic residual differences *do* exist: errors in growth models may take the form of broad average differences in productivity (along the lines of a pure "fixed effects" model), or narrowly focused differences in growth attributable to more efficient use of a single resource (an "interaction" effect).

But these effects are not purely random. In other words, the residuals in a growth model are serially correlated, so that differences in growth persist through time: Japan does consistently better, and Argentina consistently worse, than one would predict from a model based purely on factor endowments. Neither of these effects is consistent with orthodox neoclassical theory, which appears to predict *convergence*. Convergence means that there is a baseline, or average, rate of development.

Though nations may show temporary variation around this baseline, over time growth rates should converge, or become indistinguishable, as capital flows and the ability to mimic successful practices eliminates differences. Conversely, if growth rates do not converge, there must be something about the nation itself, the *context* in which economic activity takes place, that affects the quality and quantity of that activity.

The literature on convergence in growth is large, and we will not pretend to review it here. Two important recent works are Barro and Sala i Martin (1997) and de la Fuente (1997). The interesting thing about this new work, "endogenous growth" theory, is that it allows for persistent differences across nations (i.e., nonconvergence) in a neoclassical setting where all nations have access to the same technology and to resource markets. In this setting, nonconvergence arises from differences in policy, particularly investment in public goods such as human capital and physical or technological infrastructure. This is not a "culture" argument, of course, but rather a "policy persistence" view, where differences in policy cause differences in growth and prosperity. If policies persist, differences persist, apparently solving the puzzle.

We believe this is an insufficient answer. Without a theory of politics, economists cannot answer a fundamental question: Why do (apparently) suboptimal policies persist? Existing comparative politics explanations, relying on a residual conception of culture, are equally unsatisfying: "Because all countries are different!" In this chapter, we offer a suggestion of how to incorporate a broader, yet still practical, conception of "culture" into research on economic growth. Though the debt of this approach to North (1990) is obvious, we are also contradicting North in some ways that will become clear as we proceed.

Our main point is that culture can be separated analytically (though not always practically) into two distinct parts: *institutions* and *ideologies*. In particular, our argument is that ideologies, or *the shared preferences and moral codes of a society* (North, 1990; Hinich and Munger, 1994), influence economic growth and development by shaping the political preferences of competing groups. The society's institutions, or *the formal rules that govern political and economic activity* (Buchanan and Tullock, 1962; North, 1981), constrain this political conflict by ruling out certain alternatives, and advantaging certain interests.

More simply:

POLICY = Optimize f(ID) subject to (INST)
ID = A vector of ideologies, or widely held political belief systems
INST = Political and social institutions, which constrain ideological conflict
$f(\bullet)$ = Some objective function, whose arguments are the ideologies in conflict

There is general agreement that the policies (regulation, education, taxation, etc.) a government chooses affect prosperity and growth. But policies are not culture. Policy is the endogenous consequence of ideologies competing within an institutional setting. If that institutional setting persists, and if the ideologies that contest policy persist, policy may persist. To put it differently, attempts to change policies without changing the underlying institutions or affecting ideological perceptions are not likely to change the economy in line with predictions.

For example, there was hope that a "market" system in the former Soviet Union would rapidly spur growth and transform the nation. But establishing market *policies*, without first creating an *institutional* system of property rights or developing an *ideology* of legitimate free-market entrepreneurship had unexpected results. In fact:

Political Corruption
& Economic Mafias $=$ f(Socialism, Nationalism)
subject to (Collective Property Rights)

The result was not growth, at least not on the scale expected, because political corruption and economic mafias do not create confidence that investment and legitimate entrepreneurship will be rewarded. However, the policies we observe are the result of optimizing responses by what North (1990) would call "organizations," or humanly devised arrangements for carrying out economic activities. The fact that the outcomes are not optimal from the society's perspective doesn't change the fact that, given the logic of competition, organizations are responding optimally to institutional constraints.

II   Growth

If economic growth and development were simply consequences of exogenous forces (e.g., technological development,[1] resource endowments, stochastic shocks to economic systems, etc.) and individual wealth-maximizing behavior, then there would be little value in researching the causes of prosperity. A neoclassical economist would simply measure a nation's economic "capacity" in order to understand its path of economic development.

From a social scientific perspective, the neoclassical approach has some advantages. For one thing, it generates precise and testable hypotheses. Ferejohn (1991: 281) illustrates this advantage in referring to the rational choice paradigm, which is at the core of neoclassical economic theory:

> At the most abstract level, rational choice theorists are committed to a principle of universality: (all) agents act always to maximize their well-being as they understand it, based on their beliefs, preferences, and strategic opportunities. This commitment to a universal description of agents is what permits rational choice theorists to believe in the possibility of prediction as well as the ex post explanation.

Further, the neoclassical model would appear to provide a template for organizing development: follow these rules, implement these policies, and growth will happen.

However, this theoretical approach has been criticized for failing to account for differences in the empirical data. One critic of the neoclassical approach is L. E. Harrison (1992: 8):

> The world has learned a lot about development in the half-century since World War II. We know that market-oriented economic policies are a prerequisite for sustained growth. We know that political stability is also an essential ingredient. We know that extensive governmental intervention in an economy often breeds fiscal and efficiency problems and suppresses private initiative.... But for most countries, these lessons have had little impact, at least in terms of the access of the majority of human beings to the means of raising their standard of living; their ability to influence their governments' policies and actions; their equality before the law; and their equality of opportunity. What experts thought thirty years ago was going to be a fairly manageable, almost mechanical process has typically turned out to be vastly more complicated....

---

[1] It is arguable that technological development is partially a function of a society's investment in research related activities. We do not dispute this point. By technological development we mean simply to imply the "luck" or good fortune of discovering new production techniques or new products.

Thus, Harrison argues that social scientists must also account for differences in "culture." The idea that nations have idiosyncratic (within a nation) but shared (across nations) differences in rules, customs, or preferences seems to be an important point. However, is it possible to distinguish between the features that matter and those that simply reflect idiosyncratic differences in custom or taste?

We want to argue that these differences can and do matter. However, before we proceed to discuss why culture is important in explaining the performance of markets, we have to consider the nature of markets and market failure.

II.A   Market Failure

As any sophomore knows, orthodoxy allows for three kinds of market failure: information, externalities, and economies of scale. However, in some ways these are the least important "failures" of markets, as the following hierarchy (from Munger, 1997) shows.

Hierarchy of Market Failure: From General to Specific
1. Government *removes* or *fails to create* what Hayek (1935, 1945) called the "infrastructure" of market processes. Infrastructure includes a system for defining and trading property rights, a legal system for the adjudication of disputes, and a monetary system to facilitate exchange.
2. Government *creates* or *fails to remove* impediments to market processes. Such impediments might include taxes, subsidies, regulations, or standards that distort prices and information.
3. Markets fail to perform efficiently because of informational asymmetries, externalities in consumption or production, or large economies of scale in production.

Type 1 market failure arises from inadequate infrastructure, type 2 market failure results from poorly designed policies, and type 3 market failure is caused by flaws in market processes.

Blaming type 1 failure on markets is analogous to calling your car a lemon because there is no road. Charging markets with type 2 failure is akin to faulting your car for breaking down after you have put ammonia in the gas tank and molasses in the crankcase. Only type 3 is really a *market* failure; type 1 and 2 failures are malfunctions of *government management* of markets.

It is immediately clear how important this distinction is in diagnosing problems. On the face of it, the problem seems the same: in all three cases, the car (economic growth) won't go! Should you conclude the market is a lemon, and trade it in? A new car won't help if the real problem is bad roads or bad maintenance; the new car will likewise break down almost immediately. Unless we can think more fundamentally, the result will be an endless cycle of expensive trade-ins, none of which get us anywhere.

Yet this seems an apt description of much of the history of "development" economics. By excluding the cultural context in which optimizing behavior takes place, economists have left out key determinants of the extent to which self-interested action is capable of generating Pareto-superior outcomes.

II.B   Economic Growth and Institutions

Social scientists who have studied the implications of institutions for economic development and growth have approached the problem from a variety of perspectives. Economists (North, 1989; Grier and Tullock, 1989; Knack and Keefer, 1995; Clague et al., 1996) have generally defined institutions as measurable differences in the extent of liberty citizens in a nation enjoy, and the specific types of voting process used to make collective decisions.

North (1989) compares what he calls the "interdependence of political and economic institutions" against premises in neoclassical theories of economies, which maintain that population and savings are the principal determinants of economic growth. He looks at the institutional frameworks that preceded adoption of the United States Constitution and the Northwest Ordinance in early America, relating these precedents to the evolution of common law in England, where interests unconcerned with the Crown coalesced to form competing political units. The differences between England's institutional development and the comparatively centralized enforcement mechanisms of Spain, North claims, support the hypothesis that institutions have economic consequences.

Grier and Tullock (1989) use pooled cross-section/time-series data on 113 countries to investigate empirical regularities in postwar economic growth. They find that coefficient values vary widely across identifiable groups of countries, with evidence supporting the convergence hypothesis apparent only in the Organization for Economic Cooperation and Development (OECD) country sample. Among other results, they find that the growth of government consumption is significantly negatively correlated with the economic growth in three of four subsamples, including the OECD, and that political repression is negatively correlated with growth in Africa and Central and South America.

Knack and Keefer (1995) argue that the definition of property rights influences economic growth. They test this claim using indicators provided by country risk evaluators to potential foreign investors and find that rates of convergence to U.S. level incomes increase notably when these (often omitted) property rights variables are included in growth regressions. Clague et al. (1996) are more ambitious: they try to specify, and test empirically, a broader theory of property and contract rights. They claim that any incentive an autocrat has to respect such rights comes from his interest in future tax collections and national income. Consequently, the incentive to respect property rights increases with the effective planning horizon. Clague et al. find empirical evidence for a relationship between property and contract rights and an autocrat's time in power. In lasting – but not in new – democracies, the same rule of law and individual rights that ensures continued free elections appears to entail extensive property and contract rights.

Engerman and Sokolof (1994) dissent from this position, pointing out that "histories" of development are often selective and that "controls" for levels of factor endowments often understate the true differences between colonies or developing nations. In the Western Hemisphere, for example, scholars have wondered why the United States and Canada have been so much more successful over time than other New World economies. Engerman and Sokoloff argue that the divergence in paths can be traced back to sustained growth during the eighteenth and early nineteenth centuries. They argue that the roots of these disparities in the extent of inequality lay in (correctly measured) differences in the initial factor endowments of the respective colonies.

Engerman and Sokoloff explore the effects of the degree of inequality on the evolution of institutions that are conducive to broad participation in the commercial economy and to technological change. They suggest that the greater equality in wealth, human capital, and political power may have predisposed the United States and Canada toward earlier realization of sustained economic growth. Over all, they claim that "the role of factor endowments has been underestimated, and the independence of institutional developments from the factor endowments exaggerated, in theories of the differential paths of growth among New World economies."

The foregoing analysis, although it may be incomplete in many ways, is meant to suggest that institutions do matter for understanding economic growth and development through time. Specifically, institutions offer mechanisms through which a society can distribute scarce resources under conditions of uncertainty. While the analysis of institutions has much to reveal about economic development and growth through time, it is still incomplete because it does not offer insight into the problem of institutional change. This theoretical deficiency can be confronted in our opinion by understanding the interaction between what we argue are the two key components of "culture": *ideologies* as persistent determinants of political preferences and *institutions* as persistent constraints on the choices that the political process can make.

III   Alternative Frameworks

In the introduction, we argued that economic forces were *necessary* but not *sufficient* to explain economic growth and development. The gap between neoclassical theory and empirical evidence has led social scientists to propose two alternative theoretical frameworks: the institutional (e.g., Keohane, 1984; March and Olsen, 1984; North, 1981, 1990) and the ideological (e.g., Weber, 1950; Harrison, 1992; Hinich and Munger, 1994).

These two theoretical perspectives have been presented in conjunction with the classical economic explanations. We will argue that these two perspectives are not mutually exclusive but are both in fact necessary for understanding economic growth and development through time. First we will proceed by discussing the institutional perspective. Then we will relate institutions to the ideological perspective.

III.A   Institutions

The most common definition of "institutions" is now something like Douglass North's (1981) phrase, "the humanly devised rules of the game." Similarly, Keohane (1984) defines institutions as ideas about what constitutes a "good" decision, embedded in a formal framework of rules and norms. Kreps (1990) notes that institutions solve a problem in the specification and enforcement of long-term contracts, by creating expectations that may be fulfilled in equilibrium, and by providing information about defection from, or compliance with, the complex social arrangements that this equilibrium implies.

These definitions imply that institutions help groups confront two fundamental problems. The first problem is the existence of *scarcity*. By scarcity we mean to imply that a society does not have enough resources to satisfy all of the demands that are placed on it by individuals or groups of individuals within the society. Thus the scarcity of resources suggests that a society must make choices in order to determine how to distribute the resources to its individual members.

The second fundamental problem that institutions combat is *uncertainty*. We view uncertainty as having two sources. The first is very close to a statistical problem and comes from the tenuous connection between policy (which governments can change) and outcomes (which citizens care about). It is difficult to predict the effects of policies on outcomes, because (a) causal relations are complex, and (b) there are large stochastic elements in the process of generating outcomes.

The other source of uncertainty is strategic. Strategic uncertainty comes from not knowing the actions of other members of society. We are never certain about the actions other individuals will take. This is problematic because the actions we would want to take often depend upon our calculation of what others will do. If we are uncertain about what others will do, it will be hard for us to determine what course of action we should pursue.

In particular, this uncertainty about the actions of others is a problem when we believe that others will take actions that increase their own welfare but will have hurt the rest of society. Thus, as Mancur Olson (1965) and others have noted, the fundamental dilemma for a society (or the collective action problem) is how to create a context where self-interested actors have reasons to cooperate. In other words, a society must ensure that its members are able to capture the gains that result from the specialization and division of labor by discouraging certain behavior.

Institutions help a society confront the conditions of scarcity and uncertainty by providing a structure or an arena for human interaction. In particular, institutions provide structure by establishing formal rules, much as Buchanan has expressed in a variety of his writings.[2] Institutions prevent chaos by establishing a set of rules that will determine how the game will be played or, in terms of politics, how collective choices will be made. That is, institutions provide a structure or framework under which different players and groups can interact. It would be wasteful, and even dangerous, constantly to place people in a game that they had never seen before. These potential players would need to be given rules to guide or coordinate their actions.

By formalizing the rules governing collective choice, institutions allow decision makers to gain greater certainty about the political process. Ronald Heiner (1983) argues that as human interaction becomes more complex and uncertain, successful social institutions must reduce the information needed to achieve cooperation among individuals. A person's "overall behavior may actually be improved by restricting flexibility to use information or to choose particular actions" (p. 564). Thus, by limiting the choice set of possible actions, cooperation among individuals can be improved under restrictive or rigid formal rules by increasing the predictability or certainty of other people's actions. Heiner states that

> In general, further evolution toward social interdependence will require institutions that permit agents to know about successively smaller fractions of the larger social environment. That is, *institutions must evolve*

---

[2] In addition to the quoted passage from Buchanan and Tullock (1962), see Buchanan (1966) and Brennan and Buchanan (1985).

which enable each agent in the society to know less and less about the behavior of other agents and about the complex interdependencies generated by their interaction (p. 580; emphasis in original)

Institutions will reduce the uncertainty in the "game" by shrinking the choice set of all of the "players." If the rules are not formalized, the players may spend too much time arguing over the rules and less time competing in productive activities. The actual choice of institutions, however, is hard, since there are countless ways of restricting "bad" choices. What makes some institutions better than others?

III.B   Ideologies

Why should we look to ideologies to explain institutional choice and institutional change? In the beginning we defined ideologies as the shared preferences and moral codes of a society. These shared preferences and moral codes serve as organizing principles for large political groups by combating uncertainty. First we can think of ideologies helping individuals frame complex and unfamiliar problems. As Denzau and North (1994) recognized:

> Ideas matter, and the way that ideas are communicated among people is crucial to theories that will enable us to deal with strong uncertainty problems at the individual level. . . . Under conditions of uncertainty, individuals' interpretation of their environment will reflect their learning. Individuals with common cultural backgrounds and experiences will share reasonably convergent mental models, ideologies, and institutions; and individuals with different learning experiences (both cultural and environmental) will have different theories (models, ideologies) to interpret their environment. (pp. 3–4)

Thus Denzau and North refer to these belief systems as "shared mental models" because they assist individuals who lack information in making choices.

These shared mental models also help combat the uncertainty about the actions of other members of society. Since these mental models are "shared" among large groups, it helps provide, as Schofield (1985) puts it, a "common knowledge" basis. This common knowledge basis may help discourage self-interested behavior that is harmful to the general welfare of society.

The term "knowledge" is meant to imply that people have valuable information that will increase their level of certainty about the possible actions of other citizens. This increased level of certainty about the actions of others will have a self-reinforcing effect: If an individual is more confident that others will not act against the collective interest, then he or she will be less likely to act against the collective interest. Thus, this common knowledge basis will allow people to capitalize on the gains that result from the division and specialization of labor by increasing their level of confidence that others will act in the collective interest.[3]

Similarly, Hinich and Munger (1994) define an ideology as an integrated set of ideas with implications for "what is good, who gets what, and who rules." Consequently, ideologies can be religious or secular and can either be adaptable or make claims to be the exclusive conception of right and justice. The key features of ideologies, for our purposes, are two. First, they constitute legitimating rationales for existing institutions. Alternatively, ideologies can provide the intellectual basis for attacking, changing, or destroying institutions. Thus, it is this conflictual aspect of ideologies that is useful in understanding how culture can affect economic growth and development.

Unconstrained by institutions, ideological conflict prevents growth by ensuring that conflict will be unlimited and that the future gains to present investment cannot be guaranteed. If institutions are the only way out, we need to know how institutions are chosen and how they are maintained.

IV   Institutional Choice

From the perspective of neoclassical economics, growth and development are the result of individual actors pursuing self-interested goals. The pursuit of wealth and prosperity by individual actors leads to an efficient allocation of goods and resources. Thus, according to neoclassical economics, institutions are simply mechanisms that aid or assist in the efficient allocation of resources and goods. The logical conclusion to be drawn from this argument is that institutions that lead to inefficient outcomes will be abandoned or phased out of existence.

However, as North (1981, 1990) has argued, inefficient institutions can persist. Similarly, Avner Grief (1997) points out that neoclassical economics is not able to explain the existence of some institutions. "Neoclassical economics suggests that markets and the process of market integration foster efficiency and growth. Yet, it has been proved difficult to substantiate this claim based on historical data" (p. 81). So if it is not purely the pursuit of efficiency (and hence, economics growth and development) that shapes institutions, then what forces shape institutions?

Our argument is that a key determinant of understanding institutional choice and institutional change is the balance of ideological forces in a given society. Before laying out the argument, we should begin with a caveat. It is quite reasonable to assume that under certain conditions

---

[3] Garrett and Lange (1996) argue that open economies have the effect of forcing convergence in labor policies.

institutions will change for reasons of efficiency (as the neoclassical view predicts). However, what happens when there is disagreement over the nature of an efficient institutional design? In other words, what if there is a difference of opinion over what constitutes the proper institutions for a society? Or to take a more pessimistic view, what happens when one group seeks to change institutions for its own personal benefit, while disregarding the welfare of other groups?

Given our assumption that institutions affect economic growth and development (mainly through the distribution of property rights), then it is quite reasonable to assume that certain groups within a society will try to use the choice of institutions to serve their own interests. Regardless of whether one takes an optimistic or pessimistic view of human nature, the problem is still the same: Given that there exists a difference of opinion over the proper set of institutions, under what conditions will institutions change?

There appear to be two major normative schools of thought: a positive argument (Rawls) and a normative argument (Buchanan and Tullock). Rawls (1971) attempts to explain institutional choice by arguing that institutions should be chosen (as if) behind a "veil of ignorance." The veil hides the decision makers from the true state of the world. Institutions thus are chosen under uncertainty. Rawls argues that individuals in this situation can be predicted to choose institutions that protect the interests of the lowest member of the society. To put it differently, if individuals are risk averse in their choice of institutions, the result would be egalitarianism, regardless of the ethical value of this approach.

Buchanan and Tullock (1962) also argue that institutions are chosen under conditions of uncertainty. Instead of assuming that individuals are risk averse in institutional choice, they argue that institutions that benefit the average or mean member of society will be chosen. Buchanan and Tullock make this analogy quite clearly:

> Since no player can anticipate which specific rules might benefit him during a particular play of the game, he can, along with all the other players, attempt to devise a set of rules that will constitute the most interesting game for the average or representative player. It is to the self-interest of each player to do this. Hence, the discussion can proceed without the intense conflicts of interest that are expected to arise in the later playing of the game itself. (1962: 79–80)[4]

---

[4] Buchanan and Tullock (1962) also note that in a society where a sharp cleavage exists, we would not expect to see cooperation among the winning and losing coalitions. Where a sharp cleavage exists, the boundaries between political groups or ideological units are not fluid. Thus, a winning coalition will be more certain that it will remain in power because the relative sizes of the coalition's support groups are not expected to change. Therefore, in order for the incentive to provide and protect the rights of minorities to exist, the current coalition's boundaries must be fluid so that the current winners and losers will be uncertain about their future roles.

Thus, rules that promote particular interests or favor certain groups should not be adopted. However, are these notions of institutional choice under uncertainty a reasonable assumption?

While the idea of uncertainty in institutional choice is an important aspect of the process, it seems that institutions are never made under conditions of complete uncertainty. Thus there is still an opportunity to be strategic in institutional choice. But under what conditions will groups of individuals be able to act strategically in choosing institutions? While there are some preliminary answers (Riker, 1980; March and Olsen, 1984; Knight, 1992; North, 1995), the process by which institutions are developed and modified is still not clearly understood. For whatever reason, institutions often persist, and this persistence is an important aspect of any analytical explanation of economic performance.

V   Conclusion

In this chapter we have hoped to persuade the reader that cultural factors can be important in understanding long-term economic growth and development. Further, we hope to transform the conception of "culture" from a named residual, or a name for persistent policy, into a three-part concept. Specifically, culture can be broken into (a) the specific interaction of political ideologies competing in (b) an institutional context, and (c) a true (i.e., fixed effect) residual that persists in a given nation over time. While the empirical data suggest that growth and development are more than products of economic factors, we wanted to provide a framework in which to analyze the effects of culture. By arguing that institutions and ideologies are mechanisms that society utilizes to solve the problem of uncertainty, we attempted to illustrate how cultural factors (or ideologies) interacted with institutions. Although this analysis is incomplete in many ways, we believe that this chapter provides strong reasons why scholars should examine cultural factors when studying economic growth and development. More specifically, we believe that scholars interested in economic growth and development should examine the extent to which institutions mediate ideological competition.

References

Barro, Robert, and Xavier Sala i Martin. 1997. "Technological Diffusion, Convergence, and Growth." *Journal of Economic Growth* 2: 1–26.

Brennan, Geoffrey, and Buchanan, James M. 1985. *The Reason of Rules: Constitutional Political Economy.* Cambridge: Cambridge University Press.

Buchanan, James M. 1966. "An Individualistic Theory of Political Process." In D. Easton, ed., *Varieties of Political Theory.* Englewood Cliffs, N.J.: Prentice-Hall, pp. 25–37.

Buchanan, James M., and Tullock, Gordon. 1962. *The Calculus of Consent: Logical Foundations of Constitutional Democracy.* Ann Arbor: University of Michigan Press.

Clague, Christopher, Keefer, Philip, Knack, Stephen, and Olson, Mancur. 1996. "Property and Contract Rights in Autocracies and Democracies." *Journal of Economic Growth* 1(2): 243–76.

de la Fuente, Angel. 1997. "The Empirics of Growth and Convergence: A Selective Review." *Journal of Economic Dynamics and Control* 21: 23–73.

Denzau, Arthur, and North, Douglass. 1994. "Shared Mental Models: Ideologies and Institutions." *Kyklos* 47: 3–32.

Engerman, Stanley, and Sokoloff, Kenneth. 1994. "Factor Endowments, Institutions, and Differential Paths of Growth among New World Economies: A View from Economic Historians of the United States." National Bureau of Economic Research Working Paper Series on Historical Factors in Long Run Growth, Cambridge, Mass.

Ferejohn, John. 1991. "Rationality and Interpretation: Parliamentary Elections in Early Stuart England." In Kristen Renwick Monroe, ed., *The Economic Approach to Politics: A Critical Reassessment of the Theory of Rational action.* New York: Harper Collins, pp. 279–305.

Garrett, Geoffrey, and Lange, Peter. 1996. "Internationalization, Institutions, and Political Change." In Robert Keohane and Helen Milner, eds., *Internationalization and Domestic Politics.* Cambridge: Cambridge University Press.

Grief, Avner. 1997. "Microtheory and Recent Developments in the Study of Economic Institutions through Economic History." In David M. Kreps and Kenneth F. Wallis, eds., *Advances in Economics and Econometrics: Theory and Applications, Seventh World Conference, Vol. II.* New York: Cambridge University Press. pp. 79–113.

Grier, Kevin, and Tullock, Gordon. 1989. "An Empirical Analysis of Cross-National Economic Growth, 1951–80." *Journal of Monetary Economics* 24(2): 259–76.

Harrison, Lawrence E. 1992. *Who Prospers? How Cultural Values Shape Economic and Political Success.* New York: Basic Books.

Hayek, Friedrich A. 1935. *Prices and Production.* London: Routledge and Kegan Paul, 2d edition.

____ 1945. "The Use of Knowledge in Society." *American Economic Review* 4: 519–30.

Heiner, Ronald. 1983. "On the Origins of Predictable Behavior." *American Economic Review* 73: 560–95.

Hinich, Melvin, and Munger, Michael. 1994. *Ideology and the Theory of Political Choice.* Ann Arbor: University of Michigan Press.

Keohane, Robert. 1984. *After Hegemony: Cooperation and Discord in the World Political Economy.* Princeton, N.J.: Princeton University Press.

Knack, Stephen, and Keefer, Philip. 1995. "Institutions and Economic Performance: Cross-Country Tests Using Alternative Institutional Measures." *Economics and Politics* 7(3): 207–27.

Knight, Jack. 1992. *Institutions and Social Conflict.* Cambridge: Cambridge University Press.

Kreps, David. 1990. "Corporate Culture and Economic Theory." In James Alt and Kenneth Shepsle, eds., *Perspectives on Positive Political Economy.* New York: Cambridge University Press.

March, James G., and Olsen, Jonah P. 1984. "The New Institutionalism: Organizational Factors in Political Life." *American Political Science Review* 78: 734–49.

Munger, Michael C. 1997. "Kicking Competition to the Curb." *Regulation* (Summer): 69–72.

North, Douglass. 1981. *Structure and Change in Economic History*. New York: W. W. Norton.

1989. "Institutions and Economic Growth: An Historical Introduction." *World-Development* 17(9): 1319–32.

1990. *Institutions, Institutional Change, and Economic Performance*. Cambridge: Cambridge University Press.

1995. "Five Propositions about Institutional Change." In Jack Knight and Etai Sened, eds., *Explaining Social Institutions*. Ann Arbor: University of Michigan Press.

Olson, Mancur. 1965. *The Logic of Collective Action*. Cambridge, Mass.: Harvard University Press.

Persson, Torsten, and Tabellini, Guido. 1992. "Growth, Distribution and Politics." In Alex Cukierman, Zvi Hercowitz, and Leonardo Leiderman, eds., *Political Economy, Growth, and Business Cycles*. Cambridge, Mass.: MIT Press.

Rawls, John. 1971. *A Theory of Justice*. Cambridge, Mass.: Belknap Press of Harvard University Press.

Riker, William. 1980. "Implications from the Disequilibrium of Majority Rule for the Study of Institutions." *American Political Science Review* 74: 432–46.

Schofield, Norman. 1985. "Anarchy, Altruism, and Cooperation: A Review." *Social Choice and Welfare* 2: 207–19.

Weber, Max. 1950. *The Protestant Ethic and the Spirit of Capitalism*. New York: Scribner.

PART II

ELECTORAL SYSTEMS AND INSTITUTIONS

Electoral system choice, especially the distinction between proportional representation and the plurality forms of electoral rules, is widely regarded by political scientists as one of the fundamental institutional decisions made by a democratic polity. Part II is made up of contributions that examine the operation of the systems and institutions of representation. Grofman and Reynolds provide an overview of the current state of knowledge and of the cutting-edge areas of research. This includes a panoramic view of such issues as votes–seats relationships, party proliferation and government stability, as well as the nature of partisan bias, incentives for strategic misrepresentation of preferences, incentives for voter turnout, and incentives for localism and corruption.

Mudambi and his colleagues take a practical look at the effects of electoral rules on coalition strategies in the context of Italian national elections. The rules in question are an attempt to move away from a proportional system toward one incorporating elements of plurality. Since elements of both systems are present, their effects on political coalition strategies can be studied. Paul and Wilhite, on the other hand, examine the plurality system in U.S. congressional elections, focusing on effects of campaign finance considerations.

Many important characteristics of government are not included in formal constitutions. These include the organization of public administration and its relationship with the polity and, in many federal systems, with the local and regional government. It is generally argued that voters are neither interested in nor capable of exerting influence on these aspects of government. Using evidence from France, Salmon criticizes this view. He suggests that by means of their capacity to vote in ordinary elections and in a way that is mostly negative and tacit (and therefore often inconspicuous), voters do exert considerable influence in these matters.

123

Electoral Systems and the Art of Constitutional Engineering: An Inventory of the Main Findings

Bernard N. Grofman and Andrew Reynolds

I   Introduction

Electoral system choice, especially the distinction between proportional representation systems (PR) and plurality or majority forms of electoral rules, is widely regarded by political scientists as one of the three fundamental institutional decisions made by a democratic polity (the two other key elements of choice being presidentialism vs. parliamentarism, and unitary vs. federalized government).[1] Choice of electoral systems and other electorally related decisions (e.g., about number of districts, timing of elections, basis for apportioning seats, the nature of the redistricting process, etc.)[2] can be directly linked to a variety of other aspects of the political system such as the number of parties; the degree to which minor parties or minority points of view come to be represented; the degree of descriptive representation by gender, race, religion, and so forth; bias in the way in which some parties have their vote shares translated into set shares relative to other parties with the same vote share;

[1] See e.g., Lijphart (1984). However, elsewhere it has been argued (Grofman, 1996c) that there are several other elements of constitutional choice (in particular, (4) the basis of citizenship (e.g., citizenship by blood vs. citizenship by mutual choice) and (5) whether or not the constitution proclaims that citizens possess positive rights (e.g., the right to an education or to health care) and not merely protections for rights such as free speech) that are at least as important for the politics of a nation.

[2] The Introduction to Grofman and Lijphart (1986) identifies nearly two dozen aspects of electoral system choice, including rules for candidate eligibility, types of restrictions on the nature of campaigning, campaign finance rules, and procedures for ensuring the honesty of the ballot count. Despite the potential importance of fine tuning such as the actual mechanisms and standards for drawing distinct boundaries (see e.g., various essays in Grofman et al., 1982; Cain, 1985; Mair, [1986]/1994; Grofman, 1990; Courtney, MacKinnon, and Smith, 1992; Butler and Cain, 1992; Grofman, 1998) our principal focus here is on the basic aggregation rules for translating votes into seats (see e.g., Taagepera and Shugart, 1989).

the likelihood of single-party governments; cabinet durability; incentives for localistic or parochialistic attitudes on the part of legislators; electoral responsiveness of the legislature to changes in voter preferences; conflicts between president and legislature; and so on. In sum, electoral systems matter.

Electoral systems are currently a hot topic in political science, with the "third wave" of democratization having produced a large number of new (or "renewed") democracies.[3] Electoral and other results from these new democracies provide a fertile avenue for new research, especially since the number of electoral system variants available for study has increased at the same time as there has been the increase in the number of practicing democracies from which data can be obtained.[4] Because of the availability of data from more than one country using the same (or nearly the same) electoral system as well as data permitting district-level within-nation comparisons, and because of the relatively easy availability of longitudinal data sets for the long-term democracies for at least the fifty-year post-WWII period,[5] electoral systems research lends itself naturally to genuinely comparative research following the *tnt* principle (comparisons across *t*ypes of (electoral) systems, across *n*ations or other political sub-units, and across *t*ime).[6]

Electoral systems generate quantitative data (e.g., about party vote shares and seat shares) that is readily amenable to quantitative analysis.

---

[3] Much of the best work on electoral systems appears in the journal *Electoral Studies*, which came into being a little over a decade ago.

[4] The best sources for an inventory of electoral system use around the world are Reynolds and Reilly (1997) and Cox (1997). Because the major variations in electoral systems are relatively well known and have been fully described elsewhere (e.g., Rae, 1971; Reeve and Ware, 1992; Taagepera and Shugart, 1989; Reynolds and Reilly, 1997; Cox, 1997; Farrell, 1997), given space constraints we will not attempt to review those basic definitions here, but will assume that readers are familiar with the distinctions among, say, plurality, list PR, STV (the single transferable vote), limited voting systems such as SNTV (the single non-transferable vote), cumulative voting, the German double-ballot added-member system (which imposes overall proportionality), and other double-ballot mixed systems (e.g., that in Japan or Russia) whose separate PR and SMD components are not linked in any way.

[5] Hard copy versions of detailed election results for established democracies are available in sources such as Mackie and Rose (1991 et seq.), with current election results reported in journals such as *Electoral Studies* and an annual special issue of the *European Journal of Political Research*. Increasingly, data for a majority of democratic polities is available on-line. In particular, the Lijphart Archives, directed by Gary Cox at University of California, San Diego, http://dodgson.ucsd.edu/lij/ now offers election data at the district level (as well as at the national level) from elections around the world.

[6] The notion that comparative research can be phrased in terms of the *tnt* principle is due to A. Wuffle (cited in Grofman, 1999a), but the idea is certainly not original to him. Indeed, Wuffle (personal communication, April 1, 1992) recalls having heard this same general idea being advocated by David Easton nearly thirty years ago (cf. Przeworski and Teune, 1970).

With only some exceptions most of the obvious dependent variables to study (e.g., number of parties, disproportionality of votes to seats results) lend themselves to unambiguous operationalization.[7] Electoral systems analysis also lends itself to modeling because we may reason in an intuitive way about how certain structural properties of electoral systems (e.g., electoral system type, district magnitude, etc.) will impact other variables of interest (e.g., the number of parties who gain seats in the legislature).[8] Furthermore, in the electoral arena it does not seem especially problematic, even to the most hide-bound of political scientists, to try to develop models with a rational choice component to them. Political actors are likely to be attentive (at least in an intuitive way) to the same institutional features of electoral systems that the analyst is seeking to model insofar as those features can impact their electoral chances or political careers.

While as a matter of political reality electoral systems are hard to change, they are more open to change than most other key institutional practices, especially since, in many countries, electoral systems choice is not constitutionally embedded, but allows for change by legislative action.[9] Thus, of the three "fundamental" political choices identified by

---

[7] Of course, there are a number of far from trivial issues of operationalization even about matters that would seem to be obvious, like how many parties there are. What about parties that are essentially regional wings of one party (e.g., the CDU and the CSU in Germany) but that, nonetheless have distinct names even though they never contest one another and always are in (or out of) governing coalitions as a unit? Should we look at only those parties that gain seats? Should we use some (arbitrary) threshold to exclude "minor" parties from our analyses? To deal with the counting issue, Laakso and Taagepera (1979) propose that we take into account party vote or seats shares in terms of what they call the "effective" number of electoral and the "effective" number of legislative parties. Their answer (which is a variant of the Hirschman-Herfindahl index familiar to economists) has been widely accepted by political scientists. Similarly, there are at least two main contenders for a measure of disproportionality of electoral results. One is the coefficient of deviation, most closely associated with the names of Loosemore and Hanby (1971), which had become the standard measure in the literature. The other is Gallagher's more recently proposed (1991) least-squares measure, which has already begun to win converts – beginning with Arend Lijphart. But these are essentially technical questions which need not concern us here. We should note, however, that in general we will use the Laakso-Taagepera effective number of parties, which equals one over the sum of the party vote shares, whenever we talk about the "number" of parties.

[8] Moreover, certain electoral constraints (e.g., on the maximum number of parties that can gain representation, a constraint set by the size of the assembly) allow us to appeal to basic statistical principles (e.g., about the properties of bounded distributions) to derive testable inferences.

[9] We don't know exactly how many countries have electoral rules that are constitutionally embedded and thus especially resistant to change, but it is a minority of countries. Even countries that reference the electoral rules in their constitution rarely do so in a very detailed way. For example, South Africa's Constitution simply talks about the use of a proportional method of election (Reynolds, 1996). The U.S. Constitution does not specify

Lijphart (1984), electoral system choice appears to be the easiest to change. Therefore, to the extent that we can identify clear probable consequences of electoral system choice, it may be possible to implement desired changes.

In looking to choice of electoral system, the three-fold distinction between proportional, semi-proportional, and majoritarian/plurality systems is standard in the literature on electoral systems (e.g., Grofman, 1975; Taagepera and Shugart, 1989). Here we argue that it must be rethought.

First, we must distinguish between how electoral systems operate in principle to achieve proportionality and how systems operate in practice. The first is based on theoretically derived properties of electoral system like the threshold of representation and the threshold of exclusion (Lijphart, 1986), thresholds that tell us the minimum expected vote share needed to gain a seat and the maximum expected vote share which is still not large enough to guarantee at least one seat, respectively. The second is based on what, in reality, those thresholds are. In general, small parties often achieve representation with considerably fewer votes than would seem to be required by the threshold of representation, and the "effective" threshold of exclusion is usually a lot lower than its theoretical value (Rein Taagepera, work in progress). Moreover, in judging the expected proportionality of any electoral system we must also take into account complications such as national thresholds that exclude parties that fail to receive a certain proportion of the total vote.

Our second challenge to the usual classification of electoral systems in terms of their expected proportionality is quite different, and even more fundamental. Elsewhere (Grofman, 1996b; Bowler and Grofman, 1997; Grofman, 1999b) we have argued that, while proportionality is important (e.g., in affecting system legitimacy and the number of political parties), it is not necessarily the most important feature of an electoral system (see also Carey and Shugart, 1995). If we focus on other considerations that we have previously talked about, for example, the extent to which an electoral system provides options to voters to choose among candidates as well as among parties (which affects strength of party systems) or the differences in electoral systems in terms of the incentives for local-

---

the election method for members of Congress other than to say it will be by popular vote. Even the details of the electoral college method for electing the president are actually a lot more open than is commonly thought. In particular, even though, at present, all states implement the rule that the candidate who wins a plurality of the state's popular vote wins all of the state's electoral college votes, in fact states are free to choose any method they like to select presidential electors. Rein Taagepera (personal communication, February 1997) has noted that in long-term democracies that have had recent changes of electoral system (France in the 1980s, twice; New Zealand, 1993; Japan, 1996; Italy, 1993) constitutional change was not required.

ism or particularism, then we end up with quite different ways to view the question of which electoral systems are most alike.

For example, in the usual classification STV (single transferable vote) and list PR are on one end of the continuum (most proportional), while bloc vote plurality is at the other end (least proportional) and a system like SNTV (single non-transferable vote) is in the middle. However, if we classify systems according to the degree to which they are likely to strong and disciplined political parties, then, ceteris paribus, list PR is at one end, but now STV may look a lot more like SNTV than it does list PR, because both STV and SNTV allow for intra-party competition when a party nominates more candidates within a constituency than its voting strength in the electorate will permit success to, and this normally gives rise to party factionalism. Moreover, under closed list PR, the party apparatus has control over candidate placement (and thus likelihood of electoral success) which gives the party a lot of clout in disciplining errant legislators by holding over them the threat of denying them renomination (or at least placing them so low on the list that their chances of victory are much reduced). Similarly, if we classify systems according to the degree to which they foster localistically oriented representatives, then STV may look a lot more like SNTV or even a single-member district (SMD) than it does list PR, since the success of a candidate depends entirely on having enough *personal support* among voters in the local constituency – which sensitizes the candidate to local concerns. In these systems, running on the stronger party label may help, but it is not the whole story, and it is the local preferences among candidates that are decisive.

II Classic Propositions of the Electoral Systems Literature

Until quite recently, the literature on the political consequences of electoral laws emphasized three effects:[10] first and foremost, the way in which electoral systems impact on the proportionality of the translation of party shares of the vote into party seat shares in the (national) legislature; second, the impact of election rules on the number of parties; and third, the stability of political regimes, especially as measured by the longevity of governing cabinets. Key propositions with respect to each domain may be summarized (in what we might think of as "classic comic book," i.e., oversimplified form) as follows:

First, PR systems are more proportional in their translation of votes into seats than plurality/majority systems, and the most important single variable affecting degree of proportionality in PR and semi-PR systems is what has been called district magnitude, generally denoted M, the

[10] See e.g., Rae (1971), Grofman (1975), Lijphart and Grofman (1984), Grofman and Lijphart (1986), Taagepera (1986), Taagepera and Shugart (1989), and Lijphart (1994).

number of seats per district (Sartori, 1968; Taagepera and Shugart, 1989; Lijphart, 1994). For fixed M, more fine-tuned differences among PR systems are captured by the *threshold of representation* and the *threshold of exclusion*. The latter is the smallest vote share a party might receive and still obtain representation (under the most favorable circumstances); the latter is the largest vote share a party might receive and still be denied representation (under the least favorable circumstances). For most PR systems, the threshold of representation is roughly inverse to M.[11] However, certain forms of list PR[12] are more advantageous than others to smaller/larger/mid-sized parties (Gallagher, 1992).[13]

Second, with respect to the number of parties, Duverger's Law states that plurality-based elections[14] in single-member districts[15] will generally result in two-party politics. In contrast, Duverger's Hypothesis states that proportional election systems generally give rise to multi-party politics.[16] An important further generalization of Duverger is the claim that, ceteris paribus, the larger the district magnitude, M, the greater will be the number of political parties (Sartori, 1968).

Duverger posits that his "Law" operates through two factors. On the one hand, plurality elections have a very high threshold of exclusion (1/2) and thus non-majority parties may be frozen out completely, while small parties are unlikely to win representation even if more than two parties compete. This is what Duverger calls the "mechanical effect." On the other hand, voters who see their first choice having little or no chance of victory might be expected to vote (eventually) for the more preferred

[11] Values of these thresholds are given for most of the common electoral systems in use in Grofman (1975) and in Lijphart (1986), which corrects an error in the Ste. Lagüe formula given in the earlier work. Taagepera (personal communication, February 1997) has suggested using an index value that is the average of these two thresholds.

[12] The most important formulae for list PR are D'Hondt, Ste. Lagüe, and "largest remainder." These correspond, respectively, to the Jefferson, Webster, and Hamilton rules for apportioning the U.S. House of Representatives (Balinski and Young, 1982).

[13] The literature on proportionality as a function of party size (see esp. Taagepera and Shugart, 1989) draws on derived quantities such as "advantage ratio" (denoted A, the ratio of seat share to vote share for a given party) and B (the break-even vote share value such that above that value the "index of advantage" is greater than 1, i.e., the point at which larger parties come to be overrepresented).

[14] The British call such elections, "first past the post," commonly abbreviated FPTP. We will stick to the American usage.

[15] A "single-member district" (SMD) is one from which a single representative is elected. Similarly a "multi-member district" (MMD) is one from which more than one representative is to be elected.

[16] Duverger's ideas are contained in Duverger (1954). The distinction between Duverger's Law and Duverger's Hypothesis is due to Riker (1982, reprinted as in Grofman and Lijphart, 1986). Downs (1957), operating in apparent ignorance of Duverger's work, proposes something very close to Duverger's Law. Riker also traces still earlier scholarship anticipating Duverger's assertions. See also Duverger (1986), Sartori (1986), Taagepera and Shugart (1989), Lijphart (1994), and Fedderson (1992).

of the two major parties. This is what Duverger calls the "psychological effect." Clearly, too, potential candidates of small parties might be deterred from running when they realize that their party has no realistic chance of victory, and financial and other campaign support for candidates with no realistic chance of victory would be inhibited.[17] Downs (1957) provides a somewhat different argument for why single-member district competition should create two-party competition. If there is a single dimension of ideological competition, in an extension of the famous median voter argument, Downs shows that three-party politics tends to be unstable in that the pressures toward convergence toward the views of the median voter will tend to squeeze out the center party.

Third, with respect to cabinet durability, nations with two parties have the longest-lasting cabinets, and generally speaking, the greater the "effective number" of parties, the lower is cabinet durability (Dodd, 1976; see recent literature review in Grofman and van Roozendaal, 1997). Thus, combining Duverger's Law and Hypothesis with these results, we get the claim that nations using plurality-based elections in single-member districts will generally have more stable cabinets than nations using PR in large, multimember districts, that is, that cabinet stability will be inverse with M.

Note that stating each of the three basic propositions of the classical electoral systems literature in terms of M allows us to see linkages among these propositions that might not otherwise be apparent. We show those links in Figure 1.

As we see, because each is oppositely signed with respect to M, we expect that cabinet stability and proportionality of election results will be inversely related to one another. The seeming incompatibility of the two criteria of proportionality and stability has been the single most salient feature of the normative debate over electoral systems (Introduction to Lijphart and Grofman, 1984). Advocates of PR have trumpeted its proportionality and concomitant "fairness" of representation. Advocates of single-member district elections have argued that PR makes likely the election of "extremists"[18] and argued, more generally, for the incompatibility of PR and stability of policymaking (see e.g., the various essays in Lijphart and Grofman, 1984; cf. the extended discussion in Reynolds and Reilly, 1997; Farrell, 1997).

We find that the PR versus plurality debate is largely misguided.

---

[17] Ongoing work by a student of Grofman's (Collet, 1997) on minor party candidates in the United States shows that almost all of them run knowing that their party (and they) have no chance for victory. Collet's study considers in some depth the motivations of these candidates.

[18] We will look at the linkages between electoral system type and the ideological dispersion of representatives later in this essay.

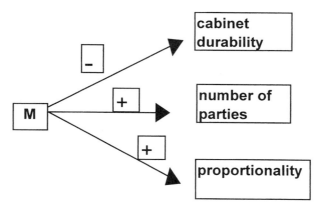

Figure 1. Hypothesized links between district magnitude M and various political consequences of electoral laws.

First, any simple-minded polar opposition between PR and plurality is mistaken because we can better think of electoral systems as organized along a continuum (according to M) than in terms of a dichotomy. Also, there are various systems that show that PR versus plurality is a false dichotomy, for example, limited voting and various types of mixed systems design that combine PR and plurality elements (such as the added member system in Germany and in the countries that have recently copied the German mixed system to a greater or lesser degree: Italy, New Zealand, Albania, Russia, Japan, etc.). Even within PR, as noted earlier, a good case can be made that the difference between the STV form of PR and list PR is more significant than the difference between STV and SMD plurality (Grofman, forthcoming b). Moreover, each of the three classic propositions laid out in Figure 1 is in need of some important qualifications.

Proportionality

While PR systems are, in general, more proportional in their translation of aggregate party vote shares into legislative seat shares than plurality systems, we must be careful not to exaggerate the magnitude of the differences. Indeed, we may actually initially get very high disproportionality of seats to votes in new democracies that adopt PR with a high district magnitude![19] The disproportionality result stated in Figure 1

---

[19] This happened in a number of the Eastern European and Baltic nations (e.g., Estonia and Russia) in the 1990s.

implicitly assumes that we are comparing across district magnitudes while holding party system (and electoral system) constant. Yet, in new democracies, the number of parties that contest elections will also rise with M and it will take time (perhaps quite a lot of time) for a weeding out of parties to occur. If most of these new parties generally fail to meet the (empirical) threshold of representation at the district level (or some national level threshold), it is quite possible that 20 percent (or an even higher proportion) of the vote may end up wasted, thus producing considerable disproportionality of vote share to seat share among the set of parties as a whole.

For SMD plurality elections Cox (1997) identifies certain non-Duvergerian equilibria that permit more than two parties to compete in situations where expectations about which party will come in third are not clear. Similarly, Cox shows that a proliferation of small parties competing for the Mth seat is possible under list PR in situations where there can be no clear expectations about which of these parties will be victorious. This suggests that the full effects of electoral systems may not occur immediately, since it may take time for key actors to realize the nature of the behaviors that constitute optimizing strategies in the new system (Reed, 1990).[20]

On the other hand, in long-established two-party systems as in the United States, where it is rare that one party's vote share for the House or Senate falls below 40 percent, disproportionality may not be that large (see, e.g., Brady and Grofman, 1991b; Brunell, 1997). Over the past several decades, the relationship between seat share (S) and vote share (V) in the U.S. House is given by

$$S/(1-S)^a [V/(1-V)]^{1.7}$$

Thus, in the United States a party with, say, a 0.55 vote share, will end up with a 0.59 seat share in the House – not that far from proportionality. Moreover, if we look over a series of elections, since parties may well alternate in power, in two-party systems the long-run disproportionality between seats and votes when these are cumulated over a large number of elections may be very small, indeed.[21]

---

[20] In the Japanese electoral context, Michael Theis (e-mail communication, SSJ-Forum: RE "Electoral System Reforms and Political Behaviour," June 15, 1995) observes that implications of 1994 electoral law change will not be immediate: "extant parties and individual incumbents and *koenkai*-based campaigning" introduce stickiness. He also makes the more general point that "new institutionalist" models should never assume that politics is a "frictionless market."

[21] The British geographer Peter Taylor (1984) refers to this long-run seats–votes proportionality in stable two-party systems as "proportionality of tenure."

Duverger's Law and Hypothesis

Similarly, there are a number of problems with Duverger's Law and Hypothesis in the form they are customarily stated. Are we to take the Law to apply to individual districts or to the nation as a whole?[22] Two-party competition at the district level can generate far more than two-party competition nationally if the same two parties do not compete in all the districts. With the notable exception of the United States, no nation using single-member district-plurality elections actually has only two major national parties! Indeed, we believe that no nation other than the United States actually has only two-party compassion even at the constituency level. Ought we not try to take into account ethnic or other cleavage lines that might create regional bases of strength for some parties (Amarin and Cox, 1997; cf. Eckstein, 1988/1992)?[23]

Moreover, even within a given single-member district, the lines of argument that would appear to necessitate two-party competition in that district are suspect. In the United States in a significant number of congressional districts the incumbent runs unopposed because the demographic features of the district, combined with party loyalty, make one party a sure winner. Cox (1997) makes the strong argument that both Duverger's Law and Duverger's Hypothesis should generally be taken as upper bounds, such that we can expect *no more than* (an "effective" number of) $M + 1$ party lists or candidates.

Also, national level outcomes and outcomes in other districts may affect the nature of competition in individual districts. Operating within the standard Downsian framework, Shvetsova (1997) has shown that when parties must pick a single ideological position and campaign under the banner of that position throughout the country, the fact that the ideological distribution (and the location of the median voter) varies from constituency to constituency makes it possible for third parties to find winning locations in some constituencies.[24] On a related note, while there may be a wasted-vote effect that acts to shrink support for regionally based parties if it becomes apparent that they will never have significant national influence, the fact that parties have zones of control in some

---

[22] Similarly, if we have k districts of size M each, do we expect to get, say, $M + 1$ parties competing nationally, or ought we to expect many more given the possibility of different sets of $M + 1$ parties competing in different districts? Recent, as yet unpublished, work by Rein Taagepera (personal communication, February 1997) addresses this question.

[23] The geographic distribution of partisan support is a key intermediating factor that shapes the extent to which electoral institutions (or changes in them) affect outcomes, especially electoral fairness in the translation of votes into seats (Gudgin and Taylor, 1979; Taylor, Gudgin, and Johnston, 1986).

[24] Cf. Grofman, Koetzle, McDonald, and Brunell 2000.

areas of the country makes it more likely that they will have the resources and the motivation to continue to compete even in areas where it initially appears their candidates have little chance. Moreover, the effects on party competition of the electoral system used to elect the national parliament may be intertwined with the effects of other political institutions such as the rules for choosing a president and the election cycles for both presidential and provincial elections (Shugart and Carey, 1992). For example, sometimes parties may choose to compete in certain legislative elections solely for the purpose of providing additional incentives to attract their supporters to the polls to vote in other contests.

Even more generally, Duverger's Law and Hypothesis attributes great weight to electoral effects, yet Taagepera and Grofman (1985) claim that, for well-established democracies, the number of political parties is better predicted by the number of issue cleavages in the society than by its electoral laws – although they recognize the potential for reciprocal causality. Amarin Neto and Cox (1997) make the argument that ethnic cleavage lines and district magnitude impact in a multiplicative fashion on the number of parties.[25] Only if there are both facilitative electoral institutions *and* a large number of potential cleavages should we expect to see a large number of parties. This analysis has been replicated by Caul, Taagepera, and Grofman (1998). Moreover, changes in election systems may give rise to equilibrating forces that moderate the consequences of the changes as voters, candidates, and parties adapt their behavior to the new institutional environment in ways that compensate for the changes, so as to partially restore significant elements of the status quo ante (Shugart, 1992; Christensen and Johnson, 1995).

Also, we must be very careful that we are comparing apples and apples. As noted previously, a given electoral law can have very different consequences as a function of its average (or effective) district magnitude. Similarly, failure to take into account national vote thresholds in which parties that fail to receive certain national vote shares (e.g., 2% or even 5%) are denied district-level representation will often lead to serious errors in estimating electoral system effects on both the proportionality of votes to seats conversions and the incentives for party proliferation (Reynolds and Grofman, 1994; Grofman, 1999c). Moreover, many electoral systems have a variety of subtleties, such as complex tiering arrangements for applying allocation rules of full or partial proportionality. Failure to take into account such complications can give rise to quite misleading comparisons across election systems. This is especially true when we are looking at mixed systems. For example, some Japanese journalists writing of the recent reform of the Japanese

[25] See also Cox (1997).

electoral rules that replaced SNTV with a mix of list PR and SMD constituencies for elections to the lower chamber of the Diet have suggested that the SMD component of the system will be the driving force and that we should expect Japan to become a two-party system. In our view that is absurd. The two components of the system will interact in a complex way and the eventual outcome will probably be something close to what might be expected from small-district PR, but which parties will emerge strengthened and which weakened may depend more upon events exogenous to the reform (such as which party is best able to take advantage of voter concerns about political corruption) than upon the change in electoral law.[26] Also, results will depend upon the geographic distribution of party strength.

Cabinet Stability

Finally, when we look at the relationship between electoral system type and stability of political institutions, it is important to recognize that the link between electoral system type and cabinet durability while strong is far from perfect. When we look at the set of parliamentary democracies, which lack a fixed term of office, some multiparty democracies were quite stable in terms of cabinet duration. Perhaps even more importantly, we must be careful not to overweight the importance of cabinet duration. As Carol Mershon (1994), and many others, remind us, the appearance of instability in countries like Italy must be taken with several grains of salt. During the post-WWII decades, when Italian cabinets were toppling left and right with remarkable rapidity, the same core of politicians was returning to office again and again, and the Christian Democrats were almost never out of power. Moreover, Schofield's re-analysis of European Party Manifestos data shows that the Christian Democrats occupied a near-core position in Italian policy space which gave them great power even when they were in coalition governments (Schofield, 1995).

III   Other Consequences of Electoral System Choice

We shall not try to go beyond our summary discussion of the three central propositions of the traditional electoral systems literature we gave above.[27] Instead, we wish to briefly turn to a variety of other vari-

---

[26] The recent Japanese electoral change is also a good example of how actors can be surprised by the outcomes of given reforms. The Japanese Socialist Party expected to benefit from the change. So far, they have been major losers.

[27] Lijphart (1994) offers a near-definitive review of the empirical evidence on the three classic propositions on electoral system effects that we identified in Figure 1. His data cover all of the long-standing democracies of the post-WWII period (see also Taagepera and Shugart, 1989; Cox, 1997). Of course, new evidence on all three propositions is continually coming in.

ables strongly affected by choice of electoral law such as the nature of partisan bias, incentives for strategic misrepresentation of preferences by voters, the range of ideological points of view that will be represented in the legislature, the strength of party organizations, incentives for voter turnout, descriptive (racial and gender) representation, and incentives for localism and corruption. We shall use several of these effects to suggest alternative ways to classify electoral systems. In addition, in a subsequent section, we will briefly inventory theories to explain choice of electoral system.

Partisan Bias

The classic comparative electoral systems literature deals only with the bias imposed by electoral systems as a function of size of party. Clearly, the larger M, the better off, ceteris paribus, are small parties. Similarly, certain divisor rules are generally thought to favor small parties (e.g., greatest remainder), others to favor mid-sized parties (modified Ste. Lagüe) and others to favor large parties (D'Hondt).[28] However, for first-past-the-post countries such as the United States (e.g., Tufte, 1973), the United Kingdom (e.g., Gudgin and Taylor, 1979) or Australia (e.g., Jackman, 1994) there is an extensive literature dealing with the expected differences in disproportionality between party vote share and party seat share as a function of factors that differ across parties such as the nature of the geographic dispersion of the party's sympathizers.

In two-party political competition, there are two basic measures of the characteristics of a seats–votes curve showing the relationship between a party's vote share and its (expected) share of the seats: partisan bias and swing ratio (Tufte, 1973), each of which can be generalized to apply to the multiparty case. Here we focus on the two-party case. The swing ratio, often denoted by β, is a measure of the responsiveness of the electoral system to change in the vote. In two-party competition, the *swing ratio* is taken to be the expected size of the percentage point increase in seat-share for each percentage point increase in a party's share of the aggregate vote above 50 percent, that is, swing is analogous to a tangent to the seats–votes curve (Tufte, 1973).[29] Partisan bias can be thought of

---

[28] See Gallagher (1992).

[29] Since the publication in 1973 of Tufte's seminal article, numerous authors have approached the analysis of seats–votes relationships in two-party systems by looking at the twin concepts of partisan bias and swing ratio (see e.g., Niemi and Deegan, 1978; Grofman, 1983; Brady and Grofman, 1991a, b; Cain, 1985; King and Browning, 1987; Campagna and Grofman, 1990; Campagna, 1991; Niemi and Jackman, 1991; King and Gelman, 1991; Garand and Parent, 1991; Gelman and King, 1994a). There are several different methods for simultaneously calculating swing ratio and bias, but two are most important. The first is the log-odds method developed by Tufte (1973) and used by many subsequent authors (e.g., Campagna, 1991; Brady and Grofman, 1991a, b). The second

as the (expected) advantage/disadvantage in seat-share above/below 50 percent received by a given party that wins 50 percent of the vote.[30] In two-party competition, *partisan bias* is customarily taken to be the difference between the seat-share a given party with exactly 50 percent of the vote can expect to win and the seat-share that it should win if both parties were treated equally by the electoral rules, i.e., a seat share of 50 percent (Tufte, 1973).

It is well known (Gudgin and Taylor, 1979; Johnston, 1981; Brady and Grofman, 1991b) that, in two-party competition, swing ratio is largely a function of the number of competitive districts. Similarly, it is well known that partisan bias is also, at least in part, a function of the asymmetry in the distribution of partisan voting strength across constituencies (Gudgin and Taylor, 1979; Johnston, 1981; Taylor, Gudgin, and Johnston, 1986; Brady and Grofman, 1991b). In particular, if one party wins most of its seats by disproportionately large vote shares and loses most of the seats it loses by relatively narrow vote shares, while the reverse is true for the other party (or parties), then partisan bias exists against the first party. Such bias may have been caused by intentional gerrymandering or by an "accident" of geography. Any districted system is potentially subject to partisan biases.

Building on earlier work such as that of Rydon (1968) and Jackman (1994), in recent work by the senior author (Grofman, Brunell, and Koetzle, 2000), it is shown that the partisan bias that arises because of differences in the distribution of party voting strength across constituencies[31] that creates differences between each party's share of "wasted votes" is only one of the three basic ways in which an electoral system may manifest partisan bias. The other two ways to create partisan bias are (a) through malapportionment – that is, differences in population across districts (see Baker, 1955; Rydon, 1968; May, 1974; Yamakawa, 1984; Jackman, 1994),[32] and (b) through differences in

is the averaging technique developed by King and Gelman (1991) and instantiated in the computer program JudgeIt used by those authors (Gelman and King, 1994a, b) and by a number of others (e.g., Garand and Parent, 1991).

[30] Customarily, in two-party competition, both swing ratio and the distributional aspect of partisan bias is estimated at a (hypothetical) vote share of 50 (Tufte, 1973), or for a range of vote shares relatively near to 50 percent and symmetrically distributed around that point. Gelman and King (1994a, b), estimate values over the 0.45 to 0.55 vote share range. Swing ratio and bias can also be specified at any point on the seats–votes curve or averaged across any range of points (Grofman, 1983), but we shall neglect such complications here. In a two-party contest, the bias for party A is simply the negative of the bias for party B.

[31] This distribution (and thus partisan bias) may be manipulated through purposeful gerrymandering (see e.g., Owen and Grofman, 1988; Grofman, 1990).

[32] Clearly, the concept of malapportionment needs to be defined with respect to some basis. In the United States, unlike most other democracies, apportionment is on the basis of total population (persons) rather than on the basis of citizen population or potentially

turnout rates across districts (Campbell, 1996).[33] However, neither malapportionment[34] nor unequal turnout, per se, generate partisan bias; it is only when population or turnout differences across districts are linked to the distribution of party voting strength that we get partisan bias.

While distributional effects, malapportionment effects, and turnout effects are not, in general, uncorrelated, we can conceptually separate them by imagining three ideal types. In the first, all districts are equally populated[35] and the same proportion of voters turn out in each (or, at least constituency population and turnout are uncorrelated with the distribution of party voting strength at the constituency level), but the distribution of voting strength across districts is such that one party's victories are costlier than the others in terms of winning its seats by larger vote shares, on the average. In the second, all districts are equally populated (or, at least district population is uncorrelated with distribution of party voting strength at the constituency level) and the distribution of mean partisan voting strength across districts does not generate any partisan bias, but one party's voters do tend to turn out at a lower level than do voters of the other party. In the third case, while the distribution of mean partisan voting strength across districts does not generate any partisan bias, and each party's voters tend to turn out at the same rate as do voters of the other party (or, at least, turnout is uncorrelated with distribution of party voting strength at the constituency level), now districts are not equally populated and the differences in population across districts is related to the partisan distribution of voting

eligible electorate (e.g., citizen voting age population) or registered voters or past turnout. Obviously, the choice as to the basis for apportionment can have important implications for what we conclude about the presence or absence of malapportionment (see e.g., Grofman, 1992; Scarrow, 1992). In the remainder of this chapter, except where otherwise indicated, the reader may take the word "population" as a generic term, referring to whatever may be the basis of apportioning seats in the country under investigation. Since, the actual data we analyze are from the United States, this usage should not be a cause of confusion.

[33] By turnout rate we mean the ratio of votes cast to the apportionment base in the district. Obviously, the actual number of voters will not be the same as the apportionment base. Implications of that fact for the equity of representation have been discussed by a number of authors (for a review of the U.S. debate see Brace, Grofman, and Handley, 1987; Grofman, 1993).

[34] While population in U.S. House districts is now almost perfectly equal within states, it is often forgotten that, across states, there can be dramatic differences in average House district size. In the 1990s apportionment, for example, the largest district in the United States had 1.7 times the population in the smallest (Grofman, 1992). Thus, despite the one-person, one-vote standard it is still quite reasonable to imagine that there might be a partisan bias in the U.S. House due to malapportionment.

[35] Recall that we use "population" as a generic term to refer to the basis of seat apportionment.

strength. We may think of these three examples as giving rise to pure forms of distributional, turnout-based, and malapportionment-based partisan bias.

All methods of calculating partisan bias have in common the need to specify each party's national share of the (two-party) vote as a baseline for calculating a seats–votes relationship from which bias is to be estimated. It is important to recognize that even though both P_i (party i's vote share in each constituency averaged across all constituencies) and R_i (party i's raw share of the total vote) can legitimately be regarded as party i's national vote share, these two estimates of national party vote share are unlikely to be identical because they measure two different things. One, R_i, is based on *raw total votes*; the other, P_i, is based on *average vote shares at the district level.* Only if the district level turnout is totally uncorrelated with the distribution of party voting strength across constituencies (a special case of which would be that in which turnout levels are constant across all constituencies) will $R_i = P_i$. But, we know that, in the United States, for example, Democratic seats tend to have lower turnout because this, along with lower income and minority status, is a disproportionately Democratic identifier (see e.g., Campbell, 1996; Grofman, Collet, and Griffin, 1998).

Clearly, whether we use R_i or P_i as our national vote share value will directly affect our estimate of bias. Say, for example, we use P_i. If, instead, we had used R_i, the effect would simply be to displace each **x** element on the seats-votes curve by an amount equal to $P_i - R_i$. But, in particular, this would mean that the seat share value when party i has a national vote share of 50% would be displaced by an amount equal to $P_i - R_i$. But that is just another way of saying that *replacing P_i with R_i as our estimate of party i's actual national vote share should (if our statistical estimation procedure were perfect) act to increase the estimated partisan bias by the amount $P_i - R_i$.* This simple link between choice of measure of national vote share and estimated partisan bias is an important observation that underpins the integrated approach to the determinants of partisan bias developed by Grofman and his co-authors.

It can be shown that R_i and P_i can be expressed in a "common language," where the difference between the two is a function of how we choose to weight constituencies. If we use P_i we are implicitly weighting constituencies equally; that is, we neglect both turnout and malapportionment effects and have only distributional effects. In contrast, if we use R_i we are implicitly weighting constituencies by turnout; that is, we incorporate turnout effects on partisan bias in addition to distributional effects. In similar fashion it becomes possible to devise an outcome measure that is weighted by the "population" in each constituency. This gives us a malapportionment-based measure, M_i. It is also possible to set up these three measures so that we can construct from them *pure* mea-

Table 1. *Three Ways of Estimating Democratic National Vote Share and Three Aspects of Partisan Bias in 1980s U.S. House and Senate Elections*[a]

Year	Chamber	P_i	M_i	R_i	Pure distribut. partisan bias	Pure malapport. partisan bias = $M_i - P_i$	Pure turnout partisan bias = $R_i - M_i$
1984	House	54.9	55.0	52.5	-1.7^b	0.1^b	-2.5^b
1986	House	57.3	57.1	54.8	-2.6^b	-0.3^b	-2.7^b
1988	House	57.0	56.8	54.1	-3.4^b	-0.3^b	-2.7^b
1984	Senate	48.5	51.9	50.7	-0.4 ns	3.4 ns	-0.8 ns
1986	Senate	50.6	51.0	50.8	2.9 ns	0.4 ns	-0.2 ns
1988	Senate	53.2	53.3	52.9	-0.2 ns	0.1 ns	-0.4 ns

Source: Grofman, Koetzle, McDonald, and Brunell (2000).
[a] Positive values of bias are pro-Republican.
[b] Significant at the 0.01 level or less.

sures of the three key effects: distributional, malapportionment, and turnout by appropriate subtractions. To illustrate the method we reproduce as Table 1 a table from Grofman, Koetzle, McDonald, and Brunell (2000) that shows the magnitude of the three sources of bias for several recent House and Senate elections in the United States. We see from Table 1 that the magnitude of partisan bias is relatively small and often not statistically significant. In the House the main effect is that turnout-related bias (cheap seats) favored the Democrats. In the Senate, remarkably, the vast differences in population among the states did not translate into statistically significant partisan bias.

Strategic Calculations and Incentives for
Strategic Misrepresentation of Preferences

Cox (1997) is the definitive study to date of the calculations on the part of voters, candidates, and parties as to optimal choice under a variety of electoral arrangements. In general, Cox views electoral institutions in game-theoretic terms and looks for equilibrium strategies, emphasizing the importance of being able to develop a stable set of expectations as to outcomes. We will not try to do justice to the richness and sophisticated modeling of his analyses here but merely offer a few quick very general summaries. With respect to nomination strategies, Cox shows that under certain election rules, such as SNTV, parties will be especially sensitive to their voting strength and be concerned not to divide their vote too thinly. With respect to voter choice, Cox reviews the literature on strategic incentives for failing to vote for one's most preferred choice and shows that, in some systems (such as plurality) these incentives can be quite strong when one's first choice has no realistic chance of being elected and it matters to the voter whether his second-best alternative will defeat his third-best alternative. Cox also considers potential for manipulation and strategic voting in more complex electoral systems such as STV and the German double-ballot system. For the latter, for example, Cox reviews evidence showing that strategic voting is taking place in which voters cast their PR ballot sincerely while they cast their constituency-level ballot for their next most preferred party – one with a chance of winning the plurality election in the constituency. Moreover, Cox shows that, because of a national 5 percent threshold showing required before any party can gain seats, coalitional concerns can motivate strategic voting in Germany even in the PR component of the system when some voters whose first loyalty is to whichever party is expected to be in coalition with the FDP (the small liberal party) switch to vote for the FDP when that party is threatened with falling below the 5 percent threshold.

The Range of Ideological Points of View That Will Be Represented in the Legislature

The bulk of the literature on the ideological consequences of electoral system choice follows Downs (1957) in positing a single dimension of ideological competition. The classic Downsian result, the median voter theorem for two-party competition, is in our view taken far too seriously by most economists and even many political scientists. As a number of authors (e.g., Rowley, 1984; Grofman, 1996b) remind us, the Downsian convergence result holds only when a large number of assumptions are satisfied.[36] When we modify those assumptions convergence under two-party competition to the views of the median voter is no longer to be expected. In the United States there is undeniable evidence for continued party differentiation (Poole and Rosenthal, 1984; Grofman, Griffin, and Glazer, 1990; Shapiro et al., 1990) even though the range of ideological variation among major party candidates in the United States may be much more limited than that in many other countries. As one of us has argued elsewhere, we must acknowledge Downsian centripetal pressures toward centrist politics while at the same time recognizing the major forces that push in a centrifugal direction, such as the role of activists and (in the United States) the role of party primaries. A veritable cottage industry has grown up in the last decade or so creating

---

[36] See Romer and Rosenthal (1979) for discussion of evidence about median voter effects in non-partisan settings.

models that give us two-party divergence even in a single dimension.[37] Here we will confine ourselves to a brief look at how nomination rules can impact convergence, focusing on the U.S. experience. We will review two models, that of Aranson and Ordeshook (1972) and that of Coleman (1971, 1972), as further developed by Owen and Grofman (1995).[38]

In the Aranson and Ordeshook model, candidates are assumed to develop expectations about the probability of victory in the primary election (P1) and the general election (P2) as a function of the policy position they associate themselves with, and are posited to choose a spatial location so as to maximize P1 × P2. The Aranson and Ordeshook (1972) model of two-stage election processes makes candidate choices the focus of their modeling. In contrast, in the Coleman (1971, 1972) model, the focus is on voter motivations. In the Coleman model some (or all) voters in the primary election are concerned with the likelihood that the primary victor will be able to win the general election as well as with that candidate's policy position, and choose among candidates accordingly. Roughly speaking, he assumes that voters maximize a function that can be thought of as the benefit derived from selecting a party representative whose location is close to their own ideal point discounted by the likelihood that such a candidate will be elected in the general election. Both models assume that candidates must be consistent in adopting an ideological position in the general election that corresponds to the views they espouse in the primary.

Both models give rise to an expectation that, under most circum-

---

[37] Approaches offered to explain candidate and party divergence include the role of ideologically committed party activists and interest groups, who are a major source of campaign resources (Aldrich, 1983; Baron, 1994; cf. Morton, 1993); candidates who have policy preferences that they wish to see implemented and not just a desire to win election (Wittman, 1983; see also Wittman, 1973, 1977); directional rather than proximity-based voting (Rabinowitz and Macdonald, 1989; Merrill, 1993; Merrill and Grofman, 1997); discounting of candidate positions (Grofman, 1985; Merrill and Grofman, 1998); multiple dimensions of issue competition (Schofield, 1995); non–policy-related motivations for candidate support such as those that give rise to reputational effects and incumbency advantage or to partisan bias (Bernhardt and Ingberman, 1985; Feld and Grofman, 1991; Adams, 1996); and strategic calculations such as concern for future entry (Brams, 1980; Palfrey and Erikson, 1994; cf. Brams and Merrill, 1991) or policy balancing across multiple contests (Alesina and Rosenthal, 1995). See the review of this literature in Grofman (1994). For more general reviews of the literature on spatial party competition inspired by Downs, see Enelow and Hinich (1984, 1990) and Grofman (1993, 1996a).

[38] Both the Aranson and Ordeshook and the Coleman works have largely been neglected in the subsequent literature. Coleman's work first appeared in an early issue of *Public Choice*, shortly after the journal changed its name from *Papers on Non Market Decision-Making*, at a time before many libraries subscribed to this subsequently well-known journal. The 1972 articles of Coleman and Aranson and Ordeshook are book chapters in an excellent edited volume that deserves to be far better known, but that was published by a firm that shortly thereafter went out of business.

stances, the primary winners can be expected to be located between the overall median voter and the median voter in their party. Owen and Grofman (1995) introduce a parameter into the Coleman model that taps the extent to which voters are oriented toward having a candidate who is able to win the general election versus concerns about ideological proximity. In general, in their model, candidate positions will be closer to the party median than to the overall median, and there are conditions under which a party may "paint itself into a corner ideologically" and remain a minor party.[39] In particular, they show that when we have an incumbent located at a centrist position, rather than Downsian convergence to the center by the nominee of the other party, we often will get divergence because voters of the "out" party will be uninterested in electing a "tweedledee" candidate of their own party.[40]

When we look at formal results on ideological placement in multi-party competition on a single dimension for $M > 2$ there are a number of results that suggest, for list PR elections, we either do not get equilibria or we get "funny" kinds of equilibria such as those with two parties that are virtual clones of one another located at each of several equally spaced focal points or even the completely non-realistic result of pure convergence (Cox, 1987, 1990; Shepsle, 1994; cf. Robertson, 1975; Sugden, 1984; Greenberg and Weber, 1985; Myerson and Weber, 1993). Neither of us knows this literature well enough to judge the extent to which these results are a product of the unidimensionality assumption or of other features of some of the models, such as positing a uniform distribution of voters' ideological locations on the dimension. More realistic results have been obtained recently by taking actual distributions of voter ideal points (in one or two dimensions) and then seeing what kinds of party locations seem to be implied by those distributions and how strong the incentives are for particular parties to move strategically from their "own" concentration of voters in order to improve either their vote share or their chance to be part of a winning coalition (Merrill, 1994; Nixon et al., 1995; Schofield, Sened, and Nixon, 1997; Schofield et al., 1997). We regard this work as particularly promising.

In looking at the empirical evidence, there seems little doubt that, for list PR, the larger the M the greater, ceteris paribus, is the likelihood that parties whose support is located at the fringes of the ideological space (or whose support comes from a minority of the electorate who attach especially high salience to some distinct issue dimension) will be able to gain representation (see also Cox, 1990, 1997). Schofield, Sened, and

---

[39] Owen and Grofman (1995) also show that a party whose supporters are more ideologically concentrated can generally be expected to do better.

[40] In the United States for example, President Clinton is often criticized by ideologues of his own party who assert that "if [the party members] wanted a Republican they would have voted for one."

Nixon (1997: 14) conclude their paper with the observation that "policy convergence does not occur in any known multiparty system." This fact has led some authors to suggest that in SMD districts "politics" is fought out at the constituency level, with the outcomes determinative of a party majority in the legislature and thus of policy; while PR systems leave political conflicts to be resolved by the legislature (or at least by cabinet coalitional bargaining) because the legislators under PR reflect a greater range of ideological (and other) diversity.

Strength of Party Organizations and the Nature of Within-Party vs. Cross-Party Competition

Certain election systems, notably SNTV and STV, generate a great deal of intra-party competition. Indeed, Gallagher (1997) shows that, under STV, Irish members of the Dail are more likely to be defeated by someone from their own party than they are by a member of the opposition. SNTV has been argued to lead to very factionalized politics since candidates seek support from particular wings of the party in their campaigns, with more representatives being nominated in some instances than the party will be able to elect (Cox and Rosenbluth, 1994; Grofman, 1996b, 1999b). In contrast, closed-list PR strengthens the hand of the central party organization that is responsible for the ordering of the party list.[41] Various other systems are intermediate in their incentives for strong party organizations (Katz, 1980). Classifying systems according to the extent to which they can be expected to foster strong parties is an alternative to classifying according to the usual PR-plurality continuum and results in creating proximacies that are often quite different from those defined in terms of an expected degree of proportionality test (see Table 2 later in the discussion section).

One other feature of multi-member district systems using some form of PR or semi-PR rules such as cumulative voting or limited voting worth calling attention to is that minorities within a region may achieve representation that they would not get if SMD were used instead.[42] This may enhance the likelihood of cross-party coalitions centering around issues of particular interest to a given region.

---

[41] In a closed-list system nothing voters may do can change the order of candidates on a party's list. Some countries (e.g., Finland) have open or partly open list systems that allow voters to affect this ordering and thus which of the party's candidates will get chosen if the full slate is not elected (see e.g., Ames, 1995; Cox, 1997, for more details).

[42] In Illinois, when cumulative voting was used for the state legislature, the two major parties sometimes agreed to limit their nominations to two candidates in various three-member districts so as to assure minority-party representation in each district, even when the dominant party might have won all three seats. Of course, in some of these

Incentives for Voter Turnout

An obvious extension of the Downsian analysis of the link between competition and turnout would suggest that electoral systems that increase the likelihood that the average voter's vote will be decisive will, ceteris paribus, induce higher turnout. Similarly, we would expect that electoral rules that increase the ideological range of candidates/parties who are competing will also increase turnout. Thus, we would expect that, ceteris paribus, turnout in PR systems should be higher than in non-PR systems. This claim has been empirically tested by Blais and Carty (1990) and Mudambi, Navarra, and Nicosia (1996), who find higher turnout in PR systems, even when other controls have been introduced.

Descriptive (Racial and Gender) Representation

Women. There is a considerable body of evidence, both cross-sectional and longitudinal, and general consensus among students of electoral systems, that, ceteris paribus, large-magnitude districts whether in list PR or semi-PR election systems or even in plurality (bloc) voting systems will tend to increase the representation of women relative to similar electoral rules with a smaller M. The basic notion is that large districts permit the parties to nominate a diverse array of candidates, whereas single-member districts provide incentives to parties to nominate only candidates from the dominant group in the party (which usually is overwhelmingly male or predominantly of one ethnic persuasion, at least in terms of party activists). For example, Rule (1997: figure 2) shows that among long-standing democracies ($N = 27$), list PR systems average far higher in women's representation in the national legislature over the period 1988–93 (average = 19.2%) than do SMD countries (average = 8.5%).[43] However, this same generalization requires an important modification with respect to plurality systems when we consider racial or ethnic minorities. Because racial or ethnic minorities, unlike women, can be (and often are) geographically concentrated, drawing multi-member districts may submerge these minorities if the voting rule is plurality, since the majority group may be able to elect all the members in the district, whereas the drawing of single-member dis-

instances the candidate of the minority party was a "stooge" for the other party, whose members controlled the nominating process for both parties in the district (Sawyer and MacRae, 1962; Brams, 1975).

[43] STV in Ireland generates only 12% women's representation, and SNTV in Japan comes in at a minuscule 2.3%. These both are, however, systems with relatively small district magnitude (around 4 for Ireland, somewhat over 3 for Japan), but it is clear that cultural factors also play a role.

tricts may permit concentration of minority voters into districts that thus become winnable by minority candidates (Grofman, 1993; Grofman and Davidson, 1994; Grofman, 1998).

Alternatively, women or ethnic or racial minorities may be guaranteed representation by way of quotas.[44] These quotas may either be imposed by the government or by the internal rules of the parties themselves.

In Nepal 5 percent of the single-member district candidates must be women. The PR systems of Belgium and Namibia require parties to field a certain number of women candidates. In Italy, women now must make up 50 percent of the candidates listed on any PR ballot, in Argentina the requirement is for 30 percent women, and in Brazil it is 20 percent. Similar rules have also been proposed elsewhere, such as for the Indian Lokh Sabha. Of course, parties may try to avoid the implications of such quotas by concentrating their women candidates toward the bottom of the list, where they are unlikely to be elected, or placing them in constituencies where they have no chance of victory. However, some laws specifically deal with this issue; for example, in Argentina there is the extra proviso that women must be placed in winnable positions and not just at the bottom of a party's list.

Political parties adopting their own informal or formal quotas for women as parliamentary candidates has become the most common mechanism used to promote the participation of women in political life throughout the world, but this mechanism has been used, until recently, almost entirely only by parties on the left: for example, by the African National Congress in South Africa, the Partido Justicialista and the Union Civica Radical in Argentina, Conscience of the Fatherland in Bolivia, the PRD in Mexico, the labor parties in Australia and the United Kingdom, and throughout Scandinavia. The use of women-only candidate short-lists by the Labour Party at the 1997 United Kingdom elections was also entirely responsible for doubling the number of female MPs, from 60 to 119.

Party list PR systems are conducive to the adoption of gender quotas and are linked to other contextual variables that are conducive to women's representation, such as a history of left government. While electoral system type (PR vs. plurality) is an important independent predictor of the level of women's national parliamentary representation in the 1970s and the 1980s; by the 1980s, the existence of quota rules became a more important predictor of women's electoral success in the developed democracies. However, strength of left government is the single strongest predictor in both decades (Caul, 1999).

---

[44] Quotas are often defended as transitional mechanisms to lay the foundation for a broader acceptance of women's representation.

Minorities

Reserved seats are one way of ensuring the representation of specific minority groups in parliament. Parliamentary seats are reserved for identifiable ethnic or religious minorities in countries as diverse as Jordan (Christians and Circassians), India (secluded tribes and castes), Pakistan (non-Muslim minorities), New Zealand (Maori),[45] Colombia (black communities), Croatia (Hungarian, Italian, Czech, Slovak, Ruthenian, Ukrainian, German, and Austrian minorities), Slovenia (Hungarians and Italians), Taiwan (the aboriginal community), Western Samoa (non-indigenous minorities), Niger (Taurag), and the Palestinian Authority (Christians and Samaritans). Reserved seats have also been set aside for women in Taiwan and other countries. Representatives from these reserved seats are usually elected in much the same manner as other members of parliament, but are often elected only by members of the particular minority community designated in the electoral law.[46] While it is often deemed to be a normative good to represent small communities of interest, structures that give rise to a representative parliament "naturally" rather than through legal obligation are clearly to be preferred.[47]

Some ethnically heterogeneous societies took the concept of reserved seats to its logical extension. With each defined community having its own electoral roll and electing only members of its own group to parliament. However, most communal-roll arrangements were abandoned after it became increasingly clear that communal electorates, while guaranteeing group representation, often had the perverse effect of undermining the path of accommodation between different groups.[48] The only example left of which we are aware is Fiji. There, the native

[45] In New Zealand, Maori electors can choose to be on either the national electoral roll or on a specific Maori roll, which elects five Maori MPs to Parliament. In New Zealand under the new electoral law, the 1996 election generated more than twice as many Maori elected "normally" than the handful who were elected via reserved seats. Thus, there are pressures to do away with the separate Maori rolls.

[46] Another possibility is the best-loser system used in Mauritius, in which the highest-polling losing candidates from a particular ethnic group are awarded some parliamentary seats in order to balance overall ethnic representation.

[47] Quota seats may breed resentment on the behalf of majority populations and shore up mistrust between various cultural groups. Moreover, parliamentarians elected from reserved or special seats may be marginalized from real decision-making responsibility.

[48] In India, for example, the separate electorates that had existed under colonial rule – for Muslims, Christians, Sikhs, and others – were abolished at independence, although some reserved seats remain in order to represent scheduled tribes and castes. Similar communal-roll-based systems used at various times in Pakistan, Cyprus, and Zimbabwe have also been abandoned. In each of these cases, the issue of how to define members of particular groups, and how to distribute electorates fairly between them, has been strewn with pitfalls.

Fijians have retained majority control of the legislature despite being a population minority by a combination of communal rolls (Fiji, Indian, other) and deliberate malapportionment. This system is under attack (Reilly, 1997).

Another way to (over-)represent certain minorities is to over-represent regions where these groups are concentrated. In essence this is the case in the United Kingdom, where Scotland and Wales have more MPs in the British House of Commons than they would be entitled to if population size alone were the only criterion. Electoral boundaries can also be manipulated to serve this purpose. The Voting Rights Act in the United States has been alleged (wrongly in our view) to require the drawing of grotesque districts for the sole purpose of creating majority Black or Latino or Asian-American constituencies. (Grofman, 1998). However, the Voting Rights Act, properly construed, is aimed simply to protect minority influence against unconstitutional vote dilution in which minority populations are (deliberately) fragmented or submerged (see Karnig and Welch, 1982; Grofman, Migalski, and Noviello, 1986; Grofman, Handley, and Niemi, 1992; Grofman and Davidson, 1992; Davidson and Grofman, 1994; Grofman and Davidson, 1994).

Incentives for Localism

Incentives to cultivate a personal vote through particularistic appeals vary significantly across electoral system types (Cain, Ferejohn, and Fiorina, 1987; Carey and Shugart, 1995; McCubbins and Rosenbluth, 1995).[49] Here we emphasize a new measure of electoral incentives for localism that one of us has recently developed (Grofman, 1999b).

We will use the letter e to refer to the number of voters who voted for a given candidate or party, and E to the *mean* value of electoral constituency size in a legislature. In candidate-centered systems e is simply the vote received by the candidate; in closed party-list systems we take e to be the vote received by the party list in the district. In STV systems calculating e is more problematic but we will take the expected e for STV to be (somewhat more than) one Droop quota.[50]

If we assume that all seats are equally apportioned in per capita terms, for a fixed legislative size L, it is very important to appreciate the fact that E can be expected to be a monotonically increasing function of mean district magnitude for some candidate-centered systems (e.g.,

[49] Myerson (1993a, b), in closely related work, has looked at the impact electoral incentives may have on incentives for corruption.

[50] While a Droop quota elects a candidate, candidates who lack strong first-place support rely on second-place, third-place, etc. ballots transferred after other candidates have won or been dropped, so that it becomes a matter of chance exactly which of the "excess" voters voting for winning candidates would be transferred to them.

plurality bloc voting), since if we, say, cut the number of constituencies in half, thus doubling M, E can also be expected to (roughly) double. However, E is a near constant function of M for some other candidate-centered systems (e.g., STV), since if we cut the number of constituencies in half, the population-weighted threshold of exclusion is $1/2(M + 1)$ as compared to $1/(2M + 1)$, and the ratio of the two thresholds, $(2M + 2)/(2M + 1)$, stays reasonably close to one even though it increases slightly. Lastly, E can be an increasing function of M for some electoral systems (e.g., closed party list systems), since for closed party list systems increasing district size will increase E, albeit (for a given M) the increase in size of E will generally be lower under closed party list systems than under plurality bloc voting because increasing district size will also permit some groupings whose size or lack of geographic concentration was not sufficient to permit them to win seats when M was low, to do so now.[51]

Looking at E suggests a new way to array electoral systems in terms of their consequences for localism (see Table 2 in the next section). What is especially interesting about this classification scheme is that, for a fixed L and for a fixed M, plurality bloc voting is at one extreme (with a high E value) and other candidate-centered systems like SNTV and STV are at the other (with a low E value), while closed list PR is in the middle, with its exact location on the spectrum depending upon the distribution of voting strength across voting blocs. More even in voting strength are the groups the more closed list PR will look like SNTV and STV in terms of expected E value (i.e., $E = 1/(M + 1)$); while if the distribution of voting strength is such that some groups are much larger than others, the E value for closed-list PR will more closely resemble that for the plurality bloc voting case (i.e., $E = 1/2$).

Interactions among Elections of Different Types

Some of the most interesting material in Cox (1997) deals with the strategic calculations involving interaction of elections at different levels of

---

[51] For example, consider three voting blocs, with bloc A having 4/7 of the vote, bloc B having 2/7+ and bloc C having 1/7− of the population. Let $L = 8$. If we have two 4-seat districts then, in each, under closed list D'Hondt PR, if each bloc's voting strength is proportionally the same in each district as it is overall, then bloc A will win 3 seats (each with an e value of 4/14 of the national vote) and bloc B will win 1 seat (with an e value for that seat of 2/14 of the national vote); while bloc C will win no seats. Thus, E will be 1/4 (= $(3 \times 4 + 1 \times 2)/(4 \times 14)$). If we have only one 8-seat district, then bloc A will win 5 seats (each with an e value of 4/7 of the national vote), bloc B will win 2 seats (each with an e value of 2/7 of the national vote), and bloc A will win 1 seat (with an e value of 1/7 of the national vote). Now E will be 25/56 (= $(5 \times 4 + 2 \times 2 + 1 \times 1)/(8 \times 7)$). The E ratio in the two cases is 1.78.

government, such as whether elections for president and legislature are or are not simultaneous (see also Shugart and Carey, 1992).

IV   Explaining Choice of Electoral System

We may divide explanations of electoral system choice (including decisions leading to the demise of electoral systems) into four types.

First and foremost we have the standard public choice model in which preferences for electoral systems are based on the expected outcomes under those systems[52] and the actual choices are the result of the interaction of preferences and power.[53] Various authors have emphasized the importance of uncertainty in this process of seeking political advantage. Parties whose strength is widely distributed but the depth of whose support is far from certain are likely to hedge their bets by opting for PR; on the other hand, parties that are geographically concentrated or parties that may be dispersed but which can expect to have a majority (or near majority) of the vote can be expected to prefer SMD. Perhaps even more importantly, in the so-called third wave of democratization, whenever electoral systems are negotiated in the midst of civil war (or threat thereof) PR is far and away the most likely outcome (Mozaffar, 1997), even in anglophone nations and even in situations when one dominant party might impose a preference for an SMD system which would guarantee itself virtually undisputed control of the national parliament (e.g., the ANC in South Africa: Reynolds and Grofman, 1994). In this context it is useful to note that, in many of these new democracies of the past decade National Conferences including participation from leading political actors and NGOs have been the forum for the negotiation of new electoral rules (Mozaffar, 1997; cf. Geddes, 1995, 1996).[54]

Second, we have what we may think of as a "standard operating procedure" model that attributes electoral system choice either to cultural legacies (e.g., anglophone nations in Africa largely chose SMD; francophone African countries inevitably adopted list PR or the (French) two-round system), or to diffusion (e.g., at present the German added-member system is currently undergoing a mini-boomlet both in terms of recent adoptions and in terms of nations where it has major proponents: Lancaster, 1997).

[52] As John Ferejohn (personal communication, 1971) once aptly put it, "Preference for outcomes conditions preferences for institutions."

[53] For example, in Russia, after the breakup of the Soviet Union, President Yeltsin could, in effect, dictate the rules for the election of the new Russian legislature. Indeed, his preferences became determinative.

[54] It is also worth noting that choice of electoral systems appears closely linked to other aspects of constitutional design (see esp. Lijphart's 1984 discussion of the features of the Westminster model vs. the consensus model).

The third explanation for electoral system choice, related to the second, is inertia. As my colleague, A. Wuffle, recently put it (personal communication, April 1, 1997): "Inertia is the strongest force for change – it's against it." Or, as Taagepera and Shugart (1989: 218) put it: "Familiarity breeds stability." In the major Western European democracies, just as party cleavages were said to have been frozen for a long time, so too were the major elements of electoral system choice (with the notable exception of France). However, recently we have seen major changes in electoral system in countries as diverse as Italy and New Zealand, and electoral system reform is even on the British agenda and not just a continuing topic of politically irrelevant agitation for the 100+ year old British Electoral Reform Society.

The fourth explanation for choice of system is that inquiring minds, steeped in the wisdom of the electoral system literature, debating the pros and cons of electoral systems in the abstract (behind a Rawlsian veil of ignorance), seek to make normatively appropriate choices. Of course, there are no known cases where this model fits the data.

V   Discussion

The combination of quantitative data, a limited number of (mostly) well-defined variables, opportunity for comparative analysis, and potential for both statistical and rational choice insights means that we ought to be able to develop good models in the electoral systems area. Still, we should not be overly impressed with formal models of electoral system equilibria if these produce results that are too widely at variance with observed reality. Moreover, although simple-minded vote maximization is a good first cut in modeling the incentives of candidates and parties, real understanding requires us to appreciate subtleties such as prospects for coalition (e.g., the German or Israeli case), relative advantage with respect to potential chief competitors (e.g., the Japanese case), and even concerns for legitimacy of outcomes (e.g., the South African case).

On the normative level, what is clear is that there are multiple "reasonable" criteria that can be used in evaluating electoral system choice, and thus no definitive answer is possible as to which electoral system is best. Most importantly, however, even the basic way of classifying electoral rules according to their expected degree of proportionality[55] misses the point that proportionality is only one aspect or consequence of electoral system choice.[56] We do not wish to suggest that the PR-versus-plurality continuum is not significant, but we would wish to argue that

---

[55] In the standard approach, STV and list PR are taken as the two pure forms of PR, with semi-proportional systems treated as in the middle on the PR vs. plurality divide but tending toward the PR side as judged by their degree of proportionality of result (Grofman, 1975).

[56] See earlier discussion.

the distinction among electoral systems between systems in which voters cast their votes for individual candidates (regardless of whether or not those candidates have an attached party label) and those in which voters' only choice is to vote for a party [57] is at least as important as that between PR versus plurality when it comes to considerations of constitutional engineering. Similarly, we would argue that incentives for localism are important elements of electoral system choice.

Note that a focus on different types of consequences gives rise to quite different ways of grouping the four main groups of electoral systems (plurality or plurality bloc voting, SNTV and cumulative voting, STV, and list PR) in terms of their similarity to one another – as shown in Table 2 (reproduced from Grofman, 1996b).

In one of these (the standard PR-versus-plurality continuum), plurality is at one end and list PR and STV are at the other, with SNTV and cumulative voting in the middle; in one (candidate-centered politics versus party-centered politics), SMD plurality, STV, SNTV, and cumulative voting are all together, with closed party list PR at the other end, and open list PR as an intermediate category; in the third (small electoral constituencies systems versus large electoral constituencies), one end of the continuum is plurality bloc voting, but now systems such as STV and SNTV anchor the other end, and closed list PR, remarkably, is an *intermediate* category.[58]

---

[57] This classification is somewhat different than that given in Bogdanor (1985: 11), although the underlying ideas are closely related. Carey and Shugart (1995) offer a similar, but much more elaborated, electoral system classification scheme in a paper that we believe is destined to become a classic. They propose a continuum of electoral systems in terms of the incentives that each provides to "cultivate a personal vote." They rank systems in terms of four variables: (a) lack of leadership control over access to ballot or ballot position, (b) degree to which candidates can be elected independent of the vote shares of co-partisans; and (c) whether the voters possess a single intra-party vote as opposed to multiple intra-party votes or a single party-level vote, and (d) district magnitude, m. They treat these variables as dichotomous and weigh the first three factors equally to arrive at a composite index. Contrary to the claim in Lancaster (1986), Carey and Shugart (1995) reach the conclusion that higher district magnitude actually increases incentives for clientalism in what they call "personal vote" seeking systems, even though it decrease such incentives in party-list systems or other systems with a great deal of centralized party control over the nomination process. Grofman (1999b), while generally sharing their views about the contingent effects of m on localism argues that we can make this idea more precise by expressing the incentives for "personal voting" in terms of E (mean electoral constituency size) rather than m (district magnitude), since the relationship between E and M will depend upon the type of election system. He argues that we can get a more fine-tuned analysis by estimating personal-vote incentives as a function of (average) e, because e is a quantitative rather than qualitative variable (albeit strength of party control over the nomination process might still need to be treated as some type of polychotomy).

[58] Of course, these are theoretically derived expectations as to placement. In particular, it would be important to look at how different electoral systems actually differ in their value of E.

Table 2. *Three Continua of Classification*

	Continuum		
	Most	Intermediate	Least
PR versus plurality (Proportionality)	list PR STV	SNTV cumulative voting mixed systems	plurality bloc voting
Candidate-centered Politics vs. party-centered politics (candidate focus)	SMD plurality STV SNTV cumulative voting bloc voting (plurality)	open list PR mixed systems	closed-list PR
Large electoral constituencies systems vs. small electoral constituencies (particularism, E)		closed list PR mixed systems	STV SNTV cumulative voting SMD plurality

Source: Grofman (1996).

Still a fourth continuum might be developed were we to try to classify electoral systems according to the difficulty voters or parties have in developing optimal strategies (see e.g., Cox, 1987, 1997).

A fifth continuum along which electoral systems might usefully be differentiated is in terms of incentives toward conciliation. It is often taken for granted that the proportionality of an electoral system is a measure of its openness to the representation of extreme points of view, but that is too simplistic. Systems like STV and list PR may, for a given M, be roughly identical in their proportionality but may have quite different consequences for extremist politics, for instance, in terms of their degree of encouraging intra-party as opposed to inter-party competition and in terms of E, expected mean electoral constituency size.

Yet another continuum that has been suggested might be called "opaqueness." Edwin Winckler (personal communication, June 1995) has argued that "Japanese and Nationalist elites chose SNTV because it is an electoral system that is singularly open to manipulation from behind the scenes, thereby reducing their risks from democracy." In like manner, some systems are easier to understand than others, with single-member district plurality high in terms of its seeming transparency.[59]

---

[59] We emphasize *seeming* transparency, because a critical feature of plurality elections, namely the way that plurality elections translate votes into seats (e.g., the balloon effect that tends to sharply advantage the largest party, the suppression effect on seat share for minor parties whose votes are not regionally concentrated) is unlikely to be understood by the average voter.

From the standpoint of constitutional engineering, we believe that these and other alternative ways of classifying electoral systems[60] can provide us at least as many insights into the real political consequences of electoral laws as the standard PR-versus-plurality classification with its emphasis on proportionality as the sole criterion of interest.[61] However, election systems cannot be understood as operating in a vacuum. Their effects are mediated by other aspects of political institutions and political culture, as well as past history and the resistance of institutions once in place to change (Grofman, 1999a). Indeed, essentially identical electoral rules may give rise to rather different types of outcomes in different political settings.[62]

References

Adams, James. 1996. "Equilibrium in Multicandidate Competition: The Case of the 1992 Presidential Election." Unpublished manuscript, University of California, Santa Barbara.

Aldrich, John H. 1983. "A Downsian Spatial Model with Party Activism." *American Political Science Review* 77: 974–90.

Alesina, Alberto, and Howard Rosenthal. 1995. *Partisan Politics, Divided Government and the Economy.* Cambridge: Cambridge University Press.

Amarin, Neto, and Gary W. Cox. 1997. "Electoral Institutions, Cleavage Structures, and the Number of Parties." *American Journal of Political Science* 41(1): 149–74.

Ames, Barry. 1995. "Electoral Strategy under Open-List Proportional Representation." *American Journal of Political Science* 39(2): 406–34.

Aranson, Peter, and Peter C. Ordeshook. 1972. "Spatial Strategy for Sequential Elections." In R. Niemi and H. Weisberg, eds., *Probability Models of Collective Decision Making.* Columbus, Ohio: Merrill.

Baker, Gordon E. 1955. *Rural versus Urban Political Power: The Nature and Consequences of Unbalanced Representation.* Westport, Conn.: Greenwood Press.

Balinski, Michael L., and H. Peyton Young. 1982. *Fair Representation: Meeting the Ideal of One Man, One Vote.* New Haven, Conn.: Yale University Press.

Baron, David D. 1994. "Electoral Competition with Informed and Uninformed Voters." *American Political Science Review* 88(1): 33–47.

Bernhardt, M. D., and D. E. Ingberman. 1985. "Candidate Reputations and the Incumbency Effect." *Journal of Public Economics* 27: 47–67.

Blais, André, and R. K. Carty. 1990. "Does Proportional Representation Foster Voter Turnout?" *European Journal of Political Research* 18(2): 167–81.

---

[60] Of course, as noted earlier, subtle variations in electoral rules may also have non-trivial consequences.

[61] For very similar views see Reed, 1994; Carey and Shugart, 1995.

[62] For example in Australia STV operates more like list PR than it does in Ireland because most Australian voters cast a "party-ticket" vote – partly because they are required to express their preferences for *all* candidates lest their ballot be invalidated (Bowler and Grofman, 1997). Similarly, SNTV systems can behave rather differently in Taiwan and in Japan (Grofman, 1999c).

Bogdanor, Vernon. 1985. "Introduction." In Vernon Bogdanor, ed., *Representatives of the People?* Aldershot, England: Gower.

Bowler, Shaun, and Bernard Grofman. 1997. "STV in the Family of Electoral Systems." *Representation* 34(1): 43–7.

Brace, Kimball, Bernard Grofman, and Lisa Handley. 1987. "Does Redistricting Aimed to Help Blacks Necessarily Help Republicans? *Journal of Politics* 49: 143–56.

Brady, David, and Bernard Grofman. 1991a. "Sectional Differences in Partisan Bias and Electoral Responsiveness in U.S. House Elections, 1850–1980." *British Journal of Political Science* 21(2): 247–56.

1991b. "Modeling the Determinants of Swing Ratio and Bias in U.S. House Elections, 1850–1980." *Political Geography Quarterly* 10(3) (July): 254–62.

Brams, Steven J. 1975. *Game Theory and Politics.* New York: Free Press.

1980. "Spatial Models of Election Competition." University Modules in *Applied Mathematics.*

1989. "Are the Two Houses of Congress Really Co-Equal?" In B. Grofman and D. Wittman, eds., *The Federalist Papers and the New Institutionalism.* New York: Agathon Press.

Brams, Steven, and Samuel Merrill. 1991. "Final-Offer Arbitration with a Bonus." *European Journal of Political Economy* 7: 79–82.

Brunell, Thomas. 1997. "Partisan Bias in the U.S. Congress: Why the Democrats Have Usually Been More Successful in House Elections than the Senate." Unpublished manuscript, School of Social Sciences, University of California, Irvine.

Butler, David, and Bruce Cain. 1992. *Congressional Districting: Comparative and Theoretical Perspectives.* New York: Macmillan.

Cain, Bruce. 1985. "Assessing the Partisan Effects of Redistricting." *American Political Science Review* 79(2): 320–33.

Cain, Bruce, John A. Ferejohn, and Morris Fiorina. 1987. *The Personal Vote: Constituency Service and Electoral Independence.* Cambridge, Mass.: Harvard University Press.

Campagna, Janet C. 1991. "Bias and Responsiveness in the Seat–Vote Relationship." *Legislative Studies Quarterly* 16(1) (February): 81–90.

Campagna, Janet C., and Bernard Grofman. 1990. "Party Control and Partisan Bias in 1980s Congressional Redistricting." *Journal of Politics* 52(4) (November): 1242–57.

Campbell, James E. 1996. *Cheap Seats: Democratic Party Advantage in U.S. House Elections.* Columbus: Ohio State University Press.

Carey, John M., and Matthew Shugart. 1995. "Incentives to Cultivate a Personal Vote: A Rank Ordering of Electoral Formulas." *Electoral Studies* 14(4): 417–40.

Caul, Miki. 1999. "Women's Representation in Parliament: The Role of Political Parties." *Party Politics* 5(1): 79–98.

Caul, Miki, Rein Taagepera, and Bernard Grofman. 1998. "Social Cleavages and the Number of Parties." Paper presented at the Annual Meeting of the Western Political Science Association, March 19–21, Los Angeles, Calif.

Christensen, Raymond, and Paul Johnson. 1995. "Toward a Context-Rich Analysis of Electoral Systems: The Japanese Example." *American Journal of Political Science* 39: 575–98.

Coleman, James S. 1971. "Internal Processes Governing Party Positions in Elections." *Public Choice* 11 (Fall): 35–60.

1972. "The Positions of Political Parties in Elections." In R. G. Niemi and F. Weisberg, eds., *Probability Models of Collective Decision Making*. Columbus, Ohio: Charles E. Merrill, pp. 332–57.

Collet, Christian. 1997. "Minor Parties in America: Evidence from the State and Local Level." Unpublished Ph.D dissertation in progress, Department of Politics, University of California, Irvine.

Courtney, John C., Peter MacKinnon, and David E. Smith, eds. 1992. *Drawing Boundaries: Legislatures, Courts and Electoral Values*. Saskatoon, Saskatchewan: Fifth House Publishers.

Cox, Gary W. 1987. "Electoral Equilibrium under Alternative Voting Institutions." *American Journal of Political Science* 31(1): 82–108.

1990. "Centripetal and Centrifugal Incentives in Electoral Systems." *American Journal of Political Science* 31: 82–108.

1997. *Making Votes Count: Strategic Coordination in the World's Electoral Systems*. Cambridge: Cambridge University Press.

Cox, Gary W., and Frances Rosenbluth. 1994. "Reducing Nomination Errors: Factional Competition and Party Strategy in Japan." *Electoral Studies* 13: 4–16.

Davidson, Chandler, and Bernard Grofman, eds. 1994. *Quiet Revolution in the South: The Effects of the Voting Rights Act, 1965–1990*. Princeton, N.J.: Princeton University Press.

Dodd, Lawrence C. 1976. *Coalitions in Parliamentary Government*. Princeton, N.J.: Princeton University Press.

Downs, Anthony. 1957. *An Economic Theory of Democracy*. New York: Harper and Row.

Duverger, Maurice. 1954. *Political Parties, Their Organization and Activity in the Modern State*. Trans. Barbara and Robert North. New York: Wiley.

1986. "Duverger's Law: Forty Years Later." In Bernard Grofman and Arend Lijphart, eds., *Electoral Laws and Their Political Consequences*. New York: Agathon Press, pp. 69–84.

Eckstein, Harry. 1988. "A Cultural Theory of Political Change." *American Political Science Review* 82(3) (September). Reprinted in Eckstein, Harry, 1992, *Regarding Politics: Essays on Political Theory, Stability and Change*. Berkeley: University of California Press.

Enelow, James M., and Melvin J. Hinich. 1984. *The Spatial Theory of Political Competition: An Introduction*. Cambridge: Cambridge University Press.

1990. *Advances in the Spatial Theory of Voting*. Cambridge: Cambridge University Press.

Farrell, David M. 1997. *Comparing Electoral Systems*. London and New York: Prentice-Hall/Harvester Wheatsheet.

Fedderson, Timothy J. 1992. "A Voting Model Implying Duverger's Law and Positive Turnout." *American Journal of Political Science* 36: 938–62.

Feld, Scott L., and Bernard Grofman. 1991. "Incumbency Advantage, Voter Loyalty and the Benefit of the Doubt." *Journal of Theoretical Politics* 3 (2): 115–37.

Gallagher, Michael. 1991. "Proportionality, Disproportionality, and Electoral Systems." *Electoral Studies* 10(1): 33–51.

1992. "Comparing Proportional Representation Electoral Systems – Quotas, Thresholds, Paradoxes and Majorities." *British Journal of Political Science* 22 (October): 469–96.

1997. "The (Relatively) Victorious Incumbent under PR-STV: Legislative Turnover in Ireland and Malta." Presented at the XVII World Congress of the International Political Science Association, August 17–21, Seoul, Korea.

Garand, James C., and T. Wayne Parent. 1991. "Representation, Swing and Bias in U.S. Presidential Elections, 1972–1988." *American Journal of Political Science* 35 (November): 1011–31.

Geddes, Barbara. 1995. "A Comparative Perspective on the Leninist Legacy in Eastern Europe." *Comparative Political Studies* 28: 230–74.

———. 1996. "Initiation of New Democratic Institutions in Eastern Europe and Latin America." In Arend Lipjpart and Carlos Waisman, eds., *Institutional Design in New Democracies*. Boulder, Colo.: Westview Press, pp. 15–42.

Gelman, Andrew, and Gary King. 1994a. "A Unified Method of Evaluating Electoral Systems and Redistricting Plans." *American Journal of Political Science*. 38 (2 May): 514–54.

———. 1994b. *Judgeit* (computer program available free via anonymous FTP from latte:harvard.edu.)

Greenberg, Joseph, and Shlomo Weber. 1985. "Multiparty Equilibria under Proportional Representation." Presented at Weingart Conference on Models of Voting. California Institute of Technology, March 22–3.

Grofman, Bernard N. 1975. A Review of Macro-Election Systems. In Rudolph Wildenmann, ed., *German Political Yearbook* (*Sozialwissenschaftliches Jahrbuch für Politik*), Vol. 4, Munich: Günter Olzog Verlag, 303–52.

———. 1983. "Measures of Bias and Proportionality in Seats–Votes Relationships." *Political Methodology* 9: 295–327.

———. 1985. "Neglected Role of the Status Quo in Models of Issue Voting." *Journal of Politics* 47: 231–7.

———. ed. 1990. *Political Gerrymandering and the Courts*. New York: Agathon Press.

———. 1992. "An Expert Witness Perspective on Continuing and Emerging Voting Rights Controversies: From One Person, One Vote to Political Gerrymandering." *Stetson University Law Review* 21(3): 783–818. (A revised and expanded version appears under the title "What Happens after One Person–One Vote: Implications of the U.S. Experience for Canada," in John Courtney and David Smith, eds., *Drawing Boundaries*, Saskatoon, Saskatchewan: Fifth House Publishers, 1992, pp. 156–78.)

———. 1993. "Toward an Institution Rich Theory of Political Competition, with a Supply-Side Component." In Bernard Grofman, ed., *Information, Participation and Choice: An Economic Theory of Democracy in Perspective*. Ann Arbor: University of Michigan Press, pp. 179–93.

———. 1994. "Should Parties Converge?" Presented at the World Congress of the International Sociological Association, Bielefeld, Germany, July 21–24.

———. 1996a. "Downsian Political Economy." In Robert Goodin and Hans-Dieter Klingemann, eds., *New Handbook of Political Science*. London: Oxford University Press.

———. 1996b. "The Place of STV in the Family of Electoral Systems." Paper presented at the University of California to Irvine Conference on STV Elections in Australia, Ireland and Malta. Laguna Beach, Calif. December 13–14.

———. 1996c. "Arend Lijphart and the New Institutionalism." Paper presented at the Annual Meeting of the American Political Science Association, August 29–September 1, San Francisco, Calif.

———. 1999a. "Preface: Methodological Steps toward the Study of Embedded Institutions." In Bernard Grofman, Sung-Chull Lee, Edwin Winckler, and

Brian Woodall, eds., *Elections in Japan, Korea and Taiwan under the Single Non-Transferable Vote: The Comparative Study of an Embedded Institution.* Ann Arbor: University of Michigan Press.

1999b. "SNTV, STV, and Single Member District Systems: Theoretical Comparisons and Contrasts." In Bernard Grofman, Sung-Chull Lee, Edwin Winckler, and Brian Woodall, eds., *Elections in Japan, Korea and Taiwan under the Single Non-Transferable Vote: The Comparative Study of an Embedded Institution.* Ann Arbor: University of Michigan Press.

1999c. "SNTV: An Inventory of Theoretically Derived Propositions and a Brief Review of the Evidence from Japan, Korea, Taiwan and Alabama." In Bernard Grofman, Sung-Chull Lee, Edwin Winckler, and Brian Woodall, eds., *Elections in Japan, Korea and Taiwan under the Single Non-Transferable Vote: The Comparative Study of an Embedded Institution.* Ann Arbor: University of Michigan Press.

ed. 1998. *Race and Redistricting in the 1990s.* New York: Agathon Press.

Grofman, Bernard, Thomas Brunell, and William Koetzle. 1997. "An Integrated Perspective on the Three Potential Sources of Partisan Bias: Malapportionment, Turnout Differences, and the Geographic Distribution of Party Vote Shares." *Electoral Studies* 16(4): 457–70.

Grofman, Bernard, Christian Collet, and Robert Griffin. 1998. "Analyzing the Turnout-Competition Link with Aggregate Cross-Sectional Data." *Public Choice* 95: 233–46.

Grofman, Bernard, and Chandler Davidson. 1992. "Postscript: What Is the Best Route to a Color-Blind Society?" In Bernard Grofman and Chandler Davidson, eds., *Controversies in Minority Voting: The Voting Rights Act in Perspective.* Washington, D.C.: The Brookings Institution, pp. 300–17.

1994. "The Effect of Municipal Election Structure on Black Representation in Eight Southern States." In Chandler Davidson and Bernard Grofman, eds., *Quiet Revolution in the South: The Effects of the Voting Rights Act, 1965–1990.* Princeton, N.J.: Princeton University Press, pp. 301–34.

Grofman, Bernard, Robert Griffin, and Amihai Glazer. 1990. "Identical Geography, Different Constituencies: See What a Difference Party Makes." In R. J. Johnston, F. Shelley, and P. Taylor, eds., *Developments in Electoral Geography.* London: Croom Helm, pp. 207–17.

Grofman, Bernard, Lisa Handley, and Richard Niemi. 1992. *Minority Representation and the Quest for Voting Equality.* Cambridge: Cambridge University Press.

Grofman, Bernard, William Koetzle, Michael McDonald, and Thomas Brunell. 2000. "A New Look at Split-Ticket Voting: The Comparative Midpoints Model." *Journal of Politics* 62(1): 34–50.

Grofman, Bernard, Sung-Chull Lee, Edwin Winckler, and Brian Woodall, eds. 1999. *Elections in Japan, Korea and Taiwan under the Single Non-Transferable Vote: The Comparative Study of an Embedded Institution.* Ann Arbor: The University of Michigan Press.

Grofman, Bernard, and Arend Lijphart, eds. 1986. *Electoral Laws and Their Political Consequences.* New York: Agathon Press.

Grofman, Bernard, Arend Lijphart, Robert McKay, and Howard Scarrow, eds. 1982. *Representation and Redistricting Issues.* Lexington, Mass.: Lexington Books.

Grofman, Bernard, Michael Migalski, and Nicholas Noviello. 1986. "Effects of Multimember Districts on Black Representation in State Legislatures." *Review of Black Political Economy* 14 (4 Spring): 65–78.

Grofman, Bernard, and Peter van Roozendaal. 1997. "Review Article: Modelling Cabinet Durability and Termination." *British Journal of Political Science* 27: 419–51.

Gudgin, G., and P. J. Taylor. 1979. *Seats, Votes and the Spatial Organization of Elections*. London: Pion.

Jackman, Simon. 1994. "Measuring Electoral Bias – Australia, 1949–93." *British Journal of Political Science* 24 (July): 319–57.

Johnston, R. J. 1981. *Political, Electoral and Spatial Systems*. London: Oxford University Press.

Karnig, Albert, and Susan Welch. 1982. "Electoral Structure and Black Representation on City Councils." *Social Science Quarterly* 63: 99–114.

Katz, Richard S. 1980. *A Theory of Parties and Electoral Systems*. Baltimore, Md.: Johns Hopkins University Press.

King, Gary, and Robert X. Browning. 1987. "Democratic Representation and Partisan Bias in Congressional Elections." *American Political Science Review* 81(4): 1251–73.

King, Gary, and Andrew Gelman. 1991. "Systemic Consequences of Incumbency Advantage in United States House Elections." *American Journal of Political Science* (February): 110–38.

Laakso, Markku, and Rein Taagapera. 1979. "Effective Number of Parties: A Measure with Application to West Europe." *Comparative Political Studies* 12: 3–27.

Lancaster, Thomas. 1986. "Electoral Structures and Pork-Barrel Politics." *International Political Science Review* 7(1): 67–81.

Lancaster, Thomas D. 1997. "The Origins of Double Ballot Electoral Systems: Some Comparative Observations." Paper presented at the XVII World Congress of the International Political Science Association, August 17–21, Seoul, Korea.

Lijphart, Arend. 1984. *Democracies: Patterns of Majoritarian and Consensus Government in Twenty-One Democracies*. New Haven, Conn.: Yale University Press.

1986. "Degrees of Proportionality of Proportional Representation Formulas." In Bernard Grofman and Arend Lijphart, eds., *Electoral Laws and Their Political Consequences*. New York: Agathon Press.

1994. *Electoral Systems and Party Systems: A Study of Twenty-Seven Democracies, 1945–1990*. New York and London: Oxford University Press.

Lijphart, Arend, and R. W. Gibberd. 1977. "Thresholds and Payoffs in List Systems of Proportional Representation." *European Journal of Political Research* 5: 219–44.

Lijphart, Arend, and Bernard Grofman, eds. 1984. *Choosing an Electoral System*. New York: Praeger.

Loosemore, John, and Victor J. Hanby. 1971. "The Theoretical Limits of Maximum Distortion: Some Analytic Expressions for Electoral Systems." *British Journal of Political Science* 1: 467–77.

Mackie, Thomas T., and Richard Rose. 1991. *The International Almanac of Electoral History*. Fully rev. 3d edition. Washington, D.C.: Congressional Quarterly.

Mair, Peter. [1986]/1994. "Districting Choices under the Single-Transferable Vote." In Bernard Grofman and Arend Lijphart, eds., *Electoral Laws and Their Political Consequences*. New York: Agathon Press, pp. 289–307.

May, J. D. 1974. "Democracy and Rural Overrepresentation." *Australian Quarterly* 46: 52–6.

McCubbins, Matthew D., and Frances M. Rosenbluth. 1995. "Party Provision for Personal Politics: Dividing the Votes in Japan." In Peter Cowhey and Matthew D. McCubbins, eds., *Structure and Policy in Japan and the United States*. Cambridge: Cambridge University Press, pp. 35–55.

Merrill, Samuel. 1993. "Voting Behavior under the Directional Spatial Model of Electoral Competition." *Public Choice* 77 (December): 739–56.

———. 1994. "A Probabilistic Model for the Spatial Distribution of Party Support in Multiparty Electorates." *Journal of the American Statistical Association* (December): 1190–9.

Merrill, Samuel, and Bernard Grofman. 1997. "Directional and Proximity Models of Spatial Two-Party Competition: A New Synthesis." *Journal of Theoretical Politics* 9(1): 25–48.

———. 1998. "Conceptualizing Voter Choice for Directional and Discounting Models of Two-Candidate Spatial Competition in Terms of Shadow Candidates." *Public Choice* 95: 219–31.

Mershon, Carol. 1994. "Expectations and Informal Rules in Coalition Formation." *Comparative Political Studies* 27 (April): 40–79.

Morton, Rebecca. 1993. "Incomplete Information and Ideological Explanations of Platform Divergence." *American Political Science Review* 87(2): 382–92.

Mozaffar, Shaheen. 1997. "Strategy, Context, and the Choice of Electoral Systems in Third Wave Democracies: Africa in Comparative Perspective." Paper presented at the XVII World Congress of the International Political Science Association, August 17–21, Seoul, Korea.

Mudambi, Ram, Pietro Navarra, and Carmela Nicosia. 1996. "Plurality versus Proportional Representation: An Analysis of Sicilian Elections." *Public Choice* 86: 341–57.

Myerson, Roger B. 1993a. "Incentives to Cultivate Favored Minorities under Alternative Electoral Systems." *American Political Science Review* 87(4): 856–69.

———. 1993b. "Effectiveness of Electoral Systems for Reducing Government Corruption: A Game Theoretic Analysis." *Games and Economic Behavior* 5: 118–32.

Myerson, Roger B., and Shlomo Weber. 1993. "A Theory of Voting Equilibria." *American Political Science Review* 87(1): 102–14.

Niemi, Richard G., and John Deegan, Jr. 1978. "A Theory of Political Districting." *American Political Science Review* 72(4): 1304–23.

Niemi, Richard G., and Simon Jackman. 1991. "Bias and Responsiveness in State Legislative Districting." *Legislative Studies Quarterly* 16(2): 183–202.

Nixon, D. C., D. Olomoki, N. Schofield, and I. Sened. 1995. "Multiparty Probabilistic Voting: An Application to the Knesset." Working Paper No. 186, Center in Political Economy, Washington University, St. Louis, Mo.

Owen, Guillermo, and Bernard Grofman. 1995. "Two Stage Electoral Competition in Two-Party Contests: Persistent Divergence of Party Positions with and without Expressive Voting." Unpublished manuscript, University of California, Irvine.

Palfrey, Thomas, and Robert Erikson. 1994. "Preemptive Spending and Entry Deterrence by Incumbents in Congressional Elections." Social Science Working Paper, California Institute of Technology (March).

Park, Chan Wook. 1988. "Legislators and Their Constituents in South Korea: The Pattern of District Representation." *Asian Survey* 28: 1049–65.

Poole, Keith T., and Howard Rosenthal. 1984. "The Polarization of American Politics." *Journal of Politics* 46: 1061–79.

Przeworski, Adam, and Henry Teune. 1970. *The Logic of Comparative Social Inquiry.* New York: Wiley-Interscience.

Rabinowitz, George, and Stuart Elaine Macdonald. 1989. "A Directional Theory of Issue Voting." *American Political Science Review* 83: 93–121.

Rae, Douglas W. 1971. *The Political Consequences of Electoral Laws*, 2d edition. New Haven, Conn.: Yale University Press (1st edition, 1967).

Reed, Steven R. 1990. "Structure and Behavior: Extending Duverger's Law to the Japanese Case." *British Journal of Political Science* 20: 335–56.

1994. "Democracy and the Personal Vote: A Cautionary Tale from Japan." *Electoral Studies* 13(1): 17–28.

Reeve, Andrew, and Alan Ware. 1992. *Electoral Systems: A Comparative and Theoretical Introduction.* London: Routledge.

Reilly, Ben. 1997. "Constitutional Engineering and the Alternative Vote in Fiji: An Assessment." In Brij V. Lajand and Peter Larmour, eds., *Electoral Systems in Divided Societies: The Fiji Constitution.* Canberra, Australia: National Centre for Development Studies.

Reynolds, Andrew. 1996. "Electoral Systems and Democratic Consolidation in South Africa." Unpublished Ph.D. dissertation, Department of Political Science, University of California, San Diego, August.

Reynolds, Andrew, and Bernard Grofman. 1994. "Choosing an Electoral System for the New South Africa: The Main Proposals." Paper presented at the Conference on Electoral Reform and Democratization, April 18–19, Columbia Institute for Western European Studies, Columbia University.

Reynolds, Andrew, and Ben Reilly. 1997. *The International IDEA Handbook of Electoral System Design.* Stockholm: Institute for Democracy and Electoral Assistance.

Riker, William. 1982. "Two Party Systems and Duverger's Law." *American Political Science Review* 76: 753–66. Reprinted in Bernard Grofman and Arend Lijphart, 1986, *Electoral Laws and Their Political Consequences.* New York: Agathon Press.

Robertson, David. 1975. *A Theory of Party Competition.* New York: Wiley.

Romer, Thomas, and Howard Rosenthal. 1979. "The Elusive Median Voter." *Journal of Public Economics* 12: 143–70.

Rowley, Charles K. 1984. "The Relevance of the Median Voter Theorem." *Journal of Institutional and Theoretical Economics* 140: 104–26.

Rule, Wilma. 1997. "Political Rights, Electoral Systems and the Legislative Representation of Women in 73 Democracies: A Preliminary Analysis." Paper presented at the XVII World Congress of the International Political Science Association, August 17–21, Seoul, Korea.

Rydon, Joan. 1968. "Malapportionment – Australian Style." *Politics* 3(2 November): 133–47.

Sartori, Giovanni. 1968. "Political Development and Political Engineering. In J. D. Montgomery and A. O. Hirschman, eds., *Public Policy* Vol. 17: 261–98.

1986. "The Influence of Electoral Systems: Faulty Laws or Faulty Method." In Bernard Grofman and Arend Lijphart, eds., *Electoral Laws and Their Political Consequences.* New York: Agathon Press, pp. 43–68.

Sawyer, Jack, and Duncan MacRae, Jr. 1962. "Game Theory and Cumulative

Voting in Illinois, 1902–1954." *American Political Science Review* 56: 936–46.

Scarrow, Howard. 1992. "'One Man–One Vote': Tracing Its Roots and Consequences." In John C. Courtney, Peter MacKinnon, and David E. Smith, eds., *Drawing Boundaries: Legislatures, Courts and Electoral Values.* Saskatoon, Saskatchewan: Fifth House Publishers, pp. 179–91.

Schofield, Norman. 1995. "Coalition Politics: A Formal Model and Empirical Analysis." *Journal of Theoretical Politics* 7: 245–81.

Schofield, Norman, Andrew D. Martin, Kevin M. Quinn, and Andrew B. Whitford. 1997. "Multiparty Electoral Competition in the Netherlands and Germany." Working Paper, Center in Political Economy, Washington University, St. Louis, Mo., April.

Schofield, Norman, Itai Sened, and David Nixon. 1997. "Nash Equilibrium in Multiparty Competition with 'Stochastic Voters.'" Center for Political Economy, Washington University, St Louis, Mo., March.

Shapiro, Catherine R., David W. Brady, Richard A. Brody, and John A. Ferejohn. 1990. "Linking Constituency Opinion and Senate Voting Scores: A Hybrid Explanation," *Legislative Studies Quarterly* 15(4 November): 599–623.

Shepsle, Kenneth. 1994. *Models of Multiparty Electoral Competition.* New York: Harwood.

Shugart, Matthew. 1992. "Electoral Reform Systems of Proportional Representation," *European Journal of Political Research* 21(3): 207–24.

Shugart, Matthew, and John Carey. 1992. *Presidents and Assemblies: Constitutional Design and Electoral Dynamics.* Cambridge: Cambridge University Press.

Shvetsova, Olga. 1997. "Duverger's Law without Two-Partyism." Paper presented at the Annual Meeting of the Public Choice Society, San Francisco, March.

Sugden, Robert. 1984. "Free Association and the Theory of Proportional Representation." *American Political Science Review* 78(1): 311–43.

Taagepera, Rein. 1986. "Reformulating the Cube Law for Proportional Representation Elections." *American Political Science Review* 80: 489–504.

Taagepera, Rein, and Bernard Grofman. 1985. "Rethinking Duverger's Law: Predicting the Effective Number of Parties in Plurality and PR Systems – Parties Minus Issues Equals One." *European Journal of Political Research* 13:341–52.

Taagepera, Rein, and Matthew Shugart. 1989. *Seats and Votes: The Effects and Determinants of Electoral Systems.* New Haven, Conn.: Yale University Press.

Taylor, Peter J. 1984. "The Case for Proportional Tenure: A Defense of the British Electoral System." In Arend Lijphart and Bernard Grofman, eds., *Choosing an Electoral System.* New York: Praeger, pp. 53–8.

Taylor, Peter, Graham Gudgin, and R. J. Johnston. 1986. "The Geography of Representation: A Review of Recent Findings." In Bernard Grofman and Arend Lijphart, eds., *Electoral Laws and Their Political Consequences.* New York: Agathon Press, pp. 183–94.

Tufte, Edward R. 1973. "The Relationship between Seats and Votes in Two-Party Systems." *American Political Science Review* 67: 540–7.

Wittman, Donald. 1973. "Parties as Utility Maximizers." *American Political Science Review* 18: 490–8.

1977. "Candidates with Policy Preferences: A Dynamic Model." *Journal of Economic Theory* 14: 180–9.

1983. "Candidate Motivation: A Synthesis of Alternative Theories." *American Political Science Review* 72: 78–90.

Yamakawa, Katsumi. 1984. "A Lorenz Curve Analysis of the Allocation of the Seats in the [Japanese] House of the Representatives by the General Elections." *Kansai University Review of Law and Politics* 5 (March): 1–26.

CHAPTER 9

Ordinary Elections and Constitutional Arrangements

Pierre Salmon

1   Introduction

It is widely held that voting in the course of ordinary elections has no significant influence on the constitutional regime or order of a country. If voters have any influence at all on the constitutional set-up, which not everybody sees as evident,[1] this is generally considered to occur only on the relatively rare occasions when constitutional questions are submitted to a referendum or to a specially elected convention or constitutional assembly. At least three arguments are provided to support that opinion. A logical consideration comes first. Ordinary elections are parts of the political game and thus logically take place *within* the rules of that game – that is, within the constitutional order or regime of the country. To assume that, at the same time as they play, players can change the rules is, to say the least, logically puzzling. The second argument refers to the motivations and possibilities of voters. Voters, this argument says, are not really interested in constitutional issues and, even if they were, are particularly ill equipped to understand their implications. The third argument rests on the observation of what obtains in practice. As a matter of fact, constitutional issues are generally absent from electoral platforms and campaigns.

In spite of its apparent strength, I will try to show that this three-pronged denial is not compelling. To defend the opposite view – that voters do exercise a substantial influence on constitutional matters simply by the way they vote in ordinary elections – I will endeavor to neutralize each of the three arguments mentioned above. The organization of the chapter reflects this objective. Thus I will explain in Section 3 why I think that ordinary elections having constitutional effects implies no logical contradiction, discuss in Section 4 voters' capacities and motivations, and argue in Section 5 that voters' influence on constitutional or institutional matters is compatible with the observation that these

---

[1] Although the assumption that they have is implicit in the way the constitutional economics school sees its prescriptive or normative role (see, e.g., Vanberg, 1994).

165

matters seldom come to the fore in electoral debates. But before proceeding to the main discussion, I must address in Section 2 the question of what one may want to include in the "constitutional regime" or "order."[2]

2   What Is Constitutional?

By definition, the question is largely semantic but (*pace* Karl Popper and Milton Friedman) this does not mean that it is meaningless. In some cases, notably that of the United States, it is at least feasible or conceivable to equate the constitutional regime or order and the formal (paper) constitution itself. If this is done, then, because formal constitutions cannot be changed by simple majorities of voters,[3] it is trivially true that the constitutional order cannot be changed in this way either. However, in many cases, it is not feasible or conceivable to equate the constitutional regime with a constitution either because there is no such thing or because the one that exists is largely irrelevant. Furthermore, even when it is conceivable, the assimilation is, I would say, generally inadvisable. It implies, for example, that countries that have the same constitution have the same constitutional regime, which is not exactly what one would want to say of all the countries whose constitution was modeled on that of the United States. It also leads to the neglect of rules of the game which, albeit absent from the formal constitution, constitute major constraints on the way the game can be played and thus deserve to be considered, in some sense, "constitutional."[4]

In a country such as France, there are at least four sets of rules or arrangements that we might want to include in the constitutional regime although they are either not addressed at all or only alluded to in the formal constitution. One is the electoral system. The other three concern the rules which govern the relations between the politicians in power in the central government in Paris, on the one side, and, on the other side, first the bureaucracy, second the sub-national elected governments (i.e., municipal, departmental, and regional governments), third the European institutions in Brussels. Whatever their origin or status, the rules or arrangements currently in force in these four areas have a considerable incidence not only on political life in general but also on matters that are addressed at length by the formal constitution.

[2] "Constitutional order" is a bit pompous; it should be understood as more or less synonymous with "constitutional set-up," "regime," "system," "set of rules," "arrangements," etc.
[3] Disregarding the case of countries, such as Britain, which have no formal constitution, only in Iceland is a 51 percent majority sufficient to change the constitution.
[4] James Buchanan (1987) refers to the "set of legal-institutional-constitutional rules that constrain the choices and activities of economic and political agents" or, somewhat more economically, to the "legal-institutional-constitutional structure of the polity."

I will refer to decentralization and to the relationship between politicians and bureaucrats in subsequent sections. At this stage let me give some illustrations of the constitutional relevance of Europe and of the electoral system. With regard to Europe, the European Court of Justice itself has repeatedly referred to the European Economic Community Treaty as, "albeit concluded in the form of an international agreement," being "the basic constitutional charter" (see Weatherill, 1995, p. 184). This is not a purely rhetorical claim on the part of an institution whose objectivity on this point could be suspected. The constitutional relevance of the European treaties can be illustrated in many ways. For instance, many scholars, especially among economists, consider the protection of individual rights of a more economic kind (property, income from capital, etc.) to be an essential task of constitutions. The French constitution does in part fulfill this function, as the Socialist government discovered in 1981 when it was compelled by the *Conseil Constitutionnel* to raise the compensation paid to the owners of the firms transferred to the public sector. But this constitution is not in France the only protector of property rights. It is more than supplemented in this task by the rules adopted in the context of European integration for promoting the free movement of goods, factors, and persons. One might even argue that, at the present stage of European integration (this could change at a later stage), the main protection of economic rights lies in the existence of these rules rather than in the constitutions of the member states. For instance, the former, not the latter, in fact prevent recourse to a level of taxation of income or capital bordering on confiscation. The European rules concerned here legally constrain governments, and thus should not be confused with the market forces referred to under the name of globalization. Because of this legally compelling character at least some of these European rules should be considered as essential components of the constitutional order currently prevailing in France, or for that matter in other member countries.[5]

Another example concerning Europe is budgetary discipline. There is a provision in the French constitution (Article 40) that says: "The proposals and amendments initiated by members of parliament cannot be taken into consideration when their adoption would either reduce the fiscal revenue or impose a financial burden on the budget."[6] In the past, this may have contributed to budgetary discipline by more transparently

---

[5] This point is particularly important in the case of a country such as Britain, where, according to Walter Murphy (1993), "Parliament is supposedly the authoritative creator, emendator, and interpreter of the constitution, restrained only by the ballot box and its collective conscience," but only inasmuch as the European Economic Community or the European Convention on Human Rights are not involved (p. 15). In other words, in Britain the only formal constitutional constraints on parliamentary sovereignty are the European institutions.

[6] See Sartori, 1994, p. 201.

making the executive branch of government responsible for any lack of it. But today the disposition has lost much of its relevance. It is overshadowed by the budgetary requirements imposed at the European level in the context of monetary unification.[7]

Let us turn to the electoral system. Its importance in the characterization of the political system of a country need not be stressed. Among many possible sources, a particularly illuminating one is Giovanni Sartori's excellent little book (1994) on "constitutional engineering." This term, Sartori indicates (p. 140), should be understood as "a shorthand that includes the electoral system, even though electoral systems are generally determined by ordinary legislation." Many examples of the close relationship between various aspects of the formal constitution and the electoral system can be found in Sartori's book: for instance, in the "English system of government," the crucial importance of plurality voting (p. 104); or, in the "Washington model," of the way representatives are induced by the electoral system to concentrate on local interests, a characteristic that contributes to avoiding deadlocks when the two branches of government are held by different parties (pp. 86–91).

A question that Sartori does not raise, at least in this book, is why electoral systems, despite their importance in constitutional matters, are seldom included in formal constitutions. One reason might be that if they were, they could well turn out to be unfortunate given other features or circumstances of the countries concerned. The Weimar constitution and the constitution adopted in France under the Fifth Republic are similar in many respects. However, the former (in its Article 22) imposed proportional representation, whereas the latter imposed nothing. It seems agreed among specialists of Weimar that the pure system of proportional representation (applied to a single national constituency) that it used at least "exaggerated the multiplicity and divisiveness of German politics in the Reichstag" (Finn, 1991, p. 145).[8] By contrast, a major effect of an electoral system like the double-ballot majority system used in France is to reduce the representation in parliament of "anti-system" parties (Sartori, 1994, pp. 67–9).[9] There are other means available for that

---

[7] For an interesting analysis of the close relationship that may exist between constitutions and treaties, see Ackerman (1997). For Bruce Ackerman (p. 776), "the (uncertain) transformation of a treaty into a constitution is at the center of the European Union today; it was also at the center of the American experience between the Revolution and the Civil War." See also Weatherill (1995, chap. 6).

[8] Sartori (1994, p. 129) writes: "*Pace* Lijphart, more than by any other factor Weimar was undermined by PR [proportional representation] (a defect remedied by the French with the double ballot majority system)."

[9] Possibly even (when access to the second round is limited to the first two runners) when one such anti-system party is the relative winner in the first round (Sartori, 1994, p. 78, note 17).

purpose.[10] Among these, a particularly illustrative one was the *apparentement* system contrived in France in 1951 by the parties of the center-left and center-right to safeguard a majority of seats endangered by the converging electoral forces of the Gaullists and the Communists.[11] Without this device, allowed by the fact that electoral rules were not too difficult to change, it is quite possible that the Fourth Republic would have come to an end earlier than it did. Among others, the opposite cases of Weimar and of the *apparentements* show that the fact that an electoral system is not part of the formal constitution, and thus can be changed more easily, may actually contribute to the survival of the constitutional regime – a consideration that constitutional framers may well have had in mind in the first place.

Electoral systems can thus be seen to be a priori less permanent or structural than the dispositions included in the formal constitutions. In practice, however, it is often the case that electoral systems prove to be more stable or enduring than many of these dispositions. In any case, I think, together with many authors, that electoral systems are an essential characteristic of political systems at the constitutional level. From the perspective of this chapter, the most important feature of an electoral system is whether it allows a swift replacement of office-holders or of policies considered as unsatisfactory by a majority of voters. Indeed, as will become clear, if an electoral system has this property, it may well turn out to be a more essential component of the constitutional order than most other components.

3   Elections and Constitutional Logic

A large part of the literature on constitutions and almost all of that small part of it which is produced by economists reflects what has been called "constitutionalism," that is, an exclusive concern with constraining, circumscribing, or binding majorities of voters.

A degree of mistrust of the majority of voters was expressed by James Madison among others (e.g., Benjamin Constant in France). For instance, Madison wrote:

> In our Governments the real power lies in the majority of the Community, and the invasion of private rights is chiefly to be apprehended, not from acts of Government contrary to the sense of its constituents,

[10] Including making anti-system parties anti-constitutional and dissolving them, as was done in West Germany.

[11] The scheme gave the electoral alliance, which obtained a relative majority, a premium sufficient for it to have the majority in parliament, although it (the scheme) maintained proportional representation within the alliance (see Sartori, 1994, pp. 6–7). A combination of proportional representation with a majoritarian premium is currently the rule in France for municipal elections. It works very well.

but from acts in which Government is the mere instrument of the major number of constituents.[12]

The reasons for constraining the freedom of decision of majorities of voters are well known. First, there is the protection of individual rights. In the long run and under a "veil of ignorance" all citizens may favor such protection, but in the short run there may be powerful incentives for a majority to transgress them. Hence the usefulness of binding (see, e.g., Buchanan, 1990). Second, in some cases, there may be the protection of perfectly identified and permanent minorities – ethnic, religious, or linguistic minorities in particular. This protection may be accepted by a majority at "a constitutional stage" because of ethical principles, or as a consequence of some constitutional logrolling, or just for the purpose of safeguarding internal peace. Third, the protection of property rights of an economic kind can be understood as an aspect of the protection of rights in general or as a means to foster investment and growth (which in turn may be deemed necessary for democratic stability, as argued by, among others Peter Bernholz, 1997). Fourth, independently of the other reasons, constraining the majority of voters may be necessary to render more credible some commitments, either promises or threats. For instance, making central banks independent may be a way to solve the time-inconsistency problem that plagues government policymaking in matters of money and inflation; or the constitutionally protected independence of judges and non-retroactivity of the law may be, as a side-effect, a means for a country to avoid being blackmailed by terrorists.

Inasmuch as constitutional rules and arrangements are seen as exclusively concerned with the task of binding majorities of voters, there is something akin to a logical contradiction in the possibility that these majorities could change the constitutional rules and arrangements. Leaving them this freedom would be akin to leaving Ulysses the freedom to unbind himself. I wonder whether, even more than a normative concern, it is not this logical issue that underlies Dennis Mueller's reaction to the view, defended in particular by Bruce Ackerman (1991), that simple electoral majorities do in fact change the constitutional order.[13] That in the United States the constitutional order has changed a lot without formal constitutional amendments has been a major theme in the public-choice and constitutional-economics literature for some time (see, e.g., Buchanan, 1975; McKenzie, 1984; Wagner, 1987; Gwartney and

---

[12] Letter of October 17, 1788 to Thomas Jefferson (quoted by Murphy, 1993, p. 6).

[13] Mueller (1996, p. 337, note 20) raises the question "To what extent does a minority remain party to the constitutional contract, if the contract can be amended whenever a substantial majority so chooses?" In reality this question is far-reaching. It points to a puzzle that affects the whole construction of constitution-as-contract (see Hardin, 1990; Ordeshook, 1992).

Wagner, 1988; Niskanen, 1990). But inasmuch as the responsibility for this phenomenon is ascribed to the Supreme Court or to politicians, it raises a possibly difficult question about constitutional enforcement but no logical problem. The specificity of Ackerman's book is the claim that the ultimate legitimate source of the change in the constitutional order is to be found in the opinion or will of a majority of voters. Pushed too far this kind of argument is destructive of the notion of constitutional binding in general. It is clear that Ackerman himself is conscious of this danger. He insists on a number of requirements to be satisfied before it becomes possible for a majority to change the constitutional rules and on the paucity of situations in which these requirements have been met. The logical problem raised by "self-unbinding" (if I may use that term) is mitigated or solved when there are obstacles and costs to unbinding. Thus it is natural to impose conditions for constitutional change brought about by elections as demanding as those included in formal amendment procedures.

Constitutions, however, have a second function that does not raise this kind of problem when considered in isolation. This second function consists in organizing the principal–agent relation between voters (the principals) and their representatives (agents). The problem then is to design institutions and rules in such a way that the preferences or interests of a majority of voters get satisfied. Under that second perspective, there is nothing strange or self-destructive in simple majorities of voters changing some rules or institutions in view of getting a better alignment between government decision making and their preferences or interests.

It is understandable that, for the majority of authors concerned with constitutional economics – that is, with individual rights – this second perspective is of little importance. Whether the government or the legislature violates the constitutional rules protecting minorities and rights because, as an agent, it does not itself respect the mandate or trust received from a majority of voters or because the majority of voters itself has an interest in these rules being violated is relatively secondary. In the vocabulary employed in some of this literature, the important issue is whether what gets favored is "predation" or "exchange" (Wagner, 1987). If, with the complicity of the courts, what gets favored is predation, it does not really matter whether the predator is a majority of voters, a set of office-holders, or, more likely, a combination of the two.

Without adopting this position, one must admit that disentangling the two functions of constitutional or quasi-constitutional rules or arrangements is not an easy task. What constitutions do, materially, is to restrict politicians, not directly voters. In so doing they at the same time, in generally unknown or undecidable proportions, fulfill the two tasks of fostering the interests of a majority of voters (the principal–agent perspective) and of restraining the same voters (the constitutionalist perspective). For instance, constitutional provisions concerned with budgetary discipline, such as the already mentioned Article 40 of the French constitution, or like the much more ambitious constitutional constraints defended for the United States by Buchanan and others, reflect a distrust indistinctly of legislators and of majorities of voters.

For the purpose of justifying my proposition, what creates a problem is when the representatives of a majority of voters change components of the constitutional order in the direction of *increased* power or freedom for themselves. Let me assume that this is done with the acquiescence of voters. If one could be sure that the change has no bearing on the first function of the constitution (concerning the relations between voters), but only on the second function (concerning the agency relationship between voters and their representatives), it could be considered as nondestructive of constitutional principles. But I am not sure that ascertaining independent effects in such a way is even only sometimes possible. Thus, as already noted, taking into account principal–agent considerations changes nothing in practice to our logical problem. Since this is the situation on which Buchanan and his followers focus, they are not inconsistent.[14] When, on the contrary, with the approval of voters as expressed in ordinary elections, representatives change components of the constitutional order in the direction of *decreased* power or freedom for themselves, the logical problem is more or less absent. Extra self-binding is much less puzzling than self-unbinding, so to say. Of course, such behavior may be puzzling for other reasons. One problem may be solved, but others arise. I turn to some of the other problems now.

4   Voters' Concerns and Capabilities

Consumers are not generally concerned with how production is organized. Similarly, it is often claimed that voters are concerned or should be, only with the outputs of governmental activity and the cost or tax prices associated with these outputs and not with the internal organization of the state. One possible reason for their lack of concern could be that they trust their representatives, the elected politicians, to organize the state in their (the voters') interests. Another possibility is that voters can rely on their assessment of policy outputs and tax prices, combined with voting, as sufficient to ensure that they are provided with the policies they want. The reason that most people think of first of all is that voters are completely ignorant of constitutional matters and know that they are.

Although apparently convincing, this last argument is possibly the

---

[14] Whether their factual beliefs or interpretations are true is another matter, discussed for instance by Wittman (1995, pp. 137–48), with regard to "takings" clauses.

weakest. It is probably true that most voters are rather ignorant of the way government is organized. However, the main features of this organization or the main problems that it raises are not more difficult for them to understand than many other issues, economic and social issues in particular, which they are not supposed to be completely unable to understand in most accounts of electoral behavior. Compare for instance the informational problems involved in deciding whether the president should be elected for five years with a possibility of being re-elected once, for seven years with this possibility also, or for seven years without it. And consider the information required to answer the question of whether a lot of influence on employment is lost when monetary policy becomes unavailable as a consequence of fixed exchange rates or monetary unification. Both questions are or recently have been part of the political debate in France. The first is typically constitutional, but it calls for considerations that many citizens are perfectly able to grasp, it seems to me. The second calls for an understanding and comparative assessment of full-blown models (involving expectation-augmented Philips curves, time inconsistency, sunspot equilibria and what have you) that should tax the analytical capacity of the most competent economists. I do not say that voters are deprived of any means of making up their mind on these matters as on others (see Wittman, 1995, chap. 1), but I refuse to adopt the widely shared presumption that issues similar to the second question, typical of the most relevant questions in the economic domain, are more easily decidable by voters than questions like the first, which are typical of the constitutional agenda.

Let me turn now to the question of whether, assuming that they are sufficiently competent, voters should be concerned with constitutional or quasi-constitutional issues, pertaining for instance to the organization of the relationship between politicians and bureaucrats.[15]

When economists discuss the relations between politicians and voters, they tend since the mid-1980s to adopt the principal–agent framework. They model bureaucrats as the agents of elected politicians. At the same time, they assume elected politicians to be the agents of voters and they treat these two agency relationships as if they were independent. This implicit assumption has unfortunate consequences. It implies that the stronger the agency relationship between politicians and bureaucrats, the better from the standpoint of voters, *whatever the state of their relation-*

---

[15] In Section 2, I mentioned three relationships whose organization should be considered, in the case of France at least, to be part of constitutional arrangements. In work published previously (Salmon, 1987, 1991, 1995), I have devoted some attention to how voters may have some influence on the relationship between central and subcentral governments and between central (member-state) governments and European institutions. For a while, in this section, I draw on an analysis of the relationship between voters, bureaucrats, and politicians adumbrated in Salmon (1997).

ship with politicians. But, when the relationship between voters and politicians is defective (as is necessarily the case in our actual, generally imperfect, world), it is far from clear that voters should wish the relation between politicians and bureaucrats to be as good or tight as possible (supposing that they should is a mistake akin to the mistake whose elimination motivated the theory of the second best). For instance, if we do not trust our president or prime minister, do we wish him to enjoy a perfectly symbiotic relationship with the head of the police? If the assumptions that could justify a positive answer to that question were stated explicitly, it would be clear that they are unacceptable, but they are usually made implicitly in the context of the study of one of the two relationships at the time. This allows many authors to suppose, as if it were obvious, that a perfect control of politicians over the bureaucracy would be a good thing for democracy, that a major problem of our democratic societies is that this control is highly imperfect.

For our purpose, what the foregoing discussion suggests is that voters could remain completely unconcerned with the organization of relations between politicians and bureaucrats only if they could fully trust their representatives, the politicians, to shape these relations in their (the voters') best interests. I have some sympathy for the minority view, defended notably by Albert Breton (e.g., 1996) and Donald Wittman (e.g., 1995), that powerful mechanisms are at work which make politicians exert themselves and respond fairly well to the preferences of voters (not worse than business firms with regard to the preferences of consumers, to use a comparison both authors make). However, even if we accept this general perspective, I think that at least two sets of considerations prevent us from considering the relationship between voters and politicians as unproblematic. One set is related to what is known as the "fear of the state": voters may be afraid or distrustful of the power of the rulers, or they may be afraid or distrustful of their fellow voters or of themselves. Even accepting Breton's view that the government or the state is not a monolith, that "governmental systems" are very competitive, the question remains of whether voters can rely in all circumstances on this competition. It is not inconceivable, for instance, that a single disciplined party could conquer many centers of power, at all levels of jurisdiction, and then that its leaders could misuse the considerable power that such concentration or monopolization would provide them with. Since the damage caused by a chain of events of that kind could be serious, a small probability of its occurrence would be sufficient to justify the fear of the state on the part of risk-averse citizens. The existence of relatively independent or protected non-elected decision makers, such as civil servants and judges, might be valuable to voters under that perspective. Even closer to counterfactual reasoning, another question arises: Is the fragmentation of the state into smaller mutually competitive units independent of the fear of the state? The checks and balances and other institutional arrangements that allow competition to develop may themselves have something to do with that fear.

A second set of qualifications is related to the fact that, while retrospective assessments necessarily play a major role in the vote, they cannot bear with the same reliability or strength on all policies or aspects of policies. To refer to my own work (e.g., 1987), I have called performance competition a mechanism based on the assumption that office-holders in one jurisdiction know, albeit with some degree of uncertainty, that many voters in their electorate compare policy outcomes in the jurisdiction to policy outcomes elsewhere. This gives office-holders an incentive to exert themselves, that is, in some sense, to move the policy mix toward the production frontier. If this mechanism worked perfectly well, voters could concern themselves exclusively with policy outputs and disregard completely the way governments are organized (provided of course that their power to dismiss is safeguarded by the electoral rules). However, a major problem that this mechanism encounters, or more generally that any mechanism based on retrospective voting encounters, stems from the fact that policy outputs are not equally measurable by voters. As a consequence, politicians may be induced to concentrate their efforts on policies whose outcomes are more easily measurable and sacrifice other policies that would also be useful to voters (see Salmon, 1991; Tirole, 1994; and, in a more general context, Holmström and Milgrom, 1991).

Policies yielding benefits only in the long run may be particularly vulnerable to distortions of that kind. Admittedly, some aspects of these policies may well be relatively easily assessable by voters before they bear fruit: voters may understand that investment in tangible or human capital may be favorable to future growth, they may welcome land reclamation or reforestation programs, they may perceive or accept the claimed causality between new laws or new agencies and some relatively distant objectives. There are, however, many aspects of long-term oriented policies which they will find more difficult to observe or assess. The literature on the interaction between the polity and the bureaucracy focuses on making and implementing rules, changing policies, creating agencies. But the major part of what the state or the government does, and should be doing, is more basic and less related to change. As a matter of course, the state (including sub-central governments) provides citizens with a regular and continuous flow of services. Maintaining the future capacity to deliver these services, at a constant and sufficient level of quality, is typically a long-term policy that cannot easily be assessed by voters. If political competition is very severe, which may be a good thing in itself, this might well have the unfortunate side-effect of literally compelling incumbents to sacrifice all policies that do not "pay" in terms of probability of re-election, this kind of policy in particular. The organization of the state, including for instance an institution such as the civil service, may mitigate that problem. But it is unlikely to follow such an objective if voters leave politicians free to shape it according to their (the politicians') preferences.

The foregoing discussion shows, I hope, that voters should not completely trust the politicians or the perfection of the agency or delegation relationship they have with politicians, and should not be unconcerned by the organization of government. The question now is whether they can and do have an influence on this organization. This type of issue seems to be more or less absent from electoral campaigns.

5   Institutional or Constitutional Issues in Elections

Many of these issues are dealt with on the occasion of formal constitution making or amending. Others, such as the ones we focus on in this chapter cannot. For instance, the relationship between the polity and the bureaucracy is not addressed in formal constitutions. The relations between the central government and sub-central governments is not based on a distribution of constitutional rights in unitary states – or even, for that matter, in all federal states (see Ordeshook, 1992, p. 167). This means that the form of institutional design that is of interest to us is not of a constitutional kind in the formal sense of that term. Received wisdom is that institutional design or change that is not of a constitutional kind in the formal sense is the business of politicians, or perhaps the result of spontaneous evolution, but cannot in any case be influenced by voters in the course of ordinary elections. In addition to the idea, discussed in the preceding section, that voters have neither the motivation nor the capacity to be concerned with these issues, what could make the influence of voters on institutions (by the means of ordinary elections) somewhat doubtful is that institutional issues seldom become salient issues in electoral contests.

Seldom is not "never" and in a sense it might not be abnormal that constitutional issues come to the fore only intermittently or discontinuously. On some occasions, it is the case that voters clearly want institutional change. Then, we can often count on political entrepreneurship to bring that change about. In the United States as in France, presidents or candidates in presidential elections are the most likely constitutional entrepreneurs. But this may be a relatively recent phenomenon (see Ackerman, 1991). An American illustration of a process starting from below is the way the Progressive movement imposed reforms at the turn of the century, in particular at the level of municipal government (see, e.g., Maser, 1985; Knott and Miller, 1987). Municipal governments were typically dominated by party machines under a generalized system of patronage. Although this often worked well or speedily in terms of policy outputs, many voters, especially in the middle classes, were revolted by at least some aspects of the system. The National Municipal League pushed for a reform including the introduction of a relatively neutral or independent civil service for government employees. The issue became a salient one in elections at the local and state levels. As a result, many municipal charters were changed. Although the story is complicated, with some moot points (see the discussion following Maser's paper and the references in Knott and Miller), it seems generally agreed that the discontent of a large part of the electorate with the existing institutions was a major cause of their reform. Other examples that come to mind are in the United States the anti-slavery movements before the Civil War and the civil rights movement in the 1960s, and in various countries the women's suffrage movement.

Even if we accept that open "constitutional politics" at the electoral level is infrequent, this fact may not reflect a disinterest of voters for institutional issues but rather the existence of an attachment of voters to the institutional status quo and the knowledge of this preference by politicians (it is natural enough that attachment to the status quo plays an important role in constitutional and institutional matters).

In the article already cited (1987), I discussed the case of the surprisingly radical decentralization law passed in France in 1982–3. Decentralization had not come out as an important issue in the 1981 presidential and legislative elections, both won by the left, and it was not clear, when the law was passed, whether it would be an asset for the incumbents at the following election. Thus, I do not deny that the influence of voters was unimportant in the decision to make the law.[16] In fact, I do not know whether the reform was an asset during the 1986 legislative election, which was dominated by economic and social issues, and which the left in any case lost (see Penniman, 1988). What is clear, however, is that the politicians who were hostile to the law (there were many of them on both sides, but they were the majority on the right) did not raise the issue during that election, nor in the following ones. Presumably, they knew that public opinion had become rapidly attached to the new sub-central institutions and to the new division of powers. Given this support, questioning the reform would have been electorally dangerous. The same kind of stories could be told about the creation of a number of independent authorities, or the granting of more independence to existing ones. Again in France, a case in point is the striking disappearance of opposition to the independence of the central bank granted in the wake of Maastricht. In earlier work (Salmon, 1995), I

---

[16] Gaston Deferre, at the time simultaneously Minister of the Interior and mayor of Marseilles, was the politician most involved in the design of the law.

have proposed a small model along similar lines to account for the roundabout nature of the transfer of powers to European institutions.

An alternative explanation of many of the phenomena mentioned here could be based on the theoretical framework proposed by Breton in his recent book (1996). Adopting his framework, one should say that what ensures the survival of sub-central governments, supra-national institutions or independent authorities is the consent that people give these power centers in exchange for the goods and services that they provide (see especially his chapter 5). Most of the time, I think, the two interpretations come to the same. Not always, though. In particular, in Breton's account, consent is related to the goods and services that an institution has produced in the past or at the limit is currently producing, whereas I can accept that consent can also be given to institutions that have as yet produced nothing or perhaps do not even exist, except on paper. To account for this possibility, I suggest that one must see voters as being, at least sometimes or to some extent, principals within a hierarchical relation rather than buyers on a market. The same need applies, I think, to an issue such as the politicization of the administration. In France, this issue has several times become a salient one in presidential elections, mostly in the form of a denunciation of, or a warning against, either the "Etat-RPR" (i.e., "RPR State") or the "Etat-PS" (i.e., "PS State").[17] The attention that some voters give to that issue constrains (perhaps increasingly) the proclivity of the party in power to politicize appointments to the top jobs. To generalize, under the perspective that I defend, only voters can be the ultimate guardians of the structural characteristics of the system, including its democratic and competitive characters.[18]

6   Concluding Remarks

The foregoing discussion has supported the claim, I hope, that an institution or a set of institutional rules can be entrenched in voters' preferences rather than in a constitution. This is how and why voters have a profound influence on institutional design, as I claimed in the last section. The discussion also suggests that it might be easier to explain why an institution or arrangement endures than to explain how or why it was established or came about in the first place.

---

[17] RPR is for Rassemblement pour la République, the name of the neo-Gaullist party; PS is for Parti Socialiste.

[18] In the United States, as Robert Inman and Daniel Rubinfeld write (1997, p. 104), "when a political institution did rise to the defense of the federalist constitution – whether it was the executive, the judiciary, or a legislative political party – a single truth prevailed: the vast majority of the citizens in that society believed the federalist constitution to be worth protecting."

To conclude, let me stress an important point. Although I recognized the possibility of constitutional change being initiated from below, all along the paper I rather assumed voters' influence to be typically of a reactive or monitoring kind, the main initiators or producers of change being the politicians. But, for voters' reactions or potential reactions to have an effect, the politicians must take them into account. This means two things. First, the electoral system must favor the influence of voter preferences on politics. In this sense, the electoral system, as noted in Section 2, is a very basic component of the system. If it is of the right, highly competitive type, all the rest follows. If not, for instance if it gives too much security to political parties, things become uncertain. Second, the substitution in the literature on elections of probabilistic voting to deterministic voting is a great help toward making the foregoing reasoning plausible. Probabilistic voting means that politicians, insecure about any individual voter's choice, take into account the preferences of all the voters, not only those of the pivotal voter as is the case in nonprobabilistic voting. As a consequence, even institutional concerns shared by a minority of voters or, if shared by a majority, considered as secondary by all, are taken into account by politicians or parties submitted to sufficiently tight electoral competition. In other words, institutional or constitutional concerns among voters may be not only negative or latent, as argued earlier, but also relatively weak, and nonetheless constitute an essential underlying cause of the shape taken by institutions.

References

Ackerman, Bruce. 1991. *We the People: 1. Foundations.* Cambridge, Mass.: The Belknap Press of Harvard University Press.
1997. "The Rise of World Constitutionalism." *Virginia Law Review* 83: 771–97.
Bernholz, Peter. 1997. "Necessary and Sufficient Conditions for a Viable Democracy." In Albert Breton, Gianluigi Galeotti, Pierre Salmon, and Ronald Wintrobe, eds., *Understanding Democracy: Economic and Political Perspectives*, Cambridge: Cambridge University Press, pp. 88–103.
Breton, Albert. 1996. *Competitive Governments: An Economic Theory of Politics and Public Finance.* Cambridge: Cambridge University Press.
Buchanan, James M. 1975. *The Limits of Liberty.* Chicago: The University of Chicago Press.
Buchanan, James M. 1987. "Constitutional Economics." In John Eatwell, Murray Milgate, and Paul Newman, eds., *The New Palgrave: A Dictionary of Economics.* London: Macmillan, vol. 1, pp. 585–8.
1990. "The Domain of Constitutional Economics." *Constitutional Political Economy* 1 (1 Winter): 1–18.
Finn, John E. 1991. *Constitutions in Crisis: Political Violence and the Rule of Law.* Oxford and New York: Oxford University Press.
Gwartney, James D., and Richard E. Wagner, eds. 1988. *Public Choice and Constitutional Economics.* Greenwich, Conn.: JAI Press.
Hardin, Russell. 1990. "Contractarianism: Wistful Thinking." *Constitutional Political Economy* 1 (2 Spring/Summer): 35–52.

Holmström, Bengt, and Paul Milgrom. 1991. "Multi-Task Principal-Agent Analyses: Incentive Contracts, Asset Ownership, and Job Design." *Journal of Law, Economics, and Organization*: 7, special issue: 24–52.

Inman, Robert P., and Daniel L. Rubinfeld 1997. "The Political Economy of Federalism." In Dennis Mueller, ed., *Perspectives on Public Choice: A Handbook*. Cambridge: Cambridge University Press, pp. 73–105.

Knott, Jack H., and Gary Miller. 1987. *Reforming Bureaucracy: The Politics of Institutional Choice*. Englewood Cliffs, N.J.: Prentice-Hall.

Maser, Stephen. 1985. "Demographic Factors Affecting Constitutional Decisions: The Case of Municipal Charters." *Public Choice* 47: 149–62.

McKenzie, Richard B., ed. 1984. *Constitutional Economics: Constraining the Economic Powers of Government*. Lexington, Mass.: D.C. Heath (Lexington Books).

Mueller, Dennis C. 1996. *Constitutional Democracy*. Oxford and New York: Oxford University Press.

Murphy, Walter F. 1993. "Constitutions, Constitutionalism, and Democracy." In Douglas Greenberg et al. eds., *Constitutionalism and Democracy: Transitions in the Contemporary World*. Oxford and New York: Oxford University Press, pp. 3–25.

Niskanen, William A. 1990. "Conditions Affecting the Survival of Constitutional Rules." *Constitutional Political Economy* 1 (2 Spring/Summer), pp. 53–62.

Ordeshook, Peter C. 1992. "Constitutional Stability." *Constitutional Political Economy* 3 (2 Spring/Summer): 136–75.

Penniman, Howard, ed. 1988. *France at the Polls, 1981 and 1986: Three National Elections*. Washington, D.C.: American Enterprise Institute (Duke University Press).

Salmon, Pierre. 1987. "Decentralisation as an Incentive Scheme." *Oxford Review of Economic Policy* 3 (2 Summer): 24–43.

   1991. "Checks and Balances and International Openness." In Albert Breton, Gianluigi Galeotti, Pierre Salmon, and Ronald Wintrobe, eds., *The Competitive State*. Dordrecht: Kluwer, pp. 169–84.

   1995. "Nations Conspiring against Themselves: An Interpretation of European Integration." In Albert Breton, Gianluigi Galeotti, Pierre Salmon, and Ronald Wintrobe, eds., *Nationalism and Rationality*. Cambridge: Cambridge University Press, pp. 290–311.

   1997. "Politicians and Bureaucrats: A Relationship Shaped by Voters." Unpublished paper.

Sartori, Giovanni. 1994. *Comparative Constitutional Engineering: An Inquiry into Structures, Incentives and Outcomes*. London: Macmillan.

Tirole, Jean. 1994. "The Internal Organization of Government." *Oxford Economic Papers* 46 (1 January): 1–29.

Vanberg, Viktor. 1994. *Rules and Choice in Economics*. London and New York: Routledge.

Wagner, Richard E. 1987. "Parchments, Guns, and the Maintenance of Constitutional Contract." In Charles K. Rowley, ed., *Democracy and Public Choice: Essays in Honor of Gordon Tullock*. Oxford: Basil Blackwell, pp. 105–21.

Weatherill, Stephen. 1995. *Law and Integration in the European Union*. Oxford and New York: Oxford University Press.

Wittman, Donald A. 1995. *The Myth of Democratic Failure: Why Political Institutions Are Efficient*. Chicago: The University of Chicago Press.

CHAPTER 10

The Cost Imposed on Political Coalitions by Constituent Parties: The Case of Italian National Elections

Ram Mudambi, Pietro Navarra, and Giuseppe Sobbrio

1   Introduction

On March 27, 1994, after about forty years of proportional representation, national elections to both chambers of the Italian Parliament took place governed by an electoral system with a strong element of plurality. Since then Italy has held one more general election under the new rules (in April 1996). In the present study, we will be concerned with observing and explaining some of the effects of the new rules on the voting behavior of the Italian electorate. Our analysis will focus on the most recent election to the Chamber of Deputies (the lower house).

The rules for the Chamber of Deputies are as follows: approximately three-quarters are now elected on a plurality basis, while the remaining quarter is elected proportionally and essentially on a regional basis.[1] This is operationalized by allowing voters to express two simultaneous votes: one for the single-member college candidate (a Plurality [PL] ballot) and the other for the party for the proportional allocation of seats (a

We would like to thank Bruno S. Frey, Bernard Grofman, and participants at the Conference on Constitutional Political Economy, University of Messina (Sicily), for many helpful comments on an earlier version of this chapter.

[1] A more detailed description of the new rules is provided here. Of a total of 630 seats, 475 were assigned on the basis of plurality, while 155 were assigned on the basis of proportionality. The country was divided into 475 single-member constituencies and each of these elected a member on the basis of plurality. In addition, the country was divided into 27 electoral regions, roughly corresponding to the 20 political regions – the number of electoral regions is larger because some of the larger political regions were divided into more than one electoral region. Each electoral region represented a certain number of seats that were assigned according to a proportional representation rule. The total number of seats assigned in this way was 155.

Each voter was given two ballots – a plurality (PL) vote to exercise in the single-member constituency and proportionality (PR) vote to exercise in the regionwide proportional system.

Proportional Representation [PR] ballot). Since each voter has two simultaneous votes available, he or she can express a double preference for a party, by voting for it in the PR ballot and for that party's candidate in the PL ballot. Alternatively, the voter can express split preferences by voting for a party in the PR ballot, but *not* for that party's candidate in the PL ballot. This phenomenon, that can be described as a "switching-voter phenomenon" (Navarra, forthcoming), can significantly influence the overall results of the elections and, consequently, the formation of the government. Indeed, it may seen that this underlies the results of the 1996 Italian general elections.

The 1996 Italian general elections were contested by two large coalitions that encompassed most major national parties together with some independent and regional parties.[2] These were the Center-Right coalition (Polo)[3] and the Center-Left coalition (Ulivo). Ulivo included the Socialists and the successors to the old Italian Communist Party. Between the two of them, these coalitions accounted for about 95 percent of the popular vote.

In the light of the switching-voter phenomenon, each party can impose a cost on its coalition. This cost is imposed by split-preference voters, who vote for their chosen party's coalition in the PR ballot but fail to support the coalition candidate in the PL ballot. In the context of the competing coalitions, split-preference voting becomes much more widespread. This is because many voters find themselves in PL constituencies with coalition candidates who are from parties other than their own. We therefore characterize split-preference voting in the following way: we assume that voters who vote for the candidate of their chosen coalition in the PL ballot will always vote for their chosen coalition in the PR ballot. However, the reverse need not be true. Thus, split-preference voters are those who support their party's coalition in the PR ballot but find themselves with a candidate from another coalition party in the PL ballot whom they cannot or will not support.[4]

In this chapter we are concerned with studying the effects of the new electoral rules on the election of the Chamber of Deputies members competing in single-member constituency races. We use data on voting patterns in the PL and PR ballots of each constituency to estimate the

---

[2] Navarra and Lignana (1997) provide a detailed picture of the process of coalition formation and the electoral strategies adopted by the various parties in Italian politics after the change in electoral rules.

[3] Polo included the recently formed grouping Forza Italia (FI), the National Alliance or Alleanza Nazionale (AN) and the successors to the Christian Democrats or Centro Cristiano Democratico e Cristiani Democratici Uniti (CCD/CDU).

[4] This means that we are assuming that all voters are affiliated to some party. This assumption may be justified on the basis of Italy's long history of PR elections, during which voting without a party affiliation was impossible.

electoral cost imposed on a coalition by each of its constituent parties. This is done by constructing an index of popularity measuring the votes gained by candidates from voters affiliated to coalition parties other than their own. We then use this index as a means of estimating the probability that a particular seat will be won or lost by the coalition.

According to the classification of Mershon (1996), it is possible to distinguish between four types of coalition theories: (1) office-driven institution-free, cooperative theories; (2) policy-driven, institution-free, cooperative theories; (3) policy-driven, institution-focused, non-cooperative theories; (4) theory-oriented empirical research. Studies predicting the formation of minimal winning coalitions belong to the first group and follow Riker (1962), Leiserson (1968), and Axelrod (1970). They highlight the costs of broader coalitions where the loss of parliamentary majority is possible through the actions of a larger number of parties. Consequently, such office-driven theories deal primarily with coalition size. On the other hand, policy-driven theories predict policy outcomes that are often consistent with coalitions of different sizes (De Swaan, 1973; McKelvey and Schofield, 1987; Schofield, 1986, 1993; Schofield, Grofman, and Feld, 1988). As far as the third school of research is concerned, it focuses particularly on the constraints that institutions impose on coalition formation (Shepsle, 1979, 1986; Shepsle and Weingast, 1987; Laver and Shepsle, 1990a–c). Finally, the fourth group of studies relates to a voluminous literature dealing with game-theoretic approaches to the composition and durability of coalitions (Dodd, 1976; Franklin and Mackie, 1983; Powell, 1982; Taylor and Herman, 1971).

This chapter is structured as follows: in Section 2, the theoretical hypotheses and their implications are discussed. The methodology, data, estimation, and results are presented in Section 3. Some concluding comments are offered in Section 4.

2   The Underlying Theoretical Hypotheses

In this chapter, we examine the electoral cost imposed on a coalition by its constituent parties. We are interested in operationalizing this cost in terms of votes that the coalition would have obtained under a PR system that it does *not* obtain under a PL system. In other words, we attribute this cost to the switching-voter phenomenon. Ultimately, we wish to estimate the effect of this cost on the probability of winning particular seats. Thus, after constructing an index to represent the magnitude of the switching-voter effect, we wish to estimate its effect on the probability of victory in the PL ballot for each seat.

The switching-voter effect is operationalized by observing the percentage of the vote obtained by the coalition in the PR ballot (x). This is compared with the percentage of the vote obtained by the coalition candidate in the PL ballot (y). If $(x - y)$ is positive, then there is a net switch of coalition support *away* from the coalition candidate. However, if $(x - y)$ is positive, there is a net switch of support *for* the coalition candidate and away from parties of the opposing coalitions. We define this measure, $(x - y)$, to be the switching index and assert that it is a measure of the switching-voter effect.

We expect the effect of this switching index to be negatively related to the probability of victory in the PL ballot in a particular seat. This expectation is the result of several factors. The first factor is the differences in party behavior driven by intra-coalition electoral competition. Parties in a coalition have two ordered objectives, over which their preferences may be considered to be lexicographic. The primary objective is a coalition-focused objective, which consists of achieving a coalition victory in each PL electoral constituency. The secondary objective is a party-focused objective, which consists of minimizing the margin of victory of candidates from *other* coalition parties while attempting to maximize the margin of victory of its own candidates.

Assuming that the intra-coalition game is played non-cooperatively with Nash strategies, we expect that each coalition party will exert maximum effort (and elicit maximum support from its adherents) only when the primary objective of a coalition victory is threatened. This will occur in constituencies where the ex ante belief in a coalition victory is weak. We define such constituencies to be "marginal" constituencies. On the other hand, in constituencies where the ex ante belief in a coalition victory is strong, the primary objective is not in doubt, so the secondary objective determines party behavior. Here parties exert maximum effort (and elicit maximum support from their adherents) only if the candidate in the PL ballot is one of their own. If not, they put virtually all their energies into fighting the PR ballot. We define such constituencies to be "safe" constituencies.

As an example, consider a seat considered, ex ante, to be a "safe" Polo seat. If the coalition candidate is from FI, then the other two coalition parties, the AN and the CCD/CDU would like the margin of victory to be as small as possible, as this will strengthen their position in subsequent seat allocations in local and regional elections. Thus, they work almost exclusively to maximize the coalition's share of the PR ballot, allowing FI to do most of the work for the PL ballot. Not surprisingly, some, and perhaps many AN and CCD/CDU supporters either vote for non-coalition regional or independent parties or abstain in the PL ballot. This ensures that the switching-voter effect is powerful and that the coalition share of the PL ballot is lower than its share of the PR ballot.

If the seat were marginal, we would expect the behavior of the AN and the CCD/CDU to be different, as the coalition victory is in doubt. Thus, they join FI in fighting to maximize the coalition share of both the

PR and the PL ballot. This minimizes the number of AN and CCD/CDU supporters who fail to support the coalition candidate (who is from FI) in the PL ballot. Consequently, the switching-voter effect is small, and the coalition share of the PL ballot and its share of the PR ballot are very close.

The second factor underlying the relationship between the switching index and the probability of victory is based on strategic behavior of voters. Many voters who rank the coalition as their second choice will nonetheless vote for it in marginal constituencies. This will occur if they feel that their first choice has no chance of victory and the victory of their second choice is in doubt. In safe constituencies, however, they feel free to vote for their first choice (which may be a regional or independent party).

Thirdly, voter apathy is likely to play a role. We expect coalition supporters to be far more apathetic in safe constituencies and less so in marginal ones.

All of these effects, which are based on parties' and voters' beliefs about the safety or marginality of a seat, become self-fulfilling as their strategic behavior changes. Thus, the switching index, which reflects these beliefs, is expected to have a negative relationship with the probability of victory in the seat.

3   The Data, Estimation, and Results

The data were obtained from the Italian Electoral Commission. They relate specifically to the electoral performance of the Polo coalition and its constituent parties, along with overall performance of the opposing Ulivo coalition. The analysis is therefore carried out for the constituent parties of the Polo coalition.

We attempt to estimate the relationship between the switching index and the probability of victory. The analysis is carried out from the perspective of the Center-Right coalition Polo. Hence, the probability of victory here is that of the Center-Right candidates in the PL ballot. The analysis from the perspective of the Center-Left coalition Ulivo, could be carried out in a like manner.

We expect the relationship to be affected by turnout and incumbency, so we normalize for these factors. The estimated equation is

$$P(\text{Victory}) = f(\text{Switching Index, Turnout, Incumbency dummy}) \qquad (1)$$

A few words about the variables used are in order. The probability of victory is a latent variable that is not observed. What we observe is victory or defeat of the Polo candidate in each PL constituency. Therefore (1) is estimated using a latent (or limited) dependent variable tech-

Table 1. *Sicilian National Election Data, 1996:*
Summary Statistics

Variable	N	Mean	Std. Dev.
Switching index	474	-1.7808	3.8430
W	474	0.3565	0.4794
Turnout (%)	474	83.026	8.0686
Vote share (%)			
Polo	474	42.704	9.6259
Ulivo	474	41.360	10.188
Incumbent party dummy	474	0.3270	0.4696

nique. The appropriate technique in this case is binomial probit. The dependent variable is therefore written as:

$$W = 0 \quad \text{Polo defeat} \tag{2}$$
$$W = 1 \quad \text{Polo victory}$$

The switching index has already been described above. Turnout is expressed as a percentage. The incumbency dummy relates to the party, rather than the individual candidate. Thus, it takes the value 1 if the current elected representative in the constituency is from the same party as the current Polo candidate and 0 otherwise.

Finally, we note that binomial probit estimators work best in situations where the normal approximation to the binomial distribution is good. This approximation is best when the probability parameter "p" (the probability of victory, in our case) takes the value of 0.5. As p diverges away from 0.5, as it would in safe constituencies for both co-alitions, the variances of the conditional distributions become smaller. The problem of heteroskedasticity appears and the estimators become inefficient.

When we examine the OLS estimates in Table 2, we note that the Breusch-Pagan test is failed, lending support to our suspicion of the presence of heteroskedasticity. We deal with this problem by obtaining weighted least squares and weighted probit estimates. The source of the problem is the varying degrees of safety of the seats from the perspective of Polo, since it is the probability of Polo victory that is the dependent variable. We generate weights by constructing a proxy for the safety of each seat from the perspective of Polo. This proxy is the normalized difference of the proportions of the vote going to Polo and Ulivo respectively. The normalization is carried out using a two sample difference-of-means procedure. These weights are denoted by "z". Since het-

Table 2. *Estimating the Probability of Victory:*
OLS and Probit Results

OLS	
Constant	0.9009 (3.70)[a]
Switching index	−0.0043 (0.72)
Turnout	−0.0074 (2.58)
Incumbent party dummy	0.1812 (3.89)
R^2(Adj)	0.5441
Log-likelihood	!308.8973
ANOVA: F (3, 470)	10.0723
Amemiya PC	0.2192
Breusch-Pagan $\chi^5(3)^b$; p value	158.772 (0.000)

Probit			
Constant	1.1023 (1.65)		
Switching index	−0.0128 (0.78)		
Turnout	−0.0201 (2.56)		
Incumbent party dummy	0.4826 (3.77)		
Log-likelihood	−294.4483		
Restricted log-likelihood ($\beta = 0$)	−308.7643		
Likelihood ratio test: $\chi^5(3)$	28.6319		
(p value)	(0.000)		
Probit prediction matrix	*Predicted*		
	Losses	Wins	Total
Actual Losses	274	31	305
Actual Wins	128	41	169
Total	402	72	474

Note: Regressand: Binary variable: $W = 0$ (Polo defeat); $W = 1$ (Polo victory).
[a] Standard "t" statistics in parentheses.
[b] The Breusch-Pagan (1979) test for heteroskedasticity.

eroskedasticity is a quadratic problem (and because it becomes severe in both tails of the distribution), we use z^2 as the weighting variable.

Summary statistics regarding the variables used as presented in Table 1. The unweighted OLS and probit results are presented in Table 2. The weighted OLS and probit results are presented in Table 3. Examining the Breusch-Pagan results, it is seen that the weighting solves the heteroskedasticity problem. The fit of the equation improves and the explanatory power of the variables becomes substantially better, as seen from the probit prediction matrix.

We focus our attention on the results in Table 3. We find that the switching index has a strongly significant negative effect on the probability of victory, supporting the predictions of the theory. Interestingly,

Table 3. *Estimating the Probability of Victory: Weighted OLS and Weighted Probit Results*

Weighted OLS (Wts = z^2)	
Constant	1.8962 (9.33)[a]
Switching index	−0.0163 (4.74)
Turnout	−0.0197 (8.46)
Incumbent party dummy	0.4496 (11.36)
R^2(Adj)	0.5592
Log-likelihood	−133.1192
ANOVA: F (3, 470)	201.0479
Amemiya PC	0.1044
Breusch-Pagan $\chi^2(3)^b$; p value	4.9965 (0.172)

Weighted Probit (Wts = z^2)	
Constant	5.0723 (5.51)
Switching Index	−0.0626 (3.88)
Turnout	−0.0713 (6.59)
Incumbent party dummy	1.4877 (8.20)
Log-likelihood	−160.6090
Restricted log-likelihood ($\beta = 0$)	−308.7643
Likelihood ratio test: $\chi^2(3)$	296.3106
(p value)	(0.000)

Probit prediction matrix		*Predicted*		
		Losses	Wins	Total
	Losses	201	104	305
Actual	Wins	81	88	169
	Total	282	192	474

Note: Regressand: Binary variable: $W = 0$ (Polo defeat); $W = 1$ (Polo victory).
[a] Standard "t" statistics in parentheses.
[b] The Breusch-Pagan (1979) test for heteroskedasticity.

the turnout is negatively related to probability of a Polo victory; the effect is statistically significant and is in line with much of the literature that suggests that a higher turnout tends to benefit the Left. Finally, we also find a strong and statistically significant effect emanating from the incumbency dummy. Again, this is in agreement with much of the literature, which stresses the advantages of incumbency.

4   Concluding Remarks

The introduction of new rules regulating the electoral market is likely to affect both the electoral strategies of politicians and the electoral behavior of voters. In this chapter we have dealt with the impact of the new Italian electoral rules governing the elections to the Chamber of Deputies. These rules are largely based on the principle of plurality (PL) with three-quarters of the seats being assigned on the basis of races in single-member constituencies. However, elements of the old system have been retained in that proportional representation (PR) is used to allocate the remaining quarter.

These rules are operationalized using a two-ballot system. Each voter is given a PL ballot to exercise in his or her single-member constituency and a PR ballot to exercise in a large multi-member constituency. Voters are therefore given the opportunity to express a preference for a party in the PR ballot and for a candidate in the PL ballot. They are able to express split preferences by voting for their chosen party's coalition in the PR ballot but not for that coalition's (party) candidate in the PL ballot.

In this study, we have two objectives. First, we are interested in measuring the electoral costs imposed on political coalitions by constituent parties. We posit that this cost appears through the phenomenon of split preference voting, since voters can support their party in the PR ballot but express disapproval of other parties' candidates (in the same coalition) in the PL ballot. We constructed an index operationalizing the electoral cost imposed by individual parties on the coalition in terms of the extent of split-preference voting.

Second, we studied the electoral strategies implemented by the competing coalitions seeking to maximize their chances of electoral success. This was done by estimating the relationship between the index measuring the extent of split-preference voting and the probability of victory in each constituency. We found a strong negative relationship between these variables. This result gave support for the hypothesis that parties in a coalition have two ordered objectives. The primary one is a coalition-focused objective that consists in achieving a coalition victory in each single-member constituency. The secondary objective is a party-focused objective consisting of minimizing the margin of victory of candidates from other coalition parties while attempting to maximize the margin of victory of its own candidate.

Our results have implications that are both practical and theoretical. In practical terms, estimating the electoral cost of individual parties on a coalition can be used to plan an optimal locational distribution of party candidates in single-member constituencies in future elections. Coalitions can therefore use this concept to refine their appeal to the electorate.

From a theoretical point of view, there are three main implications. First, coalition bargaining under the new rules occurs at the level of the single-member constituency rather than in the legislature, as was the case under the old PR system. Second, there is an underlying conflict between political parties joining political coalitions. In the pursuit of their electoral objectives these parties will be increasingly characterized by intra-coalition conflict. Third, coalitions are often composed of heterogeneous parties that have joined together for purely electoral purposes with significant differences in their political platforms. This possibility leads one to conjecture that such coalitions are likely to be unstable. Further, one would expect significant links to develop between parties of opposing coalitions in inter-election periods.

References

Axelrod, R. 1970. *Conflict of Interest: A Theory of Divergent Goals with Applications to Politics*. Chicago: Markham.

Breusch, T., and Pagan, A. 1979. "A Simple Test for Heteroskedasticity and Random Coefficient Variation." *Econometrica*, 47: 1287–94.

Budge, I., Robertson, D., and Hearl, D. eds. 1987. *Ideology, Strategy and Party Change: Spatial Analyses of Post-War Election Programmes in 10 Democracies*. Cambridge: Cambridge University Press.

De Swaan, A. 1973. *Coalition Theories and Cabinet Formations*. Amsterdam: Elsevier.

Dodd, L. C. 1976. *Coalitions in Parliamentary Government*. Princeton, N.J.: Princeton University Press.

Donovan, M. 1995. "The Politics of Electoral Reform in Italy." *International Political Science Review*, 16: 47–64.

Franklin, M. N., and Mackie, T. T. 1983. "Familiarity and Inertia in the Formation of Governing Coalitions in Modern Democracies." *British Journal of Political Science*, 13 (July): 275–98.

Hine, R. 1993. "The New Italian Electoral System." *Association for the Study of Modern Italy, Newsletter*, 24: 46–64.

King, G., Alt, J. E., Burns, N. E., and Laver, M. 1990. "A Unified Model of Cabinet Dissolution in Parliamentary Democracies." *American Journal of Political Science*, 34 (August): 846–71.

Laver, M., and Schofield, N. 1990. *Multiparty Government: The Politics of Coalition in Europe*. New York and Oxford: Oxford University Press.

Laver, M., and Shepsle, K. A. 1990a. "Coalitions and Cabinet Government." *American Political Science Review*, 84 (September): 873–90.

1990b. "Government Coalitions and Intraparty Politics." *British Journal of Political Science*, 20 (October): 485–507.

1990c. The Size Principle and Minority Cabinets. Presented at the Conference in Honor of William H. Riker, University of Rochester, October 12–13.

Leiserson, M. 1968. "Factions and Coalitions in One-Party Japan: An Interpretation Based on the Theory of Games." *American Political Science Review*, 69 (September): 770–87.

McKelvey, R. D., and Schofield, N. 1987. "Generalized Symmetry Conditions at a Core Point." *Econometrica*, 55 (July): 923–33.

Mershon, C. 1996. "The Cost of Coalition: Coalition Theories and Italian Governments." *American Political Science Review*, 90 (September): 534–54.

Navarra, P. Forthcoming. "Voting Diversification Strategy in Italian National Elections: An Explanatory Note." *Economic Notes.*

Navarra, P., and Lignana, D. 1997. "The Italian Left: Strategic Behaviour in a Risk-sharing Framework." *Public Choice,* 93: 131–48.

Powell, G. B., Jr. 1982. *Contemporary Democracies: Participation, Stability and Violence.* Cambridge, Mass.: Harvard University Press.

Riker, W. H. 1962. *The Theory of Political Coalitions.* New Haven, Conn.: Yale University Press.

Schofield, N. 1986. "Existence of a 'Structurally Stable' Equilibrium for a Non-collegial Voting Rule." *Public Choice,* 51(3): 267–84.

1993. "Political Competition and Multiparty Coalition Government." *European Journal of Political Research,* 23 (January): 1–33.

Schofield, N., Grofman, B., and Feld, S. L. 1988. "The Core and Stability of Group Choice in Spatial Voting Games." *American Political Science Review,* 82 (March): 195–211.

Shepsle, K. A. 1979. "Institutional Arrangements and Equilibrium in Multi-dimensional Voting Models." *American Journal of Political Science,* 23 (February): 27–59.

1986. "Institutional Equilibrium and Equilibrium Institutions." In H. F. Weisberg, ed., *Political Science: The Science of Politics.* New York: Agathon.

Shepsle, K. A., and Weingast, B. R. 1987. "The Institutional Foundation of Committee Power." *American Political Science Review,* 81 (March): 85–104.

Strom, K. 1990. *Minority Government and Majority Rule.* Cambridge: Cambridge University Press.

Taylor, M., and Herman, V. 1971. "Party System and Government Stability." *American Political Science Review,* 65 (March): 28–37.

CHAPTER 11

A Model of Two-Party Campaigns in Pluralistic Elections with Evidence

Chris W. Paul II and Allen W. Wilhite

Perhaps no issue is as central to the functioning of modern democratic institutions and guarantees of representation as the rules by which representatives are elected. In this respect, despite the variety of alternative election mechanisms, plurality is the predominant rule in modern democracies. "One of the consequences of using plurality rule is that it leads the outcome to a two-party system. This empirical result is known as Duverger's Law" (Levin and Nalebuff, 1995, p. 7). Consequently, elections in modern democracies usually involve a two-candidate campaign. This study develops a model of the strategic decisions faced by candidates in these campaigns. While building on previous models that address the effect of the rent magnitude, opponent spending, and third-party contributions, this model incorporates the effect of variations in candidate attributes. Specific attributes modeled are an election bias, seat bias, the political price of contributions, and the ability to convert campaign funds to personal use. The primary strategic variable is the candidate's campaign spending; however, the related issues of optimal contributions and converting contributions to personal use are also treated. A change in U.S. election law created a natural experiment that allows the theoretical implications of the model to be tested with data from U.S. congressional elections. However, the results are generally applicable to other plurality systems.

Buchanan (1980) identifies the expenditure of resources to capture political office in order to receive payments from others as a form of rent seeking. However, while discussions of rent-seeking behavior appear in empirical studies of campaign contributions (Crain, Shugart, and Tollison, 1988; Wilhite and Paul, 1989), an explicit theoretical model of its implications has not been previously presented. Since campaigning for a political office involves an expenditure of resources for the purpose of capturing an existing prize, it fits the strategic rent-seeking game form offered by Tullock (1980) and Rogerson (1982). Note that this formulation is essentially a single-contest tournament model with two players and a winner-takes-all prize. While the rent-seeking game form is applied, there are no claims concerning the level of rent dissipation and resulting social costs (see Ricketts, 1987).

Existing theoretical models of campaign behavior (Stigler, 1972; Kau, Keenan, and Rubin, 1982; Bender, 1986) are developed from a wealth- or utility-maximizing perspective.[1] While the present study assumes candidates are rational wealth maximizers, they are placed in a strategic rent-seeking environment. The strategic nature of a two-person rent-seeking game allows the formation of an explicit decision calculus for each candidate. By modeling a broadened set of attributes and activities a more general model emerges that replicates previous results and leads to new insights.

I   A Theoretic Model of the Political Campaign

Tullock (1980) and Rogerson (1982) presented a model of strategic rent seeking in which two identical players, X and Y, are buying lottery chances. Player X's purchases, x, relative to the total tickets held by both players, $x + y$, determine his probability of winning the prize, R. Player X's optimal strategy involves maximizing the expected value of playing; $E(z)$ for candidate X is

$$E(z_x) = \frac{x}{x + y}(R - x) + \frac{y}{x + y}(-x). \tag{1}$$

Y's optimal strategy involves the same process. Tullock derives reaction functions for each player and a Cournot-Nash-like equilibrium for the game. He also explores the ramifications of additional players, different functional forms, and bias.

The application of this framework to political campaigns is intuitively appealing. Campaigns are competitive games in which two or more candidates invest resources with the objective of increasing their probability of winning the contest. Measuring the effort or resources expended by two identical candidates as x and y, the probability of candidate X winning an election is $x/(x + y)$ and a strategy focusing on the expected value of running for office yields equation (1).

Paul and Wilhite (1990) offer a simple campaign model based on Tullock's structure by recognizing the role of contributions from self-interest-motivated third parties. Their thesis is that candidates must provide some quid pro quo for contributions. Specifically, political

---

[1] Stigler (1972) views candidates and voters as balancing the costs and benefits of actions; Kau, Keenan, and Rubin (1982) suggest candidates maximize the probability of being elected by balancing the desire of contributors and voters; and Bender's (1984) capital theory approach employs the supply and demand apparatus.

promises or assurances, which we will call political "I owe you's" (IOUs), are granted to contributors in return for their support. These IOUs can take many forms: vague promises of being pro-family or anti-Communist, specific legislation, or an understanding of accessibility (Sabato, 1984). Regardless of form, this exchange involves a contribution in return for some activity by the candidate if elected. Hence, contributions impose costs because they restrict the political latitude or choice set of the elected candidate, reducing the office's net or residual value. As a wealth maximizer the candidate's objective function is the maximization of the office's residual value.

Note the conditional nature of these political IOUs. If a candidate wins, the promise extended to contributors is valid and is paid by the legislator. If the candidate loses, the promise is void. This leads to an asymmetric cost structure, which changes the game's solution. The expected value to candidate X in this regime is

$$E(z_x) = \frac{x}{x+y}(R-x) - 0. \tag{2}$$

Because contributors purchase conditional IOUs, the second term is zero. The reduced cost of losing results in higher levels of campaign expenditures, increasing the resource expenditures relative to Tullock's simple lottery.

As candidates differ in numerous ways, several amendments are incorporated into the Paul and Wilhite (1990) model. One difference is the candidate's effectiveness at changing or protecting the existing allocation of property rights or the status quo. Contributors can be thought of either as seeking rents through the reallocation of existing property rights or defending rents by protecting the existing property rights allocation. See Paul and Wilhite (1991) for a discussion of rent-seeking and rent-defending behaviors. It is the ability to effect or resist marginal changes in the allocation of property rights that creates the seat's rent value. Thus, a candidate can possess a rent or seat bias as a result of the candidate's position in the law-making body. Thus, seat bias is a measure of post-election political power. An increase in a candidate's political power yields an advantage in at least two ways. One, it reduces the cost of contributions by increasing the probability that the policies favored by the contributor will be successfully advanced. Two, it provides a larger rent to exchange for contributions.

To incorporate both of these advantages of political power two variables are incorporated into the model. First, the difference in the value of the seat across candidates is modeled by the inclusion of a rent bias term. The value of winning the seat is elevated for incumbents with greater seniority who occupy positions of power, such as committee chairs and party leaders. A rent bias, r, is added to the model as a scalar on the rent value at stake for candidate X. If $r > 1$, X receives a higher value from winning the seat, $r < 1$ if Y has the rent bias in his favor, and when $r = 1$ there is no bias.[2] Second, to allow for the cost of political IOUs to vary across candidates and contributors, a price vector is included. The candidate's expenditure of his own funds is assigned a price of unity, and prices of other contributions are measured relative to that cost. If contributions are less onerous than the candidate's own resources, $p < 1$. The price reflects the degree to which the candidate's political latitude is constrained by the specific political promise.

To allow each candidate to possess different campaigning capabilities an election bias, labeled e, is added to the model. The election bias may be interpreted as either a capital or technology measure. A primary distinction between candidates is their initial endowment of political capital. Examples of political capital include name recognition and voters' predisposition toward the candidate's reputation. Interpreted as a technology variable it measures a candidate's relative ability to communicate political messages that increase net political support. This difference in candidates leads to a bias in spending effectiveness, similar to a production efficiency. This election bias term is included as a scalar to X's spending. If $e > 1$, X possesses the election advantage, $e < 1$ signifies that Y possesses an advantage; and if $e = 1$, the candidates possess equal amounts of political capital.

The assumption that all resources employed in campaigning arise from contributions is dropped. In this formulation, a candidate may apply his own resources to the campaign. This alternative source of funding enters the model through the addition of a parameter, α, the proportion of spending collected from contributors. As before, contributions are traded for IOUs which are honored only if the candidate wins, but the candidate's own resources are lost regardless of the election's outcome. Including the possibility of a candidate using his own resources in the campaign changes the cost of losing the election. The second term on the right-hand side of equation (2) is no longer zero. When candidates contribute to their campaign and lose, these resources are lost. The second term then reflects the probability of losing the election times the amount of the candidate's own resources invested in the effort.[3]

Including these considerations in the candidates' decision calculus, the expected value of campaign expenditures for candidate X becomes

$$E(z_x) = \frac{ex}{ex + y}(rR - p\alpha x - (1 - \alpha)x) + \frac{y}{ex + y}(-(1 - \alpha)x). \tag{3}$$

[2] To simplify some of the algebra, e and r are assumed ≥ 1 so candidate X is defined as the "advantaged" candidate.

[3] The largest own-cost is probably the opportunity cost of time spent stumping.

The first term on the right-hand side of equation (3) consists of the probability of winning the election, the relative resource commitments of each candidate and the bias accompanying the efforts times the value of the elected office. The post-election value of the office consists of the initial rent including any office bias, minus the price of contributions times their size, minus the value of the candidate's own resources.

Similarly, the expected value of spending by candidate Y equals

$$E(z_y) = \frac{y}{ex+y}(R - p\alpha y - (1-\alpha)y) + \frac{ex}{ex+y}(-(1-\alpha)y). \quad (4)$$

Maximizing equations (3) and (4) yields the optimal expenditures, x^* and y^*, for candidates X and Y:

$$x^* = \frac{-y(1-\alpha+p\alpha) + \sqrt{(1-\alpha+p\alpha)(p\alpha y^2 + eyrR)}}{e(1-\alpha+p\alpha)} \quad (5)$$

and

$$y^* = \frac{-ex(1-\alpha+p\alpha) + \sqrt{p\alpha e^2 x^2 + exR}}{(1-\alpha+p\alpha)} \quad (6)$$

Candidate X's optimal campaign spending strategy depends on the spending of candidate Y, the rent value of the office, bias terms e and r, and the political cost of contributions and resulting proportion of spending paid by the candidate. Candidate Y is affected similarly.

The derivatives of these reaction functions predict relationships that are amenable to empirical testing. For example, the first derivative of x^* with respect to y, $\delta x^*/\delta y$, is positive as is $\delta y^*/\delta x$. Candidates increase their spending in response to increased spending by their opponents. This result is the well known, in the tournament literature it is called the "rat race." The rent value, R, and rent bias, r, are both positively related to X's effort, $\delta x^*/\delta R > 0$ and $\delta x^*/\delta r > 0$.

For the election bias, e, $\delta x^*/\delta e > 0$, $\delta y^*/\delta e < 0$. As a candidate gains an election bias, he decreases campaign efforts. Conversely, the opponent increases his effort in an attempt to overcome the disadvantage. The second derivatives, $\delta^2 x/\delta e^2$ and $\delta^2 y/\delta e^2$, are both negative indicating diminishing returns.[4]

The price of contributions' relationship to spending and the proportion of personal funds expended leads to several interesting hypotheses. One, $\delta x^*/\delta p$ and $\delta y^*/\delta p$ are both negative. As contributions become more costly, requiring more restrictive political promises, total spending declines. This result is analogous to an input price increase reducing output. Two, the price of contributions affects the proportion of the can-

---

[4] Previous theoretical models assume the sign of these derivatives based on the expectation of diminishing returns. This assumption is not necessary in this formulation.

didate's own spending, $(1 - \alpha)$. As the political cost of contributions increases, a larger portion of the candidate's effort will be self-financed. The price vector, $p = (p_1, p_2, \ldots p_i)$, assigns a price to each potential contribution reflecting its cost. The derivative of each specific price with respect to spending is negative, and the proportion of funding from that source declines.[5]

It is useful to distinguish between a candidate's spending decision and his decision to raise money. The right to retain unspent campaign funds means spending and contributions may differ. Defining c as total contributions for candidate X and τ as the proportion of contributions spent, X's spending equals τc and savings equal $(1 - \tau)c$. The expected value of campaign contributions can be described similarly to (3). Specifically,

$$E(c_x) = \frac{e\tau c}{e\tau c + y}(rR - p\alpha c + (1-t)c) + \frac{y}{e\tau c + y}(-1(1-\alpha)\tau c + k(1-\tau)c) \quad (7)$$

The relevant difference between equations (3) and (7) is in the second term. The cost of losing the election is now composed of the probability of losing, $y/(e\tau c + y)$, times the cost of losing, $(1 - \alpha)\tau c + k(1 - \tau)c$, which consists of unspent campaign funds. These funds, $(1 - \tau)c$, times the candidate's ability to capture them, k, determine the value of a losing campaign. If the capture rate is high, candidates can pocket unspent contributions. This results in a difference between contributions and spending levels. With this embellishment, optimal contributions, c^*, equal

$$c^* = \frac{-y\tau(1-\alpha+p\alpha) + \sqrt{(1-\alpha+p\alpha)(p\alpha y^2\tau^2 + eyrR\tau^2 - ky^2r)}}{e\tau(1-\alpha+p\alpha)} \quad (8)$$

The partial derivatives of (8) have the same sign as the derivatives of equation (5). The major difference is the impact of k, the capture parameter. The derivative $\delta c/\delta k$ is positive, while the derivative $\delta x/\delta k$ can not be unambiguously signed. Note, if $k = 0$, equation (8) collapses to (5). In other words, if candidates cannot capture residual funds, the optimal level of contributions equals optimal spending and unspent funds will be zero.

II   An Empirical Test of Campaign Spending and Contributions

Using data from the 1984 congressional elections, the candidate's strategic campaign decisions on the level of campaign spending (SPENDING), the candidate's decision with regard to contributions (TOTFUNDS) and

---

[5] The specification of this price vector yields a useful model for PAC studies and other special interest political contributions from third parties.

retaining contributions for personal use (UNSPENT) are empirically estimated. As the expected coefficients for the independent variables in the SPENDING and TOTFUNDS equations are identical, they will be discussed together. The UNSPENT equation will be discussed later.

The theoretic results offer several empirical predictions. To review, candidate X will increase SPENDING and TOTFUNDS as his opponent increases spending, as his seat bias grows, and as his election bias decreases. Further, the composition of a candidate's campaign funds varies in response to their relative political price. Finally, the candidate's TOTFUNDS are influenced by their ability to capture unspent funds. These relationships are estimated with data from the 1984 U.S. House of Representatives elections.[6]

Of the theoretic determinants of campaign SPENDING, the level of opponent spending (OPMONEY), the proportion of spending from the candidate's own funds (POWN) and the ability to capture funds for personal use (CAPTURE) are directly observable. Proxy measures are employed for the test of rent bias and election bias.

As previously discussed, a candidate's SPENDING and TOTFUNDS are expected to be positively related to the level of OPMONEY. For POWN it should be noted that a candidate's spending of personal funds in his campaign is associated with a lower probability of election. This is true because an increased probability of winning results in IOUs presenting a lower cost alternative and the higher price of campaign funds reflects a poor match of the candidate to the constituency. Contributions impose no cost if the candidate loses; however a candidate's own resource expenditures are lost regardless of the election's outcome. Hence, as the political cost of contributions increases and a larger portion of campaign expenditures consists of POWN, SPENDING, and TOTFUNDS are expected to decline, ceteris paribus.

TOTFUNDS should be affected by the ability to capture unspent funds. This proposition is tested by analyzing the effect of a change in campaign funding legislation. Prior to 1980 representatives were permitted to pocket unspent campaign funds when they retired. In 1980 a law prohibited this practice, but a grandfather clause exempted sitting representatives. As a result, representatives elected before 1981 can turn unspent contributions into retirement income, while representatives elected after 1981 cannot. A dummy variable, CAPTURE, is set equal to one for representatives elected before 1980 to reflect this change. The CAPTURE variable is predicted to possess a positive sign in the

[6] The bulk of the data used in this study are from the Federal Election Commission's *Report on Financial Activity: The 1984 Senate and House Election Cycle.* They are augmented with published data in *Politics in America, 1986.*

TOTFUNDS equation but is indeterminate in the SPENDING equation. Additional insight on the behavior of CAPTURE is given by the UNSPENT equation discussed below.

Rent bias results from the candidate's ability to extract a larger rent from the political office. It is expected to be positively related to the candidate's power in the legislative body upon election. Thus, SPENDING and TOTFUNDS are predicted to be positively related to rent bias. Two proxy measures are used. POWER is a dummy variable set equal to one for representatives holding positions of power: committee chairs, ranking minority members, majority and minority leaders, and the party whips. It is zero otherwise. Years in Congress, TENURE, is used as a second measure of rent bias. Both measures are expected to be positively related to SPENDING and TOTFUNDS. Tenure squared, TENURE2, is included to capture the presents of diminishing returns.

Recall, an increase in a candidate's election bias decreases SPENDING and TOTFUNDS. Two proxy measures are included for the election bias. VOTEGAP, the margin of victory in the last election, and OPEN, a dummy variable for open seat races.[7] VOTEGAP is predicted to be negatively related to SPENDING and TOTFUNDS. The idea is that an increased election spread, a larger majority, is evidence of a greater election bias. OPEN, which carries the opposite implication is expected to be positively related to SPENDING and TOTFUNDS. In open elections the candidates generally will be more closely matched.

The third regression equation measures the impact of these explanatory variables on the unspent campaign contributions, UNSPENT. CAPTURE is the only variable that can be unambiguously signed by the theoretical model. Since OPMONEY is positively related to TOTFUNDS and SPENDING, the net effect on UNSPENT is indeterminate. However, the empirical results for equation (11) yields information on the relative importance of the explanatory variables on SPENDING and TOTFUNDS. Consequently, the UNSPENT equation is of particular interest as it provides insight into the candidate's trade-off or marginal rate of substitution between his desire for political power and direct financial gain.

Empirical Model

Using the derived theoretical results as a guide, SPENDING, TOTFUNDS, and UNSPENT should be affected by the variables given

---

[7] VOTEGAP is calculated as the absolute value of $(v - 0.5)$ where v is the percentage of the vote received by a candidate in the last election. As VOTEGAP increases, the less competitive the election becomes.

in the following equations. The predicted impact on the dependent variable appears in parentheses.

$$\begin{array}{cccc} \text{SPENDING} = f\,(\text{OPMONEY}, & \text{POWER}, & \text{TENURE}, & \text{TENURE2}, \\ (+) & (+) & (+) & (-) \\ \text{VOTEGAP}, & \text{OPEN}, & \text{POWN}, & \text{CAPTURE}) \\ (-) & (+) & (-) & (?) \end{array} \tag{9}$$

$$\begin{array}{cccc} \text{TOTFUNDS} = f\,(\text{OPMONEY}, & \text{POWER}, & \text{TENURE}, & \text{TENURE2}, \\ (+) & (+) & (+) & (-) \\ \text{VOTEGAP}, & \text{OPEN}, & \text{POWN}, & \text{CAPTURE}) \\ (-) & (+) & (-) & (+) \end{array} \tag{10}$$

$$\begin{array}{cccc} \text{UNSPENT} = f\,(\text{OPMONEY}, & \text{POWER}, & \text{TENURE}, & \text{TENURE2}, \\ (?) & (?) & (?) & (?) \\ \text{VOTEGAP}, & \text{OPEN}, & \text{POWN}, & \text{CAPTURE}) \\ (?) & (?) & (?) & (+) \end{array} \tag{11}$$

Empirical Results

The regression results presented in Table 1 are consistent with previous findings. These include Jacobson (1980), Bender (1986), Chappell (1982), Kau, Keenan, and Rubin (1982), Welch (1982), Wilhite (1988), Wilhite and Paul (1989), Wyrick (1994), and Milyo (1997). Reviewing the results for SPENDING and TOTFUNDS, estimation equations (9) and (10), all coefficients, except POWER, possess their expected sign and are statistically significant at the .01 level or better. The R^2 and F-statistics suggest a significant amount of variation is explained. In sum, the model appears to yield valid and statistically useful estimates. There are two possible explanations for the insignificant result for POWER. It may be correlated with TENURE or it may measure an election bias as well as a rent bias, which possess opposite signs.

CAPTURE, which could not be signed a priori in the SPENDING equation, is positive and statistically significant. Candidates who can legally retain unspent contributions for personal use exhibit significantly higher levels of SPENDING. This result may appear counterintuitive. A candidate who can claim residual funds has an incentive to retain contributions. However, winning the election appears to dominate the accumulation of unspent contributions in increasing the candidate's wealth position. However, those candidates that have a high probability of election increase both SPENDING and UNSPENT by elevating TOTFUNDS. Indeed, candidates who qualify to capture campaign funds

Table 1. *1984 U.S. Congressional Election*

	MODEL 1 Equation 9 SPENDING	MODEL 2 Equation 10 TOTFUNDS	MODEL 3 Equation 11 UNSPENT
INTERCEPT	162.109[a]	165.589**	3.480
	(18.489)	(19.312)	(4.877)
OPMONEY	0.369**	0.351**	−0.017*
	(0.034)	(0.036)	(0.009)
POWER	−0.296	21.049	21.345*
	(32.690)	(34.146)	(8.623)
TENURE	19.922**	20.449**	0.526
	(4.193)	(4.380)	(1.106)
TENURE2	−0.601**	−0.623**	−0.022
	(0.116)	(0.121)	(0.030)
VOTEGAP	−517.381**	−450.486**	66.894**
	(55.803)	(58.288)	(14.721)
OPEN	117.931**	123.293**	5.361
	(25.938)	(27.093)	(6.842)
POWN	−178.594**	−209.363**	−30.768*
	(55.390)	(57.857)	(14.612)
CAPTURE	73.232**	97.399**	24.167**
	(28.191)	(29.446)	(7.436)
ADJ-R^2	0.39	0.36	0.18
F-VALUE	64.303	57.798	23.391

[a] Standard errors in parentheses.
* Statistically significant at the 0.05 level with two-tailed test.
** Statistically significant at the 0.01 level or better with two-tailed test.

on average raise more money (approximately $97,000), spend more money (approximately $73,000), and retain more money (approximately $24,000). This suggests that the right to retain contributions for personal use elevates the value of the seat and, hence, the candidates' optimal levels of TOTFUNDS and SPENDING.

Turning to the other variables in the UNSPENT equation, the INTERCEPT, TENURE, TENURE2, and OPEN are all statistically insignificant. As a candidate must have some incentive to collect politically costly contributions and not spend them to generate political support, it is not surprising that the INTERCEPT term and OPEN have mean values that are not statistically different from zero in the UNSPENT equation.

Of the statistically significant variables, OPMONEY and POWN are negatively signed, while POWER and VOTEGAP possess positive coefficients. The negative coefficient on POWN is almost definitional. Using one's own funds precludes the existence of UNSPENT contributions.

The negative sign for OPMONEY and the positive sign on VOTEGAP have the same implication. As competition intensifies, the marginal political cost of UNSPENT funds increases. It appears the candidate prefers to increase his probability of winning over direct increases in personal wealth. This result suggests the rent value of the seat is substantially greater than the resources expended to win it.

The positive sign for POWER in the UNSPENT equation is interesting because it is insignificant in the SPENDING and TOTFUNDS equations. This supports the previous interpretation that POWER proxies both an election bias and a rent bias. POWER reduces the marginal political cost of contributions while increasing the marginal effectiveness of campaign spending.

Finally, reviewing the coefficient signs across equations, note the sign reversals on OPMONEY and VOTEGAP in the UNSPENT equation compared to the SPENDING and TOTFUNDS equations. These variables measure the level or intensity of election competition. As the intensity of competition is elevated, candidates increase spending to remain competitive. The resulting increase in the marginal cost of the reduced probability of winning results in a reduction in UNSPENT funds.

III   Summary and Conclusions

By developing an explicit theoretical model of campaign spending and contributions under the ubiquitous plurality rule we have been able to derive a number of implications for campaign tactics. The resulting construct is a general model that allows the researcher to investigate several questions concerning candidate attributes, election rules, campaign funding, and the value of the contested seat. To test the theoretical results for empirical validity, we were able to take advantage of a natural experiment created by a change in U.S. election laws.

The results of the empirical test confirm the model's predictions and provide additional insight into candidates' trade-off between enhancing their probability of winning the election and directly increasing personal wealth. For example, this is one of the first studies to include the candidates' ability to invest their own resources in the campaign and capture unspent contributions for personal use. Our results suggest that as the need for a candidate's own resources increases, the total level of spending drops. In other words, candidates are more willing to trade political influence for campaign funds than to spend their own money. We also found that candidates whose excess funds can be pocketed tend to raise more money.

Self-interest and wealth maximization provide a useful foundation on which to build models of candidate behavior. However, our results re-emphasize the importance of incorporating institutional arrangements into behavioral models. As democracies formulate the constitutional rules under which elections are held, they should consider the implications for candidates' strategic behavior and the resulting resource costs and policy consequences. By presenting this model of strategic campaign behavior, it is hoped that researchers from other countries will adapt and amend it to the specifics of their system with the result of increasing generality of comparisons.

References

Bender, Bruce. 1986. "The Determinants of Relative Political Campaign Expenditures." *Economic Inquiry*, 24: 231–56.

Buchanan, James. 1980. "Rent-Seeking and Profit Seeking." In James Buchanan, Robert D. Tollison, and Gordon Tullock, eds., *Toward a Theory of Rent-Seeking Society*. College Station: Texas A&M Press.

Chappell, Henry W. 1982. "Campaign Contributions and Congressional Voting: A Simultaneous Probit-Tobit Model." *Review of Economics and Statistics*, 64: 77–83.

Crain, Mark W., William F. Shugart II, and Robert D. Tollison. 1988. "Voters as Investors: A Rent-Seeking Resolution to the Paradox of Voting." In Charles Rowley, Robert Tollison, and Gordon Tullock, eds., *The Political Economy of Rent Seeking*. Boston: Kluwer Academic Publishers.

Jacobson, Gary C. 1980. *Money in Congressional Elections*. New Haven, Conn.: Yale University Press.

Kau, James B., Donald Keenan, and Paul H. Rubin. 1982. "A General Equilibrium Model of Congressional Voting." *Quarterly Journal of Economics*, 97: 271–93.

Levin, Jonathan, and Barry Nalebuff. 1995. "An Introduction to Vote-Counting Schemes." *Journal of Economic Perspectives*, 9: 3–26.

Milyo, Jeffrey. 1997. "The Economics of Political Campaign Finance: FECA and the Puzzle of the Not Very Greedy Grandfathers." *Public Choice*, 93: 245–70.

Paul, Chris, and Al Wilhite. 1990. "Rent Seeking under Varying Cost Structures." *Public Choice*, 64: 279–90.

———. 1991. "Rent-Seeking, Rent-Defending and Rent Dissipation." *Public Choice*, 71: 61–70.

Ricketts, Martin. 1987. "Rent-Seeking, Entrepreneurship, Subjectivism, and Property Rights." *Journal of Institutional and Theoretical Economics*, 143: 457–66.

Rogerson, William P. 1982. "The Social Costs of Monopoly and Regulation: A Game Theoretic Analysis." *Bell Journal of Economics*, 13: 391–401.

Sabato, Larry J. 1984. *Pac Power: Inside the World of Political Action Committees*. New York: W. W. Norton.

Stigler, George J. 1972. "Economic Competition and Political Competition." *Public Choice*, 13: 91–106.

Tullock, Gordon. 1980. "Efficient Rent-Seeking." In J. M. Buchanan, R. D. Tollison, and Gordon Tullock, eds., *Toward a Theory of Rent-Seeking Society*. College Station: Texas A&M Press.

Welch, William P. 1982. "Campaign Contributions and Legislative Voting: Milk Money and Dairy Price Supports." *Western Political Quarterly*, 35: 478–95.

Wilhite, Al. 1988. "Political Parties, Campaign Contributions and Discrimination." *Public Choice*, 58: 259–68.

Wilhite, Al, and Chris Paul. 1989. "Corporate Campaign Contributions and Legislative Voting." *Quarterly Review of Economic and Business*, 29: 73–85.

Wyrick, Thomas. 1994. "House Members as Residual Claimants: Campaign Spending in the 1980s." *Public Choice*, 79: 135–47.

PART III

CONSTITUTIONAL ISSUES FOR A FEDERAL STATE

Constitutional design for a federal state generally focuses on things like the policy jurisdictions of federal subjects, representation in and the authority of the national legislature, the nature of federal and regional courts, and procedures for amending the national constitution. Once these matters are settled, attempts at ensuring stability typically focus on economic matters like tax policy, revenue sharing, trade policy, and regional investment. At both stages, there is an inherent conflict between federal subjects and the national government. One question therefore dominates all others: How do we achieve stable and enforceable rules that guarantee the rights of subjects and allow for the evolution of these rights, and at the same time ensure the authority of the national government?

Filippov and his colleagues argue that the key requirement for stability is the establishment of a set of incentives whereby political elites at one level find it in their self-interest to cooperate and coordinate with elites at all levels. Frey and Eichenberger extend the notion of federalism further by integrating it with genuine political competition. They define and develop the concept of Federally Overlapping and Competing Jurisdictions (FOCJ) and relate it to current developments within Europe.

In Part I, Mueller pointed the importance of institutions as the foundation upon which constitutions, as sets of rules, can function or fail to do so. Here, Forte provides a practical illustration of this insight in the context of the Maastricht excessive deficit rules of the European Union. Schneider and Wagner also examine the practicalities of the European Union federal experiment. Like Filippov and his colleagues, they conclude that the division of power between different levels of government must be such that the incentive structure favors cooperation. In addition, they suggest that elements of direct democracy are an essential requirement that is necessary to break cartels of politicians and special interest groups.

205

CHAPTER 12

Ensuring a Stable Federal State: Economics or Political Institutional Design

*Mikhail Filippov, Peter C. Ordeshook, and
Olga V. Shvetsova*

Federalism is often seen as a partial solution to an array of problems that confound stability and economic growth in democratic states. For continental powers like the United States, Russia, and Australia, the goal is to encourage a rational treatment of public goods and externalities that vary in geographic scope. Federalism in Germany was identified as a way to decentralize power in accord with earlier traditions and to minimize the likelihood that a dictatorship could again subvert its constitutional order. Federalism in India seems the only way to govern a heterogeneous state that will soon be the most populous on the planet. Federal institutions in Russia are essential not only because of geographic diversity and the desire to break with the previous regime's practices of over-centralization, but also to make coherent a situation in which regional authorities cannot be precluded from asserting their autonomy against a weakened central government. And federalism in one form or another is regarded as the only structure that might contend successfully with the ethnic, religious, and linguistic cleavages that bedevil countries like Spain, Ukraine, Nigeria, Belgium, South Africa, and Canada. In fact, it is now commonly agreed that there should be some federal-like decentralization of governmental authority and responsibility even for states that are not explicitly or implicitly federal.[1]

Federalism, though, is not a notably successful governmental form. The ultimate character of American federalism, especially the legitimacy of the supremacy of federal over state law, was determined only through a civil war. Canada's stability remains precarious; Nigerian democracy has failed repeatedly; Spain continues to experience problems with regional separatist sentiments despite constitutional provisions for greater regional autonomy; federalism in Mexico as in much of Latin America is more cosmetic than real; ethnic and linguistic conflicts may

---

[1] See, for example, Bird, Ebel, and Wallich (1996).

207

yet destabilize Ukraine; the Czechoslovak and Yugoslav republics, as well as the USSR, no longer exist; only politicians and bureaucrats in Washington, D.C., and Brussels pretend that Bosnia is a viable state; a truly federal Europe is more promise than reality; and few people would argue that the survival of Russia as a democratic federation is anything but assured.[2]

The purported sources of these failures and difficulties are varied, but more often than not the blame focuses on economic matters – the unequal distribution of income, resources, and economic opportunities across regions, incoherent tax systems, an underdeveloped system of contract law, and a maldistribution of or poorly secured property rights. Recent prescriptions for encouraging political stability in Russia are typical of the advice offered political leaders: "the future of the Russian Federation depends on a well-designed intergovernmental system that matches expenditures and revenues . . . the fiscal system is at the heart of any solution" (Wallich, 1994, p. 249) and "until markets integrate Russian regions and hence locally based political interests, the country will fail to develop . . . a federal system which stimulates economic growth and imposes self-enforcing restrictions on counterproductive discretion of public officials" (Polischuk, 1996).

We are not surprised that for an economist, "political structures are of less importance: what is crucial for him is simply that different levels of decision-making do exist, each of which determines levels of provision of particular public services in response largely to the interests of its geographic constituency" (Oates, 1972) or that when attempting to treat the political-economic transformation of the Soviet Union and Central Europe, "economic reform theorists discounted politics. They focused on inflation, deficit spending, and exchange rates, and considered political issues a distraction" (McFaul, 1995: 87). The explanation for this focus is not simply that economists, armed with purportedly mathematically precise theories, easily succumb to disciplinary blindness. Political elites as well tend to give special emphasis to economic matters. Among other things they are forewarned by the fact that the conflicts that initially threatened the American federation – ostensibly, history's clearest example of a successful democratic federal state – were purely economic in character (national assumption of state debts, along with federal monetary and trade policy), just as the genesis of its civil war lay in arguments over the authority of the national versus state governments and the economic consequences of any resolution of that argument. Generally, in fact,

---

[2] We include Spain and Ukraine in our discussions even though both are constitutionally unitary states and even though the subject of federalism in them is a politically loaded one. Spain, though, already has many institutional features of a federation; and Ukraine's political divisions parallel Belgium's to such an extent that federalism in some form seems a plausible projection of its political-economic future.

the issues that confront political elites directly and which appear to require immediate solution are typically economic in character – balancing a budget, ensuring the collection of taxes, regulating banks, privatizing industries, sorting responsibilities for social welfare programs, and contending with corruption. The problems that, as we argue later, have a political institutional resolution as the only viable long-term solution, manifest themselves today as redistributive and resource allocation issues.

Bolstering this practical emphasis on economic matters is the fact that economic issues more often than not are the basis for justifying federal governmental forms in the first place. Such justifications typically focus on the economic concepts of public goods and externalities and on the argument that just as decentralized markets are thought best for the provision of private goods, some degree of decentralization is seen as best for the regulation of most externalities and for the provision of all but a handful of public goods. A central government may be best equipped to provide national defense, a common currency, and a rationalizable policy of income redistribution. But a vast array of public services such as municipal transportation and land-use regulation, have only limited geographic impact and are best treated locally, where differences in regional needs are best measured. Here decentralized decision making seems optimal. Having thus rationalized federalism with economic arguments about market failure, the efficient regulation of externalities, and the optimal production of public goods, it is only natural that attempts at ensuring stability will focus on those things that appear most directly to thwart efficient economic processes – a tax system that penalizes productive regional development, allocations of jurisdictional authority that empower the central government to regulate things best handled by local authorities and which thwart regional initiative and innovation, a monetary policy that stifles regional investment, a legal infrastructure that precludes coherent contract, antitrust, and labor law, an incoherent or non-existent system of law governing foreign ownership and partnerships, faulty bank regulation, and an income redistribution policy that makes regions wholly subservient to central directive or that encourages disruptive competition among regions.[3]

None of this is to say that political matters and especially the symbolic and seemingly irrational issues associated with ethnicity, religion, language, or race are ignored by those who are concerned with federal design or with political stability. It is an incontrovertible fact that such things have contributed importantly to political instability and even secession.[4] Nigerian democracy fell initially because of tribal rivalries,

[3] See, for example, Claque (1992).
[4] See, for example, Horowitz (1991, 1985); Gleason (1990); Diamond and Plattner (1994); Smith (1995).

pure and simple. Debate continues in Spain, Belgium, and Canada over the autonomy that will be allowed various regions and the ethnic or linguistic groups within them. South Africa's new constitution is premised on the supposition that the most dangerous feature of its society is not only the divide between black and white or rich and poor, but also the tribal divisions within its majority black population. And Ukraine's potential for instability can only be exacerbated by its linguistic and religious divisions. But even here, a properly designed and implemented economic policy is the most often cited solution. Although a recent assessment of Ukraine, for instance, cites the critical nature of its ethnic tensions, the solutions offered focus on defining "the boundary line between the public and private sectors," on establishing a "clear and stable expenditure assignment system," on formulating a rational "assignment of taxes and other revenues" along with "a transparent system of inter-governmental revenues," on reforming "budgetary systems and processes," and on developing "a system of capital financing for sub-national governments" (Martinez-Vazquez, McClure, and Wallace, 1996).

It is also true that in acknowledging the importance of politics, few people argue that economic policy can be depoliticized,[5] or that the constitutional foundations of a federal state designed to establish the rules of political action are unimportant. Anyone concerned with federal stability appreciates the "political" problem shared by all federations – ensuring a balance between the constitutionally sanctioned supremacy of the national government and the autonomy of regional governments – which derives directly from the more general problem of democratic design; namely, that "a government strong enough to protect property rights is also strong enough to confiscate the wealth of its citizens" (Weingast, 1993, p. 287) as well as the converse, that a government too weak to confiscate wealth is also too weak to protect property rights. But even here, as with other things, "proper" economic policy is assumed to be the surest route to maintaining the requisite balance. As a consequence, when things other than economic instruments are considered in the design and operation of a federal state – most notably, those explicitly political things that must be decided when writing a national constitution – the focus falls on some broadly defined topics and a traditional menu of alternatives.[6]

---

[5] However, see Boycko, Shleifer, and Vishny (1995).

[6] Generally, this list includes at least the following: (1) procedures for amending the national constitution; (2) specification of the jurisdictional boundaries of the different levels of government; (3) residual powers clauses; (4) establishment of the supremacy of federal law; (5) the structure of regional representation in the national legislature; (6) provision for special representation of ethnic, religious, or racial minorities in the national legislature; (7) specification of the official state language in linguistically divided

The secondary importance given to such constitutional matters derives from two assumptions. First, any list of commonly cited "federal" constitutional provisions raises the question as to how those provisions are enforced. Although it is commonly assumed that a constitution is the primary expression of federal balance, it is also understood that a constitution cannot by itself be anything more than a "parchment barrier." Absent physical force, why would a regional governor accede to federal law in the event that the courts judge a decision of the governor in violation of that law; why would a regional legislature refrain from passing legislation that explicitly contradicts federal law; and more generally, how can the federal government impose a constitutionally mandated action on a recalcitrant federal subject? In searching, then, for the sources of enforcement and the incentives for compliance, it seems only reasonable to assume that a federation will be stable and its constitution binding if and only if maintaining the federation is sufficiently "profitable" for all relevant decision makers – if the federation's survival is in the self-interest of all relevant decision makers, and if the national government has the resources to sanction noncompliance and reward compliance. The working hypothesis here, then, is that even if constitutions can define the broad outlines of the political "rules of the game," only prosperity and the resources that subsequently adhere to a national government from it can sustain whatever constitutional agreements are first established.

Those who emphasize economic policy when discussing political-economic reform and transitions to democracy, subscribe often to a second and stronger assumption concerning the role of economic forces – specifically, to the view that politics and the ultimate meaning of constitutional provisions are largely the endogenous product of economic interests. This view, understandable to the current generation of reformers trained within the Marxian paradigm, goes further to assert that once economic interests are made compatible with prosperity – once, for instance, society has a tax system or an initial allocation of property rights conducive to economic growth – and once people begin to experience prosperity directly, then reformers will have wide latitude in the political institutions they choose in order to sustain that prosperity and

states; (8) division of powers between the national legislature and chief executive; (9) guarantees of a common market (e.g., guarantees of the obligation of contracts, prohibitions on restrictions of interregional trade); (10) fiscal arrangements with respect to taxation and the allocation of tax instruments to levels of government; (11) income redistribution policies or oversight commissions; (12) mechanisms for the admission of new members to the federation; (13) a specification of the process whereby the boundaries or status of existing members may be changed; (14) the creation of regional judicial systems; (15) provisions for judicial review of intergovernmental disputes; and (16) secession provisions or explicit prohibitions of secession. See Saunders (1995).

its attendant political stability. Thus, as long as a constitutional design is not explicitly inimical to stable democratic process, then the direct implementation of appropriate economic policies will result in the further development of political institutions that are compatible with prosperity and stability.

Up to a point, we do not disagree with this view. But a more theoretically satisfying perspective approaches economic and political reform, along with federal design, in terms of a more explicit search for an equilibrium of economic policy, political institutions, and individual incentives.[7] Here we follow the lead of a handful of scholars who take issue with the view that economics lies at the heart of federal stability, if not political stability generally.[8] Although prosperity might make national and regional elites more conscious of the losses incurred by a disruption of federal relations, neither a jointly shared prosperity nor equality of economic opportunity can eliminate the incentive to acquire power and profit at another's expense or the incentive to undermine or wholly ignore constitutional provisions when immediate self-interest dictates doing so. No economic program, policy, or scheme is immune to political disruption, since the operation of any program, policy, and scheme depends on the distribution of property rights, which the state, with its coercive authority, can redefine. Instead, the solution to the puzzle of enforcement of constitutional restraints, the maintenance of a federal balance, and the adaptability and survival of a federal state must lie in construction of political elite incentives that look beyond mere economic interests. Those incentives may depend importantly on economic interests and circumstances – hence, economic policy must be considered at the same time as we design and implement political structures so that an overall equilibrium is achieved. But to this argument we add the more specific hypothesis that, since in a democracy at least, the ultimate basis of incentives and actions is the way in which political elites win and maintain public office, then at least as much attention needs to be paid to a state's political party system, to its electoral processes, and to the things that determine the character and structure of that system and those processes. The corollary to this argument is the hypothesis that the institutional variables most critical to the character and stability of a federal state are not merely the ones usually discussed in the context of federal design. Representation, the authority of the national legislature, and constitutionally established jurisdictional boundaries are important. But the literature on democracy, parties, and elections tells us that we must also

---

[7] See, for instance, Knight (1992).

[8] For a general statement of this view see Weingast (1993). In addition, see our earlier essays on this subject; specifically Ordeshook and Shvetsova (1995, 1997) and Ordeshook (1996).

consider such variables as the timing of national, regional, and local elections, the consistency of national, regional, and local election laws, the extent to which national and regional charters allow for direct election of a full range of regional public officials (regional governors, vice governors, prosecutors, regional judges, and so on), the frequency of elections, the methods for electing national public officials, the authority of those officials with respect to each other.

The core of our argument, then, is that a democratic federal state that provides some minimal guarantee that economic reforms and policies will serve their intended purpose and that a rationalizable balance between national and regional authority will be maintained requires careful attention to institutional variables that are not normally associated with federal design. Economic policy is important, as are the usual federal constitutional provisions. But equally important are the variables that structure political competition, which, if improperly set, doom a federation to instability, doom any attempt at encouraging stability by the mere manipulation of economic policy, and, in fact, doom most if not all economic programs to irrelevance.

1   The Premise of the Economist's Paradigm

Aside from the economic rationalization for federalism, the assumption that economics lies at the heart of political stability derives from the assumption that money (wealth) is the primary motivation for political as well as economic action, the premise that cooperative social action is least likely to arise when one person's gains necessarily entail someone else's loss, and the corollary that the likelihood of cooperative action increases with the general profitability of that action.

That the assumption with which this premise begins is valid seems self-evident. Anyone familiar with Russia, for example, could hardly fault it, since the quest for money appears to explain nearly all political behaviors, processes, and interests there. The "new Russian" not only populates kiosks and the board rooms of Gazprom and Lukoil, but also the halls of the Kremlin, the Duma, federal ministries, the military, and all regional governmental offices. The sole objection one might raise here is reference to those seemingly economically irrational events occasioned by ethnic, linguistic, religious, or racial conflicts – the Bosnias of the world in which conflict eliminates nearly everything of economic value. There are, though, two defenses of the assumption here. First, as the literature on market failures shows, there is no reason to suppose that individually rational actions yield outcomes that are socially optimal or rational – although we might deem the outcomes of ethnic conflict socially "irrational," such outcomes can easily follow from individually rational choices. Second, although a variety of social variables might appear to "explain" individual actions, those actions, once examined closely, will often reveal a purely private monetary motivation. All of us conduct our day-to-day affairs on the basis of expectations about how others will act, since otherwise it is impossible to guess the consequences of our actions. Those expectations may be based on kinship, formal titles, and prior interactions, but ethnicity, language, religion, and race should be included in any such list. Moreover, the relevance of such things can become a self-fulfilling prophecy and a basis for rational action. If each of us assumes that it is easier to cooperate with those who share, say, our ethnic heritage than with others, we may soon find that such expectations are realized for the simple reason that those who do not share our identities will interact with us as though cooperation is unlikely, whereas those who do will interact as though such cooperation is the natural state of affairs. The result is a clustering of cooperation in the pursuit of purely economic things that reinforces initial expectations about the relevance of "non-economic" variables. Thus, we cannot infer any violation of the first premise from the apparent "explanatory" relevance of a variable like ethnicity or religion with respect to individual actions or the advent of socially inferior outcomes.

The premise itself – that cooperative action is unlikely when circumstances are zero-sum but is more likely as its overall profitability increases – seems equally incontrovertible, since it is now well understood that when resources are finite and fixed, coalitions are not only inherently unstable, but that any coalition which might form will seek to extract as much value as possible from those excluded from the coalition. If the coalitional process is repeated and ongoing, we might see more universalistic forms of cooperation.[9] But if an economy is especially risky and planning horizons are short, such universalistic cooperation will not emerge. Instead, insofar as federations are concerned, what we will observe is a destructive form of bargaining between the center and federal subjects, as the center attempts to buy the compliance of federal subjects and federal subjects compete among themselves for a share of the fixed or shrinking pie. Conversely, if the situation is positive-sum, then not only are stable coalitions possible, but if the potential gains increase sufficiently with the "degree" of cooperation, then a stable coalition can even encompass all relevant decision makers. Thus, the greater the gain, the greater is the incentive to overcome the transaction costs that might preclude cooperation, the greater is the individual and collective effort to ensure the realization of those gains, and the greater is the likelihood that political elites will act to realize those gains.[10]

Without disputing this argument in its entirety, notice that there is still

[9] See, for example, Weingast (1979).
[10] See, for example, Bianco and Bates (1990).

	Comply	Don't comply
Comply	$B - T, B - T$	$B/2 - T, B/2 - P$
Don't comply	$B/2 - P, B/2 - T$	$-P, -P$

Figure 1.

an ambiguity here as to whether economic growth and prosperity are sufficient or merely necessary for stability. Naturally, we are not so fool-hardy as to suggest that democratic political stability can be achieved readily in a stagnant or declining economy. But the preceding argument pertains more to "necessity" than to "sufficiency." That is, economic growth or its potential may be necessary for federal stability, but it need not be sufficient. The particular difficulty lies with the incompleteness of the supposition that the greater the promise of cooperative gain or the greater the threat of economic loss, the greater is the likelihood of coop-eration and compliance. Since the state can undermine any economic program or policy, unless political interests are compatible with the eco-nomic structures sufficient to occasion prosperity, that prosperity will not be realized or will not be sustained. For example, the dissolution of the Soviet Union arguably derived as much from the political calculations of the instigators of dissolution (e.g., Yeltsin's desire to remove Gor-bachev from power, Kravchuk's desire to secure his political position by taking advantage of nationalist sentiment in Ukraine) as from the eco-nomic failings of the Union – failings that were hardly resolved by the USSR's dismemberment and which only magnified the economic plight of its republics.

However, rather than rely on case studies to question the economist's premise, let us examine that premise directly with a review of the apoth-eosis of the problems of collective or cooperative action, the simple two-person Prisoners' Dilemma game. Briefly (and taking an especially narrow and abstract view of the meaning of "stable"), suppose a feder-ation consists of two subjects, suppose that if both "comply" with the federal center by paying their full share of taxes (T), each receives a benefit B. But if one subject unilaterally defects so as to avoid paying T, the benefit afforded each subject declines to $B/2$. Finally, though, suppose that defections are punished in the amount P. Figure 1 portrays this situation and shows that absent any punishment (if $P = 0$), as long as $T < B < 2T$ the situation is a Prisoners' Dilemma in which the dominant choice for both subjects is not to comply even though both prefer (comply, comply) to (don't comply, don't comply). On the other hand, if punishment is sufficiently severe – if $P > T - B/2$ – then complying becomes dominant.

	Comply	Don't comply
Comply	$2(B - T), 2(B - T)$	$2(B/2 - T), 2(B/2) - P$
Don't comply	$2(B/2) - P, 2(B/2 - T)$	$-P, -P$

Figure 2.

	Don't cooperate	Cooperate
Don't cooperate	X_1 X_2	$X_1 + (1 - \alpha)tbX_2$ $X_2 - (1 - \alpha)tX_2(1 - b)$
Cooperate	$X_1(1 - t) + t(1 - \alpha)bX_1$ $X_2 + t_\alpha X_1 + t(1 - \alpha)bX_1$	$X_1(1 - t) + (1 - \alpha)bt(X_1 + X_2)$ $X_2(1 - t) + [t_\alpha + (1 - \alpha)bt][X_1 + X_2]$

Figure 3.

Now suppose the federal government increases the efficiency of its operation and programs. At this point our second premise allows for a number of possibilities. One possibility is simply that B increases, in which case we can see that if the increase is sufficiently great (if $B < 2T$), the Prisoners' Dilemma disappears, and compliance is no longer a problem. But another possibility is for increased efficiency to require increased expenditures – that is, only net benefits increase. Suppose, in particular, that the transformation doubles net benefits so as to yield the game in Figure 2.

Notice now, however, that compliance is assured only if $P > 2T - B$. That is, compliance requires a greater punishment, which is to say that the increased efficiency of the federal government has actually rendered federal stability more difficult to ensure.

To see some other possibilities, suppose federal subject I, $I = 1$ and 2, can generate X_i units of benefit from its own resources, let $X_1 \geq X_2$, and suppose that if neither player cooperates, their respective payoffs correspond to this benefit. Let cooperation entail allowing the national government to tax a region at the rate t, whereupon that government allocates its budget, tX_i or $t(X_1 + X_2)$, between subsidizing the poorer state and the production of some public good that benefits both players in the ratio α and $1 - \alpha$ respectively. Finally, suppose the benefit provided by the national government has a multiplier associated with it so that one unit spent by it on legitimate activities produces b units of benefit to each region. Our two-person game, then, is as shown in Figure 3.

Notice that "don't cooperate" dominates "cooperate" for player 1 (row chooser) as long as $b(1 - \alpha) < 1$. For player 2 (column chooser), if

1 fails to cooperate, then 2 should not cooperate, whereas if 1 cooperates, not cooperating is better than cooperating if $b < 1$. Several conclusions follow from these simple facts:

- First, the preference of the recipient of the resource transfer (column chooser) is unchanged by the magnitude of that transfer: Compliance cannot be bought as long as there is no punishment for non-compliance. The recipient's sole concern in the event that row chooser cooperates is the extent to which the national government produces net benefits from its activities with respect to public goods.
- On the other hand, row chooser never prefers to cooperate if $b(1 - \alpha) < 1$ – if the national government's "productivity," b, is less than 1 after taking its loss from redistributive policies into account. So, if $b(1 - \alpha) < 1$, then the don't cooperate outcome prevails, since column chooser should be able to anticipate row chooser's non-compliance, and act accordingly.
- Finally, suppose a subsidy is given only to the poorer of the two players (say, column chooser), and that non-compliance is punished by a withdrawal of that subsidy (with the central government pocketing the unredistributed resources). In other words, let column chooser's payoff in the lower left cell of Figure 3 be $X_2 + t(1 - \alpha)bX_1$. Then even if row chooser cooperates, column chooser prefers to cooperate only if $b < 1 - \alpha X_1/(1 - \alpha)X_2$. But recall that row chooser cooperates as well only if $b > 1/(1 - \alpha)$, and since simple algebra shows that $1 - \alpha X_1/(1 - \alpha)X_2 > 1/(1 - \alpha)$, the binding constraint for full cooperation remains $b > 1/(1 - \alpha)$. So the condition for full compliance is unchanged if the poorer region is threatened with a withdrawal of the subsidy designed to encourage its cooperation. In other words, with redistribution a possibility, cooperation may not be sustainable even when individual marginal cost of a public good exceeds each participant's marginal gain.

The general conclusion here, then, is that although an increase in productivity can induce cooperation, mere efficiency cannot do so. Specifically, although we might suppose that $b < 1$ corresponds to a corrupt or otherwise inefficient national government, b can be less than one with even an efficient central government. For example, even if $b = 3/4$ so that the overall benefit to society exceeds what the government spends, cooperation remains problematical. That is, absent some system of selective reward or punishment, a federal government that is "merely efficient" will continue to confront the general problem of compliance and cooperation.

This discussion also reveals why federal stability (here in the form of the choice of "compliance" or "cooperation") depends on things other than purely economic matters. First, although the success of a central government's economic development plan may be influenced by t, X_1, and X_2, behavior is most directly effected by b and α (and by P in Figures 1 and 2). But even if we take a narrow economic view of these parameters, their values will be heavily dependent on political things. The parameter b, for instance, is a function not only of "economic" policy – regulating the "right" industries and providing for a budget balanced "optimally" between various categories of spending (all of which is determined by political things) – but also of the degree of corruption that pervades public sector activities. And it goes virtually without saying that α and the structure of punishments and rewards will be determined by things other than utopian economic schemes. In 1995, for instance, Yeltsin sought the support of regional bosses in the upcoming parliamentary and presidential elections not by rewarding compliance with his policies as much as he pursued a federal policy of "rewarding" non-compliance. Direct federal subsidies were not allocated only on the basis of economic need, but also on the basis of the perceived likelihood that doing so would shore up his political support.

The preceding analysis also points to the importance of selective punishments and rewards in ensuring full cooperation and compliance. Absent these punishments, cooperation and compliance require a degree of productivity in the provision of public services that may not be met even though cooperation and compliance are to everyone's benefit – even though acting cooperatively as a federation is uniformly desirable. However, punishment itself, the forms it takes, and the consistency of its application are very much purely political variables. More problematical from the perspective of the purely economic view of federal stability is the fact that since the system of punishment required to avert Prisoners' Dilemma–type situations is itself a public good, there is no reason to suppose, a priori, that that system will be maintained (i.e., supplied optimally): ensuring full cooperation and compliance requires yet another system of punishments to guarantee the operation of the "first-level" punishment system, which, in turn, requires its own punishment system, and so on and so forth, ad infinitum. Put simply, reliance on purely economic instruments merely begs the question of the ultimate source of the incentives for compliance.

2   Equilibrium Selection and Bargaining

A federation that relies on economic punishments and rewards applied by a federal center to sustain itself encounters an additional difficulty in maintaining political stability and prosperity. That problem arises out of the fact that the center must also select which equilibrium to enforce from a multiplicity of alternatives. For example, suppose the national government out of necessity or as a matter of policy cannot provide a public good unless there is full compliance by all federal subjects, and suppose in particular that some program is sustained only if the federal government collects $5 billion in taxes for that purpose. If we suppose further that each of two federal subjects receives $4 billion in benefits from the program, then the program is desirable even though neither subject has an incentive to provide it unilaterally. However, with a reversion of 0 whenever less than $5 billion is collected, the free riding that characterized Figures 1–3 is not an issue – once an equilibrium is achieved in which total tax collections equal $5 billion and no one pays more than $4 billion, neither subject has an incentive to change its actions. Nevertheless, federal subjects will not be indifferent among the alternative equilibria – the outcomes in which the sum of tax collections equals $5 billion – since each prefers that others pay a larger share of the tax burden. That is, efficient equilibria span the entire contract curve, thereby opening the door to bargaining and conflict among federal subjects and between subjects and the federal center.

In fact, the potential for conflictual bargaining may be greater than this example suggests, since bargaining can arise not only over funding, but also over the specifics of production. Notice that to this point we conceptualize public goods in the traditional way – as a good whose consumption benefits accrue to all federal subjects. However, even if goods like national defense, education, and protection of the environment are truly public in *consumption*, they are private in *production*.[11] In providing national defense, someone gets the contract to build each ship or plane to the exclusion of someone else just as in the provision of education, someone pours the concrete for a new school and someone does not. Indeed, there is perhaps no public good that does not confer benefits on some people to the exclusion of others, including the bureaucrats that oversee policy. And once we allow for the private qualities of public goods in production, the conflict and bargaining associated with redistributive politics are easily seen to be an inherent part of any economic policy or program. Put simply, *the emphasis on economic matters in the search for federal political stability necessarily places redistributive issues at the head of the federation's political agenda.*

3   Forms of Federalism

Redistributive issues and the need to choose one equilibrium rather than another pose both theoretical and practical problems for any type of

---

[11] For an elaboration of this argument see Aranson and Ordeshook (1985).

federation, and too easily undermine any advice economists might offer as to how to ensure political stability. For example, in a highly decentralized or voluntary federation (actually, a confederation), if multiple equilibria exist in which different elites prefer different outcomes, there is little theory in the economist's paradigm that allows us to predict with any confidence which equilibrium will ultimately be chosen or whether in fact any equilibrium at all will prevail. There is, then, scant basis for the economist to use his paradigm to predict the ultimate consequences of his advice. At the other extreme, bargaining is no less problematical, with a strong federal center empowered to choose an equilibrium via its constitutionally sanctioned ability to coerce (punish and reward) citizens and federal subjects directly. Even if the center acts as a pure welfare maximizer and prefers only to collect taxes sufficient for an optimal provision of public goods, and even if it is indifferent among equilibrium allocations of costs and the private benefits of production, each federal subject has an incentive not merely to bargain with the federal center, but if possible, to coerce, cajole, and bribe the center in the direction of the equilibria it prefers and in the process, undermine the coherence of any overall plan. Predicting the ultimate consequences of bargaining in this context also lies outside the paradigm of economics.

Between the extremes of a confederation and a federation with an omnipotent center, there are, of course, intermediate possibilities, and we can cluster the alternatives into three broad categories:

- A *confederation* in which the central authority is essentially nonexistent and in which cooperation among federal units, if it occurs at all, occurs because all units find it in their interest to do so. If punishments for noncompliance are imposed, they must be imposed somehow by the federal units themselves. But since punishment itself (or at least its consequence) is a public good, it is unlikely to be optimally supplied.
- A *strong federation* in which, in addition to the N federal subjects, there is an $N + 1$th player empowered to punish noncompliance and to reward compliance. However, as Figure 3 shows, there may be many potentially efficient outcomes, and in this instance it is this $N + 1$th player who is empowered to choose the eventual outcome.
- A *weak federation* in which this $N + 1$th player, although empowered to punish, is not so powerful as to be able to choose unilaterally the outcome that will be enforced. Instead, federal subjects themselves choose that outcome.

Those who would emphasize economic policy as the path to federal stability are often torn between the last two extremes. A strong federation may best be equipped to implement the coercion necessary to avert disruptive bargaining, and in such a federation the consequences of an economic plan may be most easily predicted. But the very authority to coerce threatens democracy. Conversely, a weak federation seems more democratic, but it threatens the coherence of the policies economists deem necessary for prosperity and stability.

It is worth noting at this point that it is the third type of federation – a weak one – that the framers of the U.S. Constitution sought to establish. Although they provided for a president elected independently of the national legislature, there are two things to remember about that office. First, the selection of presidential electors – those who would actually cast ballots for one candidate or another – were to be selected in accordance with rules established by state governments. Second, the presidency itself was a constitutionally weak office – most powers resided in the national legislature, which implicitly in the case of the House and explicitly in the case of the Senate represented the individual states. It was there, they assumed, that the eventual outcome would be chosen, since it would be the legislature that would oversee the application of punishments and rewards imposed by the executive and judicial branches of the national government. The same choice of a weak federation was intended for Germany as well. The German chancellor may be the undisputed head of government, but he is appointed by a Bundestag that implicitly (in the single-member constituencies) and explicitly (via regional party lists) represents the *Länder*. Conversely, owing to the constitutional authority of its president (especially the authority to override or suspend regional administrative acts he alone deems unconstitutional and to issue decrees that do not contravene existing laws), Yeltsin clearly intended that the Russian Federation be a strong one in which the Kremlin alone decides which outcomes to seek and which to avoid.

Of these two forms, we feel more comfortable with the weaker one. Even if the more unitary state implied by a strong federation is better equipped to guide a transition to a market economy and to resolve the conflicts among federal subjects likely to arise when a federation is first formed, the danger to democracy itself is great here and it is difficult to see, once the transition is complete, how to move back to a weaker federation. Nevertheless, for reasons we have already outlined, the fear that a weak center will succumb to inter-sectional disputes or that its weakness will keep it from being able to ensure efficient market mechanisms cannot be dismissed out of hand. In fact, as long as the system of reward and punishment required to ensure cooperation and compliance are presumed to be the legitimate domain of the national government and as long as they are presumed to be primarily economic in nature – as long as they are presumed to entail such things as withholding or releasing subsidies for one federal subject or another, enforcing tax laws more strongly in some regions than in others, and favoring one region's industry as opposed to another's by federal tariff and trade policies – it is difficult to argue against the proposition that some version of a strong federation is required for efficiency and stability.

Here, though, we want to change the basis for choosing between weak and strong forms of federalism by more carefully examining the actors, incentives, and rewards of politicians themselves – of those with the power to use the coercive authority of the state to undermine or to reinforce any economic plan – so that we can argue that an effective decentralized system of reward and punishment can be established within the confines of a federation that does not threaten democracy.

4   Political Parties and Incentives

Our argument begins by setting forth a series of general requirements that guide our design of a mechanism for ensuring federal political stability, the first of which is the following:

Requirement 1 *Any system of reward and punishment designed to ensure federal stability should apply not to individual citizens, but to political elites since it is they, even in a democracy, who coordinate and lead a society to one equilibrium or another.*

We will, of course, be concerned later with voters and other political and economic decision-makers, but Requirement 1 focuses our attention on those who hold the coercive powers of the state. Indeed, this requirement and the fact that we are interested here only in designing a *democratic* federation, implies that *to the extent that political elites in a democracy have winning and maintaining office as their primary goal, the rules under which they do so have a direct impact on their actions, including their incentives to reach accommodating solutions to interregional and intergovernmental disputes.* However, before we pursue this argument more thoroughly, note first that our earlier discussion of the Prisoners' Dilemma and the inherent nature of bargaining in a federation highlight the fact that the goal of designing a federation in which political elites have an incentive to reach "accommodating solutions" is especially acute when speaking of regional political elites. It is they, after all, who directly respond to the incentives that otherwise establish Prisoners' Dilemma–type incentives in a federation. That is:

Requirement 2 *Federal stability requires a mechanism whereby local and regional political elites have little or no incentive to act non-cooperatively.*

Even when their election campaigns are based on purely regional issues such as a candidate's relative competence at regional management, local and regional political actors will find it difficult to resist "playing" the Prisoners' Dilemma by adding some promise in a campaign to wrestle more for their election district from the center or by displaying independence from the center when it is in their district's immediate self-interest to do so. In stable federations, such "electoral bargaining" between the national government and federal subjects usually takes a benign form, but at other times and in otherwise vulnerable federations it can threaten a federation's very stability, as when it leads to calls for secession and civil war. But even the intermediate responses of merely failing to comply fully with federal law and the edicts of a federal judiciary threaten, if not stability, at least the economic prosperity that depends on the fully coordinated implementation of that law.

A variety of institutional devices have been used in the attempt to accommodate Requirement 2. One is to mute the regional ties of political elites with national party-list proportional representation (PR) so that legislators are not tied to specific election districts and a specific geographic constituency. But these devices undermine an essential component of a federal system – direct federal subject representation in the national government. Thus, federal states like Germany and Russia seek a compromise between representation and Requirement 2 by mixing single-member districts with some form of nationally based proportional representation in the composition of their national legislature. Another device more traditional in Russia is to have regional administrators appointed by a central authority. This approach, though, threatens giving the national government the aura of an occupying army in each region, and it wholly undermines, even dissolves, the federal character of the state. In fact, both PR and direct appointment violate a third requirement:

Requirement 3 *Any mechanism that encourages federal stability must create political (office-related) rewards for national elites that dissuade them from overstepping their constitutionally legitimate authority.*

We appreciate that "constitutionally legitimate" is vague and that its very definition is often the source of conflict in a federation. Hence, our last requirement:

Requirement 4 *Federal stability requires a mechanism whereby the fates of regional and national political elites depend on the extent to which they achieve some consensus over the definition of 'constitutionally legitimate.'*

For the reasons we have outlined, we cannot look to economic policy alone in the search for a mechanism that satisfies our four requirements. Nor can we look to additional constitutional provisions, since doing so begs the question of enforcement. Instead, taking our cue from our first requirement, we look to a critically important extra-constitutional component of a democracy, federal or otherwise – its political party system – so as to consider the hypothesis that in a federation at least parties are the key to understanding the incentives for cooperation and compliance.

The supposition that parties are not only critically important to the functioning of the democratic state, but that they are especially important in maintaining a balance within a federation begins with Schattschneider's assertion (1942, p. 1) that "political parties created democracy and . . . modern democracy is unthinkable save in terms of parties," as well as Hofstader's observation (1969, pp. 70–1) with respect to the American constitutional order that "the balance of social interests, the separation and balance of powers, were meant to secure liberty, but it was still uncertain, after the instrument had been framed and ratified, whether the balance would not be too precarious to come to rest anywhere . . . [so] in a country which was always to be in need of the cohesive force of institutions, the national parties, for all their faults, were to become at an early hour primary and necessary parts of the machinery of government, essential vehicles to convey men's loyalties to the State." Finally, we have Riker's observation (1964, p. 136) that "whatever the general social conditions, if any, that sustain the federal bargain, there is one institutional condition that controls the nature of the bargain in all instances here examined and in all others with which I am familiar. This is the structure of the party system, which may be regarded as the main variable intervening between the background social conditions and the specific nature of the federal bargain."

These views all highlight the importance of parties as *the* extra constitutional mechanism for realizing a smoothly functioning democracy as well as a fully integrated yet federally decentralized state. But what precisely is it that parties do, and what is the precise nature of the mechanism of which parties and elections are a part that address our concerns about the endogeneity and enforcement of punishment as well as the indeterminacies and conflicts associated with redistributive politics?

The answer to our question lies in the determinants of the incentives of both existing and potential political elites. In particular, a "properly" designed electoral system that gives rise to an "appropriate" party system can give political elites a self-enforcing system of incentives – an automatically triggered system of rewards and punishments – to cooperate across regions and across levels of government in such a way as to facilitate economic growth and to facilitate the smooth evolutionary development of federal relations as changing circumstances dictate. Put simply, if we begin with the assumption that the primary objective of political elites in a democracy is to maintain their positions once in office by winning elections, then political systems need to be designed so that intergovernmental cooperation facilitates reelection.

To see better how a party system can establish the requisite incentives, and to see how to design our political institutions so as to encourage a party system most compatible with a stable federalism, imagine the following circumstances:

a. Politicians, both incumbents and challengers, are divided into parties, which operate at all levels of government. That is, no party competes at only one level or within one region, and all incumbents and challengers at all levels are associated with one such party or another;

b. There is a "ladder of advancement" in which electoral success at a lower level of government gives rise naturally to access and even success in the competition for higher office;

c. Politicians aspire to upward mobility, but the aspiration is not so great that they always prefer a position in the national government over one in a regional or local government;

d. Political elites at all levels within a party live in a symbiotic relationship so that electoral success at one level depends on the electoral success of elites at all other levels.

To better appreciate the meaning of this list, let us consider some systems that it excludes. For example, we exclude systems in which parties are organized wholly at the national level, in which parties have regional and local branches but which play little role in regional or local elections, and systems in which political parties have only a regional organization and compete for national office only in their region, as when ethnic parties organize only in regions populated by the ethnic groups they represent. Item b excludes a party system like Canada's. There, although candidates at all levels of government compete with Liberal and Conservative Party support, regional Liberal and Conservative organizations are wholly autonomous from their national counterparts, and those who begin a career in provincial politics rarely move on to the national political arena. Item c excludes any system with a political tradition like Russia's – a tradition in which, owing to the power that resides in it at the center, no career is thought to be complete until it results in a position in Moscow. Finally, item d excludes those presidential systems in which an incumbent presidential candidate is prohibited by law from being a member of a registered party.

We hasten to add that items a–d by and large describe the party systems of the United States and Germany, as well as some non-federal states such as Costa Rica. Consider the United States. That both the Democrats and Republicans satisfy the first condition is self-evident from even a cursory examination of its party system. With respect to the second condition, although we occasionally find the "war hero" or "Herbert Hoover" in American history – a person who achieves national prominence without holding local or regional elective office – such cases are rare. More common are the Calvin Coolidges (mayor, state senator, state lieutenant governor, governor, president), the Richard Nixons (U.S. representative, vice president, president), the Jimmy Carters (state senator, governor, president), and the Bill Clintons (state attorney general, governor, president). And in every instance, the offices held prior to succeeding to the presidency were won under the banner of the Democratic or Republican party. With respect to the third condition, it is by now part of American political lore that its parties are constantly in search of talent – of people who can win higher office under their labels. Hence the competition in 1995 for Colin Powell to declare himself a Republican or a Democrat. More commonly, though, both parties take those with a record of electoral success at one level as the talent pool from which to draw candidates for another, generally higher level, while successful candidates use their success in the competition for higher office. Presidential candidates more often than not come from the pool of state governors who have been successful in terms of their image within their states, and it is not uncommon to see candidates for governor or the U.S. Senate coming from the ranks of mayors or members of the U.S. House of Representatives. However, in accordance with item c, not all governors prefer "higher" office. More than one candidate for governor in U.S. history has come from the ranks of the U.S. Senate, just as more than one successful governor or mayor has preferred to maintain his or her position rather than "advance" elsewhere. Finally, and in accordance with the last item on this list, no candidate for higher office can be successful without the support and resources of candidates and party organizations operating at lower levels of government. A presidential candidate might raise millions by selling access to the Lincoln bedroom, but that money will be to no avail in winning re-election without the active support of local and regional party organizations across the country. At the same time, though, local and regional candidates for office know that their chances of election are improved considerably if their party's candidate for president is especially strong and stands a good chance of winning just as candidates for local office know that their chances will be diminished if they must live under the administration of an unpopular governor. Thus, the fates of local, regional, and national candidates are intertwined, and each depends on the other for electoral success.

There are many reasons why America's political system largely satisfies items a–d, why Germany's does the same, but why Canada's does not, and why Russia's is unlikely to match the German and American model. But the root cause lies with two interdependent and self-reinforcing factors: (1) The extent to which voters use party labels in deciding for whom to vote, and (2) the incentives of political elites to cultivate party labels. Each of these things depends on the other. Voters will not use party labels if politicians do not cultivate them, and politicians will not cultivate them if voters do not respond to them. However, we can disentangle this relationship along with its relevance to federalism and political institutional design by first noting that in a stable democracy at least, it is not uncommon to find a candidate's label and a voter's partisan attachment the best predictors of that voter's vote. This is unsurprising once we understand the role of partisan labels for voters; namely, they reduce voter information costs.[12] No voter can gather all available information about all candidates for all contests, identify their positions on all salient issues, identify one's own positions on those issues, weight the importance of the issues, and gauge which candidates are most likely to serve their interests. Even if such information were available, the cost of doing these things would exceed any individual's expected return. Since no voter's vote is likely to be decisive one way or another, making such an investment of time and resources cannot be rational. So instead, voters rely on a variety of cues that reduce their information costs, such as the opinions of close friends and the endorsements of newspaper editors. But included in this list is a candidate's partisan attachment, which, when parties have a historical record, can offer voters a costless cue about a candidate's general ideological orientation. Knowing that a candidate is a Democrat versus a Republican in America, a member of the Conservative versus Labor party in Britain, or a member of the Christian Democrats versus the SPD in Germany does not tell you how that person would act in specific instances if elected, but it does tell you something about their general sympathies with respect to, say, welfare, taxes, and government spending. And since a vote is unlikely to be decisive, the cost of an erroneous choice – one you would change if provided with more complete information – is slight, and is certainly smaller than the cost of securing that information.

It follows that if any significant part of the electorate relies on partisan labels in deciding for whom to vote, party leaders will want to cultivate those labels by attracting as many popular and viable candidates of

---

[12] For an elaboration of this argument see, for example, Downs (1957).

approximately similar ideological persuasion as possible to those labels. Just as it takes more than one McDonald's franchise to establish an identifiable national brand label and just as each franchise must offer a nearly identical product, so it is with establishing a party's brand label. This process of attraction, moreover, generates its own momentum: if voters come to rely on partisan labels, then unaffiliated candidates will want to associate with a label voters use, and affiliated candidates will seek to make their labels more appealing to voters. This is not to say that attracting candidates to a party is without its tensions. The ideological homogeneity required of candidates must be balanced against the necessity of forming a coalition large enough to win seats and to have some chance of participating in, if not controlling, the government. In parliamentary systems, the pressures for ideological "purity" are perhaps greater than in a presidential system. Obscuring one's ideological orientation may not win votes and might actually cost support if there are other ideologically similar parties, whereas, since in a presidential system, most election rules except simple plurality dictate that you are a loser even with 49.9 percent of the vote, party leaders will make a concerted effort at broadening their appeal at the expense of ideological purity.

The trade-off, then, will differ among political systems. But if trade-offs are made, they will require some degree of cooperation, compromise, and coordination among a party's candidates. If, say, Democrats at one level are as likely to support Republicans as Democrats at some other level, then the party's label begins to lose its currency. That currency is diminished as well by sharp policy disputes within a party, which thereby gives a party's political elites some incentive to negotiate many of their internal differences out of public view and to repress especially disruptive issues.[13] Thus, both Republican and Democratic parties today in the United States search for compromise positions within their ranks on the issue of abortion, with neither party wanting to be wholly "captured" by one extreme position or the other. But abortion is only the most evident such issue. There are others, including things more germane to federalism. For example, all state governors in the United States might chafe under the weight of federal rules, regulations, and mandated programs. But such things rarely become a point of partisan dispute in which, say, Democratic governors conflict openly with a Democratic president. Instead, states act much like other interest groups – lobbying members of the legislature for more advantageous legislation or negotiating with members of the president's administration for changes in administrative policy.

[13] Compromise is not always achievable as when an issue divides party members. This is precisely what happened before the American Civil War, when the Northern and Southern Democrats found it impossible to compromise over slavery – an issue Lincoln and the Republicans used to full advantage. On this point see Riker (1982, esp. ch. 9).

Our argument, then, is that the party system most consonant with federal stability is one that establishes a symbiotic relationship among political elites within a party across levels of government. This relationship corresponds to a decentralized system of reward and punishment that does not require any formal, constitutional concentration of power in the center that might threaten democracy itself. Indeed, speaking generally, it maintains and is maintained by decentralized democratic practice. So overall, our hypothesis about designing a stable federation can be summarized thus:

If a federation is to be democratic, stable, and prosperous, then political elites must share a symbiotic relationship in which their fates are interdependent. This relationship is best developed extra-constitutionally, within the state's party system whereby political elites in a party have an incentive to maintain the meaning and value of their party label.

Hence, the task that remains is to identify more precisely the type of party system most likely to generate this symbiotic relationship and, as a practical matter, to specify the political institutional variables and choices most likely to engender that system.

5   Institutional Design

Of the party systems that can be encouraged, the least desirable in a federation is a centralized one. In a centralized system characterized by virtual autocratic control from the top of a party's apparatus, including the selection of candidates for regional offices, the goal is to control party members directly as in a strong federation. But aside even from its incompatibility with the weaker forms of federation, a centralized system that functions smoothly is difficult if not impossible to maintain. Most likely, regional and local political leaders will, as a consequence of the tensions inherent in federalism, resist edicts from above and may too willingly bolt from the party when it is in their immediate electoral interest to do so. In fact, to the extent that voters see their regional interests undermined by some distant authority merely to advance the interests of that authority, they are likely to reward the candidate who campaigns as an "independent" against all party entanglements. Centralized systems also have difficulty resisting the pressures for parties to be little more than temporary coalitions of convenience that dissolve quickly after an election. In this instance, it is not so much a party's label with which voters identify and that political elites cultivate, but the personalities that head the party. Here, then, parties look like the creatures we see in Russia – entities that easily splinter, regenerate, and splinter again, often changing their names at each stage in the process as politicians compete to establish their public identities.

A decentralized party system is different, but only if it can be vertically integrated. In a completely decentralized system, of course, party organizations at one level of government have little or nothing to do with the organizations at another level. Organizations may share labels, but little else. This, then, is the situation that corresponds approximately to Canadian parties (Chandler, 1987). In contrast, in a vertically integrated decentralized system a party may have national headquarters, but those headquarters do little more than coordinate regional and local party members,[14] and regional and local party leaders are, in effect, their own bosses. The system is nevertheless a "system" in which candidates from different levels of government depend on each other for election and reelection. Here, if one candidate jeopardizes his chances during a campaign through scandal, through the "inappropriate" advocacy of issue positions, or through open conflict with other party members, then those actions undermine the public currency of the party's label and, thereby, discount the prospects of all other candidates who seek to cultivate and take shelter under that label.

Our overall argument, of course, is of little consequence if we cannot prescribe some ways to facilitate the development of a party system and corresponding system of elite political incentives that best encourages federal stability. After all, if such systems cannot be "engineered" and if party systems are the function only of historical accident and a society's sociological character, then we are left with little choice but to seek stability through the manipulation of economic policy alone. To this end, then, we offer a new list of institutional variables not normally associated with federal design but which greatly influence the structure of a state's party system. Briefly, these variables fall into three general categories – those that treat electoral processes, those that treat issues of centralization of political authority, and one that concerns the general matter of the extent to which the political system will rely on "leadership" rather than the direct (and potentially oppressive) application of power. Those variables are as follows:

1. the timing of local, regional, and national elections;
2. in the case of presidential systems, the timing of national legislative and presidential elections;
3. the number of local and regional offices filled by direct election;

---

[14] For example, if one attempts to look up the telephone number for, say, the Republican Party in the San Gabriel Valley of California, one finds instead telephone listings for "Republican Party of Alhambra," "of Arcadia," "of Whittier," "of West Covina," "of the 59th Assembly District," and of "Los Angeles."

4. the methods of electing local, regional, and national offices;
5. the autonomy of regional governments with respect to the administration of their elections;
6. the authority of regional governments in determining the method of electing their representatives to the national legislature;
7. the general authority of the national government versus regional governments over local governments;
8. in presidential systems, the constitutional authority of the president relative to that of the legislature.

To see how each of these items impacts the character and operation of parties and a state's federal structure, let us consider each of them briefly, one at a time.

Elections. A civics textbook view of democratic elections interprets such events as an opportunity to measure the "will of the people." As such, then, it seems that holding elections for more than one office simultaneously or allowing people to vote for a multitude of things can only confuse that measurement. In fact, though, the practical importance of elections is rarely anything more than an opportunity for voters to "throw the bums out" or at least to make certain that "the bums" do nothing that is blatantly inimical to their interests. With a view to developing a stable federal system based on a decentralized yet vertically integrated party system, however, an institutional arrangement is called for that is wholly different from what appears to comply most with some utopian (and unrealistic) view of democracy. More specifically,

1. Simultaneous national, regional, and local elections encourage party development by encouraging party leaders to organize voters by presenting them with slates of candidates across levels of government. This, in turn, encourages "coattails" and symbiosis – the national candidate whose popularity helps elect local and regional candidates and the local and regional candidate who finds it in his or her interest for the national candidate on his or her slate to do well.

2. For an example here of an institutional configuration inimical to stable federalism, consider Russia. There, elections to the State Duma are held in December, whereas elections to the presidency are held six months later, in June. Rather than encouraging symbiosis, this system renders the Duma contest much like a presidential primary and discourages any party consolidating role for that contest (Ordeshook, 1996). Instead, especially when combined with party list proportional representation, "parties" in the Duma election become little more than campaign vehicles for presidential aspirants.

3. Most new democracies allow few regional public offices to be filled by direct election – usually only a governor, a regional legislature, and the corresponding offices at the local level. By discouraging the development of ladders of political career advancement, and a corresponding symbiotic relationship among political elites with a region, such practices are more likely to occasion forms of boss rule in which local elections focus on candidate personalities rather than partisan attachments. And with weak partisan attachments, these local and regional candidates' interests are typically best served by campaigns that set regions in opposition to any national authority. However, by increasing the number of offices filled by direct election, the value of the party label to voters is increased (if only because the informational demands of voting are increased as well), thereby giving greater value to national partisan attachments. And the opportunities for building an integrated party within the region that can subsequently attach itself to a national label are increased as well.

4. It is by now well understood that election laws have an important influence on the types and number of parties in a political system. Less well understood is the influence of election systems in which one method is used to elect the national legislature and another for regional assemblies. One reasonable hypothesis, though, is that similar elections systems such as we find in the United States, Germany, and Spain encourage parallel party systems that are readily vertically integrated. Also, a national party list proportional representation system such as Russia's seems inimical to the development of a decentralized party system, or at least to a decentralized vertically integrated one, since that national list is most likely to be controlled by people at the federal center. In contrast, the German system, in which party lists are organized and seats allocated at the *Länder* level, encourages decentralization and vertical integration.

Centralization. Too many states merely adopt the label "federal" without giving it real meaning to the extent that most power and authority are centered in the national government. Here we do not want to debate the pros and cons of federal versus unitary government. We assume simply that the concept of federalism is to have real meaning. Nevertheless, the temptation is great, especially in disruptive economic circumstances, to try to implement economic policy by central directive so as to avoid the incoherence that seems an essential part of decentralized decision making. Without disputing this view, and without entering into a discussion of the legitimate policy domains of federal subjects versus the national government, we offer here only some suggestions that most directly impact party development.

5. A common assumption, especially in transitional democracies, is that regional and local level politics are more readily corrupted than are national politics – hence the argument for federal regulation if not outright federal control of regional and local elections. Ideally, of course, the regulation of those elections should lay in the hands of the courts, which can rely on constitutional guarantees of republican or democratic regional governance. But even if the judiciary is poorly formed, centralized regulation and control poses the threat that the center will find it impossible to resist the temptation to regulate parties and discourage their decentralized development. As with inefficient markets, moreover, there is only one long-term solution to the elimination of political corruption – competition – which can arise at the regional level only if there is something worth competing for, including the right to regulate regional elections.

6. Most constitutions give the central government the power to determine the methods whereby offices for the national legislature are filled. In countries using single-member districts, though, a critically important process is that of drawing district boundaries, which is laden with political meaning since boundaries can be drawn to favor one party or candidate over others (gerrymandering). Indeed, this process is very much like a constant-sum game among parties (the constant being the number of seats in the legislature), which, if played at the national level, can disrupt all other political processes. Decentralizing this decision, then, keeps such conflicts from "bubbling up" to the federal center. As a general rule, in fact, it is best to decentralize those decisions that are inherently zero- or constant-sum-like so as to keep them from disrupting national politics and the vertical integration of parties.

7. Giving the national government direct authority over local governments as in Russia establishes a system whereby the national government can attempt to "play off" local authorities against regional ones in its contest with regional governments for supremacy. This strategic situation, though, wholly disrupts the development of an integrated party since it more often than not makes it impossible for regional and local members of the same party to coordinate their election campaign. Instead, we are likely to see the same conflicts within the region that bedevil a poorly designed federation – local political elites who campaign primarily on the basis of their opposition to the regional government.

Leadership. Too often those who hold national political office attempt to rule by the direct application of their constitutionally sanctioned powers. As we noted earlier, however, the American presidency is a constitutionally weak office. Thus, any person holding this office cannot govern through the direct application of power. Rather, he must govern more informally, through "leadership." Leadership is, of course, difficult to define, but part of its practical meaning is using one's position as head of a party so as to encourage the party's candidates for lesser office to coordinate and comply with presidential actions. Leadership, then, not only requires a vertically integrated party system, its exercise also helps develop that system by giving all participants an interest in that development. In contrast, those political systems that give excessive powers to a president or prime minister, or which even preclude these officeholders from being associated with any party, undermine the essential integrating function of parties and, thereby, the potential for a stable and prosperous federation.

8. Finally, then, the constitutional authority of a chief of state (president) and head of government (president or prime minister) needs to be prescribed carefully. Too much authority threatens the absence of leadership; too little threatens a national government that cannot function. Too often, though, this balance, if it is achieved at all, is achieved as the product of legislative-presidential conflict, with little or no attention given to the ultimate consequences for political party development and, ultimately, federal relations. Russia here and the exceptional powers its constitution gives to its president is perhaps the clearest example of a constitutional design wholly inimical to stable federal relations.

6   Conclusions

Nothing we say here should be interpreted to mean that we place the same low priority on economic policy that we believe too many economists place on political institutional design in the search for the sources of federal stability and economic prosperity. There are, in fact, two levels of decisions that political-economic reforms confront. The first level concerns immediate problems – putting out the fires that currently burn. The second level is more long term, and consists essentially of making the federal state fireproof. And although distinctions are not perfect, the first level is more economic in character, while the second is more political, or at least "political institutional." That attention needs to be paid to both levels is attested to by the fact that, absent attention to the first – absent putting out today's fire with proper economic measures – there may be little need to make any longer-term second-level decisions; there may be nothing left to burn. Just because we succeed in extinguishing today's fire is no guarantee, however, absent long-term fireproofing, that there will not be fires tomorrow, the day after that, and so on so that all the resources of society are spent on merely fighting the fire of the day. The arguments we offer here are directed at fireproofing and as such are of only modest value to those concerned solely with today's issues. Indeed, because party systems take years if not decades to develop, the rewards that might derive from paying attention to the political institutional design variables outlined here will not interest those who are concerned with immediate payoffs. This essay, then, is addressed only to those who intend to establish a durable and prosperous federation, rather than those afforded the luxury of long-term planning and design or who seek immediate political and economic advantage.

References

Aranson, Peter H., and P. C. Ordeshook. 1985. "Public Interest, Private Interest, and the Democratic Polity." In Roger Benjamin and Stephen Elkin, eds., *The Democratic State*. Lawrence: University of Kansas Press, pp. 87–178.

Bianco, William T., and Robert H. Bates. 1990. "Cooperation by Design: Leadership, Structure, and Collective Dilemmas." *American Political Science Review*, 84(1): 133–47.

Bird, Richard M., Robert D. Ebel, and Christine I. Wallich. 1996. *Decentralization of the Socialist State: A World Bank Regional and Sectional Study*. Brookfield, Vt.: Ashgate Publishing.

Boycko, Maxim, Andrei Shleifer, and Robert Vishny. 1995. *Privatizing Russia*. Cambridge, Mass.: MIT Press.

Chandler, William M. 1987. "Federalism and Political Parties." In H. Bakvis and W. M. Chandler, eds., *Federalism and the Role of the State*. Toronto: University of Toronto Press.

Claque, Christopher. 1992. "The Journey to a Market Economy." In C. Claque and Gordon C. Rausser, eds., *The Emergence of Market Economies in Eastern Europe*. Cambridge, Mass.: Basil Blackwell.

Diamond, Larry, and Marc F. Plattner, eds. 1994. *Nationalism, Ethnic Conflict, and Democracy*. Baltimore: Johns Hopkins University Press.

Downs, Anthony. 1957. *An Economic Theory of Democracy*. New York: Harper and Row.

Gleason, Gregory. 1990. *Federalism and Nationalism*. Boulder, Colo.: Westview Press.

Hofstadter, Richard. 1969. *The Idea of a Party System*. Berkeley: University of California Press.

Horowitz, Donald. 1985. *Ethnic Groups in Conflict*. Berkeley: University of California Press.

——— 1991. *A Democratic South Africa?* Berkeley: University of California Press.

Knight, Jack. 1992. *Institutions and Social Conflict*. Cambridge: Cambridge University Press.

Martinez-Vazquez, Jorge, Charles E. McClure, Jr., and Sally Wallace. 1996. "Subnational Fiscal Decentralization in Ukraine." In Richard M. Bird, Robert D. Ebel, and Christine I. Wallich. 1996. *Decentralization of the Socialist State: A World Bank Regional and Sectoral Study*. Brookfield, Vt.: Ashgate Publishing.

McFaul, Michael. 1995. "Why Russia's Politics Matter." *Foreign Affairs*, 74(1): 87–99.

Oates, Wallace. 1972. *Fiscal Federalism*. New York: Harcourt, Brace Jovanovich.
Ordeshook, Peter C. 1996. "Russia's Party System: Is Russian Federalism Viable?" *Post Soviet Affairs*, 12(3): 195–217.
Ordeshook, Peter C., and Olga Shvetsova. 1997. "Federalism and Constitutional Design," *Journal of Democracy*, 8(1): 27–42.
   1995. "If Hamilton and Madison Were Merely Lucky, What Hope Is There for Russian Federalism?" *Constitutional Political Economy*, 6: 107–26.
Polishchuk, Leonid. 1996. "Russian Federalism: Economic Reform and Political Behavior." Mimeo. California Institute of Technology, Humanities and Social Sciences.
Riker, William H. 1964. *Federalism: Origin, Operation, Significance*. Boston: Little, Brown.
   1982. *Liberalism against Populism*. Prospect Heights, Ill.: Waveland Press.
Saunders, Cheryl. 1995. "Constitutional Arrangements of Federal Systems." *Publius*, 25(2): 61–79.
Schattschneider, E. E. 1942. *Party Government*. New York: Holt, Rinehart and Winston.
Smith, Graham, ed. 1995. *Federalism: The Multiethnic Challenge*. London: Longman.
Wallich, Christine I. 1994. "Whither Russia." In C. I. Wallich, ed., *Russia and the Challenge of Fiscal Federalism*. Washington, D.C.: World Bank.
Weingast, Barry. 1979. "A Rational Choice Perspective on Congressional Norms." *American Journal of Political Sciences*, 23 (May): 245–62.
   1993. "Constitutions as Governance Structures: The Political Foundations of Secure Markets." *Zeitschrift für die gesamte Staatswissenschaft*, 149(1): 286–311.

CHAPTER 13

A Proposal for Dynamic European Federalism: FOCJ

Bruno S. Frey and Reiner Eichenberger

I   Beyond Traditional Federalism

The economic theory of federalism yields one clear and overriding result: a federal (i.e., decentralized) state is superior to a centralized one in the sense that it fulfills the demands of the citizens more effectively. A federal constitution that endows the federal units (provinces, *Länder*, states, cantons, or communes) with sufficient decision-making rights and taxing power has three major advantages over a unitary state:

Advantage 1: More Flexible Politics. In all societies, citizens differ widely in their demand for services provided by the state. These differences in demand are not only the result of heterogeneous tastes due to differences in tradition, culture, language, and so on, but also of unequal economic conditions. The latter are caused by, for example, leads or lags in the general business cycle and, of course, special structural conditions such as differences in infrastructure, unemployment, the concentration of particular industries etc. These differences in the demand for public services must be met by differentiated supply policies if citizens' preferences are to be fulfilled. Federal sub-units are best able to meet this challenge. The politicians in charge are better endowed with information about the local requirements. They have the incentives to provide these services according to the preferences of the citizens because they are directly accountable for the local policy and their reelection depends on the satisfaction of the voters they represent.[1] In contrast, centralized states tend to produce unitary policies which respond less to differences in local demands.

---

[1] It could be argued that locally elected politicians in central states also face incentives to care for local preferences. However, in many countries, the members of the national parliament are only partly, or not at all, elected in local precincts. In the Federal Republic of Germany, for instance, a substantial share of the members of the Bundestag are not elected by winning in a particular precinct but because they are placed on a list that is controlled by the party they belong to. Moreover, in national parliaments, a local delegate's accountability is low, as he is only one of several hundred parliamentarians.

Advantage 2: More Efficient Provision of Public Services. The efficiency of the public sector is extremely important due to the very large size of today's public sectors in terms of the share of government in national income, the proportion of public officials in total employment, the dependence of a substantial portion of the population on income redistributed by government (e.g., in the form of subsidies, social security, and old age pensions) and, of course, the many resources affected by tax collection. In federally organized states, efficiency is enhanced by the mechanism of exit and entry. Individuals and firms not satisfied with the balance between the supply and cost of public services may move to jurisdictions where this balance is more favorable. Exit and entry thus establish competition among the various local suppliers of public services, giving them a strong incentive to be efficient. The exit/entry-mechanism does not depend on the full mobility of individuals or firms (there are, of course, costs of moving); it suffices if *some* such mobility is induced (in analogy to the marginal traders leading to equilibrium prices on normal goods markets). Indeed, spatial competition between jurisdictions in a federal system mimics competition among firms for the supply of private goods and services (Tiebout, 1956).

Advantage 3: More Innovation. In a federal system, innovations in public goods supply or taxation can be implemented first in those local units where the conditions are ideal for success. Moreover, a particular local unit finds it less risky to undertake innovations in public goods supply or taxation because the effects are limited and can be better observed and controlled. If the innovation is unsuccessful, not much is lost. However, if it proves to be successful, other jurisdictions and eventually the entire nation will quickly adopt it. For this Hayekian process to take place, the innovators must reap at least some of the benefits. This is much more the case when the innovation starts from a clearly defined local jurisdiction where the success (or failure) can be clearly attributed to the respective politicians and governments.

In spite of these heavyweight advantages, federalism is not an ideal system. But there is *no* ideal system. Following the well-established *comparative analysis of institutions*, it is fruitless to judge any existing system with a theoretical optimum. Rather, a comparison must be made with systems existing in reality. In the case of federalism, it is appropriate to compare it with a centralized state. From this point of view, it has often been alleged that a federal constitution is faced with four major problems:

Problem 1: Spillover Effects. Spatial positive and negative externalities produce systematic distortions in the allocation of publicly supplied goods and services. "Fiscal equivalence" (Olson, 1969; Oates, 1972) is not secured: some benefits of local public supply go to citizens of other jurisdictions who have not paid the corresponding tax cost (which induces undersupply); some costs are carried by citizens outside a particular jurisdiction (which induces oversupply). This cause for the distorted allocation of public services cannot be neglected. In reality, it can often be observed that such spillovers are substantial. Part of the fiscal crises of cities can be attributed to that factor. As an example, consider the cultural institutions (e.g., the opera house) whose costs are carried by the local taxpayers but whose benefits are enjoyed by many people living and paying taxes outside the city. Acknowledging that such positive and negative spillovers may be serious under many circumstances, we hereby propose a solution: the size of the jurisdiction should correspond to the "geography of the problems."

Problem 2: Smallness. In traditional federalism, jurisdictions are often too small to exploit economies of scale. Think, for example, of nuclear power plants or universities, which normally require heavy capital investments for a local jurisdiction (city, commune) to run efficiently. In our proposal for a new federalism, we are trying to confront the problem directly. We envisage flexible (functional) jurisdictions, which are able to adjust to the lowest cost size.

Problem 3: Need for Coordination. It is often claimed that federalism makes cooperation difficult or impossible. However, this is only part of the real problem. In federal states, cooperation among the various national sub-units emerges endogenously because it is obviously advantageous for all actors concerned. Moreover, it should be noted that coordination problems also exist within unitary states, in particular among the various national ministries whose competencies and interests overlap. Thus, a unitary state is neither a necessary nor a sufficient condition for effective cooperation.

Problem 4: Redistribution of Income. This argument says that when a local unit tries to tax the rich in order to support the poor, the rich will leave and the poor will enter. The redistribution policy therefore cannot be maintained in a federalist state but is only feasible in a unitary state. This argument has some truth in it. However, empirical evidence shows that federalist structures allow for a substantial amount of income redistribution (see, e.g., Gold, 1991). An example is Switzerland where the (partly very small) 26 cantons together with about 3,000 communities levy more than 80 percent of total income and capital taxes. Although each canton is free to set its own tax schedule, all cantons rely on progressive taxes and engage heavily in income redistribution (see Kirchgässner and Pommerehne, 1996). Moreover, quite a large amount of redistribution exists between rich and poor cantons. Nevertheless, the problem of redistribution in a decentralized governmental system has to be taken seriously. In our proposal for a new kind of federalism, we argue that this is one of the functions for which the national state is sometimes an appropriate jurisdiction.

240   **Bruno S. Frey and Reiner Eichenberger**

In this contribution, we pursue two major goals. The first is to develop a *new type of federalism* that exploits the strong advantages of federalism spelled out above, but which at the same time avoids the problems as discussed. The second goal is to suggest an *application to the case of the European Union*. We believe that our concept – called FOCJ – is well suited for a future European Constitution designed to meet the wishes of the citizens (other than those of the *classe politique*). The present state, as well as the future plans for the European Union have led to considerable dissatisfaction among the population of the various countries in the Union, most notably the new members Austria, Sweden, and Finland (see the regular public opinion surveys in the *Eurobarometer*). The problems cannot possibly be solved within the existing "constitution" when the European Union is to be enlarged to the East. Even if the present institutional structure *were* satisfactory – which, from a politico-economic perspective, it is definitely *not* – an increase from fifteen to twenty-five members (the three Baltic states, Poland, the Czech Republic, Slovakia, Slovenia, Hungary, Bulgaria, and Romania) *absolutely requires new institutional structures*. A reformed constitution should take into account the widely different level of development as well as the different economic structure of the new members. If this requirement is not met, the European Union will either completely change its nature by becoming a loose association, or will dissolve itself over time. Our proposal suggests a new way to deal effectively with the basic issue of integrating unequal units while maintaining democratic rights and fostering economic development.

The new kind of competitive federalism we put forward may seem radical in various respects. But we will show that the concept has been successful in the past as well as today. Thus, we believe that it constitutes an idea worthy of serious consideration. The remainder of this chapter is organized as follows. Section II specifies the concept of FOCJ, puts it into theoretical perspective, and discusses its main beneficial effects. The third section compares FOCJ to actual and proposed federal institutions in the European Union. The next section shows that FOCJ exist partially in European history and today, and the relationship to U.S. special districts and in particular to functional communities in Switzerland is emphasized. How FOCJ can be institutionalized in Europe is discussed in the fifth section. The last section offers concluding remarks.

II   FOCJ: The Concept

The federal units proposed here are named FOCJ according to their four essential characteristics:

- *Functional (F)*. The new political units extend over areas defined by the tasks to be fulfilled.

- *Overlapping (O)*. In line with the many different tasks (functions) there are corresponding governmental units extending over different geographical areas.
- *Competing (C)*. Individuals and/or communities may choose to what governmental unit they want to belong, and they have political rights to express their preferences directly via initiatives and referenda.
- *Jurisdictions (J)*. The units established are governmental; they have enforcement power and can, in particular, levy taxes.

These functional, overlapping, and competing jurisdictions form a federal system of governments that is not dictated from above but emerges from below as a response to citizens' preferences. For this to become reality, a fifth freedom has to be enacted, which in some way is the political counterpart to the four economic freedoms. It simply allows for such FOCJ. Such a fifth freedom requires a *constitutional decision* (see, e.g., Frey, 1983; Mueller, 1996) which ensures that the emergence of FOCJ is not blocked by existing jurisdictions such as direct competitors or higher level governments. Every citizen and community must have the right to directly appeal to the European Court if barriers to the competition between governments are established. The European Constitution must give the lowest political units (communities) a measure of independence so that they can engage in forming FOCJ. The citizens must be given the right to establish FOCJ by popular referenda, and political entrepreneurs must be supported and controlled by the institution of popular initiatives. The FOCJ themselves must have the right to levy taxes to finance the public services they provide.

The concept of FOCJ is based on theoretical propositions advanced in the economic theory of federalism. It nevertheless leads to a governmental system that is completely different from the one suggested in that literature. While the economic theory of federalism (see Oates, 1991; Bird 1993, or the various contributions on federalism in the fall 1997 issue of the *Journal of Economic Perspectives*) analyzes the behavior of *given* political units at the different levels of government, FOCJ *emerge* in response to the *"geography of problems."*[2]

---

[2] As always, there are precursors to FOCJ. The general idea has already been advanced by Montesquieu (we owe this information to one of the referees), but it has, to our knowledge, not been applied to the European Union. In the economics literature a related concept has been pioneered by Tullock (1994), who somewhat misleadingly speaks of "sociological federalism". Casella and Frey (1992) discuss the concept and refer to relevant literature. A recent Centre for Economic Policy Research Publication (CEPR 1993) shortly mentions the possibility of establishing overlapping jurisdictions in Europe (pp. 54–5) but does not work out the concept nor does it refer to previous research (except for Drèze, 1993 on secession).

We will now compare FOCJ with existing federal institutions and theoretical concepts, pointing out both similarities and differences and the beneficial effects of FOCJ.

A   The Main Characteristics

1 Functions. A particular public service that only benefits a certain geographical area should be financed by the people living in this area, that is, there should be no spillovers. Under this rule, the different political units can cater for differences in the populations' preferences or, more precisely, to its demands. To minimize cost, these units have to exploit economies of scale in production. These may strongly differ between functions (e.g., between schools, police, hospitals, power plants, and defense). This creates an additional reason for governmental units of different sizes with narrow functional fields. While this idea is central to "fiscal equivalence" as proposed by Olson (1969) and Oates (1972), the endogeneity of the size of governmental units constitutes an essential part of FOCJ. Moreover, fiscal equivalence theory has been little concerned with decision making within functional units. The supply process is either left unspecified or it is assumed that the mobility of persons (and of firms, a fact rarely mentioned) automatically induces these units to cater for individual preferences. This criticism also applies to a closely related concept of fiscal federalism, namely "voting by foot" (Tiebout, 1956). This preference-revealing mechanism makes comparatively efficient suppliers grow in size, and the others shrink. According to this model of federalism, the political jurisdictions are exogenously given, are multi-purpose, and do not overlap, while the political supply process is left unspecified. In contrast, we emphasize the need to explicitly study the political supply process. In line with Epple and Zelenitz (1981), exit and entry is considered insufficient to eliminate rent extraction by governments. Individuals must have the possibility to raise voice in the form of voting. Buchanan's "clubs" (see Buchanan, 1965; Sandler and Tschirhart, 1980) are similar to FOCJ because their size is determined endogenously by club members' benefits and costs.

2 Overlap. FOCJ may overlap in two respects: (a) two or more FOCJ catering for the same function may geographically intersect (e.g., a multitude of school FOCJ may exist in the same geographical area); (b) FOCJ catering to different functions may overlap. The two types of overlap may coexist; however, a constitutional decision can be taken to restrict FOCJ of specific functions to the second type because this alleviates free-riding problems (see below). An individual or a political community normally belongs to various FOCJ at the same time. FOCJ need not be physically contiguous, and they need not have a monopoly over a certain area of land. In this respect the concept of FOCJ is similar to Buchanan-type clubs, which may intersect, but it differs completely from archaic nationalism with its fighting over pieces of land. It also breaks with the notion of federalist theory that units at the same level may not overlap.

3 Competition. In FOCJ, two mechanisms guarantee that empowered politicians conform closely to their members' preferences: while the possibility for individuals and communities to exit mimics market competition (Hirschman, 1970), their right to *vote* establishes political competition (see Mueller, 1989). It should be noted that migration is only one means of exit; often, membership in a particular functional overlapping competing jurisdiction (which we will call FOCUS) can be discontinued without changing one's location. Exit is not restricted to individuals or firms; as said before, political communities as a whole, or parts of them may also exercise this option. Moreover, exit may be total or only partial. In the latter case, an individual or community only participates in a restricted set of FOCUS activities. This enlarged set of exit options makes "voting by foot" a real constraint for politicians.

"Secession," that is, exit of jurisdictions such as states or regions, has been recognized in the literature as an effective mechanism for restricting the power of central states (e.g., Zarkovic Bookman, 1992; Drèze, 1993). Secession has been suggested as an important ingredient for a future European constitution (Buchanan, 1991; European Constitutional Group, 1993). The right to secede stands in stark contrast to the prevailing concepts of nation states and federations where this is strictly forbidden and often prevented by force, as is illustrated, for example, by the American Civil War (1861–5), by the Swiss "Sonderbundskrieg" (1847), or more recently by the wars in Katanga (1960–3), Biafra (1967–70), Bangladesh (1970–1), and in this decade in the former Yugoslavia. Current European treaties do not provide for the secession of a nation from the European Union, and a fortiori for part of a nation or even for communities. A future European constitution thus plays a crucial role in shaping the possibility for lower-level jurisdictions to exit at low cost from particular sub-units (nations, states, *Länder*, autonomous regions, etc.) or even from the European Union as a whole.

For FOCJ to establish competition between governments, exit should be as unrestrained as possible. In contrast, entry need not necessarily be free. As for individuals in Buchanan-type clubs, jurisdictions may be asked a price if they want to join a particular FOCUS and benefit from its public goods. The existing members of the particular FOCUS have to decide democratically whether a new member pays an adequate entry price and thus is welcome. "Free" mobility in the sense of a disregard for the cost imposed on others is overcome by internalizing the external cost of movement. In addition, FOCJ do not have to restrict entry by administrative and legal means such as zoning laws. Explicit, openly declared entry fees substitute implicit restrictions, resulting in high land prices and housing rents. The commonly raised concern that pricing could be exploitative and mobility strongly curtailed is unwarranted as FOCJ are subject to competitive pressure. Moreover, the possibility of imposing an explicit entry fee gives incentives to FOCJ governments to care for the preferences not only of actual but also of prospective members.

However, the exit option does not suffice to induce governments to act efficiently. Thus, competition needs to be enhanced by political institutions. The citizens should directly elect the persons managing the FOCJ and should be given the right to initiate popular referenda on specific issues. These democratic institutions are known to raise efficiency in the sense of caring well for individual preferences (for elections, see Downs, 1957, and Mueller, 1989; for referenda, Cronin, 1989, and Frey, 1994).

4 Jurisdiction. A FOCUS is a democratic governmental unit with authority over its citizens, including the power to tax. According to the two types of overlap, two forms of membership can be distinguished: (a) The lowest political unit (normally the community) is a member, and all corresponding citizens automatically become citizens of the FOCJ to which their community belongs. In that case, an individual can only exit via mobility. (b) Individuals may freely choose whether they want to belong to a particular FOCUS, but while they are its citizens, they are subject to its authority. Such FOCJ may be non-voluntary in the sense that one must belong to a FOCUS providing for a certain function, for example, to a school FOCUS, and must pay the corresponding taxes (an analogy here is health insurance, which in many countries is obligatory but individuals are allowed to choose an insurance company). The citizens of such a school FOCUS may then decide that everyone must pay taxes in order to finance a particular school, irrespective of whether one has children. With respect to FOCJ providing functions with significant redistributive effects, a minimal regulation by the central government may be in order so that, for example, citizens without children do not join "school FOCJ" which in effect do not offer any schooling but have correspondingly low (or zero) taxes. In this respect, Buchanan-type clubs differ from FOCJ, because they are always voluntary while membership in a FOCUS can be obligatory.

FOCJ as jurisdictions provide particular services but do not necessarily produce them themselves if contracting out to a public or private enterprise is advantageous. It is noteworthy that present-day outsourcing by communities does not automatically lead to FOCJ. The former is restricted to production, while FOCJ care for provision and are directly democratically controlled. FOCJ also differ from existing functional and overlapping institutions such as the various kinds of specific administration unions (or *Zweckverbände* as they are aptly called in German-speaking countries). These institutions normally do not have the legal status of governments but are purely administrative units. The same applies to the many types of corporations that usually have no power to tax but have to rely on charges.

B   Beneficial Effects of FOCJ

Because of its four essential characteristics, FOCJ compare favorably to traditional forms of federalism. One aspect concerns the governments' incentives and possibilities to satisfy heterogeneous preferences of individuals. As a consequence of the concentration on one functional area, the citizens of a particular FOCUS have better information on its activity and are in a better position to compare its performance to other governments. As many benefits and costs extend over a quite limited geographic area, we envisage FOCJ to be often small, which is also helpful for voters' evaluations. The exit option opened by the existence of overlapping jurisdictions is not only an important means to make one's preferences known to governmental suppliers, but it also strengthens the citizens' incentives to be informed about politics (see Eichenberger and Serna, 1996).

On the other hand, FOCJ are able to provide public services at low cost because they are formed in order to minimize interjurisdictional spillovers and to exploit economies of scale. When the benefits of a specific activity indivisibly extend over large areas, and there are decreasing costs, the corresponding optimal FOCUS may cover many communities, several nations, or even Europe as a whole. An example may be defense against outward aggression where the appropriate FOCUS may most likely extend over the whole of Europe (even beyond the European Union). That such adjustment to efficient size is indeed undertaken in reality is shown by the Swiss experience. Communities decided by referendum whether they wanted to join the new canton Jura established in 1978, and in 1993 communities in the Laufental opted to belong to the canton Basel-Land instead of Berne. Communities also frequently change districts (the federal level below cantons) by referendum vote, which suggests that voters perceive the new size of jurisdictions and the new bundle of services to be more efficient. The same holds for American special districts.

The specialization on one or a few functions creates advantages that result in cost efficiency. As FOCJ levy their own taxes to finance their activity, it pays to be economical. In contrast, in All Purpose Jurisdictions (APJ) financed from outside, lacking such fiscal equivalence, politicians have an incentive to lobby for ever increasing funds, thereby pushing up government expenditures. The incentive to economize in a FOCUS induces its managers to contract out whenever production cost can thereby be reduced. While FOCJ are more market oriented than APJ, they reduce the size of the public sector.

However, they differ from today's one-shot privatization, which usually does not impact on the government's basic incentives and thus is often reversed by re-regulation and deprivatization. In contrast, in a system of FOCJ privatization emerges endogenously and is sustainable, as the politicians' incentives are changed fundamentally.

The threat of dissatisfied citizens or communities to exit the FOCUS, and the benefit of new citizens and communities joining, gives an incentive to take individual preferences into account and to provide the public services efficiently. Quite another advantage of FOCJ is that they open up the politicians' cartel (*classe politique*) to functionally competent outsiders. While all-purpose jurisdictions attract persons with broad and non-specialized knowledge to become politicians, in FOCJ, rather, persons with a well-grounded knowledge in a particular functional area (say, education or refuse collection) are successful.

The possibility to form FOCJ helps to deal with issues raised by fundamentalist sentiments. Political movements focused on a single issue (e.g., ethnicity, religion, environment, etc.) are not forced to take over governments in toto but can concentrate on those functions they are really interested in. An ethnic group need not disassociate itself completely from the state in which it resides but may found FOCJ that care for its particular preferences. South Tyroleans, for example, unhappy with the language domination imposed by the Italian state, need not leave Italy in order to have their demands for cultural autonomy fulfilled but may establish corresponding FOCJ. Such partial exit (e.g., only with respect to ethnic issues) does not lead to trade barriers, often going with the establishment of newly formed all purpose political jurisdictions. FOCJ thus meet the criterion of market preserving federalism (see Qian and Weingast, 1997).

A federal web composed of FOCJ certainly affects the role of the nation states. They will certainly lose functions they currently do not fulfill according to the population's preferences, or which they produce at higher cost than FOCJ designed to exploit cost advantages. However, the scheme does not purport to do away with nations but allows for multinational as well as small scale alternatives where the citizens desire them. Nation-states subsist insofar as they provide functions efficiently according to the voters' preferences.

III   FOCJ Compared

FOCJ differ in many crucial respects from scholarly proposals for a future European constitution. One of the most prominent was

Buchanan's (1991) who stresses an individual nation's right to secede but, somewhat surprisingly, does not build on Buchanan-type clubs. The European Constitutional Group (1993) focuses on the example of the American constitution and presents constructivist proposals with respect to the houses of parliament and the respective voting weights of the various countries. Overlapping jurisdictions and referenda are not allowed for, and the exit option is strongly restricted. Other economics scholars (e.g., Blöchliger and Frey, 1992; Schneider, 1992) suggest a strengthening of federalism in the traditional sense (i.e., with multi-purpose federal units) but do not envisage overlapping jurisdictions. The report by the Centre for Economic Policy Research (1993) criticizes "subsidiarity" (as used in the Maastricht Treaty) as an empty concept arguing that good theoretical reasons must be provided for central government intervention. But the report does not deal with the institutions necessary to guarantee that policy follows such theoretical advice. The idea of overlapping, not geographically based jurisdictions is shortly raised (CEPR, 1993: 54–5) but is not institutionally or practically worked out, nor is the need for a democratic organization and the power to tax acknowledged.

The recent proposal from politicians (Herman report of the European Parliament, 1994) mainly deals with the organization of the parliamentary system (the houses of parliament and the national vote weights) and to a substantial extent accepts the existing treatises as the founding blocks of the European constitution. The idea of competition between governments (which is basic for FOCJ) is neglected or even rejected in favor of "cooperation" between governments.

FOCJ are also quite different from the regions envisaged in existing *European treaties* and *institutions* (see, e.g., Adonis and Jones, 1991). A major difference is that FOCJ emerge from below while the "European regions" tend to be established from above. Moreover, their existence strongly depends on the subsidies flowing from the European Union and the nation states (Sharpe, 1993). In contrast, the concept of FOCJ corresponds to Hayek's (1960) (and Buchanan's) non-constructivist process view. It cannot a priori be determined from outside and from above which FOCJ will be efficient in the future. This must be left entirely to the competitive democratic process taking place at the level of individuals and communities. The central European constitution must only make sure that no other government units, in particular the nations, may obstruct the emergence of FOCJ (see Section V). In contrast to Hayek, however, our scheme allows for a (closely restricted) set of central regulations, as mentioned above. Moreover, Hayek measures efficiency by survival in the evolutionary process, while we define efficiency more directly in terms of the fulfillment of citizens' demands.

"Subsidiarity" as proclaimed in the Maastricht Treaty is generally recognized to be more a vague goal than a concept with content (see, e.g.,

Centre for Economic Policy Research, 1993: 19–23; Hösli, 1995). Even if subsidiarity were taken seriously, it would not lead to a real federal structure because many (actual or prospective) members of the European Union are essentially unitary states without federal sub-units of significant competence (examples are the Netherlands, France, and Sweden). The "regions" existing in the European Union (examples are Galicia and Catalonia in Spain, and South Tyrol and Sicily in Italy) are far from being units with significant autonomous functional and fiscal competencies.

The Council of Ministers is a European decision-making institution based on federal principles (but nations only are represented) and organized according to functional principles (or at least according to the corresponding administrative units). However, this council is only indirectly democratic (the ministers are members of governments that are democratically legitimized by the representative system) and the deliberations are not public. Exit from the European Union is not formally regulated, and exceptions to specific aspects of agreements reached (as in the Maastricht Treaty concerning the European Monetary Union and the Protocol on Social Policy, or in the Schengen Treaty concerning the free movement of persons) are granted reluctantly. Indeed, they are seen as damaging the "spirit of Europe." Whether differential degrees of European integration are framed as models of variable geometry, multi-track, multi-speed, two-tier, hard core, concentric circles, or as Europe à la carte (*The Economist*, Oct. 22, 1994; Survey of the European Union, p. 15; Pitschas, 1994), it always evokes fierce opposition. In a system of FOCJ, in contrast, functional units not covering everyone are taken as a welcome expression of heterogeneous demands among Europeans.

IV   Promising Opportunities, Successful Contemporaries, and Noble Ancestors

A   Opportunities for the Future

A careful consideration reveals that there is a wide range of functional issues to which FOCJ could profitably be applied. A practical example is the policing of Lake Constance, which borders on two German *Länder*, two Swiss Cantons, and one Austrian *Land*. This involves the regulation of traffic, environmental protection, the suppression of criminal activities, and the prevention of accidents. Formally, the various local police departments are not allowed to directly collaborate with each other, not even to exchange information. Rather, they must advise the police ministries of the *Länder* and cantons, which then have to notify the respective central governments, which then interact with each other. Obviously, such a formal procedure is in most cases vastly inefficient and unnecessarily time consuming. In actual fact, the problems are dealt with by direct contact among the local police commissioners and officers. However, this is outside the law and depends to a substantial extent on purely personal relationships (which may be good or bad). A FOCUS committed to policing the lake would allow a pragmatic, problem-oriented approach within the law – and would, moreover, be in the best "spirit" of Europe.

FOCJ are not restricted to such small-scale functional issues but are relevant for all levels of government and major issues. An example would be Alsace, which, while remaining a part of France in other respects, might partially exit by joining, say, the German social security or school system (with German as the main language), or might join a university FOCUS involving the Swiss university of Basle and the German universities of Freiburg and Karlsruhe. Actually, the first steps for establishing such a university FOCUS are under way. But these efforts contrast with the idea of regions as set out in the Maastricht Treaty (and elsewhere), not least because one of the participants (the University of Basle) is not part of the European Union. Another example refers to Corsica, which according to Drèze's (1993) suggestion should form an independent region of Europe because of its dissatisfaction with France. However, most likely the Corsicans are only *partially* dissatisfied with France. This suggests that one or several FOCJ provide a better solution in this case; they may, for example, especially focus on ethnic or language boundaries, or on Corsica's economic problems as an island. This allows the Corsicans to exit France only partially instead of totally. Quite generally, tourism and transport issues, in particular railroads, are important areas for FOCJ. It should be noted that, despite the membership of various countries in the (then) European Community, railroad policy was not coordinated to exploit possible economies of scale; a FOCUS may constitute a well-suited organization to overcome such shortcomings.

B   Contemporary and Historical Examples

The European Community started out as a FOCUS designed to establish free trade in Europe, and was from the very beginning in competition with other trade areas, in particular North America, Japan, and the European Free Trade Area (EFTA). Due to its economic success, it has attracted almost all European countries. But entry has not been free but the nations determined to enter had to pay a price. They have (with partial exceptions) to accept the *acquis communautaire* as well as to pay their share to the communities' outlays, which to a large extent serve redistributive purposes. In several respects there exist FOCJ-like units within Europe such as with respect to police, education, environment, transport, culture, or sports though they have been prevented to become autonomous jurisdictions with taxing power.

Most of these functional units are not congruent with the area of the European Union. Some are smaller (e.g., those organized along ethnic or language functions), and some are larger. EU non-members like Switzerland and many East European countries are nonetheless fully involved in, for example, European culture, education, and crime. FOCJ of the nature understood in this paper may therefore build upon already existing structures, and are in the best of European traditions.

There are two countries in which functional, overlapping, and competing jurisdictions exist (though they do not in all cases meet the full requirements of FOCJ specified above).

United States. Single-purpose governments in the form of "special districts" play a significant role in the American federalist system (ACIR, 1982, 1987; Burns, 1994). Their number has strongly increased, between 1967 and 1972 by 30.4 percent, between 1972 and 1984 by 19.7 percent, in both cases more quickly than other types of jurisdictions (Zax, 1988). There are both autonomous and democratically organized as well as dependent special districts (e.g., for fire prevention, recreation, and parks). Empirical research suggests that the former type is significantly more efficient (Mehay, 1984). Our theoretical hypothesis of the opposition of existing jurisdictions against the formation of special districts is well borne out. In order not to threaten the monopoly power of existing municipalities statutes in eighteen states prohibit new municipalities within a specified distance from existing municipalities (ACIR, 1982; Zax, 1988: 81); in various states there is a minimum population size required and various other administrative restrictions have been introduced (see, e.g., Nelson, 1990). Empirical studies reveal that these barriers imposed by Local Agency Formation Commissions (LAFCO) tend to reduce the relative efficiency of the local administration (Di Lorenzo, 1981; Deno and Mehay, 1985), and tend to push upward the local government expenditures in those municipalities that have introduced LAFCOs (Martin and Wagner, 1978).

Switzerland. Many Swiss cantons have a structure of overlapping and competing functional jurisdictions that share many features of FOCJ. In the canton Zurich (with a population of 1.2 million), for example, there are 171 geographical communities, which in themselves are composed of three to six independently managed, direct-democratically organized communities devoted to specific functions and levying their own taxes on personal income. Besides general purpose communities, there are communities that exclusively provide for elementary schools and other ones specializing in junior high schools, and there are the communities of three different churches. All these governmental units have widely differing rates of income taxes. Moreover, there are a vast number of "civil communities" (*Zivilgemeinden*) that are direct-democratic and finance themselves by user charges levied on their provision of such things as water, electricity, and TV antennas. These communities often overlap with neighboring political communities. In addition there are 174 functional units (*Zweckverbände* as they are aptly called in German-speaking countries) whose members are not individual citizens but communities. These *Zweckverbände* take care of, for example, waste water and purification plants, cemeteries, hospitals, and regional planning. The canton Zurich is no exception in Switzerland concerning the multitude of types of functional communities. A similar structure exists, for instance, in the canton Glarus or Thurgau (for the latter, see Casella and Frey, 1992). Various efforts have been made to suppress this diversity of functional communities, usually initiated by the cantonal bureaucracy and politicians. However, most of these attempts were thwarted because the population is mostly satisfied with the public supply provided. The example of Switzerland – which is generally considered to be a well-organized and administered country – shows that a multiplicity of functional jurisdictions under democratic control is not a theorist's wishful thinking but has worked well in reality.

Decentralized, overlapping political units have also been an important feature of European history. The competition between governments in the Holy Roman Empire of German Nations, especially in today's Italy and Germany, has been intensive. Many of these governments were of small size. Not few scholars attribute the rise of Europe to this diversity and competition of governmental units, which fostered technical, economic and artistic innovation (see, e.g., Hayek, 1960; Jones, 1981; Weede, 1993; and Baumol and Baumol, 1994 who also give a lively account of how the musical genius of Wolfgang Amadeus Mozart benefited from this system of government). While the Chinese were more advanced in very many respects, their superiority ended with the establishment of a centralized Chinese Empire (Pak, 1995; Rosenberg and Birdzell, 1986). The unification of Italy and Germany in the nineteenth century, which has often been praised as a major advance, partially ended this stimulating competition between governments and led to deadly struggles between nation-states.[3] Some smaller states escaped unification; Liechtenstein, Luxembourg, Monaco, San Marino, and Switzerland stayed politically independent and at the same time grew rich.

The aforementioned governmental units were not FOCJ in the sense outlined in this contribution, but they shared the characteristic of competing for labor and capital (including artistic capital) among each other. However, history also reveals examples of jurisdictions close to FOCJ.

---

[3] According to Sperber (1994: 24), in the first half of the nineteenth century average income was higher in strongly decentralized Germany than in strongly centralized France, which may at least partly be attributed to the difference in the degree of centralization.

The problems connected with Poland's strong ethnic and religious diversity (Catholics, Protestants, and Jews) were at least partly overcome by jurisdictions organized along these features, and not along geography (see, e.g., Rhode, 1960; Haumann, 1991). The highly successful *Hanse* prospered from the twelfth to the sixteenth century, and comprised inter alia Lübeck, Bremen, and Köln (which are today in Germany), Stettin and Danzig (currently in Poland), Kaliningrad (currently Russian), Riga, Reval, and Dorpat (today in the Baltic republics), and Groningen and Deventer (today in Holland); furthermore, London (England), Bruges and Antwerp (currently Belgian), and Novgorod (currently Russian) were *Händelskontore* or associated members. It clearly was a functional governmental unit providing for trade rules and facilities and was not geographically contiguous.

V   Institutionalizing FOCJ in Europe

Our proposal is purely process oriented. It is neither necessary nor possible to determine at the European and at the national levels all the functions that should be provided by FOCJ and how these entities should be organized. The internal organization of a particular FOCUS lies alone in the competence of the communities and individuals who decide to found such a jurisdiction. Nevertheless, it is possible to specify the conditions for FOCJ to emerge and to fulfill their tasks effectively. Thus, our approach follows the logic of constitutional economics, which aims at designing beneficial decision processes without closely defining the outcomes (Buchanan and Tullock, 1962; Mueller, 1996).

One condition is crucial for FOCJ to work properly: They have to guarantee economic and political competition. Thus, economic markets in FOCJ have to be open; in particular, the four freedoms referring to the free movement of goods, services, and capital, and the free mobility of individuals have to be secured. At the same time, the political markets of FOCJ have to be competitive; that is, human rights and the fundamental democratic rights have to be secured to the full extent. This includes the right of the citizens to make use of the instruments of direct democracy.

Not only traditional governments but also the governing bodies of FOCJ pursue their own interests and tend to undermine competition and to build cartels or even monopolies. Therefore, the respective rules have to be monitored by a "competition supervisory board." This body has also to fix rules for determining the ceiling on entry and exit fees. If they are too high, mobility is hampered. However, such prices for mobility prove effective in preventing individuals from exploiting the redistributive policies in FOCJ. Regulative measures may also be necessary to enable FOCJ to supply public services effectively – as we have discussed for the case of school FOCJ. In such cases, it may be advantageous to declare membership in a FOCUS to be obligatory and to fix minimum levels for the services to be supplied. The competition supervisory board must be given the competencies to step in if such regulations are violated. This board has to be empowered in a constitutional decision at the European level. It would be mistaken to delegate the monitoring of competition among FOCJ to the national bureaucracies that are interested in restricting FOCJ. Rather, an independent agency seems appropriate. A possible solution is a constitutional court (in the European Union, the European Court). Although even such institutions tend to favor national at the cost of regional and local interests, they tend to decide with less bias than national political institutions.

In light of the stiff resistance functional jurisdictions will meet, they will only emerge successfully if two conditions are met:

(1) To found and to operate FOCJ must be a constitutionally guaranteed right – the *fifth freedom*, as we would like to call it. The newly founded political units must be allowed to operate as jurisdictions with (restricted) enforcement rights. The power to tax in order to finance a clearly specified service is the key to efficiency. However, this right of FOCJ will be disputed by other political units with which FOCJ will compete for the same tax base.

Principally, the communities (as the lowest level political units) as well as individuals in the constitution should be allowed to form FOCJ. However, depending upon the function to be fulfilled, membership may be restricted to the former. It is, for instance, quite possible that individuals form a FOCUS that provides a special type of schooling; for other services, especially for those with stronger public good appeal, for example, waste water treatment or local police, communities or parts of them are the "natural" agent. It is important to note that the decision as to which of those two classes a function belongs can be left to the local level itself. This decision should not be transferred to the European level.

(2) Existing political units may not hinder the formation of FOCJ. As a most important consequence, the higher level political units have to appropriately reduce the taxes of those citizens who become members of a FOCUS or of various FOCJ providing governmental services. The competition supervisory board has to force the existing units to openly declare the cost, that is, the tax prices of the various services they provide. These "tax price lists" can then serve to fairly rebalance the tax rate of the citizens who receive services from newly emerging FOCJ instead of from traditional political units. The existing governments' tendency to underrate the cost in order to minimize tax reductions to FOCJ members can be broken simply by demanding that the tax prices for a specific service not only serves to compensate exiting citizens, but also to tax

former and newly entering service recipients. This rule makes the market for politics contestable. The potential existence of FOCJ is enough to compel all levels of government to give an account of the real cost of their services. However, it need not be said that existing political units will use all possible measures to impede the new competitors. The competition supervisory board has no easy job. Again, the constitutional court seems to be the appropriate institution to undertake this task. It could rely on the competencies of the audit office (the *Rechnungshof*) to control the calculations of the tax prices. This latter institution has the necessary knowledge that has so far been wasted as audit offices are typically only allowed to formulate non-binding recommendations that are most often ignored by the political decision makers.

VI   Conclusions

Our concept of functional, overlapping, and competing jurisdictions provides a radical alternative to today's policy in Europe. The fifth, political freedom guarantees that FOCJ emerge from below and finance their services themselves. Nevertheless, they are "European" several respects. Most importantly, this concept relies on diversity as a main characteristic of Europe. Thus, it takes up the favorable properties of a Europe of variable geometry, multi-speed, concentric circles, flexible integration or even of a Europe à la carte. FOCJ provide an opportunity to promote European integration without abandoning democracy and diversity. They make it possible to broaden and deepen Europe at the same time. It seems impossible for the many Eastern European countries to enter the European Union by accepting the *acquis communautaire*. The differences in income between them and today's members are much too wide; the transfers necessary to integrate them in the "old style" cannot be financed. The one remaining alternative to the EU – to maintain its structure and exclude the Eastern countries – threatens to end in stagnation and even disintegration. In contrast, the other alternative – to foster flexible integration – seems much more promising. Such flexible integration can be favorably achieved by FOCJ. But European integration can also be deepened by FOCJ, provided that integration is not understood as progressive standardization of political, societal, and economic conditions but as reciprocal recognition of diversity and the cooperation in catering for diverse preferences. Functional, overlapping, and competing jurisdictions are able to break up dividing national borders and separating political structures. The fifth freedom guarantees that the map of political authority is designed according to the geography of problems, and it gives Europe a unified framework to foster the political influence of the citizens directly concerned.

References

Adonis, Andrew, and Stuart Jones. 1991. "Subsidiarity and the European Community's Constitutional Future." *Staatswissenschaft und Staatspraxis*, 2: 179–96.

Advisory Commission on Intergovernmental Relations (ACIR). 1982. *State and Local Roles in the Federal System.* Report A-88. Washington D.C.: U.S. Government Printing Office.

——— 1987. *The Organization of Local Public Economies.* Report A-109. Washington D.C.: U.S. Government Printing Office.

Baumol, William J., and Hilda Baumol. 1994. "On the Economics of Musical Composition in Mozart's Vienna." *Journal of Cultural Economics*, 18: 171–98.

Bird, Richard M. 1993. "Threading the Fiscal Labyrinth: Some Issues in Fiscal Decentralization." *National Tax Journal*, 46: 201–21.

Blöchliger, Hansjörg, and René L. Frey. 1992. "Der schweizerische Föderalismus: Ein Modell für den institutionellen Aufbau der Europäischen Union?" *Aussenwirtschaft*, 47: 515–48.

Buchanan, James, and Gordon Tullock. 1962. *The Calculus of Consent.* Ann Arbor: University of Michigan Press.

Buchanan, James M. 1965. "An Economic Theory of Clubs." *Economica*, 32: 1–14.

——— 1991. "An American Perspective on Europe's Constitutional Opportunity." *Cato Journal*, 10: 619–29.

Burns, Nancy. 1994. *The Formation of American Local Governments: Private Values in Public Institutions.* New York: Oxford University Press.

Casella, Alessandra, and Bruno S. Frey. 1992. "Federalism and Clubs: Towards an Economic Theory of Overlapping Political Jurisdictions." *European Economic Review*, 36: 639–46.

Centre for Economic Policy Research (CEPR). 1993. *Making Sense of Subsidiarity: How Much Centralization for Europe?* London: CEPR.

Cronin, Thomas E. 1989. *Direct Democracy. The Politics of Initiative, Referendum and Recall.* Cambridge, Mass.: Harvard University Press.

Deno, Kevin T., and Stephen L. Mehay. 1985. "Institutional Constraints on Local Jurisdiction Formation." *Public Finance Quarterly*, 13: 450–63.

Di Lorenzo, Thomas J. 1981. "Special Districts and Local Public Services." *Public Finance Quarterly*, 9: 353–67.

Downs, Anthony. 1957. *An Economic Theory of Democracy.* New York: Harper and Row.

Drèze, Jacques. 1993. "Regions of Europe: A Feasible Status, to Be Discussed." *Economic Policy*, 17: 266–307.

Eichenberger, Reiner, and Angel Serna. 1996. "Random Errors, Dirty Information, and Politics." *Public Choice*, 86: 137–56.

Epple, Dennis, and Allan Zelenitz. 1981. "The Implications of Competition among Jurisdictions: Does Tiebout Need Politics?" *Journal of Political Economy*, 89: 1197–1217.

European Constitutional Group. 1993. *A Proposal for a European Constitution.* London.

Frey, Bruno S. 1983. *Democratic Economic Policy.* Oxford: Blackwell.

——— 1994. "Direct Democracy: Politico-Economic Lessons from Swiss Experience." *American Economic Review*, 84: 338–42.

Gold, Steven D. 1991. "Interstate Competition and State Personal Income-Tax

Policy in the 1980s." In Daphne A. Kenyon and John Kincaid, eds., *Competition among States and Local Governments*. Washington D.C.: Urban Institute Press, 205–17.

Haumann, Heiko. 1991. *Geschichte der Ostjuden*. Munich.

Hayek, Friedrich August von. 1960. *The Constitution of Liberty*. Chicago: Chicago University Press.

Herman, Fernand (reporter). 1994. *Zweiter Bericht des Institutionellen Ausschusses über die Verfassung der Europäischen Union*. Europäisches Parlament, Sitzungsdokumente (A3-0064/94).

Hirschman, Albert O. 1970. *Exit, Voice and Loyalty*. Cambridge, Mass.: Harvard University Press.

Hösli, Madeleine. 1995. "The Political Economy of Subsidiarity." In F. Loursen, ed., *The Political Economy of European Integration*. Amsterdam: European Institute of Public Administration, pp. 63–89.

Jones, Eric L. 1981. *The European Miracle*. Cambridge: Cambridge University Press.

Kirchgässner, Gebhard, and Werner W. Pommerehne. 1996. "Tax Harmonization and Tax Competition in the European Community: Lessons from Switzerland." *Journal of Public Economics*, 60: 351–71.

Martin, Dolores, and Richard Wagner. 1978. "The Institutional Framework for Municipal Incorporation." *Journal of Law and Economics*, 21: 409–25.

Mehay, Stephen L. 1984. "The Effect of Governmental Structure on Special District Expenditures." *Public Choice*, 44: 339–48.

Mueller, Dennis C. 1989. *Public Choice II*. Cambridge: Cambridge University Press.

1996. *Constitutional Democracy*. New York: Oxford University Press.

Nelson, Michael A. 1990. "Decentralization of the Subnational Public Sector: An Empirical Analysis of the Determinants of Local Government Structure in Metropolitan Areas in the U.S." *Southern Economic Journal*, 57: 443–57.

Oates, Wallace E. 1972. *Fiscal Federalism*. New York: Harcourt Brace Jovanovich.

1991. *Studies in Fiscal Federalism*. Aldershot, England: Elgar.

Olson, Mancur. 1969. "The Principle of 'Fiscal Equivalence': The Division of Responsibilities among Different Levels of Government." *American Economic Review*, 59: 479–87.

Pak, Hung Mo. 1995. "Effective Competition, Institutional Choice and Economic Development of Imperial China." *Kyklos*, 48: 87–103.

Pitschas, Rainer. 1994. "Europäische Integration als Netzwerkkoordination komplexer Staatsaufgaben." *Staatswissenschaft und Staatspraxis*, 4: 503–40.

Qian, Yingyi, and Barry R. Weingast. 1997. "Federalism as a Commitment to Preserving Market Incentives." *Journal of Economic Perspectives*, 11: 83–92.

Rhode, Gotthold. 1960. "Staaten-Union und Adelsstaat: Zur Entwicklung von Staatsdenken und Staatsgestaltung in Osteuropa, vor allem in Polen/Litauen, im 16. Jahrhundert." *Zeitschrift für Ostforschung*, 9: 185–215.

Rosenberg, Nathan, and L. E. Birdzell. 1986. *How the West Grew Rich: The Economic Transformation of the Industrial World*. London: I. B. Tauris.

Sandler, Todd, and John T. Tschirhart. 1980. "The Economic Theory of Clubs: An Evaluative Survey." *Journal of Economic Literature*, 18: 1488–1521.

Schneider, Friedrich. 1992. "The Federal and Fiscal Structures of Representative and Direct Democracies as Models for a European Federal Union: Some Ideas Using the Public Choice Approach." *Journal des Economistes et des Etudes Humaines*, 3: 403–37.

Sharpe, L. J., ed. 1993. *The Rise of Meso Government in Europe*. London: Sage.

Sperber, Jonathan. 1994. *The European Revolutions 1848–51*. Cambridge: Cambridge University Press.

Tiebout, Charles M. 1956. "A Pure Theory of Local Expenditure." *Journal of Political Economy*, 64: 416–24.

Tullock, Gordon. 1994. *The New Federalist*. Vancouver: Fraser Institute.

Weede, Erich. 1993. "The Impact of Interstate Conflict on Revolutionary Change and Individual Freedom." *Kyklos*, 46: 473–95.

Zarkovic Bookman, Milica. 1992. *The Economics of Secession*. New York: St. Martin's Press.

Zax, Jeffrey S. 1988. "The Effects of Jurisdiction Types and Numbers on Local Public Finance." In Harvey S. Rosen, ed., *Fiscal Federalism: Quantitative Studies*. Chicago: University of Chicago Press, pp. 79–106.

CHAPTER 14

The Maastricht "Excessive Deficit" Rules and Creative Accounting

Francesco Forte

I   Introduction

Constraining rules are bound to give rise to opportunistic behaviors designed to elude them. In examining the Maastricht budgetary rules, therefore, one should expect opportunistic accounting behaviors. These may be called "creative accounting" in the sense that they do not reflect reality but rather are designed to demonstrate that constraints are met. Such behaviors may be considered kinds of intended or unintended fiscal illusion.[1] The study of creative accounting is therefore at the core of the issue of budgetary transparency.

Because of the scope for opportunistic behaviors, some have expressed skepticism about the possibility of truly enforcing constitutional fiscal rules, consisting of parametric constraints (Von Hagen, 1991). However, it is argued here that in the context of the Maastricht rules, it is possible to limit substantially the scope of opportunistic behavior. The real problem is the willingness of the relevant authorities to accept *inescapable* constitutional fiscal constraints. Thus far, the authorities have tolerated or even fostered a climate in which the political considerations of a smooth launch of the European Monetary Union (EMU) have been held to be more important than the application of the constraints.

This chapter, presented in a preliminary draft at the Conference on Constitutional Political Economy held in Messina, is the result of a research undertaken in Summer and Fall 1997 when I was a guest of the Fiscal Affairs Department of the International Monetary Fund in Washington D.C. Particular thanks are due to Vito Tanzi, Director of that department, to Jeffrey Davis, Assistant Director of the same department, to Adrienne Cheasty and O. Cangiano with whom I had the opportunity of discussing general ideas and the various drafts of this paper. Obviously, the responsibility for what is written and the remaining errors is exclusively mine.

[1] On fiscal illusion see Puviani, 1903; Fasiani, 1951; Wagner, 1976; Buchanan and Wagner, 1977; Alesina and Perotti, 1994; Dollerey and Worthington, 1996; Forte, 1997a.

II The Inadequacies in the Accounting Setting of the Maastricht Fiscal Constitution Rules

A The Maastricht Fiscal Constitution

The Treaty of Maastricht of 1992 introduces a set of rules constraining the budget and the public debt for the countries expected to become members of the EMU. These rules may be seen as a *fiscal constitution*, as they cannot be modified by the laws of the member countries and generate penalties if and when violated. These fiscal rules aim to hinder the accumulation of an "excessive deficit"[2] in the general government budget. They are given for the ratios of the planned and actual deficit and debt to GDP, setting the following limits:

- 3% for the ratio to GDP of the general government *deficit*, understood to be *net borrowing*, as defined in the European System of Integrated Economic Accounts (ESA);
- 60% for the ratio to GDP of the general government *debt*, understood to be *gross debt* at nominal value outstanding at the end of the year, as defined in the ESA.

B Relationship of the 3% Deficit Ratio and the 60% Debt Ratio to GDP Growth

Why just 3% for the deficit and 60% for the gross debt as ratios to the domestic GDPs? If a country's debt amounts to 60% of its GDP and it cannot grow at least at the nominal rate of 5%, it cannot maintain a deficit of 3% of GDP unless it benefits from a devaluation of its liabilities or sells financial assets. Indeed, to keep the ratio of gross debt to GDP invariant at 60%, when GDP grows by 5%, ceteris paribus, the maximum allowable increase in net liabilities is 3% of GDP. Denoting the maximum deficit allowed by d, debt by G, GDP by Y and setting the rate of growth of GDP equal to 5%, the value of d that keeps the ratio G/Y constant, is given by the proportion $d / 0.05 = G / Y$. Thus, when

$$G/Y = 0.6 = d/5$$

it follows that

$$d = 0.6 \times 0.05 = 0.03.$$

---

[2] No consideration is given to the size of the public sector relative to gross domestic product (GDP), on the expenditure side or to the tax and social security burdens relative to GDP. Thus these rules appear essentially as a fiscal constitution for *monetary* purposes; neither for purposes of equilibrium between the *private market* economy and the *government* and *public sector* nor for the objectives of growth and employment. In both these cases, government size may be very relevant.

In the 1979–92 period, the European Union (EU) has experienced a real rate of growth of GDP of 2.2%.[3] The Maastricht inflation target was that of the best performing countries. The German rate had been around 3% until German reunification; and it was considered excessive. Thus, assuming a rate of inflation of 2.5% and a rate of real GDP growth of 2.5%, one would get precisely that 5% rate of growth of GDP. However, as such, the 3% of deficit rule, without any further qualification, is inherently *pro-cyclical*. Indeed, in years of depression and low inflation, when the rate of growth of nominal GDP could easily be as low as 2.5–3% (inflation at 1.5% and real GDP growth at 1–1.5%), the permitted deficit would be only 1.5–1.8%. Unless the flexibility with respect to the parameters[4] underlying the ratio of debts to GDP was interpreted loosely – a deficit of 3% could not be allowed, unless in the boom years the deficit was *below the 3% level*. Creative accounting may, implicitly, be allowed at the European level, to ease the strictures thus created.

The reasons for the setting of the 60% ceiling on the ratio of debt to GDP also appear to be of a practical kind. With a ceiling lower than 60%, Germany would have been disqualified, because the burden of the East German debt pushed total gross debt to a level close to 60%. The Federal Republic had maintained a debt/GDP ratio of no more than 40% for about fifteen years, and so the 60% ceiling did appear to be an extreme limit.

One may thus conclude that both the 3% and the 60% parameters are "applied economics" parameters, grounded in practical experience and feasibility, rather than on theoretical principles. Thus opportunistic accounting, as a means of easing the rules without openly abandoning them, could appear to be a pragmatic solution. This solution is appropriate for the countries lagging behind, but it is also attractive for the best performing countries as an acceptable way out, to *speed up* the realization of Monetary Union. But from a *structural, medium-term* perspective, the attractions of this approach are not equally clear.

C   *ESA 78, ESA 95, EC Regulations' Accounting Inadequacies*

The Maastricht fiscal rules are currently assessed under Council Regulation 3605/93, which refers to the second (old) edition of the ESA (ESA 78). The third edition (ESA 95) was officially adopted by a Council Regulation on June 25, 1996. However, application of ESA 95 to the Maastricht fiscal rules has been postponed to 1999. Several accounting possibilities, prevented or dubious under the new accounting framework,

---

[3] The Maastricht Treaty was drafted in 1991, when the forecasts of main economic indicators for 1992 were likely to have been available to the experts in Brussels, as well to those in the EU member countries.

[4] Allowed by Article 104c, 2, para. 2.

are thus still allowed. Regulation 3605/93, by restricting the Maastricht definition of *the increase of gross debt*, in order to arrive at a meaningful concept, unintentionally opens up some further avenues for creative accounting. Government debt, according to this regulation,[5] is constituted only of currency and deposits, bills and short- and long-term bonds, other short-term loans and other medium- and long-term loans as defined by ESA 78. Thus, short- and long-term *trade loans, accounts payable*,[6] and *technical reserves* of assurances are excluded from gross debt. Only the deficit of the cash budget, broadly defined as *besoin de financement*, whether through bonds or any other financial instruments, plus (or minus) the change in value of public debt[7] denominated in foreign currency, is relevant for the gross indebtedness of the considered year. This definition of the deficit, while per se well grounded,[8] also opens the way to some creative accounting practices, to contain gross debt.[9]

Regulation 3605/93, following ESA 78 and ESA 95, defines government, whether central or local, in a subjective way, excluding the commercial operations of non-government institutions. Thus general

---

[5] See Article 1, para. 5, second indent of Regulation 3605/93.

[6] ESA 78, para. 558 (p. 106) defines "accounts receivable and payable" as "financial claims resulting from the time lag which sometimes occurs between the conclusion of certain transactions and the actual receipt of the payments involved." Obviously postponing payments for public expenditure, by using cash policies, will not reduce the deficit, because in the Maastricht definition the deficit is measured on an accrual basis, with the inclusion of credits payable. However, such an action reduces the debt. This is a very important effect for those countries that satisfy the Maastricht deficit requirements but have problems meeting the debt ceiling.

[7] According to that ESA, assets and liabilities must be assessed at their value at the end of the year. Regulation 3605/93, Article 1, 5, indents 3–5 state that "the nominal value of a liability outstanding at the end of the year is the face value" but that "the nominal value of an index-linked liability corresponds to its face value adjusted by the index-related capital uplift accrued to the end of the year" and that "liabilities denominated in foreign currency shall be converted into the national currency at the representative market exchange rate prevailing on the last working day of each year."

[8] Indeed, if all government non-financial liabilities were included in the gross debt, a misleading relation between the deficit on an accrual basis and the debt would emerge, with the gross debt increasing in an amount greater than that of the deficit. This would occur through including some government obligations on the expenditure side of the budget, without considering the corresponding credits of the government on the revenue side. It is true that in doing the opposite, the increase in debt may be smaller than the increase in the deficit. But at least in this case one gets the nice figure of the liquidity constraint, which is very relevant not only from a solvency point of view, but also from the point of view of the monetary effects of fiscal policy. See the discussion in the text below.

[9] As we shall see below, it is possible to reduce the increase of gross public debt by delaying payments of current expenditures (V.E.18). It is also possible to reduce it by fictitious revenue generation. Examples include the sale of gold obtained from the central bank, the issue of commercial loans; the sale of public debt to (partially) funded social security institutions and cash obtained – to redeem public debt – from financial institutions, credited with accounts payable (IV, C, 12, 13, 14 and D).

government "comprises only institutional units producing non-market services as *their main activity* (italics added)" As a result, autonomous public entities running deficit-generating public services, which finance their investment by debt, are left outside the realm of government. This is because they are defined as commercial operations by ESA, even if they actually supply impure public goods[10] and results in substantial *off budget* accounting. Other opportunistic accounting practices are made possible by ESA's narrow definition of *liabilities*, which excludes the debts of public enterprises for which the government is fully liable. Recent public accounting rules, in some countries, require that government guarantees to private or public entities should be recorded as liabilities, in official statements. However, given their non-market nature, they do not appear among the gross liabilities in ESA 78 financial assets and liabilities accounts. They are therefore excluded from Maastricht accounting. Under ESA 78, all assets must be recorded at their *nominal value* or at their *purchase value*. ESA 95, while still not considering government guarantees because of their non-endowed market value, adopts more realistic valuations for assets and liabilities relevant for government accounting, taking into account their market price or the present discounted value of their future returns.[11] Thus the net lending nature[12] of government purchases of assets dictated by public policy may be recognized.

ESA 78 considers neither the methodological problems of ex ante valuations, nor those of the medium-term Maastricht requirements.[13] Parameters like those specified in the Maastricht Treaty can only be assessed in a convincing way using a medium-term perspective.[14] But the "planned

[10] See Regulation 3605/93, Article 1, para. 2, and ESA 78, Chapter II, 239–40, p. 31, and ESA 95, Chapter II, 2.68–2.74. The IMF accounting methodology (IMF1986 known as *GFSM*) adopts a distinction between general government and public enterprises based on the nature of the activities that they perform rather than on institutional or legal classification (Stella 1993). Obviously, grants given to these entities by governments enter the expenditure side of the budget. But the purchase of their assets by the government, which has a grant component, is not recorded as government expenditure. The problem may be particularly delicate for municipal and regional transportation services and for some corporations in the "ecological" sector. See subsequent discussion of the problems for *economic policy* created by purchases of financial assets.

[11] See ESA 78, Chapter V, 706, p. 128, and ESA 95, Chapters 7, 7.25–7.32 and 7.47–7.57, pp. 131–4.

[12] In the sense of GFS1986. See Blejer and Cheasty, 1991, pp. 1647–8.

[13] ESA 95, Chapter 12 (Quarterly Economic Accounts), particularly 12.04 and 12.05, begins to consider the problem of ex ante estimates for the quarterly accounts of the last part of a year whose ex post data are available for the first quarters.

[14] Tanzi (1993) notes that there are *one-off* measures which, while reducing the size of the deficit in the short run, do little or nothing to improve the fiscal situation. He points out that for this reason it would be desirable to present a measure of the fiscal deficit that would remove the impact of such short-term measures. "This adjustment would give an underlying or *core deficit* [italics added] that would better reflect the fiscal situation of the country over the longer run."

deficit" mentioned in the Maastricht Treaty[15] merely refers to the next year, and Regulation 3605/93 only requires the member states to present "before March of year n, an up-to-date estimate of their actual government deficit for year $n - 1$, and their actual government deficits for years $n - 2, n - 3$ and $n - 4$."

In the present Maastricht accounting framework (particularly due to Regulation 3605/93) gross indebtedness is virtually a liquidity constraint, that is, the cash deficit in the broad sense of *besoin de financement*. The only additions considered are the changes in value of assets denominated in foreign currency. In a monetary union, as that envisaged under the Maastricht Treaty, it would have been paradoxical not to have a measure of the liquidity constraints of the governments of the member countries. It is not enough to keep a measure of the deficit on an accrual basis, though this may be a meaningful fiscal policy figure in terms of real economic resources. Provided that the deficit as a net cash requirement is necessary for monetary policy coordination,[16] it would appear better, from a transparency point of view, to require that this figure be given and constrained, as an additional *deficit* figure, rather than as a *debt* figure. The level of indebtedness should be a comprehensive *accrual* figure, since it has to do with stocks and not flows.

Obviously, one may argue that if it is correct to maintain the general government debt as a stock affecting net wealth, such a measure should include all debt. However it may be misleading to add the non-financial debt of the government to its financial debt. This is because a part of the former is matched by credits for revenues. This addition would lead to a level of indebtedness inconsistent with the accrual deficit and is likely to be systematically bigger. However, by this reasoning all the non-financial debt of the government can be excluded from the official figure for public debt. A bias is introduced, again disconnecting the gross indebtedness from the accrual deficit figure. And this new accounting bias may induce the government to run up non-financial indebtedness, throwing part of its financial problems on the private sector market economy. Some governments are already in the grip of this bad habit and it does not need further stimulus.

Inconsistencies and biases (in both directions) would be avoided and the concept of gross debt would be better approached if the algebraic sum of government non-financial debt were added to government financial debt, at the end of the year. This last total, indeed, is a rough measure

---

[15] See Article 104c, 2, second indent of the Maastricht Treaty and Protocol 5, Article 1, first indent annex, and Article 4, 1–3 of Regulation 3605/93.

[16] In the terminology of French public accounting this is the "*besoin de financement*," while in the German it is the "*Finanzierungsaldo*." The present Italian budgetary accounting system uses the word "*fabbisogno*" for the above cash-deficit concept, while the accrual budgetary deficit is called the "*saldo netto da finanziare*." On the usefulness of this concept in Italian fiscal policy, see Balassone and Franco (1996).

of the stock of financial requirements drawn from the economy by the government, in the production and distribution process over and above that resulting from its economic resource gap. It also takes account of the time lags involved in the relevant transactions. With average time lags on the revenue side equal to the average time lags on the expenditure side, the only gap would be the resource gap. The government would have no financial requirement with regard to circulating capital.

D   *Value and Fiscal Policy Effects of*
       Economic Policy Financial Assets

As noted, under ESA 78 the deficit is viewed as the sum of liabilities net of any asset purchases. There is no rationale based on the definition of government wealth or fiscal policy for mixing purchases of assets for reasons of economic policy with purchases for mere liquidity management (Blejer and Cheasty, 1991). The former, given their concessional character, are general government *net lending* in the IMF GFS 1986 terminology and may be particularly relevant in the case of public enterprises, because of their hidden grant component. They have an economic effect similar to those of unrequited capital and current expenditures directed at similar destinations. Their real and monetary macroeconomic impact may be greater through the hidden grant component because of a leverage effect on the aggregate financing capability of the beneficiaries. From a genuine government wealth Ricardian perspective, these assets more often than not have a small or zero worth and sometimes even a negative one.[17]

Of course, governments may purchase assets of industrial and financial corporations that are not expected to have systematic losses. But as it has been stressed by Tanzi (1993), if these public enterprises had to raise their finance entirely on the market, their investment behavior and pricing policies would likely be less expansionary. However, to consider as government wealth financial assets that officially belong to the government, but whose real value these enterprises are able to increase through reinvesting their profits, is untenable and ideologically biased. The public technocrats who manage these enterprises are not financially liable to the government in terms of profits distributed or negotiable capital gains. These are, for the taxpayer, *abstract property rights.* These assets, therefore, should not be assessed as government wealth unless there is a prospect of their realization (with likely receipts discounted) or revenue for the government (with likely flows capitalized).

---

[17] An example of zero value is Section V, A, no. 9 (see Table 3). Possible cases of negative value may take place within category n. 6. This can occur if in addition to the lending, a guarantee has been given to the aided bad bank, so that the net result is a loss additional to that of the loan plus interests thereof.

Government purchases of new shares of (public) corporations might be employed to cover their losses. Such purchases function as direct grants. As it is well known, both grants and disguised grants to (public) corporations are forbidden in the EU, except in some particular situations, because such support may distort competition. Given the movement toward privatization in the EU, such activity may not be considered important.[18] More important is the purchase of stocks and bonds of public entities of mixed public and private corporations guaranteed by the government, to finance public utilities and infrastructures, replacing direct investment. These quasi-public or quasi-market operations may be helpful in solving the problems of providing public services and collective infrastructures at a reduced cost for the government. Thus, per unit of public expenditure, such activities can have a greater real and monetary impact than similar direct public investments. But the government's guarantees to these operations create contingent government liabilities. Again, to assess whether here there are any true government assets, it is necessary to assess how much property (to be monetized in the future) the government has effectively bought in terms of stocks and flows. Weighed against this, it is necessary to assess the liabilities that the government may take on with the above guarantees. The sum, for some items, may be negative, rather than positive. The transparency of the budget may be compromised by sometimes putting in a positive entry instead of a negative one.

Finally, some public financing consists of giving loans at concessional rates to public or private entrepreneurs without any government responsibility in their results. Here, clearly, there is a grant component, with real and monetary effects particularly relevant if these low-rate loans are long term. From a government wealth perspective, these loans should be recorded, in the balance sheet, at a value discounting their concessionary component, while in the budget the transfer component should be recorded on the expenditure side with the full loan on the revenue side. However, from a fiscal perspective, this recording may be misleading because the expansionary effect of this activity may exceed the difference between the market value of the assets and the expenditure necessary to purchase them.

As noted previously, adopting the financial assets valuation rules of ESA 95 could reduce the opportunistic accounting and lack of transparency arising in this area. However, the correct asset value of the government's investment is *not* obtained by capitalizing the expected flow of revenues of these enterprises. The correct value is obtained by capi-

---

[18] However, the Maastricht fiscal rules are also likely to be employed to assess the financial requisites of countries seeking admission to EU. In many such countries, public sector enterprises are still a large part of the economy.

talizing the flow of revenues that the government's budget is likely to be able to withdraw.[19] Nor would it be correct to consider the market value of the stocks of these enterprises, insofar as the government is not expected to be willing to dispose of them.

III   The Limits of National Income Statistics in Fiscal Constitution Accounting

A   Accounting, the Fiscal Constitution, Opportunistic Behavior

There is no such entity as a "best" accounting system. Maastricht accounting must meet several functional objectives. It must also be transparent and take into account the incentives for opportunistic behavior. Functional perfectionism may lead to complexities that reduce transparency, such as the ease with which figures can be interpreted. ESA 78, as the accounting framework for the Maastricht fiscal rules, was a well-known, ready-made system that was supposedly impartial. However, it was put to a use for which it had not been designed.

ESA 78 was conceived as an accounting system for national income statistics and not for operational government budgetary planning. Therefore its definitions – while open to unforeseen incentives for opportunistic behavior – sometimes lack the perspective relevant for fiscal analysis. For instance, the notion of *obligation due*, for a national income statistician means that the statistician should assess on an objective basis whether and when it is due. In budgetary accounting, one must specify who – whether the administration or the taxpayer or some third impartial observer, like the national income statistician – has to assess whether it is due. And rules on when obligations are due need to be more specific, to avoid opportunistic choices of time period.

National income accounting statisticians, indeed, have no property rights or other similar direct interest in the situations that they record. However, private and public administrators have a direct interest in the institutions that they manage. Thus, they may interfere with their internal documentation and adjust their administrative behaviors and legal institutions. They can window dress their results by fiscal illusions created by opportunistic accounting behaviors.

B   Influence of Keynesian Ideology on ESA

Accounting may be heavily influenced by ideologies. This appears to be the case for the UN system of national accounting and for ESA, which

---

[19] Thus the criterion of putting the entire amount of this "net lending" above the line suggested Blejer and Cheasty (1991) might be, on balance, the best on practical grounds.

is its most notable derivative. It has a strong ideological bias, in terms of Keynesian flows reflecting the belief in short run planning. It has a conception of the government as a benevolent productive institution. The essence of the market was *pricing*, not *property rights*. Distribution as a process of payments for the factors of production appears the same for the market economy and the public economy; and it is mixed with redistribution, in a unique view of distributive transactions.[20] The wealth approach is not relevant. This methodology cannot be of much help in medium term budgetary planning with credible forecasts.

The ESA view of social security reflects the ideology of pervasive welfare protection intrinsically different from that offered by insurance. Thus social insurance is distinguished from social security. For ESA, social security consists of only the general regimes; the sectoral ones, whether funded or unfunded, are recorded as social insurance and excluded from government. Even state employees' social insurance, therefore, is generally excluded from social security.[21]

The lack of an accepted accounting framework for medium-term structural budgetary analysis of ESA induces a formal interpretation of the Maastricht fiscal rules. The exceptions laid down in the Maastricht Treaty[22] are precise in terms of the specification of the deficit and debt parameters but are presented in merely numerical terms. Those who maintain a "political interpretation" of these parameters may easily adopt, as an argument in their favor, the fragility of such a numerical interpretation of the Maastricht rules together with the lack of an accepted

---

[20] For ESA 95, Chapter 4 (Distributive Transactions), 4.01, these transactions consist of those "by means of which the value added generated by production is distributed to labor, capital and government and of transactions involving the redistribution of income and wealth." Which government transactions are meant not to be distributive but redistributive remains unspecified.

[21] ESA 78, Chapter II, 2.24–2.25, defines as social security funds all central and local government units whose principal activity is to provide social benefits and whose main resources are derived from compulsory social contributions paid by other units. Thus, the social insurance funds run by institutions different from the central or the local government are not part of the security sector. This is so even if they serve as a replacement for employees exempted from the general system and raise compulsory contributions and give social benefits. ESA 95 Chapter II, 2.74, p. 29, and Chapter IV, 4.88, p. 79 consider as social security schemes only those "covering the entire community or sections of the community which are imposed, controlled and financed by governments units." The word "section" means an entire class of income receivers. Even social insurance schemes organized by the government for their own employees are classified as private schemes (see para. 4.89), by ESA 95. GFS 1986 excludes from social security "funded government employee pension schemes invested in the capital market or in loan and securities other than those of the employing government," if they are segregated from the employing government fund and do not cover other employees (such as those of the local governments).

[22] See article 104c, n. 2 (a) and (b).

framework for structural fiscal analysis. Thus, short-run opportunistic accounting may help in the alternative political interpretations of the parameters.

C   *Accrual versus Cash*

In accounting terminology, accrual has a strong conceptual basis in terms of economic resources, whereas cash is a more concrete term, referring simply to "money going in or out." Thus the former, if not carefully and consistently specified, is open to definitional manipulations. Cash data, however, may refer to effective economic resources in a divergence between the fiscal economy and the market economy. This can occur, for example, through postponing payment of standing obligations and artificial acceleration of revenues with one-off effects.

Any accounting system, whether of business or of government or of national income, must be in accrual terms if it is to give a truthful and comprehensive representation of revenues and expenditures and of the meaning of government gross debt. The mere accounting flows can be deceptive if the changes in the stocks are not taken into account. Flows of revenues are overvalued when they cause a clear diminution in stocks and are undervalued when accompanied by clear increments in stocks. Flows of expenditures are undervalued, when new liabilities linked to them are overlooked or overvalued and give rise to clear increases in stocks. On the other hand a complete accounting of stocks and flows, considering all stock fluctuations inclusive of the probabilistic expectations, may imply excessive informational requirements and may lead to inconclusive results, thus lacking transparency. The Herculean efforts of Buiter (1984, 1992) are testimony to this.[23]

Obligations that are relevant for accrual, particularly if related to peripheral branches, may sometimes go unnoticed when incurred; or their value may be misrepresented due to inadequate documentation. Thus for budgetary short-term accounting it raises the delicate question of assigning obligations to the years in which they came into existence. It is argued that this must be done retroactively. This is actually done in ESA accounting. But the expectation of such retroactive re-allocation of obligations may tempt authorities to be lax in terms of the recording of current obligations. And this behavior fosters fiscal illusion. Increasing the deficits of the past has no effect on the current financial flows. However, the obligations pertaining to the past that are discovered now do create present problems of disbursement.

---

[23] On a measurement of the deficit inclusive of all capital variations and future claims and liabilities see *pro*: Eisner, 1986; Auerbach, Gokhale, and Kotlikoff, 1994; *contra*: Havemann, 1994. Some notes of caution are provided by Stotsky and Sunley, 1994.

*D   Dual Meaning of the Time Dimension of Obligations:
How Time Discretion in Accrual Can Become
Similar to That under Cash Accounting*

According to the standard accounting definition (SNA, ESA 83, ESA 95, IMF 1996[24]) a positive or negative flow "is accounted for, under the accrual method when an economic value is created, transformed, or extinguished, or when claims and obligations arise, are transformed or are canceled." But what is meant when it said that "economic value is created" or when it is said that "obligations arise"?

To begin with the first question, in the context of the government's supply of goods and services, ESA gives different answers, distinguishing among the purchase of intermediate goods, value added for collective consumption and capital formation. In the case of the purchase of intermediate goods, the time of recording is generally that of purchase. However, for goods withdrawn from stocks (strategic stocks, emergency stocks, and stocks held by regulatory organizations) the time of recording is delayed until the goods are drawn from the stocks to be employed. This definition from national accounting appears wrong for the government's accrual accounting.

For the supply of collective consumption goods, time of recording, under ESA 78 is when the costs are incurred. Here, however, ESA 78 contradicts itself stating that the *compensation of employees*[25] shall be recorded, when *payment is due.*[26] Thus, delayed obligations relating to wages may be recorded after the time when the corresponding services were performed.[27] As a general rule, under ESA 78, capital goods should be recorded when made available to the purchasers. And when production extends over several periods, the value of the works made available in each period should be accounted for in that period. However, buildings and construction works whose construction extends over several periods and for which a buyer (in our case the government) has been found during a previous period are recorded at the end of the accounting period. Thus, time of recording of public works expenditures may be postponed. Under ESA 95, the room for discretion in this last area is not reduced.

---

[24] See ESA 78, Chapter V, section "Time of Recording Transactions," pp. 129ff. More precisely, see ESA 95, Chapter I, para. 1.57 (Time of Recording), pp. 13–14, where a general definition of accrual is given. As to the time "when economic value is created, transformed or extinguished, or when claims and obligations arise, are transformed or are canceled" see IMF 1996, Chapter III, paras. 64–72 (Basis of Recording) which, basically, follows the same definition.

[25] See ESA 78, Chapter 7, 707, *Final consumption*, second indent, p. 129 and Chapter 3, 317 p. 47.

[26] See ESA 78, Chapter 7, 708, *Compensation of employees*, p. 130.

[27] See below, Section V, n. 3.

Capital goods purchased by the government, are accounted for when the fixed asset is transferred; and for construction works extending over several periods, the output produced in any given stage is treated as being sold to the purchaser as the latter takes *legal possession* of the output.[28] However, compensations to employees are always recorded in the period during which the work is done, thus recognizing the accounting difference between the payments to the factors of the production as *distribution* and transfers as *redistribution*.

Proceeding to the second question pertaining to *obligations*, the legal complexity of this notion seems to escape to ESA economists. Indeed, in several unilateral and bilateral transactions, there is an initial obligation consisting of a legal commitment to do or undertake something, under given conditions and terms and a terminal obligation consisting of the specific execution of that commitment. An order for an aircraft by a minister of defense implies both an *initial obligation* to pay for it when delivered and a subsequent, *terminal obligation* of making payment because the aircraft has been delivered, as stipulated. A central government may be mandated by the yearly budget to credit the local governments with a given amount of transfers but only after it has decided to distribute them does an obligation to pay arise. Too often ESA postpones accrual to the last possible phase for expenditures, when principles of prudent fiscal management[29] would suggest the opposite.

In contrast to accrual, cash budgeting is open to ad hoc maneuvering to hide the real financial situation, as when currently due payments are postponed and tax collection is accelerated. On a cash basis, these behaviors cannot be defined as creative accounting per se, but help in opportunistic *accrual* accounting. Operational cash budgets may be employed as a basic first step to obtain the accrual budgets, adding credits for revenues and debts for expenditures to the revenue and expenditure items.[30] If the procedure of payment by the government starts with a request for authorization issued by the Treasury to the various spending units, credits without this authorization cannot give rise to payment obligations. This cash deferral, per se perfectly orthodox, is endowed with formal accrual effects and may lead to opportunistic behavior if accrual is not defined in a substantive way.[31] A symmetric game may be played on the revenue

---

[28] See ESA 95, Chapter 3, 3.52 and 3.59 and 3.112, first indent.
[29] On prudent fiscal accounting and fiscal responsibility management it is particularly interesting to see New Zealand's Fiscal Responsibility Act (1994) (The Treasury 1995).
[30] See European Commission, 1995, II422/95, EN, II, C.2, p. 9, "Most public accounting systems register government revenue and expenditure on a predominantly cash basis, whereas national accounts are, predominantly, based upon an accrual basis; consequently, an adjustment will often have to be made so as to include the *accounts receivable and payable* [italics added]."
[31] The Italian Court of Accounts, 1997.

side, with respect to direct taxes and social security contributions, by the acceleration of requests for payments, because here the accrual basis is that of "payment due."[32]

The *phenomenology* of cash may be deceptive about the true level of outlays because not all financial obligations imply an immediate disbursement of interest. ESA 78 follows the concept of accrual as a terminal payment obligation, so that *imputed* interest must be recorded only when the whole credit to which they are linked expires. This allows for extensive creative accounting.[33]

E   Four Meanings of Payment Due

ESA 78 states that in principle, wages, salaries, rents, interests and all unilateral transfers,[34] must be recorded when the payment is due. Here, the word *due* can have four different meanings. It can mean any one of the following: (a) that the obligation to pay exists according to the Public Administration; (b) that an obligation to pay exists from an objective point of view; (c) that an obligation to pay a particular amount has been specified to exist; (d) that a payment cannot be avoided. The second meaning (together with the last) is adopted for current taxes on income and wealth, where ESA 78 specifies that "this [date when the payment is *due*] is the last date on which they may be paid without penalty." For indirect taxes, ESA 78 adopts the first and the third meanings, stating that taxes linked to production and imports are recorded at the time when the goods and services are *produced, sold, or imported*. This expression allows the recording, as indirect taxes *due*, those amounts that the tax administration claims to *be due*, even if the taxpayer resists in court and is able to delay the payment – without penalties. In the social security area, both for contributions on wages and salaries and for those on other incomes, ESA 78 again adopts the first and the third meanings, stating that "they [the social security contributions] should be recorded when they are due."

ESA 95, however, excludes the first meaning for both direct and indirect taxes. It specifies that "the amounts to be recorded in the system are determined by the amounts due for payment only when evidenced by tax assessments, declarations or other instruments which create liabilities in the form of clear obligations to pay on the part of taxpayers." For social security contributions, however, even with ESA 95, the possibility of recording receipts merely due according to the public administration remains.

---

[32] The same cannot happen as for consumption taxes because here the time of recording is that of the production of the goods and services to which they are linked.

[33] In Section V of this chapter we examine how ESA 95 corrects this imperfection.

[34] Taxes and social security contributions are listed by ESA among the transfers.

For wages and pensions to public employees, the first and the fourth meanings may be applied, thus recording them not when a *general liability* to pay them arises, but when the treasury decides to authorize their payment. Normally, this option is not available to the European government for the regular sums of wages, salaries, and pensions that are due monthly. But it is available for *increases* in wages and salaries and for the pensions of newly retiring people, even if the obligations retroactively cover the entire period from when these rights originate. The option is also available for miscellaneous current and capital transfers and investment grants.

IV   Categories of Opportunistic Behaviors in Maastricht Budgetary Accounting – The Revenue Side

A   *Ideal Matrix of Opportunistic Behaviors in Maastricht Budgetary Accounting*

Any set of parametric rules on debt and on deficit entices governments to engage in opportunistic behaviors, whether through mere accounting "creativity" or by more subtle operations, including formal changes in institutions and contracts. Some of these opportunistic practices are listed in Tables 1, 2, and 3, in the light of the Maastricht parameters. We may analyze the opportunistic behaviors to meet Maastricht deficit and debt targets, disaggregating the transactions into their constituent components, namely their subjects, their objects, and their time period.

Obviously some opportunistic behaviors or "creative accounting behaviors" simultaneously bear on more than one of the three components in terms of the phenomenon to be circumvented. Thus, it is not easy to review these behaviors by a strict application of this three-dimensional disaggregation. Nonetheless, an attempt is made and the resulting three-dimensional disaggregation is explicitly presented in Tables 1 and 2.

We are thus able to build a "creative accounting matrix," for both the revenue and the expenditure sides of the budget. The matrix is applied to the deficit as well as the debt rule, following the three dimensions of the transactions entering the general government budget – that is, subjects, objects, and time. This creative-accounting matrix is presented in Table 3. This matrix presents a shorthand summary of the analysis explained in detail in B and C below and in A and B of Section V.

B   *Categories for the Deficit Rule*

Opportunistic behaviors in the revenue accounting to elude the *deficit* rule may consist in recording as revenues:

Table 1. *Categories of Opportunistic Behaviors for the Deficit Rule Based on the Components of the Transactions*

For the subjects of the transaction:
1. Overly restrictive definition of government, so that part of true government obligations are off budget
2. Some revenue merely consists of taking resources from other institutions that should be considered part of the government

For the objects of the transaction:
1. Optimistic definition of credits and assets on the revenue side, so that items are recorded at a book value higher than actual value
2. Recording credits that will not be collected as revenues
3. Recording revenues that are collected but must be reimbursed
4. Restrictive definitions of obligations, debts, and liabilities on the expenditure side, so that they are not recorded even if already in existence or with a strong chance of coming into existence
5. Underassessment of obligations for public expenditures such as increases in wages, pensions, and maintenance costs
6. Considering expenditures for the purchases of assets that have a real value lower than the price paid as revenue-neutral transactions

For the time period of the transaction:
1. Shifting extant obligations to future budgets by not considering them "mature"
2. Anticipating future budget revenues to the present
3. Shifting to past budgets, debts that currently come into existence but have to do with previous obligations

1. *One-off revenues which may be reimbursed.* It may be the case of an extraordinary tax which, in fulfilling political promises, will be reimbursed in the future. This functions as a sort of compulsory loan at a zero interest rate. Obviously, this device lacks transparency.

2. *Revenues* from the transfer of the technical reserves of social insurance funds run by corporations to the general government budget. This occurs by merging this insurance with the government *general social security* system. The government commits to paying the future pension liabilities through its pay-as-you-go system. However paradoxical,[35] this opportunistic accounting behavior is, at least, transparent.

---

[35] This possibility arises because of the restrictive definition of social security by ESA 78 and retained in ESA 95. Paradoxically, this "nationalization" may be a useful component of a privatization process, allowing a state company managing social insurance to be privatized. Its funds, however massive, might be insufficient to deal with the case of the peculiar pension liabilities deriving downsizing, which arise from the early retirement of large numbers of personnel.

Table 2. *Categories of Opportunistic Behaviors for the Debt Rule Based on the Components of the Transactions*

For the subjects of the transaction:
Overly restrictive definition of government, so that debts of government institutions are not consolidated in government debt

For the objects of the transaction:
1. Formal definition of public debt, so as to exclude some elements of government debt
2. Exclusion of contingent liabilities for guarantees from public debt
3. Provision of government guarantees rather than concessional loans or grants

For the time period of the transaction:
1. Consideration of public debt as of 31 December, so that accounting may retard its appearance
2. Exclusion of partially matured contingent pension liabilities from public debt

3. *Anticipation of one-off taxes due in future years, reducing the future revenues.* From a medium-term perspective, this revenue vanishes. An example is the one-off anticipation of the taxes on the benefits due to the employee from the employer, at the termination of a labor contract. Normally, they are collected through withholding, when the benefits are distributed rather than in the years in which their rights mature. If the anticipation is rendered permanent, there will be a one-off revenue in the initial period. Because the distribution of the losses over future budgets is difficult to assess, this measure may be classified among the non-transparent ones.

4. *Recording of apparent revenues* consisting of claims by the general government of taxes and social security contributions that pertain to the distant future or those that will never actually be paid.[36] Obviously, this is non-transparent creative accounting.

5. *Recording of apparent revenues* by assessing taxes gross rather than net of the reimbursements due to the taxpayers. This non-transparent accounting behavior is important both for the provisional withholding taxes on wages and interest incomes and for the value-added tax on exports.[37]

---

[36] This case has been already examined above in Part III. As seen, ESA 95 considerably reduces its relevance.

[37] ESA 95 seems to suggest that value-added taxes should be assessed, by sector of activity, net of rebates. The net tax, when rebates are due, is negative. It might then be classified as a subsidy. In this case, ESA normally applies the same time reference as for value-added taxes. See ESA 78, para. 708, p. 130, and ESA 95, para. 9.44–9.45, p. 219.

Table 3. Creative-Accounting Matrix

Side of the budget		Impact on	
	Revenue	Deficit	Debt
Restrictive definition of government	IV.2 Social insurance	+	+
	IV.7 Leasing back	+	+
	IV.9 Dividends from or taxation of apparent capital gains of a separately owned public entity	+	+
	IV.13 Shifting separately owned public entities outside of government		
Liberal definition of revenues	IV.1 Revenue to be reimbursed	+	+
	IV.4. Bad tax credits	+	+
	IV.5 Taxes gross of rebates	+	+
	IV.6 Expansion of money supply	+	+
	IV.8 Apparent operational capital gain from indexed public debt	+	+
	IV.9 Apparent capital gain on property sold	+	=
	IV.11 Debt disguised as revenue	=	+
	IV.12 Debt disguised as revenue	=	+
Consumption of future revenues	IV.3. Anticipation to the present of taxes at the expense of future tax credits	+	+
	Expenditure		
Restrictive definition of government	V.10 Nationalization of debts of public entities	+	−
	V.9 Loans from the government to public non-profits	+	+
	V.11 Deficits of public service public enterprises	+	+
	V.14 Debts of public service public enterprises	=	+
Restrictive definition of expenditures	V.6 Recording at nominal value the supply of assets under concessional conditions for economic policy reasons	+	+
	V.12 Guarantees and insurance instead of grants	+	+
Shifting public expenditures backward and forward	V.1 Apparent postponing of investment expenditures	+	+
	V.2 Apparent postponing of financing public investments undertaken by quasi-market or market entities	+	+
	V.3 Shifting pension expenditures backward	+	+
	V.3 Apparent postponement of public wages and pensions	+	+
	V.4 Shifting forward rebates due to taxpayers	+	+
	V.6 Shifting the cost of the zero coupon bonds to the year of reimbursement	+	+
	V.7 Shifting the principal and interest due on post office "capitalization" saving deposits to the time of encashment	+	+
	V.13 Postponement of currently due transfer credits that need Treasury authorization to become debts	+	+
	V.15 Delay of payments of debts due	+	=

6. *Revenues obtained as dividends from a revaluation of the gold reserves of the central bank* of which the government is a stockholder. This operation can only be performed if the central bank concurs, or by issuing a special piece of legislation.[38] The revaluation of gold reserves, recorded at a lower purchase value, does not produce any real capital gain. Therefore to claim a dividend from the central bank would imply a reduction in its real assets. The government merely expands the money supply. This method is worse than if it just drew banknotes from the central bank.[39] This is a sophisticated case of fiscal illusion, mentioned here only for the record.[40]

7. *Capital gains from the sale of real property with subsequent renting or leaseback.* This may be the case with the sale of public service infrastructure to an entity, which finances the purchase by raising funds on the financial market, with government guarantee.[41] Even if the purpose of such operations may be to reduce the size of government through "outsourcing" (in addition to obtaining financial savings and a more efficient provision of the services), the accounting of these receipts as revenue appears to be a non-transparent opportunistic accounting behavior.[42]

8. *Apparent revenue from the purchase of outstanding public debt instruments in exchange for indexed bonds sold at a price higher than their face value.* This is possible because the indexed bonds have an interest rate too close to that of the non-indexed bonds. This is another case of fiscal illusion. The (apparent) capital gain is compensated by a higher (future) flow of interest. Accrual accompanied by a comprehensive accounting of government net wealth would dispel this illusion.

9. *Revenues drawn by the government as dividend from a public*

---

[38] A proposal of this type was recently mooted in Germany. However, it had to be withdrawn almost immediately because of an overwhelming consensus of dissent, encompassing public opinion, the central bank, the parliament, and the government. The reasons are given in the text and in the next footnote.

[39] Worse because here, the net effect is a reduction of the reserves of the central bank plus an exogenous increase in the money supply.

[40] With ESA 95 requiring that assets be recorded at their true market value, this kind of creative accounting behavior would be precluded.

[41] However, if the institutions acquiring the relevant properties are capable of raising funds on the market on their own, these operations should be left out of creative accounting. Then this becomes a true means of reducing the scope of government without reducing public services, by securing an increased role of the market in their provision.

[42] However, this has been allowed by the European Statistical Office, because the more comprehensive treatments of leasing adopted after ESA 78 and before ESA 95 are not relevant for the Maastricht definition of the deficit. With ESA 95 this category of creative accounting will lose relevance.

holding. This consists of a realization of (part of) the nominal capital gains obtained on the holding by selling the asset on the market at a price higher than their previous book value, which does not reflect their actual value.[43] Here, again, the opportunistic accounting behavior implies a lack of transparency.

10. *Nominal capital gains resulting from the sale of land of the domain.*[44] Here, the land may be recorded in the books at a low value but may already possess a good market value. Privatization of real estate may be a sound policy, particularly for a heavily indebted country. Under accrual, correctly interpreted,[45] only a change of destination may give rise to a real asset revaluation and a reduction in net borrowing. The comments made in the context of 9 above apply here as well.

C   *Categories for the Debt Rule*

Budget accounting to reduce net liabilities may also automatically affect gross liabilities, that is, the ratio of public debt to GDP. This occurs for cases 1–9 above. In other words, activities related to the deficit also affect the level of debt. In addition, opportunistic accounting may reduce the gross liabilities of general government, as in the following cases:

11. *Sale by the central government of gold purchased from the central bank in exchange for long-term commercial loans.*[46] This operation does not affect the deficit, because the revenue for the government is matched by its debt with the central bank. However, a reduction in public debt can arise if the government employs these revenues to purchase its bonds. This occurs because of the exclusion of short- and long-term commercial loans from the public debt, set forth in Regulation 3605/93. This opportunistic accounting practice disguises borrowing by the government from the central bank and implies money creation by the Treasury as a substitute for public debt. The lack of transparency here relates to the government's monetary behavior.

---

[43] Again, ESA 95 makes this creative accounting practice impossible. Anyway, the case is different if the increase in stock value is caused by the fact that the government renounces its control or management of the company (for example, by liquidating a golden share). Here the increase in value is real and should be accounted for on the revenue side of the budget.

[44] This opportunistic accounting practice is not possible in countries where the receipts of sales of assets, whether non-financial or financial, are excluded from budget revenues and are deposited in a fund for the amortization of public debt.

[45] As indeed with ESA 95.

[46] The loan is a commercial one, because the gold has to be demonetized if it is to be sold on the free market.

12. *Temporary sale (for less than a week) of public debt at the end of the year 1 to autonomous financial institutions, to be repurchased in year 2.* The purchase by the financial institution is recorded in year 1 and that of the government in year 2, following ESA 78 accounting rules. The temporary flow of money going to the government goes unrecorded, being the counterpart of a financial transaction.[47] Because the ratio of public debt to GDP is that of the last working day of the year, this window-dressing operation creates the illusion that government debt has been *permanently* reduced. Being a financial transaction, this operation has no impact on the deficit, except for the (small) difference between the excess of the reimbursement by the government over the cash received, a payment for its short-term use of funds. Obviously, under ESA 78 this difference will be imputed to the budget of the year of debt repurchase.

13. *Transformation of enterprises formerly included in the government into autonomous legal entities.* These entities are still controlled and guaranteed by the (central or local) government. This action shifts the debts related to their investments off the government's balance sheet. If the government guarantees on this debt are maintained, this is non-transparent creative accounting.

V   Categories of Opportunistic Behaviors in Maastricht Budgetary Accounting – The Expenditure Side

A   Categories for the Deficit Rule

Beginning with the net deficit limit, the following categories deserve consideration.

1. *Apparent postponing of public investment expenditure by delaying the legal recognition of the purchase of work done.*[48] Outstanding debts are thus hidden and transparency violated. This operation cannot be done on a large scale and for a long period of time, because the contractors may legally question the delay. Thus the following *escamotage* may be pursued.

2. *Apparent postponing of financing of public investments*, undertaken by autonomous market economy corporations or by quasi-private entities. This can be done by delaying the official approval of their grants, but guaranteeing their debts on the

---

[47] See footnote 9. *The Wall Street Journal* has severely criticized this exotic brand of creative accounting in a number of articles. ESA 95 makes this impossible.

[48] See above, Part III.

market so they can pay their contractors. Thus, the investment may be made on time (most probably with some additional costs), without appearing as an expenditure in the year of realization.[49] Obviously this disingenuous device implies non-transparent creative accounting.

3. *Artificial containment of pensions and wages expenditure* in a given year by shifting backward or forward the time of the obligation. This can be done by manipulating the legal aspect of the procedures leading to the payments due. The first policy (*shifting back*) may be particularly applied for claims of additional benefits on existing pensions, while the second policy (*shifting forward*) may be adopted for the new early retirement pensions. The latter policy can be used to reduce the pressure for system reforms arising from high pension cost by shifting the examination of the claims from the end of one year to the beginning of a subsequent year. For wage increases, the operation may consist of retarding their recognition (shifting back), in the individual cases, to conceal their real cost. While payment does not appear in full in the present budget, it will be subsequently recorded in it, once its examination has been officially completed and approval given.[50] Clearly, the aim here is to render budgetary burdens non-transparent.

4. *Postponement of legal quantification of the rebates* due to taxpayers for taxes paid in excess[51] considering them due only when the individual credits have been officially ascertained.[52] Thus both the revenue and the expenditure are made non-transparent.

5. *Apparent reduction of the expenses for public investments* through an assumption by the government of the obligation of

---

[49] According to ESA 78, Chapter VII. O7, para. 3, indent 3, p. 707, the output of goods whose production extends over several periods of *time* is to be recorded at the end of each period on the basis of the value of the work carried out during that period. Thus, if the relevant expenditure was directly undertaken by a contractor for the government, its costs should be recorded when the work is realized in spite of the fact that no legal obligation for the payments due was yet specified. But if the government deals with an autonomous market or quasi-market entity, which in turn contracts out the work, there is no direct relation between the government and the contractor. Thus the ESA rule on accounting for expenditures on goods whose production extends over a period of time may be eluded.

[50] Normally, the beneficiaries are familiar with the content of the clauses directly affecting them and are aware of the quantitative effects on their pay and fringe benefits.

[51] See above, Part IV B, point 5 for the corresponding creative accounting device on the *revenue side*.

[52] This opportunistic behavior may not be convenient for the government if the law specifies that rebates paid after a given time period will be increased by high interest rates.

making the interest and amortization service payments on debt issued by the subsidized autonomous entities actually engaged in the projects. This may be a sound practice, to reduce public intervention and public debt. However, it is an inherently non-transparent behavior and may create an illusion about the costs of public projects, which can only be dispelled by long-term budget planning.[53]

6. *Recording at nominal value the purchases of bad assets of corporations and financially autonomous entities.* This may be a particular problem, when the subscription of new shares is used to replenish the capital of enterprises that are systematically in deficit. For example, banks burdened by non-performing loans may be "rescued" with a package in which the bad credits are sold at non-market prices.[54] Obviously, these transactions are mostly non-transparent subsidies and not purchases of assets.

7. *Issuance of zero coupon bonds* recording the implicit interest consisting of the difference between the issue price and the face value, exclusively in the year of reimbursement, as allowed by ESA 78. ESA 95, adhering more consistently to the accrual method, adopts the transparent imputation of the implicit interest cost to each year in the life of the bonds.

8. *Accounting of imputed interest on Post Office capitalization–savings deposits* in the year of withdrawal of the deposits, on the basis of the aforementioned ESA 78 rule. ESA 95 adopts the transparent device of allocating the interest credited to the savers on a year-by-year basis.

9. *Loans to nonprofit institutions that are not included in the government* as defined by ESA 78, because more than 50% of their costs are covered by sales. In practice, a large part of these sales are actually purchases by social security institutions on behalf of their beneficiaries.[55] This is off-budget non-transparent accounting.

10. *Direct assumption, by the government, of loans and other financial instruments* issued by institutions whose debt service (both interest and amortization) it was committed to bear. This debt

---

[53] This issue is dealt with below in Part VI, together with that arising in the case mentioned in Part IV B, point 7.

[54] In principle, the EU forbids these kinds of rescue operations because they distort competition, and violate the rules in force after the adoption of the "unique market" changes of the Rome Treaty approved in 1985. However, cases of this kind, particularly in the banking sector, are always coming up.

[55] These peculiar kinds of revenues, which actually have a government source are also included in market revenues by ESA 95, Chapter III, 3.34, p. 42. Its dirigistic ideology prevents it from distinguishing the true market economy from the quasi-market created by government purchases from its own autonomous entities.

nationalization ensures that only interest expenditures enter the government budget. By definition, amortization charges do not form part of the government budget. Examples of this include public utility entities such as state railways, where the EU allows infrastructural costs to be substantially borne by the state. The EU requires that as far as possible, economic criteria be used in making these expenditures, to avoid the distortion of competition. While unintentionally creative, this is transparent accounting.

11. *Non-consolidation of deficits of public enterprises* owned by the state or by the local authorities, in the aggregate deficit of the government. These enterprises run public services, and the government is responsible for their debts. This possibility of hiding deficits in off-budget entities arises because of the formal definition of government by ESA.[56]

12. *Concessions to financial institutions* in the form of guarantees in the raising of finance or insurance to support risky operations, replacing more costly but more transparent grants. This type of operation is similar to net lending (in the terminology of IMF GFS 86) because of the implicit grant component.

13. *Postponement of obligations due for transfers to public and private entities*, for given years, by denying that these credits are *due* and hence denying the Treasury authorization to make payment. The burden is thus shifted, in a non-transparent way, onto the future budgets. While this postponement may be a legitimate cash operation, to reduce the solvency constraint and postpone the creation of public debt, it nevertheless creates a transitory illusion of expenditure reduction in the primary budget. The operation may be particularly justified, from the perspective of liquidity, when interest rates on public debt are falling so that the primary budget's surplus requirement is also expected to diminish in subsequent periods.

B Categories for the Debt Rule

Most of the above finance and accounting techniques by which governments may elude Maastricht deficit constraints on the expenditure side, also automatically limit the ratio of debt to GDP. This is true for items 1–6, 8, 9, and 11–13. However, the opposite may happen in the case of items 7 and 10. Zero coupon bonds, being sold at a price lower than face

---

[56] To avoid these problems, IMF 1986 GFS, I, 46, distinguishes government as such and *government activities* and includes them in government even when carried out by formally autonomous entities.

value to reflect the imputed interest rate, as required by the market, artificially increase the debt outstanding in the year of their issuance. Debt nationalization has the same effect, but with a greater leverage. Here the effective increase of the public debt consists of the value of the assets involved.[57]

In addition, on the expenditure side, one may list the following categories of opportunistic non-transparent accounting that can be used to contain the debt:

14. *Omitting to record the existing stock of net[58] liabilities* of autonomous public enterprises and of nonprofit institutions formally not included in general government, which nevertheless functions are their guarantor.[59]
15. *Delaying payments* (with or without recognition of interest) to reduce the debt ratio. This possibility arises from the definition, in Regulation 3605/93, of gross debt as a cash concept. Again, this postponement may be an appropriate use of discretionary cash balances. However, excessive delays imply a hidden transfer of the burden of financing the public budget on households and firms. They may be a non-transparent *escamotage* to reduce the level of public debt to within the limits permitted by the Maastricht rules, without the effective motivation of the liquidity constraint.

VI   Contingent Liabilities

A   Inadequacies of Maastricht Accounting in This Borderline Area

Under the present Maastricht budgetary accounting framework, three important areas of potential deficits and debts remain hidden due to the combination of ESA 78 and Regulation 3605/93. These are guarantees, assets purchased for economic policy purposes and pension debt. All of these may be defined as issues of *accounting for contingent liabilities*. They fall in the borderline area between the conventional notions of the government budget and of public debt and the quasi-government and quasi-market activities that have sprouted in areas traditionally reserved for the government provision of public goods.[60]

---

[57] Imagine a debt of 120% of GDP, a nominal growth rate of GDP of 3.5% (a low rate indeed) and a deficit of 3.2% of GDP. Even in this pessimistic case there will be an automatic reduction of 0.36% in the ratio of debt to GDP.

[58] Net and not gross because the consolidation of autonomous public enterprises should be carried out only for their net deficits and debt and not for their total revenues, expenditures, assets, and liabilities in order to avoid presenting a misleading picture of the government sector.

[59] See footnote 10.

[60] For similar issues in the Asian "Tiger" economies, see Heller (1997).

B   *Recording Government Guarantees as Derivatives in a Collateral Account*

Depending on how they are used, government guarantees to non-government institutions can be perverse instruments or part of sound public finance regime. When they are abused, such guarantees can broaden the sphere of public intervention in the economy. When used appropriately, they can reduce direct government activities in the provision of public goods by replacing them with private investment initiatives and quasi-market operations (Sawkins and McMaster, 1997; H. M. Treasury, 1995). Cases of this second kind are considered here, where the granting government guarantees is a sound financial choice. However, even in this case, it is important to record them as contingent liabilities using some prudential accounting criteria, so that the potential risks arising from them and their beneficiaries are made transparent.

ESA 95 allows the recording of derivatives, when they are negotiable and therefore endowed with a sort of market value. On the other hand, derivative accounting is a topical question and raises peculiar problems, not only for public accounting but also in business accounting.[61] To put the guarantees, assessed as derivatives, in the general budget, may be too confusing. Nor would it result in a transparent picture of the burden of the existing stock of government guarantees. It would seem better to list them at their face value in appendices to the budget, adding their hidden grant component (assessed by prudential accounting) as a net liability, in footnotes.

C   *Recording of Contingent Liabilities of Social Security Pension Debts in a Collateral Account*

A substantial part of these debts consists of standing liabilities of social security institutions for currently mature rights of present workers. The institutions may expect to fund these net liabilities out of future contributions. However, these existing liabilities cannot be separated from future liabilities that are not yet mature. Thus, from the point of view of pay-as-you-go government institutions, their pension debt is a global contingent liabilities issue. The central government is politically (even if not always legally) responsible for these liabilities, so that they might be considered a type of option at the general government level and thus viewed as financial derivatives.

The future deficits, discounted to the present at a given rate of interest, give rise to the present pensions debt (Towe, 1993). From the social

---

[61] See ESA 95, Chapter V, 5.65–5.66, and Chapter VII, 7.50, first and second indent. The problems of prudential accounting for general government contingent liabilities are briefly dealt with below in the "Concluding Remarks."

security institution's perspective, these deficits may be considered contingent liabilities, insofar as their size depends on the level of aggregate future incomes from which future social security contributions will be drawn. In principle, this may not be the case when the system is based on actuarial fairness or even on actuarial balance because by definition, deficits should not appear (Towe, 1993). But many regimes (like the one in Italy) are based on actuarial balance in principle, but have a long transition period and suffer from exceptions that lead to a sizable future deficit (Rostagno, 1997; Hamann, 1997). The time dimension of the flow, as seen from the social security institution's perspective, should be that relating to the maximum period in which the existing potential liabilities will be translated in pension rights. Based on the present rules on retirement age, this period is forty years.

The European Commission (EC II/422/95–EN), analyzing the measure of gross debt adopted by the Maastricht Treaty as complemented by Regulation 3605/93, recognizes that, on theoretical grounds, the inclusion of *all* contingent liabilities in government debt improves the comparison of government indebtedness among different countries. However, it maintains that they have not been included in the official definition of gross debt, because of the difficulty of choosing a noncontroversial rate of interest. It has proved to be very difficult – it writes – to come up with an accurate and clear quantification of contingent liabilities, as the calculation depends crucially on the discount rate used to calculate their present value. Considerations of data availability and transparency militate in favor of a relatively simple concept that can be easily produced and monitored.

Just because the measurement of pension debt is a controversial issue, it does not follow that disregarding it, even in accounts collateral to that of the debt stock, improves fiscal transparency. Such a policy may simplify the data, but the transparency suffers. This is because this debt, partially mature but not yet liquid and partly non-mature (however measured), often represents an important part of the entire public debt burden. A serious and undesirable fiscal policy consequence of this "accounting deficit" is the unilateral emphasis laid on whether the 3% limit is *exactly* respected, while overlooking a *major* – and for some countries – *the* major source of structural deficits.

It should be noted that as a derivative, this contingent liability appears to be a marginal one in the sense that the liability is certain, up to a given amount. Further, the discount rate may be less controversial than the EC asserts, given the existence of official European interest rates based on the Maastricht Convergence rules. These European convergence rates of interest may be used to represent the opportunity cost of unfunded liabilities in each EU country (Kune, Petit, and Pinxt, 1993; Rostagno, 1997; Kotlikoff, 1984; Towe, 1993).

VII   Concluding Remark0s

As we have seen, the adoption of ESA 95 will preclude a host of categories of opportunistic accounting behaviors both on the revenue and on the expenditure side. This applies equally to behaviors undertaken to camouflage the deficit and, par consequence, to debt. Dubious direct and indirect tax revenues could not be accounted as revenues due, in the accrual-basis budget. The same rule could be extended, by interpretation, to social security contributions. Rebates on withholding taxes should be excluded from revenue, because they do not imply a tax obligation. Value-added taxes should be accounted net of rebates, as stated by ESA 95, in the relevant sectors of activity.[62] Apparent capital gains resulting from the sale of assets valued in the books at prices lower than their true market value should also be prevented by adoption of ESA 95. The same will be true for the apparent revenue from the revaluation of the book value of gold.[63] On the expenditure side, ESA 95 precludes the postponing of the accounting of the imputed interest on bilateral financial transactions that must be recorded when the transaction first takes place. Purchases of assets for economic policy reasons, under ESA 95, will give rise to an expenditure equal to the difference between the assets' nominal value and their effective value, based on the capitalization of their expected revenues or realization.[64]

It does not appear difficult to introduce, for the purposes of the Maastricht rules, some changes in ESA definitions to ensure a more comprehensive definition of the general government sector. There is no reason why the definition of gross debt should not be the comprehensive one theorized here. However, if the member states were obliged to report their planned deficits and levels of government debt on a pluri-annual basis, accounting manipulations that consist of artificially shifting obligations relating to pensions, wages, transfers to private and public entities backward and forward would lose much of their relevance.

For the taxpayer, general government debt is a currently extant debt. However, the net liabilities of "commercial" public enterprises, which may become a government liability, the pension debt and the contingent liabilities relating to the government guarantees, are liabilities that may be substantially reduced or even removed by timely interventions, to the benefit of the taxpayer. Alternatively they may become oppressive for the future taxpayers, if satisfying the letter of the Maastricht Treaty leads to illusory budgetary accounting. In any event, in the absence of a gov-

[62] For withholding taxes, accounting for them gross of rebates is (correctly) also precluded under ESA 78, because rebates do not form part of the tax due.

[63] However, this is mere money creation and the government should be precluded from undertaking this action.

[64] See ESA 95, Chapter V, Accounting Rules for Financial Transactions, pp. 11–113.

ernment balance sheet requirement, it seems important to record them in collateral accounts.

The budgetary accounting system relevant for the Maastricht fiscal constitution at the EU level is likely to underlie the standard budgetary accounts presented by EU countries. These accounts will also be presented outside the EU, to the international institutions, and to the international markets. Furthermore, in the next decade, at least eleven countries will seek admission to the EU in one form or the other. It is likely that their budgetary accounting will be scrutinized using the present Maastricht accounting framework. Thus, these opportunistic budgetary accounting behaviors, while analyzed here in the context of the early years of convergence to the EMU, will become increasingly important rather mere matters of technical curiosity.

References

Alesina, A., and Perotti, A. 1994. "The Political Economy of Budget Deficits." International Monetary Fund Working Paper WP/94/85, August.

Auerbach, A. J., Gokhale, J., and Kotlikoff, L. J. 1994. "Generational Accounting: A Meaningful Way to Evaluate Fiscal Policy." *Journal of Economic Perspectives*, 8 (1 Winter): 73–94.

Auerbach, A. J., and Kotlikoff, L. J. 1987. *Dynamic Fiscal Policy*. Cambridge, Cambridge University Press.

Balassone, F., and Franco, D. 1996. "Il fabbisogno finanziario pubblico." *Temi di discussione del Servizio Studi*, No. 277, Rome: Banca di Italia.

Blanchard, O. J., Chouraqui, J., Hageman, R. P., and Sartor, N. 1990. "The Sustainability of Fiscal Policy: New Answers to an Old Question." *OECD Economic Studies*, No. 15, Autumn. Paris: OECD.

Blejer, M., and Cheasty, A. 1991. "The Measurement of Fiscal Deficits: Analytical and Methodological Issues." *Journal of Economic Literature*, 29 (December): 1644–78.

Buchanan, J., and Wagner, R. E. 1977. *Democracy in Deficit*. New York: Academic Press.

Buiter, W. H. 1984. "Measuring Aspects of Fiscal and Financial Policy." NBER Working Paper 1332. Cambridge, Mass., National Bureau of Economic Research.

———. 1992. "Measurement of the Public Sector Deficit and Its Implications for Policy Evaluation and Design." In M. Blejer and A. Cheasty, eds., *How to Measure the Fiscal Deficit: Analytical and Methodological Issues*. Washington, D.C.: International Monetary Fund, pp. 297–344.

Buiter, W. H., and Corsetti, G., and Roubini, N. 1993. "Excessive Deficit: Sense and Nonsense in the Treaty of Maastricht." *Economic Policy*, No. 16, pp. 57–100.

Castellino, O. 1987. "Debito pubblico e debito previdenziale: analogie e differenze." In F. Bruni, ed., *Debito pubblico e politica economica*. Collana Giorgio Rota, No. 1. Rome: Società Italiana di Economia Pubblica.

de Callatay, E., and Turtelbom, B. 1996. "Pension Reform in Belgium." International Monetary Fund Working Paper WP/96/74, July.

Dollery, B. E., and Worthington, A. C. 1996. "The Empirical Analysis of Fiscal Illusion." *Journal of Economic Theory*, 10(3): 262–95.

Eisner, R. 1986. *How Real Is the Federal Deficit.* New York: The Free Press, Macmillan.

European Commission. 1995. "Methodological and Operational Aspects of the Reporting of Government Deficits and Debt Levels in the Context of the Excessive Deficit procedure." *Directorate General II, Economic and Financial Affairs*, II/422/95–EN.II.C.2.

European Community. 1993. "Council Regulation (EC) No. 3605/93, of November 22, 1933, on the Application of the Protocol on the Excessive Deficit Procedure Annexed to the Treaty Establishing the European Community." *Official Journal*, No. C324,1.12.93, (EC).

European Union. 1993. *Treaty Establishing the European Community* (Adjourned with the Maastricht Treaty's Amendments). Brussels and Luxembourg (EU).

Eurostat. 1979. *ESA 78, European System of Accounts*. 2d edition. Brussels and Luxembourg (EC).

——— 1996. *ESA 95, European System of Accounts*. Brussels and Luxembourg (EC).

Fasiani, M. 1951. *Principi di scienza delle finanze*, Vol. I. Book I. Turin, Italy: Giappichelli.

Forte, F. 1996. Myths and Paradoxes of Pensions Schemes as Intergenerational Social Contracts, unpublished manuscript, presented at the 1996 SIPI (Societá Italiana di Economia Pubblica) meeting at University of Pavia. (The Italian version is forthcoming in D. Da Empoli and G. Muraro, *Verso un nuovo stato sociale*, Milan: Angeli, 1997.)

——— 1997a. "The Measurement of 'Fiscal Burden' on GDP instead than on National Net Value Added Produced: A Chapter in Fiscal Illusion." *Quarterly Review Banca Nazionale del Lavoro*, No. 202, p. 337.

——— 1997b. "I bilanci pubblici italiani alla luce della costituzione fiscale di Maastricht." *Economia Pubblica*, No. 4, pp. 5–56.

——— 1999. "The Italian Republican Fiscal Constitution: Reasons for a Failure." *European Journal of Law and Economics* 7(2): 103–16.

Hamann, A. J. 1997. "The Reform of the Pension System in Italy." IMF *Working Paper*, WP/97/18.

Haveman, R. 1994. "Should Generational Accounts Replacte Public Budgets and Deficits?" *Journal of Economic Perspectives* 8 (1 Winter): 95–111.

Heller, P. S. 1997. "Aging in the Asian 'Tigers': Challenges for Fiscal Policy." International Monetary Fund, private circulation.

Treasury, H.M. 1995. *Private Opportunity, Public Benefit. Progressing the Private Finance Initiative*. London: H.M Treasury.

International Monetary Fund. 1996. *Government Finance Statistics Manual. Annotated Outline*. Washington, D.C.: International Monetary Fund.

——— 1986. *A Manual of Government Finance Statistics*. Washington, D.C.: International Monetary Fund.

——— *World Economic Outlook*, issues from May 1993 to May 1997.

Kotlikoff, L. J. 1984. "Economic Impact of Deficit Financing." *IMF Staff Papers*, 31 (September), pp. 549–82.

Kune, J. B., Petit, W. F. M., and Pinxt, A. J. H. 1993. "The Hidden Liabilities of Basic Pension Systems in the European Community." CEPS Working Document, 80.

Mackenzie, G. A. 1993. "Are All Summary Indicators of Stance of Fiscal Policy

Misleading?" In M. Blejer and A. Cheasty, *How to Measure the Fiscal Deficit*. Washington, D.C.: International Monetary Fund, pp. 21–51.

Merton, R. C. 1977. "An Analytic Derivation of the Cost of Deposit Insurance and Loan Guarantees." *Journal of Banking and Finance*, 1 (June): 3–11.

Puviani, A. 1903. *Teoria dell'illusione finanziaria*. Re-edited by F. Volpi. 1973, Milano, ISEDI.

Rossi, N. 1988. "Government Spending, the Real Interest Rate, and the Behavior of Liquidity–Constrained Consumers in Developing Countries." *IMF Staff Papers* 35 (March): 104–40.

Rostagno, M. 1997. "Il percorso della riforma: 1922–1995. Nuovi indicatori di consistenza e sostenibilita' per il FPLD." In F. Padoa Schioppa, *Agenda e nonagenda: limiti e crisi della politica economica*. Bologna: Il Mulino, 1997, pp. 325–97.

Sawkins, J. W., and McMaster, R. 1997. "Quasi Markets for Water Services: Reviving the Auld Alliance?" Hume Monograph, No. 1, The David Hume Institute, Edinburgh: Pace Print.

Selling, T. I., and Stickney, C. P. 1986. "Pension Accounting and Future Cash Flow." *Journal of Accounting and Public Policy*, V (Winter): 267–85.

Stella, P. 1993. "Toward Defining and Measuring the Fiscal Impact of Public Enterprises." In M. Blejer and A. Cheasty, eds., *How to Measure the Fiscal Deficit*. Washington, D.C.: International Monetary Fund, pp. 207–35.

Stotsky, J. G., and Sunley, E. M. 1994. "The Tax System of the United States." *Tax Notes International*, 9 (Dec.): 1755–83.

Tanzi, V. 1977. "Inflation, Lags in Collection and the Real Value of Tax Revenue." *IMF Staff Papers*, March 24 (I): 154–67.

1993. "Fiscal Deficit Measurement: Basic Issues." In M. Blejer and A. Cheasty, eds., *How to Measure Fiscal Deficit*. Washington, D.C.: International Monetary Fund, pp. 13–20.

Tanzi, V., Blejer, M., and Teijero, O. 1988. "The Effects of Inflation on the Measurement of Fiscal Deficits." In M. Blejer and K. Chu, eds., *Measurement of Fiscal Impact: Methodological Issues*. Washington, D.C.: International Monetary Fund.

Towe, C. 1993. "Government Contingent Liabilities and Measurement of Fiscal Impact." In M. Blejer and A. Cheasty, eds., *How to Measure Fiscal Deficit*. Washington, D.C.: International Monetary Fund, pp. 363–89.

The Treasury. 1995, 1996. *Fiscal Responsibility Act, an Explanation*. Wellington, New Zealand: Treasury.

United Nations. 1868. *A System of National Accounts*. SNA. New York: UN.

Von Hagen, J. 1991. "A Note on the Empirical Effectiveness of Formal Fiscal Restraints." *Journal of Public Economics*, 44: 199–210.

Wagner, R. E. 1976. "Revenue Structure, Fiscal Illusion and Budgetary Choices." *Public Choice*, No. 25, pp. 45–61.

Wildavsky, A., and Zapico Goni, A., eds., 1993. *National Budgeting for Economic and Monetary Union*. Maastricht: European Institute of Public Administration.

CHAPTER 15

Subsidiarity, Federalism, and Direct Democracy as Basic Elements of a Federal European Constitution: Some Ideas Using Constitutional Economics

Friedrich Schneider and Alexander F. Wagner

1   Introduction

We are currently observing the final steps in the process toward forming the European Monetary Union (EMU). Hence, the next step is to create not only an economic but also a monetary union, toward which major progress has been made with fixed agreements about the next stages in the Maastricht Treaty. In order to enable the functioning of such a dual union, some (minimal) European federal union will be required. In this chapter some basic elements of a federal European constitution, like subsidiarity, federalism, and direct democratic institution are elaborated with the help of the constitutional economics. This chapter builds on a large literature of positive economics and tries to provide some normative suggestions. The authors think that while the proposals made may be controversial, the evidence found in the literature is, on balance, in their favor. In any case this article is meant to be thought provoking and should be discussed thoroughly.

In Section 2 six propositions, which should be key elements of a European constitution, are introduced. In Sections 3–5 an attempt is made to scientifically justify these propositions. The design of European legislation is discussed in Section 3, the subsidiarity and federalism principle in Section 4, and direct democratic institutions in Section 5. Finally Section 6 provides a summary and gives some conclusions.

Based on a paper presented at the annual Public Choice meeting in New Orleans, March 12–15, 1998. We would like to thank Hilton Root (Stanford) and Robin Grier (CIDE-Mexico) as well as other discussants for their comments.

2   Six Basic Elements of a Future European Federal Constitution

The completion of the European Internal Market provides the opportunity to achieve a number of efficiency gains when creating such a big economic unit. It also provides the opportunity to stimulate the growth rates of Western European economies. This involves the dissolution of national regulations, the strengthening of competition in the markets, and the lifting of entry barriers to markets. Furthermore, competition is promoted between member states by lowering the direct and indirect tax burden and by weakening state-owned monopolies. However, there is also the danger that the positive influences would be weakened, if national regulations were replaced by EC regulations, if European cartels were allowed, if new (trade or other) barriers against non-Community countries were created or the existing ones increased, and finally if a "new federal" government at the EC level were "created" without operating in a carefully designed institutional framework.[1]

As has been argued in detail in Schneider (1996), it is generally recognized that representative (and to a much lesser extent direct) democratic systems show a long-term tendency toward rising influence of interest groups, a growing share of government expenditures in GNP, and increasing regulation. Such developments can lower overall efficiency by introducing distortions in the markets, the capability to innovate, and productive investment, and thus may finally lead to a smaller growth rate of GNP. This usually happens if a democratic regime is not restricted with respect to its expenditure, revenue, and regulation sides by constitutional or other arrangements, so that shifting majorities in parliament, which are only inadequately controlled by rationally uninformed voters, can impose their will on the great majority of the population. With at least two parties competing for votes and the necessity of financial assistance to cover the costs of their organizations and election campaigns, this results in regulation by government, tax loopholes, and subsidies to special pressure groups whenever the majority of voters is rationally uninformed about the issues.[2] This is the case as decisions only marginally affect the economic situation of citizens, since they then have little reason to inform themselves, given the fact that the influence of individual votes on election outcomes is negligible. As a consequence, we observe, for example, protection of certain industries against foreign competition, fixing of agricultural prices to above-market clearing levels, and subsidies to special industries (like the shipping and coal industries). Only if such economic developments (like rent increases to special inter-

---

[1] Compare Alesina and Perotti (1994), Alesina and Rodrik (1992), Kirchgässner and Pommerehne (1995), Lybeck and Henrekson (1988), and Wagner (2000).

[2] For example, compare the studies by Bernholz (1990b, 1993).

est groups) are perceived by a majority of voters/taxpayers as resulting in an additional tax burden for them will government action favor the majority, for example, either by imposing rent-seeking controls or cutting the subsidies.[3]

From all these factors it is to be expected that state activity will grow over time. In a system of competing parties, a democratic government responds to the demands of various groups of voters and of special interest groups with additional expenditure.[4] Thus, it is often argued, the older a democracy, the higher the level of regulations, of taxes, subsidies, and transfers one would expect with comparable levels of per capita incomes (Olson 1982, 1983). But since excessive state activity can also lead to less efficiency and innovation, one would also expect negative consequences for real economic growth, a result that seems to be corroborated by empirical evidence.[5] As has just been argued, the completion of the European Internal Market can be seen as an attempt to break down national barriers, regulations, cartels, subsidies, and so forth, which have led to a sclerosis in some European states (e.g., Great Britain and Germany) and to poor growth performance in these states compared to newly industrialized economies like Japan. This could have served as one motivational factor in the work undertaken under the heading of "Europe 1992."

But then there should be careful consideration given to creating a federal European constitution in order to limit protection, regulation, subsidies, cartels, a growing share of European federal government expenditures, and the influence of interest groups. Buchanan (1990: 1) has drawn attention to the fact that "Europe is now presented with a historically unique opportunity. . . . The [constitutional] contract must be such as to ensure mutual gains from trade. . . . The only constitutional structure that is consistent with the historically constrained setting of the 1990s is that of a federal union. . . ." Buchanan (1990: 10) also stresses that "a central political authority must come into being with some sovereignty over citizens in all of the nation-states." Following Buchanan, it seems advisable to support the introduction of a federal European constitution.

It has already been stressed in Schneider (1993, 1996) that democratic systems with market economies, if unchecked, show a strong tendency toward increasing state activity and interest group influence. As a con-

---

[3] See, e.g., Downs (1957) and Buchanan and Tullock (1962). Bartel and Schneider (1987, 1991) analyze the situation in Austria especially in the context of the state-owned industry.

[4] See, e.g., Olson (1965), Bernholz (1966, 1969), Borcherding (1985) and for empirical evidence on representative democracies compare Schneider and Frey (1988).

[5] Compare the studies by Bernholz (1990a), Marlow (1986), Peden and Bradley (1989), Weede (1986, 1990), and De Haan and Siermann (1995, 1996).

sequence, the motivation of individuals to work efficiently, to engage in risky productive activities, and to innovate is weakening. Whereas the removal of intra-European barriers to the movement of people, goods, capital, and services might weaken the influence of special-interest groups and bureaucracies in EU member states, a growth at the federal European level has to be expected as soon as Europewide interest groups and parties have been fully established. A European constitution thus has to contain provisions to counterbalance such tendencies.

The following suggestions should in one way or the other be part of such a constitution:[6]

1. The European Commission should be turned into a European government with strictly limited tasks (e.g., the ones set up in point 2), the Council of Prime Ministers into a second chamber of Parliament where each country has the same weight of voting power. The simple majority approval of both chambers (the European Parliament and the European Council) is necessary for any legislation passed. The European Parliament and the second chamber should solely have the full authority and responsibility for all European budgetary and federal items. If the two chambers cannot agree on a legislative or budgetary item, the parliament can overrule the decision of the second chamber by a qualified (e.g., two-thirds) majority.

2. The jurisdiction of the European federal government should consist mainly of defense, foreign policy, foreign trade policy, the enforcement of free intra-community movement (of people, goods, services and capital), anti-cartel and anti-monopoly policy and environmental policy (using whenever possible market consistent measures) concerning community-wide pollution and other environmental problems. All these policy issues should only be taken over by the European government, if there is consensus of the member states that the highest federal unit should do it, and if a referendum over these issues is approved by simple majority of the European voters and by simple majority of the member states.

3. For the federal European government it should not be possible to run or accumulate deficits on its (current) budget over a legislative period. If a budget deficit still occurs at the end of a legislative period, either expenditures should be cut or revenues

---

[6] For a recent discussion of constitutional issues, see Gwartney and Wagner (1988), Vanberg and Buchanan (1989), Schneider (1993), Kirchgässner (1994), and Holzmann (1996). For fiscal federalism, see Frey (1977), Oates (1977, 1985), Blöchliger and Frey (1992), and Eichenberger (1994).

should be increased, given that the political conditions for a tax rate increase are fulfilled (compare suggestions 4 and 5), so that the budget will be balanced again. Longer (than a legislative period) lasting public debt at the European federal level should only be allowed for financing investment expenditures and only if the federal government has the financial capacity to pay the interest and amortization of the debt out of its current budget.[7]

4. The activities of the Community should be financed by one specifically labeled tax, like a proportional (indirect) tax. Increases of the rates of this tax should be subject to two-thirds majority of the European Parliament and of the second chamber, and to the approval of a popular referendum.

5. The institution of a popular referendum should be introduced for major, clearly in advance specified policy issues (like a change of the constitution, change of tax rates, etc.). Furthermore, a popular referendum should be held, if a certain number of voters ask for it and if at least a certain percentage of all people entitled to vote participate. The precise figures under what conditions a referendum has to be held and is accepted have to be specified; the important point is that there exists a way to force the European government to hold a referendum over a certain issue. The issue, over which the referendum is held, is only accepted, if it is approved by simple majority of the European voters and by simple majority of the member states (which protects smaller member countries).

6. EU member states should have the right to secede from the European federal union. A member state should, by a qualified (two-thirds or three-fourths) majority vote of their population, be able to leave the European federal constitution and become again an independent state. However, the political and all other procedures for the secession should be precisely fixed in advance and a transition period of a considerable length of time (e.g., five or ten years) should be allowed. If an EU member state fails to reach such a qualified majority, the next attempt should be possible after twenty years.

After writing down these six important propositions, a scientific justification is given in the following sections why these six suggestions should be key elements of a future European constitution. It is shown that they

[7] Whether the European economic and monetary integration provides incentives to increase public deficits is investigated in Horstmann and Schneider (1994). Compare also Feld and Kirchgässner (1997).

might help to avoid some major problems, which trouble a lot of representative democracies today (like large budget deficits, voters' and taxpayers' dissatisfaction with the government, an increasing shadow economy, etc.).

3   The Design of the European Legislation

As the first basic proposition in Section 2 demands the formation of a European government with a two-chamber system, the first chamber, the European Parliament and the second chamber, the Council of Prime Ministers, and obviously the control of both chambers over all federal items, which are delegated to the European union, some general remarks will be made to justify this proposition. It is difficult to find studies analyzing the separation of powers from the perspective of positive constitutional economics. In a review-article Posner (1987) writes that the separation of powers increases the transaction costs of governing. This would hold for welfare-enhancing as well as for redistributive or even exploitative measures. The concept of separation of powers can be classified into the horizontal separation (legislature, executive, judiciary) and vertical separation (federalism). The structure of isolated powers can vary to a considerable extent.

Some progress has been made in analyzing the effects of separation of powers and political accountability. For example, Persson, Roland, and Tabellini (1997) show in a formal principal–agent model that separation of powers improves the accountability of elected officials, and thereby the utility of voters, but only under appropriate checks and balances. Two central provisions are needed: There must be a conflict of interest between the executive and the legislative. Moreover it must be impossible to implement any policy unilaterally, that is, without the consent of both bodies. The basis for these results lies in the modeling of real-world political constitutions as "incomplete contracts": "Elected politicians are not offered an explicit incentive scheme associating well defined payoffs with actions in all states of the world. Political constitutions only specify who has the right to make decisions, and according to which procedures for which circumstances. This makes it hard to tie specific rewards or sanctions to the contents of those decisions" (Persson et al.: 5). The application of these results to the European Union is worth further research but is not undertaken here.

Buchanan and Tullock have first analyzed the various effects of unicameral and bicameral legislators from a public-choice perspective in their famous book "Calculus of Consent" in the year 1962. One of their major conclusions in their analytical framework is that that decision rule is optimal which leads to a minimum of the sum of external and decision costs (interdependence costs). Buchanan and Tullock (1962: 235) conclude that, in comparison with unicameral systems, bicameral systems have higher decision costs and that, on the other hand, if the basis of representation can be made significantly different in the two houses, the institutions of bicameral legislature may prove to be an effective means of securing a substantial reduction in expected external costs of collective action without incurring as much added decision making costs as a more inclusive rule would involve in a single house. The larger the majority required to reach a certain decision, the lower the external costs connected with that decision, because a number of opponents to a decision is negatively correlated with the required majority. However, it will become increasingly difficult to reach a decision at all, because the decision costs are positively correlated with a required majority.

In a more recent study Levmore (1992) investigates the advantages and disadvantages of a bi- versus a unicameral system. He concludes that a bicameral system might be better suited than a corresponding qualified majority in a unicameral system, to reduce the power of the agenda setter (mostly the government). Bicameral systems are often interpreted as a "break" against overly active legislatures. Summarizing the effects of bicameral systems, one could conclude that the legislative activities in bicameral systems are indeed lower than in unicameral ones and this should be reflected in a lower government consumption of economic output and in higher growth rates.[8]

Some papers in constitutional economics (compare, e.g., the review article of Moser and Schneider, 1997) try to give an analysis of the consequences of a change in the power and competencies of European (government and legislative) bodies.[9] Within the European Union, the strengthening of the European Parliament can be seen as the introduction of a second force in addition to the second chamber. Also in our first proposition the bicameral system is demanded, as it reduces the capability of rent seeking, because it is much more difficult to get a majority in both chambers than in only one.[10] The draft report of the European Constitutional Group (1993) stresses the importance of competition as a mechanism to best fulfill consumers' preferences. Competition, however, is not only crucial for the working of economic but also of polit-

---

[8] A similar conclusion is reached and first empirical evidence is given by the studies of Feld and Kirchgässner (1996), Feld and Savioz (1997), and for a more general view of this aspect see Weingast (1993).

[9] Compare Peters (1996a, b) and Steunenberg (1994).

[10] The introduction of a bicameral system not only reduces attempts of rent seeking but is also important to strengthen the federal structure of the European Union. The second chamber, in which the prime ministers of every EU member state have equal voting power, can be seen as an institution that solely represents the interests of the EU member countries, like the German Bundesrat or the Schweizer Ständerat. It might especially help to take care of the interests of the smaller EU member countries.

ical markets. This concept of institutional competition has a long tradition (starting with Tiebout's "voting with feet"). Lately, Frey and Eichenberger (1997, 1999) have dealt with the implementation of so-called functional, overlapping, and competing jurisdictions. They contend that "Europe owes its rise to an economic and intellectual centre to the competition among governmental units" and show applications where the introduction of this kind of competition seems feasible. Of course, this approach is not without problems. Competitive economic or political markets require free entry and exit and the absence of regulations, which prevent suppliers from being successful with the best product – be it goods or services in the form of policies – and prevent the citizens from choosing freely. Free choice as argued above is not guaranteed if the citizens are neither part of the agenda setting (free entry) nor of the actual decision making process. A better implementation of the separation of powers, turning the commission into a European government, the Council of Prime Ministers into a second chamber and strengthening the European Parliament, giving these two chambers the full legislative power, can be seen as a first step applying the democratic principle to a European Union. This can be one way to reduce the political inefficiencies, which are normally discussed when investigating the democratic deficit of the European Union.

4   The Subsidiarity and Federalism Principles as Safeguards against Government Growth

4.1   The Subsidiarity Principle

In the second proposition as a key element of a European federal union, the tasks of the European federal government are defined. This basic proposition comes from the idea of using the subsidiarity principle, which is in substance a constitutional norm. Vanberg (1994) argues that it is meant to provide a criterion for what can be considered as a desirable constitutional order, a criterion that concerns an allocation of political authority in a multilayer system of government. To say it simply, it requires that in a multilevel policy the distribution of power should be in favor of lower level governments, and hence, smaller jurisdictions. In other words, it demands that the political authority be always located at the lowest possible level, that is as close as possible to the citizens, the ultimate sovereign.

In the commission report of the European Council on the adaptation of existing legislation to the subsidiarity principle (Com 93: 545) one reads, "the aim of the subsidiarity principle is to see to it that decisions are taken as close as possible to the citizen, a constant watch being kept to ensure that action taken at community level is justified in the light of the means available to national, regional or local authorities." Of course, the phrase "as close as possible" is in urgent need of interpretation, if the subsidiarity principle is to have specific normative content.[11] Of course the constitutional norm to allocate political authority in favor of more local levels of governments is in itself not a very operational instruction for the design of constitutional frameworks, and the question of how the general principle is to translate it into more specific constitutional provisions is by no means a trivial issue.

Judgments on the preferability of particular constitutional arrangements (e.g., using the subsidiarity principle in a strict way) over others always refer to somebody to whom these alternatives are claimed to be preferable. In other words, all such judgments are directed to some addressee to whose interests they appeal. In democratic systems the ultimate addressees of constitutional proposals are, of course, the citizens who constitute this union. This means, if the subsidiarity principle is claimed to be a desirable constitutional norm for the European Union, such claims must be supported by arguments that can convince its citizens that it would be in their interest if efforts in the constitutional construction are guided by this principle. More precisely, these citizens would have to be convinced that adopting this principle would be in their constitutional interest, that is, the interests that would form their choice if it were up to them to select the rules for the polity, in which they live.

What kind of arguments could one put forward in support of the subsidiarity principle as a constitutional norm? In other words, what kind of arguments could be made in favor of this principle when designing a federal European constitution?

One major argument for this principle is the central concern on the part of the members of any democratic organization about the principal–agent problem. That is the issue of how power delegated to agents can, on the one side, be ensured to be used to the benefit of the

---

[11] As Feld and Kirchgässner (1996: 195) write, "the origin of the principle of subsidiarity dates back to the days of Aristotle and was further developed by Saint Thomas Aquinas and the scholastics. Saint Thomas Aquinas noted that an excess of unification and standardization would threaten the polity consisting of different units in the same way as symphony and harmony of voices would disappear if all were singing the same note. In its proper sense, the principle can also be found in the theory of Althusius (1557–1638), one of the first modern theorists of federalism. The principle became more precisely defined in the course of the nineteenth century. In 1848 Kettler wrote in an open letter that the family in the community should remain autonomous. Abraham Lincoln stated in 1854 that "the legitimate object of government is to do for a community of people whatever they need to have done, but cannot do at all, or cannot do so well for themselves in their separate and individual capacities. In all the people can do individually as well for themselves, government ought not to interfere" (quoted from Nell-Breuning, 1990: 88).

principals and, on the other side, be prevented from being used against the principals' interests. As far as democratic politics are concerned there is a long tradition of inquiry, in the political economy as well as in other social sciences, into the advantages of de-centralization in political organizations. The results of this inquiry are of direct relevance for the subsidiarity principle.[12]

However, it is obvious that the subsidiarity principle alone neither constitutes a basis to regulate the intergovernmental relations in a future European Union, nor does it protect the collectivities at the grass-roots level (Feld and Kirchgässner, 1995: 4).[13] Moreover, the authors argue that the introduction of the subsidiarity principle in the Maastricht Treaty has in fact shifted the burden of the proof at least somewhat more toward the centralists. The notion of subsidiarity nevertheless remains very general and open to many interpretations. Hence, subsidiarity does not solve the dynamic organizational problem, under which condition competencies should be given to lower governmental units. From a public choice point of view, there is a need for constitutional rules, which might prevent the "misuse" of instruments by politicians, bureaucrats, and interest groups. Therefore the subsidiarity principle must be "filled with life," and the theory of federalism may represent an operational means to regulate the horizontal and vertical relationship between governmental units in the light of a potential leviathan.

4.2   Fiscal Federalism in a European Constitution

Federalism is a crucial institution that serves to establish competition within the political arena. There has been a lot of investigation into the economic theory of federalism.[14] We argue that it should be taken more seriously. Costs rise for the voters/taxpayers if certain groups are able to appropriate the benefits of a publicly supplied good, but do not have to pay the price for it. These groups can be politicians or bureaucrats, who are self-interested rent seekers, or special-interest groups, who try to reach their selfish goals. Although it is not argued here that politicians and bureaucrats always seek to maximize their own utility up to the extent of actively exploiting the citizens and taxpayers, politicians and bureaucrats will do it from time to time, if they have the opportunity. Thus federal competition helps to act as a "safeguard" against decision

---

[12] See, e.g., Oates (1977).

[13] In this context it is not surprising that Delors (1991: 12) argues that "subsidiarity does not enact any restriction for the commission to take political action" and he continues to argue "solely on the base of the Maastricht treaty subsidiarity is not judicable"). See also Sachverständigenrat zur Begutachtung der gesamtwirtschaftlichen Entwicklung (1992), Vaubel (1993, 1995), and Möschl (1993, 1995).

[14] Compare here the pathbreaking study from Brennan and Buchanan (1980).

makers taking unfair advantage of their discretionary power. Federal competition and federal institutions might also be a very crucial argument in a future European constitution. As has been discussed the highest federal unit in the European Union should only be given those tasks, which bring additional benefits (e.g., due to EU-wide spillovers, homogeneity of preferences to a certain degree, scale effects) to voters/citizens, if they are fulfilled by the highest federal unit, like foreign defense policy and environmental policy. The limitation of these tasks is necessary so that a more or less automatic centralization of tasks (especially in the area of redistribution) at the highest federal level will be avoided. All other tasks should be provided by the EU-member states (at which level within the EU member states is not discussed here).[15]

As already argued, the European federal government will be constitutionally restricted in its domain of action, severely so. Within its assigned sphere however, the central government would be strong, sufficiently so to allow it to enforce economic freedom or openness over the whole of the EU-territory. The federal European authority would prevent EU member states from placing barriers on the free flow of resources and goods across their borders. In order to guarantee, additionally to the already suggested constitutional arrangements, that the central power does not take over either fiscal or other items from the EU member states, following Buchanan (1995), we suggest thinking about an exit option in the following way: The EU member states are constitutionally empowered to secede from the federal European Union. Secession or the threat thereof represents the only means through which the ultimate powers of the European federal government might be held in balance. Without this secession prospect, the federal European government may, by overstepping its constitutionally assigned limits, extract

---

[15] One could go a step further and put forward the idea of federal competition between and within EU member states when providing goods and services, but also financing them. As has been shown in the extensive research for Switzerland by Kirchgässner and Pommerehne (1995), and Pommerehne, Kirchgässner, and Feld (1995), there is extensive tax competition in Switzerland, e.g., between the cantons on very small local distances. This tax competition did not result in a breakdown of public-goods supply in Switzerland, and there is no indication of an underprovision of public goods. According to Feld and Kirchgässner (1995: 8), the income taxes in Switzerland vary quite a lot between the different cantons. Taking the value of the (weighted) average for Switzerland as 100, in 1990 the index of burden in the form of personal income and property taxes was ranked from 56.1 in the canton of Zug to 154.1 in Valais. For instance a family with two children that earns a gross income of SFr 175.000 had to pay SFr 16.083 in cantonal and local income taxes in Zug, but SFr 34.475 in Bern, two cities only about 100 km apart! For critical view of the issue of tax competition see Genser (1992) and Sinn (1990).

surplus value from the citizenry almost at will, because there would exist no effective means of escape.[16] With an operative secession threat on the part of the EU member states, the European federal government could be held roughly to its assigned constitutional limits, while the EU member states could be left to compete among themselves in their capacities to meet the demand of citizens for collectively provided goods and services.[17]

Considering the arguments about federalism and subsidiarity, which policies should now be allocated at the European federal level? As proposed in Section 2 about the jurisdiction of the federal government, the European federal government should be responsible for competition policy including the enforcement of free intra-community movement (cf., e.g., van den Bergh, 1997, who also shows a list of pros and cons of [de]centralization of competition policy), defense, foreign policy, foreign trade policy, and environmental policy, all those areas where one can expect EU-wide spillovers, so that the single EU-citizen profits from them. The rationale for EU-wide environmental policy is first of all given by the global nature of some of today's environmental problems: for example, the shrinking of the ozone layer and the danger of global warming by increased CO_2-pollution. Coordinated environmental policy is often also demanded, however, with respect to local or regional pollution. There the argument is not based on international spillovers, which would justify at least some international cooperation, but on the implications of different environmental standards on economic competition. It is supposed that different environmental standards in the member states of the union have considerable impact on the international competitiveness in the different countries. Another argument in favor of coordinated environmental policies throughout Europe is the intended avoidance of environmental dumping.

4.3   The Tax Base of the European Government

In Kirchgässner (1994) and Schneider (1993, 1996) it is argued that the activities of the European government should only be financed by pro-

---

[16] Compare here again the pioneering work of Buchanan and Faith (1987), Allen Buchanan (1991), and James Buchanon (1995).

[17] The (threat of) secession should be seen here as an ultimate "weapon" for every EU-member country in order to avoid a development not wanted by EU-member states and their citizens. In principle it gives the single countries a power over (for them) critical issues and if it is used one might end up in a Prisoners' Dilemma situation. But as the execution of the secession for a single EU-country is not so easy (e.g., a qualified majority of voters in that country is necessary), it is unlikely that this instrument will be used frequently only for tactical reasons. In terms of game theory, the threat is unlikely to be credible.

portional (indirect) taxes. The rationale behind this idea lies in the different control possibilities (coming from the public-choice literature) that exist on different governmental levels. First any government will act more in accordance with the preference of the individual voters, the more the citizens are able to control it. At the lower levels, with smaller communities, the citizens have better possibilities to force the government to act according to their preferences; hence, this is just another argument to assign government activities to the lowest possible level again using the subsidiarity principle in a very strict way. Second, as Feld and Kirchgässner (1996: 23) argue, it implies that tasks as well as financial means, which are easier to control, are more suited to a higher governmental level than those, which are difficult to control. The proposed indirect tax can only be changed via changing a law, which means that any relative increase of the government share has to be decided via parliamentary process and also via referendum as suggested here. This ensures a public discussion, and at least as long as the European government seeks its reelection, it will hesitate to increase this tax and it might face difficulties in getting an approval from the Parliament and the voters. Such proportional taxes leave relatively little room for a leviathan behavior of a European federal government, especially if an increase in the tax rate has to be carried by a two-thirds majority in both chambers of the European Parliament and the approval of a popular referendum. Therefore, at the European top federal level only the revenues from this indirect tax should be available.

5 Institutions of Direct Democracy in a Future European Constitution

Beside the important issues of federalism and subsidiarity, institutions of direct democracy like popular initiatives and (obligatory) referenda could also be a crucial factor in a future European constitution. They should be seen as a necessary supplement for the institutions of the representative democracy such as parliament (here the proposed two-chamber system) and the government. There are two crucial institutional features when introducing institutions of direct democracy. Referenda do not simply consist of a choice between given alternatives but should also be seen as a quite important "political education" process extending over time. According to Frey (1994) and Frey and Bohnet (1994) three stages can be differentiated. The first stage is the pre-referendum stage, in which the possibility of undertaking a referendum stimulates discussion as well among citizens as between politicians and voters. Pre-referendum discussion produces a number of important effects. Preferences are articulated, enabling mutually beneficial bargaining and exchange. Moreover, the agenda of alternatives is in a great part determined by the citizens, thus constituting the relevant decisions space. The pre-referendum stage screens the alternatives to be voted upon, reduces the number of relevant alternatives (quite often to only two) and makes the preferences somewhat more homogeneous, thereby lowering the chance that the preference aggregation paradox will occur.[18] The second stage is the formal decision situation, in which it can be seen that voters clearly express approval or disapproval of a proposed referendum and quite often give a government a clear task what to do. At the third, the post-referendum stage on the one side, as just argued, the government has a clear task what to do, and on the other side, quite often, initiators of a referendum force the government in changing their policy by only threatening to bring an issue into a popular referendum.[19] But in some cases the government can also undertake unpopular measures (like tax increases), if they were supported in a popular referendum.[20]

In general one can conclude that a referendum is quite influential on policy outcome, which is demonstrated in quite a lot of (empirical) studies. Unfortunately, most of these studies have been undertaken in Switzerland, which has a long tradition of direct democracy. Nevertheless, one can learn something from their experience. The most famous study was undertaken by Pommerehne (1978), who provided an analysis for public expenditures in 111 Swiss municipalities. The sample includes municipalities, that reach collective decisions in direct town meeting procedures as well as those that rely on purely representative assemblies. Theoretical considerations lead Pommerehne (1978, 1990) to expect that the introduction of representative elements into the democratic decision-making process will create enough leeway to weaken the link between voter preferences and the actual outcome of collective decision making and will result in higher spending per capita, ceteris paribus. The empirical results from Pommerehne (1978) and Pommerehne and Schneider (1978, 1982) strongly support this hypothesis. The use of the median voter model in analyzing public spending in communes with direct democracy has yielded significantly better results than the use of traditional models. However, in municipalities using representative democratic procedures, the explanatory power of the median voter model is not significantly higher in any spending category than using traditional models. Thus, it seems that the institutional differences do matter. In addition, it turns out that in representative systems the existence of an optional or obligatory referendum on budgetary item adds enough of a constraint on the behavior of decision makers to improve

[18] Compare Bohnet and Frey (1994) and Frey (1994: 339).
[19] Compare Frey (1994) and Frey and Bohnet (1994: 339).
[20] E.g., the referendum might help the government to undertake unpopular measures in the environment policy; compare Frey and Schneider (1997).

significantly the performance of the median voter model.[21] In order to demonstrate the higher explanatory power of the median voter model, Pommerehne and Schneider (1982) examined forty-eight Swiss municipalities operating as direct democracies. They first estimated a median voter demand function for seven public expenditure items for the year 1965 and then made forecasts for 1975. In a second step, the estimated coefficients of the expenditure equations of the forty-eight municipalities with direct democracies were used to simulate what the levels of government spending would be in the year 1975 in the sixty-two Swiss municipalities operating as representative democracies. It turned out that the aggregate, as well as all of the individual expenditure categories, were underestimated using the parameter estimate of the expenditure equations derived from the data on direct democracies. In total, municipalities with representative democracies spent about 30 percent more than predicted using spending equations based on the data for direct democracies. Moreover, among those Swiss cities that operate as representative democracies but where either the citizens had the additional right of calling a referendum and thereby the possibility of reversing government decisions or the government had to approve certain (spending) decisions by a referendum, the growth of government activity has been significantly lower than in those representative democracies without referendum constraint (although still significantly higher compared to set of direct democracies). This strongly suggests that the representative form of government substantially changes (the nature of) the outcome of the political process; that is, it increases government activity to a level greater than would be reached, if it were directly determined by voters/taxpayers.

It is sometimes argued that the fact that governments have grown larger over time simply reflects the citizens' preferences. Trying to reduce the size of the public sector (by introducing referenda in the political process) would then be inconsistent with what people want. However, the crucial point is, if people want larger governments they can vote for them in the referenda! The evidence cited above seems to show that voters' preferences are not very well fulfilled in a representative system. Therefore, it also seems quite improbable that politicians use referenda to get around the representative system in order to push through their plans.

To summarize, the empirical results suggest, that the presence of a representative and fiscally centralized government, in contrast to a

---

[21] The median voter approach can also be used to explain government growth coming from the supply side – opposite to the quite often-used demand side approaches. See, e.g., Mueller (1987, 1989), Lybeck and Henrekson (1988), Kirchgässner and Pommerehne (1996), Feld and Kirchgässner (1996), and Feld and Savioz (1997).

decentralized and more direct democratic government, increases the weight of the supply side in the political process and hence, government grows faster or has a bigger size.

The institutions of direct democracies have also other important effects, like that they can be used by the voters to break politicians' cartels directed against them. As Frey and Bohnet (1994: 151) put forward, rent-seeking theory argues that representatives have a common interest in forming a cartel to protect and possibly extend political rents.[22] Referenda and initiatives can be means to break politicians' coalition against voters. Initiatives require a certain number of signatures and if the initiators get these signatures, they can force the government to undertake a referendum on a given (mostly disputed) issue. They are a particularly important institution, because they take the agenda-setting monopoly away from the politicians and enable outsiders to propose issues for democratic decision, including those that many elected officials might have preferred to exclude from the agenda. As has been demonstrated in public choice theory,[23] the group determining which propositions are voted and in what order has a considerable advantage because it decides to a large extent which issues will be discussed when and which ones will be left out. Referenda, whether obligatory or optional, enable the voters to state their preferences to the politicians more effectively than in a representative democracy. In a representative system, deviating preferences with respect to specific issues can only be expressed by informal protests, which are difficult to organize and to make politically relevant.

If one summarizes these findings, one can draw two conclusions:

1. Cumulating research on the properties of a popular referendum has revealed two major aspects on which the economics of institution has to focus. One is the importance of discussion in the pre-referendum state (Frey, 1994: 341). It implies that the number of propositions and the frequency of ballots must be low enough that the voters have an incentive and the opportunity to collect and digest the respective information in order to participate actively in the decision.

2. The second element is that direct democratic institutions enable voters to break politicians' and parties' coalitions directed against them. Direct participation serves to keep the ultimate agenda-setting power with the voters. Initiatives and referenda are effective means by which the voters might regain some control over the politicians.

---

[22] The literature on rent seeking was developed by Tullock (1967), and one of the latest surveys is by Tollison (1982).

[23] Compare Denzau (1985) and Mueller (1989).

Hence, the introduction of direct democratic institutions like the referendum at the highest constitutional level in a European constitution is an absolute necessity.[24]

The question for which issues a referendum should be mandatory is left open here. We think that especially if the European federal government wants to change the tax structure or introduce new taxes or wants to run a deficit or wants to take over new policy fields, this should only be implemented if it is approved by the legislation of the two chambers and by a popular referendum and if it is approved by a majority of the states. Hence, the introduction of direct democratic elements would be crucial for a future European constitution so that the European government strictly keeps to its given tasks.

The empirical evidence as discussed in this part strongly supports that with the introduction of direct democratic elements, government growth will be lower and the majority of voters' preferences will be better fulfilled. Hence, one can conclude that the institutions of referenda and popular initiatives provide citizens with a greater influence on political decisions and better possibility to control the political agents. To summarize, direct democratic institutions will serve as efficient constitutional means.

6   Summary and Conclusions

In this chapter an attempt has been made to provide some basic propositions of a future European federal constitution. In Section 2, six basic elements have been put forward, including that the European Commission should be turned into the European government, the Council of Ministers into a second chamber and that the European Parliament should get full control and responsibility over all federal items together with the chamber. The jurisdiction of the European federal government should consist of a few specific items that are best suited at the highest federal level, like foreign defense and environmental policy. The activities of the federal European government should be financed by one proportional (indirect) tax, and direct democratic institutions should be introduced in a European federal constitution, such as the possibility of a referendum. These elements are then justified by arguments found in the literature on positive economics dealing with the subsidiarity principle, the idea of federalism, and the research about the effects of direct democratic institutions. As has been demonstrated, these elements are best suited to limit the domain of central European authority in the long run, even if we observe a strong tendency to centralization in nearly all federal states during the last decades.

---

[24] Such a conclusion is also reached by Bernholz (1990b), Feld and Kirchgässner (1996), and Vaubel (1993, 1995).

306 Friedrich Schneider and Alexander F. Wagner

Moreover, the idea is brought forward that the structure of the constitution should be designed in such a way, that any attempt of a future concentration of government activities at the European federal level will be prevented by explicitly assigning specific governmental functions to each level of government and to put in additional safeguards like the subsidiarity principle and the direct democratic institutions so that the federal European government cannot take over tasks that are not approved by the majority of voters and European member states. From another perspective it is also very difficult for the European government to take over additional tasks, because the necessary widening of the tax base can only be done, if a majority of European voters/taxpayers (and also a majority of the member states) approve it. The European government is, moreover, not allowed to accumulate large deficits, which might serve as another safeguard to limit the domain of a future central authority in Europe.

Two central features, direct democracy and fiscal federalism, should be key principles in a future European constitution, which have shown in other federal units like Switzerland and the United States that they are strong safeguards against policies not in line with a majority of voters' preferences. Moreover, direct democratic elements provide the possibility for European citizens in a federal state to participate actively in political decision making, to break politicians' and interest groups' cartels and prevent a shifting of responsibilities from EU member state levels to the EU federal government level. Also a proper assignment of the tax competencies may help to restrain centralization.

With respect to the actual political discussion, such constitutional perspectives (e.g., the introduction of a two-chamber system, both being fully responsible for all federal items, and the possibility of a referendum) would be very fruitful and important. If the individuals in the pre-constitutional stage decide to build up an economic (and a future political) federal European union, they know that in the post-constitutional situation such a union will be accepted by the vast majority of citizens/taxpayers. Given that, according to Downs (1957), rational voters are rationally ignorant, it is necessary to build the European Union in a way that at least some advantages of this Union can be perceived by the ordinary citizens as well, even if they are not well informed. Up to now, however, the large advantages of the European process for the citizens are very indirect and often not at all obvious, while the public discussion focuses on the interests of producer interest groups and the influence of the Brussels bureaucracy. Thus, today the political opinion of ordinary citizens about the European Union varies between apathy and hostility; hence the public support for the European process is rather small in most EU member countries. If in the actual political process such a constitutional perspective could be provided, this could lead to a higher acceptance of the European Union process by the ordinary voter/ taxpayer.

References

Alesina, Alberto, and Perotti, Ronaldo. 1994. "The Political Economy of Growth: A Critical Survey of the Recent Literature." *World Bank Economic Review*, 8/3, pp. 351–71.

Alesina, Alberto, and Rodrick, Dani. 1992. Distribution, political conflict, and economic growth: A simple theory and some empirical evidence. In A. Cukierman, Z. Hercowitz, and L. Leiderman, eds., *Political Economy, Growth, and Business Cycles*. Cambridge, Mass.: MIT Press, pp. 23–50.

Bartel, Rainer, and Schneider, Friedrich. 1987. "Die Ursachen der Krise in der verstaatlichten Industrie." *Wirtschaftspolitische Blätter*, 34/3, pp. 275–301.

1991. "The "Mess" of the Public Industrial Production in Austria: The Typical Case of Public Sector in Efficiency?" *Public Choice*, 68/1, pp. 17–40.

Bernholz, Peter. 1966. Economic politics in a democracy. *Kyklos*, 19/1, pp. 48–80.

1969. Einige Bermerkungen zur Theorie des Einflusses der Verbände auf die politische Willensbildung in der Demokratie. *Kyklos*, 22/3, pp. 276–87.

1990a. The Completion of the European Market: Opportunities and Dangers from an Institutional Perspective. In C. E. P. S., eds., *The Macroeconomics of 1992*. C. E. P. S. Paper No. 42. Brussels.

1990b. Grundzüge einer europäischen Verfassung: Ein Bundesstaat mit begrenzter Zentralgewalt? In Frankfurter Institut, ed., *Argumente zur Europapolitik*, 3, pp. 2–12.

1993. "Institutional Aspects of European Integration." In S. Borner and H. Grubel, eds., *EC after 1992: Perspective from the Outside*. London: Macmillan Publishing Company.

Blöchliger, Hans-Jörg, and Frey, René L. 1992. "Der Schweizerische Föderalismus: Ein Modell für den institutionellen Aufbau der europäischen Union?" *Außenwirtschaft*, 47/3, pp. 515–48.

Borcherding, Thomas E. 1985. "The Causes of Government Growth: A Survey of the U.S. Evidence." *Journal of Public Economics*, 28/3, pp. 358–82.

Brennan, Geoffrey, and Buchanan, James. 1980. *The Power to Tax: Analytical Foundations of a Fiscal Constitution*. Cambridge: Cambridge University Press.

Buchanan, Allen. 1991. *Secession: The Morality of Political Divorce from Fort Sumter to Lithuania and Quebec*. Boulder, Colo.: Westview Press.

Buchanan, James M. 1990. *Europe's Constitutional Opportunity*. Fairfax: Virginia Center for Study of Public Choice, George Mason University.

1995. "Federalism as an Ideal Political Order and an Objective for Constitutional Reform." *Publius: The Journal of Federalism*, 25/2, pp. 19–27.

Buchanan, James M., and Faith, Roger. 1987. "Secession and the Limits of Taxation: Toward a Theory of Internal Exit." *American Economic Review*, 91/5, pp. 1023–31.

Buchanan, James M., and Tullock, Gordon. 1962. *The Calculus of Consent: Logical Foundations of Constitutional Democracy*. Ann Arbor: University of Michigan Press.

[Com 93] Commission Report to the European Council on the Adaptation of Existing Legislation to the Subsidiarity Principle. 1993. Brussels.

De Haan, Jakob, and Siermann, C. L. J. 1995. "A Sensitivity Analysis of the Impact of Democracy on Economic Growth." *Empirical Economics*, 20/1, pp. 197–215.

1996. "New Evidence on the Relationship between Democracy and Economic Growth." *Public Choice*, 86/2, pp. 175–98.

Delors, Jacques. 1991. "The Principle of Subsidiarity: Contribution to the Debate." *European Institute of Public Administration*, pp. 7–18.

Denzau, Arthur T. 1985. "Constitutional Change and Agenda Control." *Carnegie Papers on Political Economy*, 47, pp. 183–217.

Downs, Anthony. 1957. *An Economic Theory of Democracy*. London: Harper & Row.

Eichenberger, Rainer. 1994. "The Benefits of Federalism and the Risk of Overcentralization." *Kyklos*, 47/3, pp. 403–20.

European Constitutional Group. 1993. *A Proposal for a European Constitution, Report by the European Constitutional Group*. European Policy Forum. London.

Feld, Lars P., and Kirchgässner, Gebhard. 1995. "*Omne agends agendo perficitur*: The Economic Meaning of Subsidiarity." In R. Holzmann, ed., *Maastricht: Monetary Constitution without a Fiscal Constitution?* Baden-Baden: Nomos Publishing Company, pp. 195–226.

1997. Public debt and budgetary procedures: top down or bottom up? Some evidence from Swiss municipalities. Discussion Paper 9717. Universität. St. Gallen, Volkswirtschaftliche Abteilung.

Feld, Lars P., and Savioz, Marcel. 1997. "Direct Democracy Matters for Economic Performance: An Empirical Investigation." *Kyklos*, 50/4, pp. 507–38.

Frey, Bruno S. 1994. "Direct Democracy: Politico-Economic Lessons from Swiss Experience." *American Economic Association Papers and Proceedings*, 84/2, pp. 338–42.

Frey, Bruno S., and Bohnet, Iris. 1994. "The Swiss Experience with Referenda and Federalism, IDIOMA." *Revue de linguistique et des traductology*, 10/2, pp. 147–60.

1994. "Direct Democratic Rules: The Role of Discussion." *Kyklos*, 47/3, pp. 341–54.

Frey, Bruno S., and Eichenberger, Rairier. 1997. "FOCJ: Creating a Single European Market for Governments." In D. Schmidtchen and R. Cooter, eds., *Constitutional Law and Economics of the European Union*. Aldershot, England: Edward Elgar Publishing, pp. 195–215.

Frey, Bruno S., and Schneider, Friedrich. 1997. "Warum wird die Umweltökonomik kaum angewendet?" *Zeitschrift für Umweltpolitik und Umweltrecht*, 20/2, pp. 153–70.

Frey, René L. 1977. *Zwischen Föderalismus und Zentralismus*. Bern: Lang Publishing Company.

Genser, Bernd. 1992. "Tax Competition and Harmonization in Federal Economies." In Vosgerau Hans-Jürgen, ed., *European Integration in the World Economy*. Heidelberg: Springer, pp. 184–205.

Gwartney, J. D., and Wagner, Richard E. 1988, *Public Choice and Constitutional Economics*, Greenwich, Conn.: J. A. I. Press.

Holzmann, Robert, ed. 1996. *Maastricht: Monetary Constitution without a Fiscal Constitution?* Baden-Baden: Nomos-Publishing Company.

Horstmann, Winfried, and Schneider, Friedrich. 1994. "Deficits, Bailout and Free Riders: Fiscal Elements of a European Constitution." *Kyklos*, 47/3, pp. 355–83.

Kirchgässner, Gebhard. 1994. "Constitutional Economics and Its Relevance for the Evolution of Rules." *Kyklos*, 47/3, pp. 321–39.

Kirchgässner, Gebhard, and Pommerehne, Werner W. 1995. "Public Spending in Federal States: A Comparative Econometric Analysis." In Dennis Meulders, ed., *Public Expenditure and Taxation: Recent Econometric Research*. London: Routledge & Sons, pp. 112–36.

1996. "Tax Harmonization and Tax Competition in the European Union: Lessons from Switzerland." *Journal of Public Economics*, 61/2, pp. 66–82.

Levmore, Samuel. 1992. "Bicameralism: When Are Two Decisions Better Than One?" *International Review of Law and Economics*, 12/1, pp. 145–62.

Lybeck, Johann A., and Henrekson, Marcus, eds. 1988. *Explaining the Growth of Government*. Amsterdam: North Holland Publishing Company.

Marlow, Martin L. 1986. "Private Sector Shrinkage and the Growth of Industrialized Economies." *Public Choice*, 49/2, pp. 143–54.

Möschl, Werner. 1993. "Eine Verfassungskonzeption über die Europäische Union." In Herbert Gröner and Andreas Schüller, eds., *Die europäische Integration als ordnungspolitische Aufgabe*. Stuttgart: Verlag Gustav Fischer, pp. 21–39.

1995. Subsidiaritätsprinzip im Zwielicht. *WiSt*, 5, pp. 232–6.

Moser, Peter, and Schneider, Gerald. 1997. "Rational Choice and the Governance Structure of the European Union: An Introduction." *Außenwirtschaft*, 52/1–2, pp. 64–82.

Mueller, Dennis C. 1987. "The Growth of Government: A Public Choice Perspective." *IMF Staff Papers*, 34/1, pp. 115–49.

1989. *Public Choice II*. Cambridge: Cambridge University Press.

Nell-Breuning, Otto von. 1990. *Baugesetze der Gesellschaft: Solidarität und Subsidiarität*. Freiburg: Verlag Herder.

Oates, Wallace E., ed. 1977. *The Political Economy of Fiscal Federalism*. Lexington, Mass.: Lexington Books.

1985. "Searching for Leviathan: An Empirical Study." *American Economic Review*, 75/4, pp. 578–83.

Olson, Mancur. 1965. *The Logic of Collective Action*. Cambridge, Mass.: Harvard University Press.

1982. *The Rise and Decline of Nations: Economic Growth, Stagnation and Rigidities*. New Haven, Conn.: Yale University Press.

1983. "The Political Economy of Comparative Growth Rate." In Dennis C. Mueller, ed., *The Political Economy of Growth*. New Haven, Conn.: Yale University Press, pp. 222–47.

Peden, E. A., and Bradley, M. 1989. "Government Size, Productivity and Economic Growth: The Postwar Experience." *Public Choice*, 61/3, pp. 229–45.

Persson, T., Roland, G., and Tabellini, G. 1997. Separation of Powers and Political Accountability. Center for Economic Studies at the University of Munich, Working Paper No. 136, June.

Peters, Thorsten. 1996a. "Decision-Making after the EU-Intergovernmental Conference." *European Law Journal*, 2/3, pp. 251–66.

1996b. "Voting Power after the Enlargement and Options for Decision Making in the European Union." *Außenwirtschaft*, 51/11, pp. 223–43.

Pommerehne, Werner W. 1978. "Institutional Approaches to Public Expenditure: Empirical Evidence from Swiss Municipalities." *Journal of Public Economics*, 9/1, pp. 163–201.

1980. "Public Choice Approaches to Explain Fiscal Redistribution." In K. W. Roßkamp, ed., *Public Choice and Public Finance*. Paris: Kujas, pp. 169–90.

1990. "The Empirical Relevance of Comparative Institutional Analysis." *European Economic Review*, 34/3, pp. 458–69.

Pommerehne, Werner W., Kirchgässner, Gebhard, and Feld, Lars P. 1995. "Tax Harmonization and Tax Competition at the State-Local Levels: Lessons from Switzerland." In G. Pola, R. Levaggi, and G. Francke, eds., *New Issues in Local Government Finance: Theory and Policy*. Aldershot, England: Edward Elgar, pp. 201–55.

Pommerehne, Werner W., and Schneider, Friedrich. 1978. "Fiscal Illusion, Political Institutions, and Local Public Spending." *Kyklos*, 31/3, pp. 381–408.

1982. "Unbalanced Growth between Public and Private Sectors: An Empirical Examination." In Robert H. Haveman, ed., *Public Finance and Public Employment*. Detroit: Wayne State University Press, pp. 309–26.

Posner, Robert. 1987. "The Constitution as an Economic Document." *George Washington Law Review*, 56/1, pp. 4–38.

Sachverständigenrat zur Begutachtung der gesamtwirtschaftlichen Entwicklung. 1992. *Für Wachstumsorientierung gegen lähmenden Verteilungsstreit*. Jahresgutachten 1993. Stuttgart: Verlag Poeschl.

Schneider, Friedrich. 1993. "The Federal and Fiscal Structures of Representative and Direct Democracies as Models for a European Federal Union: Some Ideas Using the Public Choice Approach." *European Economy Report and Studies*, 5, Brussels, pp. 191–212.

1996. "The Design of a Minimal European Federal Union: Some Ideas Using the Public Choice Approach." In José Casas Pardo and Friedrich Schneider, eds., *Current Issues in Public Choice*. Cheltenham, England: Edward Elgar, pp. 203–22.

Schneider, Friedrich, and Frey, Bruno S. 1988. "Politico-Economic Models of Macroeconomic Policy: The Political Economy of Money, Inflation, and Employment." In Willett Thomas, ed., *The Political Business Cycle*. Durham, N.C.: Duke University Press, pp. 239–75.

Sinn, Hans-Werner. 1989. "Economic Models of Policy Making in Independent Economies: An Alternative View on Competition among Policies." Working Paper No. 390, Institute of World Economics, University of Kiel, Germany.

1990. "Tax Harmonization and Tax Competition in Europe." *European Economic Review*, 34/4, pp. 489–504.

Steunenberg, Bernhard. 1994. "Decision-Making under Different Institutional Arrangements: Legislation by the European Community." *Journal of Institution and Theoretical Economics*, 150/3, pp. 642–63.

Tollison, Robert D. 1982. "Rent-Seeking: A Survey." *Kyklos*, 25/4, pp. 575–602.

Tullock, Gordon. 1967. "The Welfare Costs of Tariff, Monopolies and Theft." *Western Economic Journal*, 5/3, pp. 224–32.

van den Bergh, Roger. 1997. "The Subsidiarity Principle and the EC Competition rules. The Costs and Benefits of Decentralisation." In D. Schmidtchen and R. Cooter, eds., *Constitutional Law and Economics of the European Union*. Aldershot, England: Edward Elgar Publishing, pp. 142–83.

Vanberg, Viktor. 1994. "Subsidiarity, Responsive Government and Individual Liberty." In Knut Wolfgang Nörr and Thomas Oppernmann, eds., *Subsidiarität: Idee und Wirklichkeit zur Reichweite eines Prinzips in Deutschland und Europa*. Tübingen: J. C. B. Mohr, pp. 253–69.

Vanberg, Viktor and Buchanan, James M. 1989. "Interests and Theories in Constitutional Choice," *Journal of Theoretical Politics*. (1/1), pp. 49–62.

Vaubel, Roland. 1993. "Perspektiven der europäischen Integration: Die politische Ökonomie der Vertiefung und Erweiterung." In Horst Siebert, ed., *Die zweifache Integration: Deutschland und Europa*. Tübingen: J. C. B. Mohr, pp. 3–31.

——— 1995. "Constitutional Safeguards against Centralization in Federal States: An International Cross-Section Analysis." Discussion Paper 532/95. Beiträge zur Angewandten Wirtschaftsforschung, Universität Mannheim, Germany.

Voigt, Stefan. 1996. "Positive Constitutional Economics: A Survey." *Public Choice*, 89/1–2, pp. 1–43.

Wagner, Alexander. 2000. Institutions and Growth: Theoretical Foundations and Empirical Evidence. Dissertation. Department of Economics, Johannes Kepler University of Linz, Linz, Austria.

Weede, Erich. 1986. "Catch-up Distributional Coalitions and Government Growth or Decline in Industrialized Democracies." *British Journal of Sociology*, 37/2, pp. 194–220.

——— 1990. *Wirtschaft, Staat und Gesellschaft*. Tübingen: J. C. B. Mohr.

Weingast, Barry. 1993. "Constitutions as Governance Structures: The Political Foundations of Secure Markets." *Journal of Institutional and Theoretical Economics*, 149/3, pp. 286–311.

Index

accounting
  accrual concept, 268–9
  cash, 268
  creative, 258, 260–1
  opportunistic, 259–62
  United Nations system, 266
  See also European System of
    Integrated Economic Accounts
    (ESA)
accounting, Maastricht Treaty
  collateral account, 283
  contingent liabilities, 282
  of ESA under, 259–68
  expenditure side in budgetary, 278–82
  national income statistics in fiscal
    constitution's, 266–72
  revenue side in budgetary, 272–8
  Social Security pension debts, 283–4
Ackerman, Bruce, 28n23, 170–1
Althusius, Johannes, 72
Amarin, Neto, 135
Anarchy, State, and Utopia (Nozick), 82
Aranson, Peter, 143
Aristotle, 72, 91–2

Barro, Robert J., 108
Beard, Charles, 16
Before Resorting to Politics (Jasay), 90–1
beliefs
  of constituencies, 184–5
  ideologies as systems of, 116
Bobbio, N., 71–2
Bohnet, Iris, 301, 304
Bork, Robert H., 87–8
Breton, Albert, 174, 178
Brunell, Thomas, 141
Buchanan, James M., 5, 17, 86–7, 118,
  166n4, 192, 247, 291, 294–5

candidates for office
  exchange in political campaign, 193–6
  test of campaign spending and
    contributions, 197–202

variations in attributes of, 192–5
Carey, John M., 153n57
Caul, Miki, 135
Centre for Economic Policy Research, 247
choice
  constitutional, 2, 34, 41–2
  in economic constitution, 34
  of institutions, 117–19
  post-constitutional, 2
choice, collective
  choice set with increased
    dimensionality, 62–3
  constitutionalization of variables, 63–7
  institutions formalize rules for, 115
  multidimensional, 60–3
  relation of costs to dimensionality,
    62–3
  role of institutions in, 115–16
  rules and dimensionality of, 58–60
  rules reduce costs of, 58–63
  rules reduce dimensionality of choice
    set, 58–63
  two-dimensional, 60–1
choice of electoral system, 123–4, 127–36
  attributed to culture or diffusion, 151
  inertia, 152
  normative choices, 152
  public choice model, 151
civil society
  Bork's perspective, 87–9
  Buchanan's perspective, 86–7
  characteristics of Western, 89
  consent legitimates, 71
  contractarian approach (Buchanan), 85
  creation of (Hobbes), 79
  Epstein's perspective, 93–4
  Gray's perspective, 83–5
  Hayek's perspective, 92
  of Hobbes, 4, 70–5, 78–80
  Jasay's perspective, 90–1
  of Locke, 4, 7, 75–8, 80–1
  Nozick's perspective, 82–3

313